D0423222

STRATEGIC HUMAN RESOURCES MANAGEMENT

A Guide for Effective Practice

Fred K. Foulkes, Editor

School of Management
Boston University

PRENTICE-HALL, Englewood Cliffs, New Jersey 07632

Library of Congress Cataloging-in-Publication Data

Main entry under title:

Strategic human resources management.

Includes index.
1. Personnel management—Addresses, essays,
lectures.   I. Foulkes, Fred K.
HF5549.S886   1986   658.3   85–25702
ISBN   0–13–851031–8

*Editorial/production supervision and
   interior design: Joan L. Stone
Cover design: 20/20 Services, Inc.
Manufacturing buyer: Ed O'Dougherty*

© 1986 by Prentice-Hall
A Division of Simon & Schuster, Inc.
Englewood Cliffs, New Jersey 07632

All rights reserved. No part of this book may be
reproduced, in any form or by any means,
without permission in writing from the publisher.

Printed in the United States of America

10   9   8   7   6   5   4   3   2   1

ISBN 0-13-851031-8   01

PRENTICE-HALL INTERNATIONAL (UK) LIMITED, *London*
PRENTICE-HALL OF AUSTRALIA PTY. LIMITED, *Sydney*
PRENTICE-HALL CANADA INC., *Toronto*
PRENTICE-HALL HISPANOAMERICANA, S.A., *Mexico*
PRENTICE-HALL OF INDIA PRIVATE LIMITED, *New Delhi*
PRENTICE-HALL OF JAPAN, INC., *Tokyo*
PRENTICE-HALL OF SOUTHEAST ASIA PTE. LTD., *Singapore*
EDITORA PRENTICE-HALL DO BRASIL, LTDA., *Rio de Janeiro*
WHITEHALL BOOKS LIMITED, *Wellington, New Zealand*

HF
55~~34~~
.~~9~~886
1986

26.29

4.9.87

*To the individual contributors
to this volume,
all leaders in the human resources field*

211432

Contents

v

PART III
THE HR FUNCTION ITSELF—PURPOSE AND MISSION, ROLE AND ORIENTATION   115

PART IV
SELECTED TOPICS OF CONTINUING AND STRATEGIC IMPORTANCE TO BOTH HUMAN RESOURCES AND LINE MANAGERS   179

PART V
NEW DIRECTIONS   331

Preface

Many books on the subject of personnel management fail to put the field in the proper perspective. Effective human resources management does not exist in a vacuum but must be related to the overall strategy of the organization. Practitioners and students alike need to relate both the human resources policies of the company and the personnel function itself to the goals of the enterprise.

This unique collection of readings is written by and for human resources practitioners, line executives, consultants, academicians, and students of the human resources profession. It is intended to be helpful to those concerned with managing people in the late 80s. The authors are leaders in the human resources field: chief executive officers, union leaders, human resources executives, academicians, and consultants. One can learn much from the experiences, insights, and reflections of these individuals who are determining the direction of personnel management today.

In Part I, an introductory section, top human resources executives discuss their work and role. Their thoughtful comments lay the groundwork for the remainder of the book.

Part II focuses on human resources in relationship to top management goals, company strategy and planning, and organizational culture. If companies are to survive—possibly even prosper and flourish—more insight and innovation are essential in relating human resources management to business purpose. Too many personnel managers have a tendency to create and function in their own little worlds, forgetting that their primary value is helping to realize top and line management goals. The readings in this section will help the reader understand how strategy is formulated and implemented, what is meant by "organizational culture," and what the requirements for effective personnel management are. The views of top management as well as those of academicians and consultants are represented.

Part III is concerned with the role of the human resources function itself—namely, its purpose, goals, and orientation. Although the practitioner must coordinate particular policies and practices with the overall goals of the organization, he or she must also operate from within an appropriately defined role in the company. The readings in this section give practical advice about the nature of the modern personnel function. These selections demonstrate that strong and distinctive personnel policy can work to a company's competitive advantage.

Part IV contains four groups of readings on topics that are of continuing and strategic importance to both human resources managers and line managers. The subjects treated include labor and employee relations, pay and executive compensation, the quality of working life, and the increasingly important fields of human resources planning and management development.

Part V, the concluding section, deals with the directions in which human resources management is moving. In the first group of articles, leading senior personnel executives discuss various policies and practices that they believe will improve long-run business performance in the '80s. In the second group of articles, senior line managers, including chief executive officers, describe what they expect to find in the human resources managers they seek. Together, these selections provide a picture of the challenges and opportunities facing practitioners today.

This book is intended to be used either as a stand-alone volume or as a supplement to a basic textbook of human resources management. Although it suggests a conceptual approach to personnel management, it is designed to emphasize practice, not theory. The material presented is the best available. It reflects the experience of successful chief executive officers, human resource executives, and others who are in a position to know what will and what will not work. It is my hope and expectation that readers will find the selections interesting, useful, and stimulating.

This volume would not have been possible had it not been for the hard work of over 40 individuals. Because they cared and took the time to organize their thoughts, others can learn from their experiences, insights, and reflections. I cannot express adequately my appreciation and gratitude to them. I do, however, sincerely thank them, and, in deep respect, dedicate this book to them. A brief biographical sketch and a photograph of each author appear at the end of the book.

In addition, I am grateful to the publishers for granting me permission to reprint these readings. I must also thank Dean Henry Morgan, a friend and colleague for over 15 years, for his support and encouragement. Finally, I want to express my gratitude to Alison Reeves, Gay Auerbach, and Carmen Jacobson. I thank Alison for her patience, support, and wise counsel. I thank Gay for superb editorial assistance. And Carmen's cheerful attitude and administrative and organizational skills contributed enormously to the successful completion of this volume.

Fred K. Foulkes
Boston, Massachusetts

Part I

Introduction: Top Human Resources Executives Talk about Their Work and Role

Within the past 12 years, Bank of America, Chase Manhattan, Johns-Manville, and the Marriott Corporation all recruited new heads of human resources from outside their industries. Bank of America hired Robert Beck, who had been a distinguished personnel executive with IBM for almost 20 years. Chase Manhattan selected Alan Lafley, an experienced labor and personnel professional with years of experience with General Electric and then, briefly, with Clark Equipment. Johns-Manville enticed Eileen Decoursey, an officer of the Squibb Corporation, to leave New York and move to Denver to head its employee relations organization. The Marriott Corporation hired Cliff Ehrlich, an experienced personnel executive who came from the Monsanto Company.

In this section, these four pros talk about their work and role. Bob Beck, of Bank of America, contrasts his initial impressions of the bank with his impressions of IBM. He discusses the banking industry and the personnel initiatives that appear to him to be needed. He also discusses his own management style and his personal goals.

Alan Lafley, too, was attracted to the financial services industry because of its opportunities and challenges. Viewing the upgrading of the quality of the bank's management as one of his most significant responsibilities, Lafley played a critical role in the turnaround and improved performance of Chase Manhattan. In this interview, he zeroes in on the "people challenges"—recruiting, training, and developing managers—as the essential tasks of the human resources manager in the banking industry.

Characterizing the employee relations field as "the most exciting game in town" that she hopes will attract "the best and brightest talent available," Eileen Decoursey talks about the way her own career developed, some of the changes she enacted at Squiob and Johns-Manville, and her views on the importance of company and employee relations. She also talks candidly about some of the special career challenges she faced because of her sex.

The Marriott Corporation, with over 125,000 employees, is in a labor-intensive service business. Effective management of employees is a priority at the company, for the company's success depends on the performance of its hourly and management people. Cliff Ehrlich, Senior Vice President, Human Resources, talks about the challenges of managing people and gives advice on creating a climate that helps employees find satisfaction in their jobs.

One cannot read these four interviews without recognizing the importance these experts attach to relating human resources policies and practices to the goals of top management. Beck, Lafley, Decoursey, and Ehrlich all maintain that personnel policies and practices must further the business objectives of the organization.

Throughout the interviews, one senses something of their own personalities and styles. Their views provide an excellent introduction for the sections of this book that follow.

BOB BECK: AN INTERVIEW WITH THE NEW HEAD OF CORPORATE PERSONNEL

IBM is considered a leader in the personnel area. Can you tell us about your work there and about IBM's programs?

There are a lot of similarities between IBM and Bank of America. A.P. Giannini and Tom Watson, Sr., IBM's founder, were friends and had a lot of the same attitudes about corporations, about people, and about customers and service. When I was considering changing companies, I wanted a company whose culture and traditions were in keeping with the training and experiences I'd had at IBM.

Based on its personnel policies and practices, IBM is what I call an enlightened employer. There are many companies that offer good pay and good benefits, but the big difference to me is not the pay and benefits. What makes an employer distinctive in today's environment is something more. The big difference is the treatment of employees, how they're managed.

One thing that is a hallmark of excellence at IBM is their emphasis on good people management. They make a tremendous investment in their managers to make them people-oriented, good leaders of others. For instance, at IBM you can't be a manager of people anywhere in the U.S. without going to management school within 30 days of your appointment. These people go through a week's class, studying mostly people issues—not technical or business issues.

The three IBM basic beliefs are respect for the individual, the pursuit of excellence in everything you do, and the best customer service in the world. Mr. Watson started those back in the early 1900s, and IBM has built everything around them. Those beliefs are very compatible with what I've found here at Bank of America.

I was fortunate in my IBM career to have the opportunity to follow a career development path that led me through a variety of assignments and gave me a well-rounded experience. I went from headquarters to manufacturing to research laboratories, to field operations, back to headquarters, into an international job, and then back to headquarters again. I spent two-thirds of my time out of the U.S. for a couple of years. Because of that broad

"Bob Beck: An Interview with the New Head of Corporate Personnel," by Doug Bartholomew, from BankAmerican, November 1982. Reprinted with permission.

exposure, I feel I'm a better personnel generalist with a wide perspective, rather than a technical specialist.

What aspects of your experience at IBM do you feel are transferable to BofA?

Managing change and managing people are going to be the real tests of corporations in the decade of the '80s, and our people have to be prepared to deal with that change. That takes an investment in our managers through a strong management development program.

We're now putting together a worldwide management development strategy for the bank. This is something for which my experience at IBM—where we implemented a worldwide management development plan several years ago—has been very helpful.

Does IBM hire executives at your level?

No. Their basic philosophy is promotion from within. However, this requires a real investment in succession planning. We already have the beginnings of a succession planning system at the bank.

The goal is to develop an effective working tool so that senior executives won't have to be hired. We need to build our management team strongly enough so that all the key jobs will be filled from within. We'll soon be implementing a program that will oversee our management development plans on a worldwide basis—for international assignments, U.S. assignments, reentry assignments, and assignments across division lines. This will be part of the succession plan process.

What are your impressions so far of the personnel programs here at Bank of America? Can you share some of your ideas for possible change?

Well, overall it's clear that one of the reasons that Bank of America is the leader in its industry is because the bank has been developing the state of the art in personnel policies and practices. One of the concerns I have is that banks in general tend to look only among banks when comparing their programs. Companies like IBM or Xerox, however, look across all industries and try to glean the policies and practices that are best for them from a wider horizon. So when you compare Bank of America against all the leading banks, we look very good. While we have areas where we can make further enhancements, I think we are in a very positive position. We have programs such as our opinion surveys, Open Line, and other employee feedback channels that are very enlightening.

I plan to enhance the things we're doing, and at the same time further reduce bureaucracy. We still have a little bit too much bureaucracy, in my opinion, in terms of certain formal procedures and ways of getting things done.

One of the things I've seen here that has been so pleasing to me in the first few weeks on the job is the willingness to change, the open mind that Bank of America people have. I've been out talking to people at all levels— in senior management, in administration, and in the branches and regions—and there's really an open attitude. There's no one putting up a fight of "not invented here," or "you're an outsider coming in." In fact, from the beginning, I didn't feel at all like an outsider. I was concerned about that, coming in as I did at a high-level position. . . .

With banking undergoing sweeping changes, training of our employees to meet the new demands of the marketplace and the workplace is likely to become more critical. Will we be doing more training and career counseling to help our people meet these changes?

Another one of my top priorities is employee development. The financial services industry is going through at least a sweeping evolution, if not a revolution. We need to better understand how that is impacting people so we can anticipate future change and plan for it by redirecting people's careers. We'll be grouping all of our training, retraining, and development efforts under employee development. This means not just training, but development of people, so that when certain jobs aren't needed anymore, or product or technology changes dictate new positions, we will have people prepared for these new careers.

Development means having meaningful careers that people can move through. By that I'm not talking just about promotions, but about horizontal development as well. Keeping people growing—that's the kind of society we have. We have a much more educated work force today than we had 30 or 40 years ago. People today are demanding continual learning and growth. . . .

I think most people come to the bank for a career. And that's why we want to develop better career path progressions. The supervisor has to sit down with each employee and ask, "Where do you want to go? What would you like to do? How much effort are you willing to invest?" Developing careers is not a one-way street—it's not just the company providing training and direction. Employees have to be willing to learn new jobs and take some risks if they want to advance or move into new career paths. There is always risk in change, but the payoff can be very rewarding.

In order to provide our employees with these development opportunities and career path progressions, we in Personnel need to have strategic plans that support the bank's strategic plans. This type of personnel planning is one of the key ingredients in making the whole process work. It is imperative that our planning process be closely aligned with the business planning process.

How about our benefits and salary policies? Is the bank considering so-called "cafeteria-style" or flexible benefits that enable employees to pick and choose benefits to meet their individual needs? Is our compensation package competitive with those of other organizations?

Let's take benefits first. We're in quite good shape with our benefits plans, especially our survivors' benefits and our pension and medical plans. In the benefit area, I'd like to see us become more flexible. Most benefit plans were designed in the 1930s and 1940s when the typical employee was male, had a non-working spouse, and three to five children. You don't find many of those anymore. You have a much wider range in the demographics of the work force. There are more single people and more working couples, there are employees with dependent parents. The traditional benefit package doesn't fit individual employees' needs as it once did.

But to go to a cafeteria-style, flexible benefits program overnight isn't easy. Some companies are trying it overnight, and it's turning out to be extremely difficult for them.

One of the most important things about any benefits program is to ensure that it's soundly funded and the company can afford it over the long haul. To have, for instance, a pension plan that's not properly funded is really unfair to the people who go on retirement. People want to be able to count on those benefits. So you should build your plans in a responsible manner, knowing you can afford them over the next 10, 20, and 30 years, not just today. . . .

In medical, for example, we offer multiple HMOs. Why not consider offering three medical plans, some that are more preventive-oriented than major-illness oriented? That's what we're working on, trying to gradually build in more flexibility for individuals—in their time-off provisions, survivors' benefits, and medical programs. You can manage it plan-by-plan, but not all at once. To get there, we've got to walk before we can run.

On the pay side, it's a little early for me to comment on the competitiveness of our salary programs. I will say that I'd like to see a strengthening of our performance-based pay system. It's clear that over the past 15 to 20 years, pay schemes that are based on length of service are not successful. Even the U.S. government is moving off that system and going to a merit-based system. It's the key to productivity and the key to success in the future. We have to have a pay system that rewards performance and challenges people. As long as performance plans are fair and mutually set by the employee and the manager, and the employee knows where he or she stands and what is expected, then you can provide greater rewards to people who make more significant work contributions.

Our system at the bank is generally designed to do that, but we need to put more emphasis on the performance side. That's the feedback I've gotten from talking to people. And we need to make sure that people are challenged and that we expect more from them each year than the previous year because of their greater experience and training.

What are your thoughts on incentive programs to promote employee initiative and contributions to productivity and quality of service?

If you look at opinion survey data, you'll find that many people say that if the conditions were right, they could improve their performance. And often the things they're talking about are either better tools or equipment to do their jobs, or simply eliminating bureaucracy and unnecessary rules and regulations.

I'd like to see us develop more of a culture and climate that rewards people in a general sense for being part of—and contributing to—the success and well-being of the company. If their company is successful, profitable, and growing, employees are going to benefit from it. We'll be able to provide better training, better pay, better benefits, and more opportunities and promotions.

The environment has to encourage people to be creative. At many companies, when a manager gets a suggestion, it seems like his or her first thought is how do I knock this off? How can I get rid of this? Because, you know, I can't let other people be suggesting ideas, I'm supposed to think of them.

I'd like to get people's attitudes to something like, "Say, this is probably a good idea. I ought to try to find some way to implement it and reward the employee for being creative." And if the solution that they've suggested isn't exactly right, but it stimulates us to do something similar to it, we ought to try to find a way to reward the employee.

It's an attitude that recognizes our employees have good ideas, and we're all on the same team. The quality circle idea is what's bearing that out. Employees today are well educated. They have good ideas. They want to be heard. They want their company to be successful. It's to their benefit. It should be a team spirit that we foster in the bank.

This is such a competitive business, we need every good idea we can get. I welcome personnel policy ideas from all employees. Particularly those ideas that will help us run the business better and make us more human relations-oriented.

What is your philosophy of managing people? How would you describe your management style?

One thing is that I trust people. I give them as much lead and challenge as they can take on. If I find that they are having difficulties, then I step in and help them overcome the hurdles.

Another philosophy I have is to surround myself with the very, very best people. Some managers try to surround themselves with weaker employees, so they won't challenge the system. I feel, however, that if my people are successful, I'll be successful. Developing people is a basic responsibility of management. I spend a lot of time trying to challenge my people—to stretch them, to help them grow, and to help their ideas come to fruition.

I also feel very strongly about treating people fairly and with respect. I heard a saying in a commercial that I'd like to paraphrase: "We don't treat our people like employees, we treat our employees like people."

Along the same lines, I believe in dealing on a first-name basis. We shouldn't get caught up in layers of bureaucracy so that, for example, I can't talk to someone three levels down from me simply because I'm supposed to go through two layers of management to get to them.

What do you see as the greatest challenge facing you at Bank of America?

I see a pent-up demand by the managers for many new personnel programs. Management development, strong succession planning, strong career-development programs—those kinds of things. The demand is here today—it's not as if they're saying, "Bob, you can take the next year to do these things at a gradual pace." It's more like "Okay, you have some good solutions, let's do them tomorrow."

It's going to be difficult for the personnel community in the bank to move and do those things in the time frame that people want. It's going to be a major challenge for us. It's not a matter of finding out what to do, it's how to do it in an orderly fashion.

What would you like to accomplish in your first year?

First, I think I need to develop a good understanding of and appreciation for the tradition and the culture that made this bank great, so that I can help build on those strengths.

Second, I'd like to ensure that we have developed the strategic directions in our personnel policies and practices that will help the bank meet its business objectives. We need a game plan in the personnel side of the business just like the business side has for its programs and products.

And I'd like to feel comfortable that we have begun to build the personnel community as a professional part of the corporate whole—in California, in the U.S., and worldwide. That means we're going to put a lot of emphasis on development of the personnel team.

There is no university anywhere that could give me the kind of development and education in personnel management that I got at IBM. But that was a deliberate plan—a combination of seminars, developmental programs, rotational assignments, and career objectives that got me to where I am. That's my goal—to make sure we have that for all our personnel people worldwide. Then our personnel community will be ready to take on whatever challenges the bank faces.

What things attracted you to Bank of America?

One is the fact that the financial services industry is going through this rapid change. I see the financial business just getting ready to explode into whole new sectors. The customer set is different, the products and delivery systems are changing, and it's an exciting time for me to be in a new industry. And with a company that is committed to being number one.

Also, in my employment interview with Sam Armacost, I became convinced that he wants this bank to be the greatest place to work from a personnel standpoint, from a human relations standpoint. That was important to me.

I also was impressed with the attitude of flexibility and openness to change that I found here. You always read in personnel research studies about resistance to change—a kind of mind set that makes changing anything in an organization difficult—product changes, organizational changes, whatever. I don't see that here. The attitude of openness here is a unique gift that must have started back in the early 1900s when the bank was founded and continues to this day. That makes me excited about the future.

AN INTERVIEW
WITH ALAN F. LAFLEY

What special traits, abilities, and knowledge are we looking for in the Chase managers and bankers of the future?

One of the most important for senior managers will be an ability to think strategically. The success of Chase is going to depend very heavily on how we plan for the future in this rapidly changing banking environment. Related to this ability, successful managers will increasingly have to pay as much attention to the long term as they do to the short term. In the management of their components, they must be capable of implementing successfully the strategies determined.

The banker of the future will also have to be more concerned about the external environment—on a truly worldwide basis. The competitive, regulatory and social environment in which our managers and bankers operate continues to become increasingly complex. This will have a greater impact on business strategy, direction and decision making, and on the way in which Human Resources will be managed.

Lastly, our managers should have the ability to establish effective working relationships not only externally, but also vertically and horizontally within the organization, and with subordinates and peers in their own components. They will need to have a broad capacity to deal with the newly emerging human resources issues of the 80s.

What are the major "people challenges" that confront us?

The key "people challenge" facing us today is our ability to manage the changing work force—managers and professionals who are more self-oriented, less concerned with job security, more focused on their professions and who expect other satisfactions beyond money for their efforts.

The population dynamics worldwide are considered by Peter Drucker and many others to be the most significant forces challenging managers in the decade of the 80s. There is an imminent shortage of young people coming into the work force. The situation will become increasingly severe dur-

"An Interview with Alan F. Lafley," from The Chase Quarterly, *Third Quarter ended September 30, 1980. Reprinted with permission.*

ing the next few years. The 1980 college graduates are the last of the post World War II baby boom.

An even more serious problem facing us in this decade will be the large number of workers—the baby boom generation—reaching middle age. Arnold Webber, the highly respected labor economist, describes this age bulge in terms of the problems it offers as a "pig passing through a python."

These demographic changes will affect us in several ways. Competition for recruitment of the best talent from college campuses will increase dramatically; starting salaries will be higher relative to salaries of more experienced employees. The bulge of experienced workers in the 35–45 age bracket, while giving us a large number of qualified managers and professionals, more continuity in positions and an environment more favorable for sound manpower development, will at the same time mean less opportunity for advancement, and therefore increased dissatisfaction for these employees.

It is these forces that will have a major impact on Human Resources management in the 80s.

Considerable leadership skills will be required of managers in this environment to attract, retain, and aid in developing talented people, to set challenging but realistic goals, and to establish a climate which motivates these employees to achieve both desired individual and organization performance results. The ability to manage human resources effectively in this rapidly changing environment will be a critical consideration in manager selection and will be a real test for all management as we move into the 80s and beyond.

What is Chase's policy regarding promoting from within versus hiring from the outside?

Chase's expressed desire and its long-term interest is to promote from within the bank. I believe that a strong organization must have a policy that emphasizes opportunity and promotion for people within the institution.

Following on that policy, staffing and development approaches must be implemented to ensure internal depth of managerial and professional people of high quality—on a continuing basis.

As we achieve this, however, I think it unwise to staff only from within Chase. In trying to fill each position, we need to examine all possible internal candidates. If we find that our internal people do not have the qualifications and experience to meet the standards we have set for staffing the position, we must look outside. Hiring from outside can add new thinking and experience to the organization. But certainly our focus and our emphasis must be and are on developing Chase people and promoting from within.

How successful has Chase been in attracting graduates of top-level business schools?

It is much easier to answer this question favorably today than it was a few years ago. Last year was the most successful year we've had in college recruiting for a long time. In the U.S., we interviewed over 1,900 graduates with bachelor degrees on 29 college campuses. We made 148 offers and got 108 acceptances—or 73 percent. We recruited at 17 graduate schools of business and hired 68 MBA graduates. In addition, we hired another 35 graduates with masters degrees from another 6 universities.

Our recruiting schedule was so full that we had to assign more Chase people than planned to meet the requests for interviews at the key business schools. Most important, the best graduates were among those requesting interviews with Chase.

We do not, of course, restrict our search for capable people to a few schools in the U.S. We recruit people with a wide range of backgrounds from different kinds of schools throughout the world. We think this variety has helped strengthen Chase.

How would you assess the depth of management talent at Chase?

Chase continues to view the building of management depth as a top priority, and we have made real progress in this area.

Our assessment of the depth of management talent is naturally affected as we continue to raise standards regarding the kind of experience and performance expectations we want from people in key positions. In the past, we did not fill the manpower pipeline at the entry levels on a regular basis. Nor did we pursue the kind of development activities required. Therefore we did not have sufficient depth of experienced people to meet our business needs.

Today, however, we recruit, select and develop people with the need for management depth firmly in mind, both for the long term as well as for current requirements. . . .

How competitive with industry are bank benefits and salaries?

At one time, banks offered exceptional benefits but low salaries. Individuals looking for job security and excellent pensions could find what they wanted at banks. Over approximately the last five years, however, banks have moved aggressively to design and structure compensation plans very competitive with those in industry. Today, bank salaries and total compensation are competitive with leading industrial companies for comparable positions and performance results. Similar incentive plans have been introduced, and more incentive arrangements are expected in banking in the future to meet specific business needs. Banks continue to be leaders in core benefit plans, particularly in profit-sharing arrangements.

Chase's excellent compensation package has been a factor in both attracting and retaining highly capable people.

What is Chase doing in the area of staff development?

Over the past three years, we've made a significant investment in staff development in terms of people and dollars. We've initiated a wide spectrum of activities—from an advanced management program, that has now been attended by about 300 key officers, to a refinement of Chase's highly regarded credit training program. We are now providing individually focused development programs on a worldwide basis, including marketing and sales training, management skills training, supervisory training, and operations training. Additionally, we are focusing, with Chase's various business units, on tailored development plans to meet their particular needs. This incorporates informal on-the-job activities in addition to formal programs.

Is there a "youth movement" afoot in terms of Chase management?

Not really. Every organization should seek a balance in the age of its management—that is, a balance between the people who move into managerial jobs at a young age with those who are more experienced. When there is a reasonable balance—as I think there is now at Chase—the energy and vision of the younger managers complements the wisdom and perspective of the more experienced managers.

EILEEN DECOURSEY:
MAKING THINGS HAPPEN

You have had a rather unusual career path—teaching, consulting with two firms, employee relations positions with five major corporations. Why did you take that route?

Much of what I've done interrelates so well that it may appear I had some kind of long-range career plan based on sampling many employee relations experiences. Actually, there has been no long range plan other than a desire to learn and do as much as possible in each situation—always with the expectancy that new challenges would emerge as I was ready for them. In time, as I felt prepared for new responsibilities, I defined my goals and actively sought to achieve them where I was. In some instances I sought merely a broadened responsibility; in others I developed a concept in which the company was interested, including rationale, staffing, budgeting, and presented it as an opportunity for both the company and for me. . . .

Tell us about your education and background.

My initial interest while attending college was not related to the personnel field. Rather, I planned a teaching career with special emphasis on speech therapy. A brief period of classroom teaching, while enjoyable in many respects, was disappointing in the lack of professional curiosity and outside interests of the staff. Also, I frankly enjoyed competition and found a system where everyone proceeds on the basis of seniority rather than individual merit not particularly to my liking. An opportunity opened up at Warner-Lambert Company which was then in the process of relocating its headquarters from New York City to New Jersey. My job was in the benefits and records section of the corporate personnel function. One of the first things I had to do was conduct exit interviews with dozens of employees who had elected not to move with the company. Many of these people had been born, raised and still lived in the neighborhood near the plant. The company had been a major part of their lives but they could not bring themselves to leave the old neighborhood. . . . It made a lasting impression in terms of the depth of feelings many employees have towards a company.

"Eileen Decoursey: Making Things Happen," reprinted from the September 1976 issue of The Personnel Administrator, *copyright 1976, The American Society for Personnel Administration, 606 North Washington Street, Alexandria, VA 22314.*

For some, the friendships and interactions and identity associated with their job exceeded anything they had in their personal lives.

Today, with the breakdown in so many institutions—family, religion, government—I wonder if business is not missing an opportunity because many people have an even greater need for identification, a sense of belonging, a need to contribute rather than merely take. Obviously, it's not a simple question and it cannot be accomplished in ways that worked 20 years ago—but the need for both the individual and the company is so much greater than ever—it is a point worth exploring.

What kind of progression did you make?

After three-and-a-half-years with Warner, I moved to New York City and joined the research staff of an executive recruiting firm. Soon after another job offer led me to the employee benefits consulting department of Johnson & Higgins and a chance to work with many Fortune 500 companies in designing and developing improvements in their benefit packages. It was a time for original thinking and a chance to see many of our own ideas incorporated in major programs. For me personally it was an opportunity to consult with a diverse group of companies with very distinctive philosophies—a great way to learn flexibility and the fact that there are many viable solutions to any given problem. It also was good schooling in determining how a company sees itself—what it is, how it wants to communicate itself—and then developing programs which reinforce its philosophy, its style.

In employee relations we have many opportunities to help reinforce the company's philosophy and what we are as an organization. Unfortunately, we often overlook such basic chances to add to the clarity and integrity of the organization.

After Johnson and Higgins came a brief encounter with the glamorous world of Time, Inc., and then I accepted a job at Bristol Myers. . . . Bristol, like so many companies in the late '60s, was actively engaged in a program of mergers and acquisitions and I soon became involved with the special problems of employees whose company had been acquired—the psychological aspects of "what happens to me now" as well as the actual change in policies and programs and new ways of doing business.

The impact of change on people's lives was very apparent and we looked for ways that employee relations programs could be utilized to help ease the strain.

You used employee relations programs to ease the strain of change?

Yes, for example, Bristol had an outstanding benefit program. Fairly soon after a merger we would approach the new company about Bristol benefits. This was one of the first formal contacts between the companies.

Many had heard good things and were receptive; others were instinctively cautious about the first step in being "absorbed". Our concern was twofold, the surface message to talk about benefits but, more importantly, to open lines of communications—not only in the benefit area but in any employee related area. Obviously, open, frank, interactive conversations in one area can set the stage for other similar discussions. . . . What we were doing was not merely presenting a new program but using that as a means of communicating company philosophy and attitude and providing a way to ease tension and smooth transition. There is nothing startling or innovative about this approach—just another means of defining and clarifying the philosophy and integrity of the corporation through an employee relations program. The startling thing is how few corporations use routine programs to transmit an advertisement for themselves. We spend millions in corporate image campaigns and overlook all the day to day chances to deliver an "important word from our sponsor."

Are there any other examples you can give which apply the idea of consciously transmitting company philosophy and integrity through an employee relations program?

When I joined Squibb Corporation early in 1971, I entered an environment where the operating companies were almost completely autonomous and where the corporate staff acted more as a negotiator, conciliator, advisor, rather than having direct line responsibility. This was clearly the philosophy of the company and yet in certain employee relations areas it was apparent we were duplicating costs and re-inventing the wheel many times over. This was particularly evident in the benefit area because of the soaring costs of benefits and the fact that each company was purchasing benefits separately, using different benefit consultants and generally designing its own package without consideration for the other companies. Employees of the more prosperous companies were happy while employees of the less prosperous companies (sometimes sitting only an office away) were understandably concerned.

We therefore set out to design a program which would control costs, make benefits competitive while enhancing the individuality and autonomy of each company. Our solution of a master plan with separate but parallel benefit tracks, centralized purchasing based on operating company demographics, met all of the stated objectives, preserved the general autonomy of the operating companies and yet provided employees with benefits which while not uniform were compatible with the overall corporation and competitive externally. . . .

Similar approaches were also used in salary administration, executive compensation, affirmative action, etc.—all designed consciously to be competitive, responsive, while maintaining the individuality and autonomy of the respective companies.

It was at Squibb that you first became a corporate officer—did that have an impact on you?

Not the officer's title itself but the increased access to the CEO and the Board of Directors certainly broadened my understanding of the total corporate functioning. Auditing monthly Board meetings and working closely with the compensation committee of the Board deepened my appreciation for the seriousness with which most Board members take their responsibilities.

Actually, from my initial days at Squibb as Assistant to the President, I was in a unique position and involved in many decisions which were unrelated to the employee relations function. They were invaluable experiences in general management problems which is essentially the best possible vantage point from which to make employee relations decisions. It has confirmed in my mind the need of employee relations executives to have the broadest management exposure if they are going to successfully fill their major responsibilities of supporting both management and employees.

Where does the employee relations department fit in terms of changing attitudes and working conditions?

In dead center of a three-dimensional continuum—with management, employees, union, government, surrounding it.

Employee relations has got to come to grips with many of the early warning noises it hears—or should hear—of how varying interest groups perceive the organization. Incorrect perceptions are real to those who have them and must be handled accordingly.

It is not the job of employee relations to field every employee related problem that comes along—but it is its job to keep management alert to change, to problems and to develop programs which, while being responsive, will be consistent with company philosophy—even to the point of recommending changes in philosophy if that seems warranted.

Personally, I feel management, employees, unions, have long since "come-of-age" and we should be dealing with each other adult to adult— with all its responsibilities as well as its privileges. Unfortunately, some of these roles are so deeply established (management the tyrannical fathers, employees the maligned children, unions the fearless interloper) that we continue to perpetuate them as attitudes even while we are adopting new approaches.

We're all familiar with the experience encountered in open communications meetings—a great opportunity for advancing adult to adult concepts—when the employee, rather than asking a question, hurls a challenge—and the management representative, rather than positively restructuring the point, fires back at this insubordination of his authority.

This is a typical occurrence and it just points up the problem we face in "laying on" new programs without helping supervisors not only to understand the philosophy but how to apply it in everyday actions. Very basically it points up the need to train supervisors in how to deal with their own attitudes as well as the ones the company wishes to implement.

You say that management and employee should be dealing adult to adult but retraining of old attitudes may be necessary. How are you handling this at J-M?

First let me say we are currently working on our statement of employee relations philosophy at J-M and therefore I'm now advancing many of my own thoughts which may or may not be part of the philosophy finally adopted by the company.

In trying to establish relationships on an adult to adult basis, as on any other philosophical point of view, I believe you must incorporate them in your basic employee relations plans so that they become an automatic way of life rather than an add-on program which does not have daily reinforcement and which can easily be discarded.

At Johns-Manville, for example, we have just introduced a completely new salary administration program as well as a work planning appraisal and review program. The programs are interrelated and supportive of one another. Basically they clarify the responsibility of the job, set out the agreed upon work plan for the next period, provide an on-going vehicle for clarification of responsibilities, appraisal and development in present job as well as in potential growth assignments. . . .

These are good programs and have been well received but we would be kidding ourselves to think the attitudes necessary to make these programs a success are going to happen just by providing some new tools. Rather, we view this as an ongoing educational process which will be provided through a number of vehicles—presentations at plant and staff meetings, articles in company and employee publications, auditing of results and return of those which do not follow the plan.

Perhaps most importantly, we will be providing a two or three day training program for all supervisors in what we are trying to accomplish and how we make it happen through work planning, appraisal and review. Each supervisor will have opportunity for handling difficult appraisal situations and hopefully through role playing and video tape will begin to understand the process, learn how to administer the programs properly and, in doing so, reinforce the attitude of mutual responsibility as understood and accepted between two adults.

You have mentioned company philosophy toward employee relations several times. Obviously you think this is important.

Yes, just as you need a philosophy for managing the financial resources of a corporation, you need a philosophy for managing the human resources. Defining and clarifying goals, objectives and attitudes provides the opportunity to consciously integrate the philosophy within the daily activities of the corporation. It is particularly important in a large company with many locations where there is a tendency for the local philosophy to prevail unless there is an established concept communicated to everyone. Even in a small company, however, there are advantages in developing a philosophy because the mere action focuses clarification of who you are as a company and what you want to become.

Fred Foulkes at Harvard has done some interesting research on large non-union companies where he has found two basic evolutions of employee relations philosophy. One which emerged by sheer personality of an individual. Marriott, for example. And a second which evolved out of a way of doing business which just naturally impacted employee relations— for example some of the high technology businesses which have flourished since the Second World War.

Obviously, a company that wants to can find a third way—by determining what the philosophy should be and then seeing that it is integrated into its total policies, programs and activities. Of course, whatever is adopted must have integrity and be "at home" within that particular company—otherwise the result will be a pervasive and damaging loss of credibility.

Does today's corporate structure call for functioning through the employee relations department to accomplish human resource management goals?

If by "functioning" you mean that everything related to employees must be channeled through the employee relations department, *the answer is no.* [Italics added.] On the other hand, there must be a genuine understanding between what line and staff and across all functional responsibilities of what we as a corporation are trying to do in the human resource area. That's why I think a philosophy—developed, analyzed and adopted by senior management—is so important to the operations of a company.

I also feel there is a strong interaction needed between the employee relations department and other parts of the business. As a service and support function, employee relations has got to be aware of business plans, changes in direction, organizational problems. We also need to know how programs we have developed are being received. Basically, we should be able to "tune-in" to the organization and we certainly can't do that without a lot of interaction with those outside the employee relations department.

How does this interrelationship between employee relations and other functional areas help J-M achieve some of its human resources goals?

A good example is the workings of our President's Review Committee. This is a group of officers representing major functional areas who meet every two weeks to help resolve the problems of otherwise capable employees who are without permanent assignment because of reorganization or because their last position was not a good match for their capabilities. The primary responsibility of the group has been to place these dislocated employees in meaningful work situations. A secondary result has been tighter control of new jobs and greater opportunity to direct minorities and women into viable job openings.

What difference do you think it has meant to your career that you are a woman?

I think one of the reasons I changed companies so often can be attributed partially to being a woman in that *few companies took seriously the desire of a woman to move ahead.* [Italics added.] No one thought to consider my next career move because in most cases I had already gone farther than any other woman. The reaction to my request was usually genuine surprise. Whether I might have gone as far by staying with one company is doubtful. In any event, I've learned a lot from the moves I've made and that was what I was seeking.

Another related difference in being a woman is the need to re-establish yourself and your credentials with each job change. A man will generally be accepted until proven inadequate. A woman must prove herself before being accepted. It's a little like the difference between the American and English system of justice—except it's England here only for women.

How do you think the employee relations department should be viewed from the outside?

With respect for its integrity and professionalism—the same as from the inside.

Where do you see employee relations developing as a profession in the next few years?

I think it's going to be the most exciting game in town and hopefully we are going to attract the best and brightest talent available. I expect it will become a regular stepping-stone to general management such as sales and finance. We are going through enormous changes as we head into a "post-industrial" society and the impact on employees as well as our entire way of doing business will be greater than anything since the design of the assembly line. Knowledgeable, prepared employee relations professionals must be able to anticipate the changes before they occur so we are in a position to support and assist the transition—not merely to record its happening.

BUILDING ON
SATISFIED EMPLOYEES

Clifford J. Ehrlich

Some American companies seem to have rediscovered how involved employees can help them succeed. What brought about this realization?

Productivity surfaced as a major concern of American business about 10 years ago. Many companies were facing serious competition from abroad and turned to automation for answers. After all, the Japanese and West Germans had developed reputations for providing superior products by using state-of-the-art technology.

People eventually came to realize, though, that lasting improvements in quality and productivity required more than advanced technology. As a result, companies began to look at their management processes and decided to increase the amount of involvement employees were given in business decisions that affected them.

How does this apply to Marriott?

We have fewer opportunities to introduce technology into our businesses. That's why we have to concentrate on the "people systems" that build in our employees a sense of commitment, a commitment that leads to improved productivity and high quality.

When managers give employees the chance to participate in the business by listening to suggestions and exchanging ideas, they show a respect for employees. And that builds employee commitment to the success of the business.

What role does a manager play in human resources?

The manager is a team captain. He or she not only has to provide direction to employees but also encouragement and support. In the service business, it's vital that employees are "up" and feel they are a part of a

"Building on Satisfied Employees," an interview with Clifford J. Ehrlich, Marriott Manager, No. 3, 1984. *Reprinted with permission.*

team. They are part of the product we offer to the consumer, and to the extent that they are better and more highly motivated than the employees of our competitors, we have a competitive advantage.

Marriott doubles in size every four to five years. How does the company ensure that it has the managers to fuel that kind of growth?

Our company is very decentralized, and each business is responsible for recruiting and developing the managers it needs. Each business has to establish good sources of applicants, whether through four-year or two-year colleges, or by seeking people with particular types of experience. Each must hire and train qualified managers, introducing them to Marriott systems.

It's important that the people who do the hiring and training take pride in Marriott and look for job candidates who will have that same kind of dedication. We're not looking for job hoppers. We want people who know a good company when they see one and can settle in, learn our systems and make a meaningful contribution.

What does a manager have to do to have a successful career with Marriott?

Anyone who joins us for a management career has to make a commitment to learn and must be willing to adapt to meet Marriott performance standards. I saw a poster two years ago that said "the key to success is the ability to do ordinary things extraordinarily well." It's very true and reflects the attention to detail that our management positions require.

People who put that kind of extra effort into their jobs are always in short supply and will find Marriott a rewarding place to work.

Marriott guarantees fair treatment to employees. How does the company keep its promise?

The Guarantee of Fair Treatment was formulated by the company decades ago. It says that if you've got a problem, you have the right to take it to whomever you think can help you solve it. It doesn't make you follow a chain of command. It doesn't say you have to go to your boss to get the problem aired.

It's realistic because sometimes we've found that the employee considers the boss to be the problem. In those instances, to require the employee to go to the boss isn't the way to get the problem resolved. In most cases, though, employees will find that the boss *is* the place to go.

The goal of the Guarantee is to ensure that employees are treated respectfully and that on-the-job problems don't distract employees from doing their jobs well.

Marriott prefers to operate union-free. What's the reasoning behind that?

We want to deal directly with our employees, but if a union is present, we don't have that opportunity. A union represents a third party, someone through whom you have to deal to reach your employees.

Employees unionize when they feel the employer isn't treating them fairly and with respect. To prevent that from happening, our company guarantees fair treatment. We also make sure that their benefits and wages are competitive for our industry and that they have good working conditions.

We have to take great interest in our employees because the success of the business depends on them. Unions, on the other hand, frequently have their own agendas, which can be very divisive.

Beyond their paychecks, what keeps managers working for Marriott?

Let's never underestimate the importance of monetary rewards. Marriott, however, offers much more than money. We offer tremendous career opportunities. Marriott's growth is unrivaled in the industry, and people who work for us know that if they do a good job, they can advance.

We also try to recognize people for a job well done through awards, incentive programs and promotions.

How can managers balance the needs of their people with demands for bottom line results?

The primary job of a manager is to make money. Everyone accepts that. But at Marriott, what's important is *how* you make money. In making money, you have to honor the values and principles that have come to mean Marriott—respect for employees; helping them when they need advice, counsel or additional training; providing them with opportunities for advancement. This is what sustains the enthusiasm of our employees so that they deal properly with our customers.

Marriott spends about 35 percent of every dollar it makes on labor. How does the company control these people costs?

Our systems and procedures are designed to use people efficiently and effectively. From labor forecasting in Hotels to productivity studies in In-Flite, we spend a lot of time with our employees to tailor systems that make efficient use of their skills.

How has the Marriott Medical Plan been affected by high health care costs?

For the past few years, medical costs have risen at a rate much greater than the cost of living. As a result, we've been looking at how to better manage and administer our Medical Plan. We started by fine-tuning administrative parts of the plan during '83 and by changing the deductible at the start of '84.

At the same time, we wanted to make the plan more flexible. We currently have a one-size-fits-all plan. But the needs of today's employees are different from those of the employees in years past. Some need a lot of coverage, others can get by with less.

To meet these different needs, "Multi-Med," a program that will replace our current Medical Plan, will be introduced in the fall. Multi-Med will give employees four plans from which to choose. Each will have different costs depending upon the level of coverage the employee selects.

After we've explained Multi-Med, employees who participate will choose the coverage they want by the end of 1984. The new coverages will be effective at the start of 1985.

As Marriott's top human resources executive, what do you want to accomplish in your job in the next year?

I have to make sure that Marriott's human resources activities are contributing to the strategic direction of the company. That means our compensation programs, benefit plans, employee communications programs, etc., must all be focused on helping us meet our business needs.

I'm now working with a consultant and with executives in all of our divisions to be certain that the time, energy and dollars we spend are in tandem with Marriott's strategic plan.

What do you see as your main focus?

My job is almost a single-focus job. I see it as being sure that we provide a climate within Marriott Corporation that assists our managers to grow. I want our managers to be satisfied in their jobs and have pride in being part of a great team, a great company. If we're able to do that with more than 12,000 managers, I'm confident that they will take care of our 100,000 hourly employees.

Part II

Human Resources in Relationship to Top Management Goals, Company Strategy, and Organizational Culture

The readings in Part II concern human resources in relationship to top management goals, company strategy, and organizational culture. The readings were selected because they bring together the views of leaders from three relevant groups: top management, academicians, and consultants. If human resources management is to help advance the long-range goals of the company, then it must take into account the values, attitudes, and philosophies of top management, the unique needs of the business, and the culture of the organization.

Kenneth R. Andrews of the Harvard Business School borrowed from Emerson to say "a corporation is essentially the lengthened shadow of a man."[1] Both employees and observers of such corporations as IBM, Polaroid, and Wang Laboratories know that it is impossible to understand either the culture or the personnel management approaches of those companies without first understanding the philosophies of Thomas Watson, Dr. Edwin Land, and Dr. An Wang, respectively, the founders and long-term leaders of those organizations.

Both personnel and line managers must understand the unique attitudes and approaches of the leaders of their organizations toward people and human resources management if they are going to be effective in their jobs. In "Managing People in the '80s," Preston Parish, vice-chairman of the Upjohn Company, reviews his company's philosophy of employee relations. He claims that

[1]Kenneth R. Andrews, *The Concept of Corporate Strategy* (Homewood, Ill.: Dow-Jones/Richard D. Irwin, Inc., 1971).

the company's employee relations guidelines stem directly from the six basic principles set forth by Dr. W. E. Upjohn, the company's founder. From across the Atlantic, the president of England's Marks and Spencer, the largest retail store chain in the United Kingdom, describes how his company, too, was guided by similar principles. Lord Sieff of Brimpton outlines his company's philosophy, which has proven to be a successful approach to both employee and customer relations. Lord Sieff appreciates the value of a "policy of good human relations at work."

Even though the cost of labor as a percentage of the cost of goods sold is generally low in the high-technology industries, nevertheless, many of the leaders of "hi-tech" long ago recognized that the effective management of human resources is critical to the success of their companies. In fact, many of the most progressive employers, from an employee relations point of view, are high-tech companies. In "Human Resources—The Limitations to High-Technology Growth," Ray Stata, the founder, chairman, and president of Analog Devices, makes the compelling argument that "human resources are, today, the major limitation to growth for many segments of the high-technology industry and will become a significant limitation for other segments as well in the future." He provides some solutions for the shortage of qualified labor in the high-technology industries.

Many now believe that, especially during times of deregulation and rapid technological and industrial change, it is important to understand a company's culture. Some mergers have not worked because of different and incompatible cultures. Changes in strategic direction, too, have been thwarted at some companies because of a poor fit between the new strategy and the old culture. Risk, responsibility, and reward are part of the new culture at General Motors, but many managers have not grown up accustomed to taking risks or acting in an entrepreneurial manner. The article by Howard Schwartz and Stanley Davis ("Matching Corporate Culture and Business Strategy") focuses on these issues in a very practical, realistic, and systematic way. They actually suggest ways to measure "cultural risk."

In "Corporate Strategy: The Essential Intangibles," Kenneth R. Andrews, the pioneer of the corporate strategy field, discusses the evolution of strategic planning, including some of its shortcomings, weaknesses, and fads. Recognizing that "people populate organizations," Andrews notes that the "problems of motivation, will, and desire" must not be left out of the strategy equation. With regard to human resources management, Andrews states:

> But a strategically managed company has not only defined its business by identifying the products and markets it is best equipped to serve in some way different and better than its competitors. Its sense of purpose must extend to the kind of human institution it is to be, for the kind of implementation we have to compete successfully means that the members of our organizations not only know and accept the company's economic strategy but see it embedded in a context of rela-

tionships satisfying their own needs, promising reward for their achievement, and stimulating their own development to greater capability.

This is a broad and comprehensive view of strategy. Andrews' message is profound. Moreover, it is a central theme of this collection of readings.

The article by Donald Meals and John Rogers ("Matching Human Resources to Strategies") also addresses the interconnectedness of human resources management and business objectives. They write specifically about the problems of matching human resources to business strategies in light of the realities of managing diverse corporate activities. Challenging the past traditions of uniform personnel policies and practices, they state:

> Implicit in the view of the corporation as a portfolio of diverse business assets is the concept that human resource systems must be congruent with the strategy of the business unit they are meant to support, even if this leads to considerable variation in programs across the corporation.

Arguing effectively for "differentiated human resource systems," they give examples in five different areas—namely, compensation, benefits, training, performance assessment, and management selection. They conclude by speculating about four effects that they believe the adoption of their principles will have on the human resource management field.

The speech by David McLaughlin ("The Turning Point in Human Resources Management") is an appropriate way to conclude Part II of this volume. It not only defines today's challenges but also suggests the new directions that human resources management must take. An experienced consultant, author, and speaker who also has been a practitioner (he was personnel vice-president for Eastern Airlines when he was 28 years old), McLaughlin has contributed to the development of the human resources profession, making it more strategic and managerially relevant than was the case in the past. McLaughlin argues persuasively that "we are going to have to build a better contextual framework for the management of people in the turbulent 80's."

MANAGING PEOPLE IN THE '80s

Preston S. Parish

The title of this discourse suggests that issues and programs fall into a neat pattern of 10-year intervals. Obviously such is not the case, but the beginning of a new decade provides a readily identifiable benchmark for such examination. Earlier decades have been variously described as the roaring twenties, the me generation of the '70s, and so forth. A title for the '80s might be "greater expectations." I say this because the expectations of employees of U.S. corporations—indeed the expectations of the people of the world—have changed markedly.

In the business world, the proper management of people has occupied the attention of industrial managers and observers of the industrial scene for several decades. And much more has been written in these first two years of the decade of the '80s about effective employee management as the key to a turnaround in declining U.S. productivity. Peter Drucker in his most recent book, *Managing in Turbulent Times*, draws attention to management's need to reexamine this responsibility noting that:

> Management's job is to make human strength productive. . . . The steady upgrading of competence in the work force represents a very large increase in the potential of human strength. Yet by and large managements . . . have not taken the initiative in converting this potential.

William Bowen writing in the *Fortune* series on American renewal under the title "How to Regain our Competitive Edge" emphasizes the need for management to work with employees, citing the following study of coal mining operations:

> In 20 similar coal mines in Wyoming, production in tons per worker-day ranged from 58 to 242, a disparity of better than 4 to 1 though the companies were all mining the same kind of coal with much the same equipment under the same regulations. The main difference was how company management worked with its employees. The most productive firm provided its employees with the greatest amount of individual responsibility and involvement with decision making.

. . . There is nothing startling or novel in this revelation. Perceptive managers have long recognized that people are their most important asset.

Preston S. Parish, "Managing People in the '80s," Kalamazoo Management Association, Inman's of Galesburg, April 14, 1981. Reprinted with permission.

They have sought to encourage worker interest in the corporation through a variety of mechanisms, most of which have been directed to pay, benefits, and job security. These three issues are still of major concern to employees and must provide the foundation for any successful employee relations program. But other concerns, indeed other demands, are beginning to be voiced. As our society has become more affluent (even in the face of inflation) and more leisure time has become available because of the shortening workweek, employees want more control of their work life. The monotonous routine of the production line is becoming less acceptable almost no matter what the wage rate. Employees recognize the impact of their work style upon their life style, and they want to exercise some influence on their individual workplaces. . . .

. . . Daniel Yankelovich called attention to these changes in his book, *A World Turned Upside Down:*

> A generation ago, the typical worker was a man working full time to provide full support for his wife and children. Today, fewer than one out of five persons who work conform to that standard. By the late 1970s, for the first time in U.S. history, the majority of American women (51 percent) were working outside the home. By 1980, more than two out of five mothers of children aged six or younger worked for pay. In families earning more than $25,000 a year, the majority now depend on two incomes: the husband's and the wife's.
>
> Most jobs are still organized as if these changes had not taken place; they continue to be full time, five-day-a-week, regular-hour jobs, with pay and fringe benefits based on the assumption that the job holder is the sole earner in the family. We can expect vast changes in the future in how paid work and child care are organized.

Occupational stress, heretofore accepted as a hazard primarily for executives, is increasingly recognized at all levels of work in an organization. Marital strains, depression, and debt are problems that may be extant in any area of responsibility from blue collar to white.

Workers in growing numbers feel they have a right to participate in decisions affecting their jobs. Curiously enough, this interest does not reflect a desire to encroach on corporate management but rather is directed to their immediate work assignments. Of course, the temptation to expand the scope of influence may be difficult to control, and permitting participation may encourage a broader interest.

Democracy at work relates to a comparison of workplace conditions with conditions in other aspects of one's life. Democracy in this sense does not mean election of management by employees as the term might imply. It does, however, acknowledge employee rights to free speech, to dissent, to privacy, to fair and equitable treatment. It identifies expectations of a work environment more closely resembling nonwork (or away from work) environment.

Quoting again from Yankelovich's book:

> What has actually changed . . . is not our willingness to work, but what we want to get out of a job or a career. Many workers, both young and old, seem to be seeking a whole new set of psychological satisfactions from their jobs. . . . Bigness, newness, excess power, and the other elements of conspicuous consumption are not as important as they once were, not worth the endless sacrifice.

Employees' perception of management's attitude toward them has also changed considerably in the last two decades, as Van Nostrand Reinehold observes in his book *Work in America—The Decade Ahead:*

- In 1977 only 17 percent of clerical workers felt they were treated fairly compared to 66 percent prior to 1960.
- In the period 1975–1977 only one third of hourly workers felt they were treated with respect as individuals.
- In 1977 only 33 percent of hourly workers and 38 percent of clerical workers felt companies were willing to listen to their problems and complaints.
- Eighty-four percent of managers felt they were treated fairly prior to 1960 compared to 45 percent in 1977.

The four issues identified earlier—alternative work schedules, occupational stress, participation, democracy in the workplace—are all part of a program of workplace improvement defined as quality of work life (QWL).

QWL has assumed growing importance and occupied increasing attention of the leaders of American unions. Just last year, 20 international unions convened in Washington, D.C. to address QWL improvements efforts.

The attention devoted to QWL improvements focuses upon changing employee values as described in a recent American Management Association publication authored by Mindell and Gordon. They commented that:

> The value profile of a traditional employee may be characterized as an individual who "places a much higher priority on his work role than on his family role and has high needs for job security. Further, this employee is extremely loyal to his or her organization. Of less importance are . . . having different kinds of things to do on his job, and taking part in decisions affecting his work.
>
> In contrast, the value profile of a 'contemporary' employee indicates that this individual who places a much higher priority on his work role, has high recognition needs, desires job duties that are varied and nonrepetitive, and likes to identify job related problems and develop solutions to those problems independently. This individual does not place as high a value on job security or company loyalty. . . .

Having now acknowledged and noted these changing values and concerns, can we really say that there will be differences in the management of people in the '80s? Not really; the basic principles of employee management have not changed. Good employee relations at all levels demand that the dignity, integrity, and value of the individual be recognized and accepted. But there is no question that the increased expectations of employees to be involved in some measure in decisions affecting their work lives must receive appropriate management response.

The Upjohn Company is generally thought to be uniquely successful in its relationship with its employees. The company's philosophy of employee relations stems directly from its founder's own manner of working with people. That philosophy dates back to 1886 when Dr. W. E. Upjohn founded the company. At the risk of appearing parochial, but at the same time realizing that an actual example is more convincing than a hypothetical one, let me review the principles which still provide the employee relations guidelines used by The Upjohn Company management. There are six:

- *He supported his employees.* Dr. W. E. believed in people's inherent desire to do a good job and believed people would respond affirmatively as long as they recognized management's confidence in them.
- *Dr. Upjohn dealt fairly with his employees.* He firmly believed in the principles of "Do unto others as you would have them do unto you." He would not tolerate any action that suggested taking advantage of an individual.
- *He listened to employees.* Dr. W. E. was willing to consider any suggestion no matter how divergent it might be from his own views as long as he was convinced it was offered in good faith. Furthermore, if the proposal made sense, he would take steps to see that it was implemented.
- *Dr. Upjohn adhered to stated policies.* He was adamant in his position that sound policies were the foundation upon which principles of doing business were based. He would not accept deviation from those policies unless there was general agreement that they should be modified.
- *He provided opportunity to those deserving of it.* The early history of The Upjohn Company is replete with stories of people hired or promoted by Dr. W. E. based on his personal observation of their special capabilities.
- *He made a special effort to recognize individual accomplishment.* This personal characteristic was urged upon each new Upjohn supervisor or manager as the business grew. Dr. W. E. believed that people's greatest desire was for recognition of personal achievement.

On the surface these traits are hardly unusual . . . yet because of the pressures of our daily assignments we often ignore these fundamental principles. The . . . corporate manager, therefore, is not considered to be compassionate and understanding. Corporate managers are thought to be only profit-oriented, heedless of individual and social concerns. This characterization, which is often translated to a corporate attitude, runs counter to increasing demands by individual employees to be heard and to be considered in corporate decisions. And as I have just noted, this employee attitude will intensify in the coming years.

That is not to say that the demand for individual rights will interfere or collide with institutional growth. But it does say that individual concerns must be recognized and included in the planning for growth. Therein lies a challenge to corporations as a whole and a special challenge to those of us involved in management.

Perhaps the most difficult concept to communicate is an understanding of management's concern for the individual. That concern seems to fly in the face of other demands upon members of management to meet financial goals. The real and presumed pressure to perform effectively in areas by which management is judged (the balance sheet, the earnings statement) tends to blur our focus on the concern for the individual employee. For some reason, supervisors feel that attention to employee concerns comes after we have achieved the other goals set by our individual business operations. Yet, it must be obvious that they go hand in hand. One cannot operate a successful business without capable, creative, productive employees. Employees with those qualities will help to improve the balance sheet, to reduce expenses, and to increase earnings. Employees who recognize management's interest in their well-being will be far more effective in accomplishing those objectives than employees who are suspicious of management's attitude toward them. . . .

Offering leadership, providing stimulation, and encouraging development are supervisory responsibilities that must be practiced within the framework of established principles of management of people. It is necessary for all members of a corporation to understand that concern about employees is not only the province of the employee relations group. Quite the contrary, it is principally the province of the manager, because it is the manager to whom an employee looks for direction. Most managers understand the principles of leadership, but occasionally in responding to business pressures, they overlook or ignore certain of those principles. . . .

. . . I have already noted increasing interest among employees about issues other than wages, benefits, and job security. In addition, they are curious about the posture of the corporation in regard to issues of broader concern, especially social issues. It is increasingly true that employees . . . care about a company's relationship to the community, to the nation, and even to the world. This expanded interest on the part of employees adds a new dimension to the process of management. It requires broader management skills and greatly increased communication skills.

Issues which will dominate the business environment during the 1980s will be issues that will also be foremost in the mind of many employees. For example, . . . uncertainty about the future of the U.S. economy, especially in light of continuing high inflation and declining productivity, increases employee concerns about unemployment.

The impact of government growth and government regulation, which now reaches into the core of business activities, is . . . another issue of the eighties. Employees fear that regulation in industries will have a negative impact on the development of products and thus limit continued growth.

Employees recognize that global interdependence is making traditional political and economic boundaries obsolete. . . . Nationalism and protectionism may fragment the world and reduce chances for constructive business policies. The ability of other countries to match our technology and our products quickly and cost-effectively is recognized as a major source of trade problems. Employees worry that the kind of inroads made in the automobile industry by foreign competition may also impact other industry. They already recognize that U.S. products no longer dominate the world markets. . . .

. . . Employees are also apprehensive about future tradeoffs between technological advances and employment. New technology may greatly increase productivity and profits, but the problem of retraining and relocating employees is regarded as a serious threat to individual opportunity.

I think it is fair to say that the new generation of employees have a deepseated apprehension about the impact of external factors on corporations of which they are members. They are concerned not only about the ability of management to function effectively in the light of these pressures, but they are also worried about the impact upon their own opportunities for the future. We must be alert to these concerns, and we must insure that they are factored into all of our decisions related to employee relation practices. It will test our communication skills to the utmost to make certain that the employees realize that we understand their interest in substantive national issues that affect corporations for which they work and thus their own personal lives. . . .

I'd like to conclude with some quotations from Crawford Greenewalt, former president of Du Pont, who in 1960 wrote a remarkable little book entitled *The Uncommon Man*, which I commend to your reading. These quotations are taken from a lecture series (based upon his book) which Mr. Greenewalt presented at Princeton University in March 1961. The observations are as appropriate today as they were then.

> The problem of our present society, a problem which is common to each of its many elements, is how best to preserve the creative power of the individual in the face of organizational necessity. . . .
>
> An organization does not flourish by virtue of the superior talents it enlists. All organizations fish in the same general pool and it is unlikely that any nets a catch appreciably better than others. Its advancement will derive from having provided for its people a climate of achievement in which men of ordinary stature are somehow stimulated to extraordinary performance. The extent to which any given individual can produce beyond his rated capacity may be very small, yet the sum of these, added together, will make the difference between a great organization and an indifferent one.
>
> Obviously this process, through which common men perform uncommon deeds cannot endure in the face of anything that deprives the individual of his dignity or his importance. Nor can it exist in our intricate day and age in an at-

mosphere of anarchy which ignores the need for close relationship and group effort. Somewhere between the two lies the middle ground through which men can find their way to satisfying careers and on which the organization can find its most effective pace.

Those corporations most likely to provide the appropriate "climate of achievement" that will be demanded by the employee of the '80s will be those practicing sound principles of people management. In so doing, they will stimulate the "extraordinary performance" that will be required if we are to successfully meet our national needs of this and following decades.

THE IMPORTANCE OF GOOD HUMAN RELATIONS AT WORK

Lord Sieff of Brimpton

Mr. President, ladies and gentlemen, how delighted I am to have received an Honorary Degree from Babson College and to join the distinguished ranks of those who have been similarly recognised; it gives me much pleasure. . . .

I am going to talk mainly about two subjects. First, that in this day and age real leadership in industry entails an understanding by top management of the importance of implementing a policy of good human relations at work. Second, that with the problems of high unemployment due sometimes to lack of demand, the decline of many traditional industries and the transition to new industries, it is necessary for successful private enterprise to understand our social responsibilities in the community and act accordingly.

I am a third generation shopkeeper. I have worked for Marks and Spencer for 50 years with two breaks, one during World War II and the second when I spent from 1948 to 1951 in the newly created State of Israel.

Throughout my business career I have been involved in wealth creation for the benefit of our shareholders, our employees, our pensioners, and the communities where we operate. We have made progress and been successful, but this would not have been possible without close co-operation with many companies in manufacture, agriculture, building, transport, with scientific and technological institutions worldwide, and with schools and universities. My experience therefore is perhaps wider than one might think from working for the same company for 50 years.

Let me tell you briefly about Marks and Spencer. We are retailers with some 260 stores in the United Kingdom, nine stores on the mainland of Europe, the controlling interest in 200 small stores in Canada, and we export to 30 countries. Our group turnover in the financial year to March 1984 was £2,854 million, and our profits before tax were £280 million, after tax, £166 million. Our turnover and profits have doubled in the last five years. We have 54,000 employees in the group.

Our approach is simple; we are in some ways an unusual and perhaps

"The Importance of Good Human Relations at Work," commencement speech at Babson College, May 19, 1984, by Lord Marcus Sieff. Reprinted with permission.

old-fashioned operation in that we are still largely a cash business and, though we are retailers, we seldom advertise. We sell a limited range of clothing, home furnishings, fancy goods, and foods, but the items we carry, whether it be sweaters or poultry, we carry in depth. We manufacture nothing, but co-operate closely both with our suppliers of finished goods and those who supply the raw materials, including farmers and food processors.

Although we are a retail firm, we have some 300 scientists, technologists, and supporting staff at our headquarters. We learned a good deal about a retailer controlling the quality of the goods he sells from our contacts with Sears Roebuck in Chicago in the 1930s.

We sell about 16 percent of the clothing sold in the United Kingdom under one brand name, St. Michael; we are the greatest supporters of British womanhood as we sell nearly 40 percent of the bras in Britain.

This year is our centenary year. My grandfather, Michael Marks, a poor immigrant from Lithuania, the founder of the business, started a stall in Leeds Open Market in Yorkshire in 1884. I do not suppose he visualised what his stall would become 100 years later.

People ask me what are the reasons for such success as we have enjoyed. I explain it is because we have a philosophy and principles to which we adhere. While our merchandise policy is flexible, our principles are sacrosanct. They are:

1. We are concerned with high quality and good value, not cheapness; if we cannot get what we want, we do not knowingly sell an inferior line. We are not interested in the "quick buck."
2. We buy British goods and foodstuffs wherever possible. Over 90 percent of St. Michael goods are made or grown in the United Kingdom. We only import if we cannot find the quality and value we seek at home.
3. We believe and implement a policy of good human relations at work. We implement a policy of constructive involvement in the communities in which we operate. . . .

If we are to have a dynamic free enterprise sector within a mixed economy, then responsible industrial leadership is vital, and to be responsible, industrial leadership must create good human relations at work. I am talking about more than industrial relations. We are human beings at work, not industrial beings.

You cannot legislate good human relations. In the United Kingdom, both Labour and Conservative governments introduced legislation in the last 15 years with this in view. Both were total failures. Such relations must come from the heart and the head and can only develop if top management believes in their importance and then sees that such a philosophy is dynamically implemented.

My experience is that everyone in senior management, be it private enterprise, government, trade union, or state-controlled industry, says he or she believes in the importance of good human relations, but in fact some top managements merely pay lip service and do not care a damn about them; others believe in them but do not know how to implement them. An increasing number of leaders implement a policy of good human relations successfully, but they are still too few.

It is easy to say one believes in good human relations, but it costs time, effort, and money, as well as determination, to implement such a policy; but it is time, effort, and money well spent. It is a continuous task, not something for which one makes an effort from time to time. It must be based on respect for the individual.

Many senior managers do not really appreciate the conditions under which their fellow employees work, and quite a few don't even know. Management must know what working conditions are like on the factory and shop floor.

They cannot know how good or bad staff amenities are unless they make use of them themselves, eat in the staff canteens, see whether the food is decent and well-cooked, determine whether the place is clean, or visit the staff cloakrooms, lavatories, and such other amenities as are provided. If amenities are not good enough for those in charge, they are not good enough for any employee.

Management must recognise and implement its social responsibility and exercise just and firm leadership. Then union leaders and all employees have to recognise their responsibility and obligations as well as accept the benefit such a policy brings. Our experience and that of many manufacturing and service organisations, large and small, with whom we work, is that the great majority of employees do so.

There is need for more open management. There is very little need for secrecy. But I find, certainly in the United Kingdom, that too many in top management still believe in secrecy and tell their employees as little as possible of what is happening instead of as much as possible. Good communications both up and down are most important.

I think we were always good employers by the standards of the day, but let me tell you how this policy which has proved so successful and profitable became one of the foundations of our business. . . .

At the time of the Depression, we were a moderate size but successful business. My father and Simon Marks, then chairman, were visiting stores . . . and found one or two members of our staff were hungry. On investigation they found that, though we paid quite good wages, . . . when other members of the family were out of work the one wage earner's pay was being shared, and, as unemployment payments in those days were below subsistence level, people were hungry.

So the heads of Marks and Spencer installed kitchens, dining rooms, and rest rooms in every store and provided good meals at a nominal price. Today this would be normal, but it was a revolutionary step 50 years ago, and it led us into the whole area of looking after our staff's welfare—medical and dental care, early detection of breast and cervical cancer (the majority of our staff are women)—and into many other activities, such as chiropody and hairdressing facilities for the staff and eventually noncontributory pensions and profit-sharing.

Our staff appreciated our efforts, became more identified with the business (many considered themselves partners, not employees), and they worked harder and were always open to change. This is part of the reason for our profitable progress.

We discuss our personnel policies openly. Some heads of other companies are critical that we spend a great deal of money on employee benefits—their cost last year was over £50 million—and so much time on personnel problems. Our personnel department is over 900 strong.

They say to me: "You must be soft in the head." And I reply: "I suppose we are, but you know if you look at the bottom line—our profits—we can't be all that mad." We have long been convinced that this constructive involvement with people is one of the best investments we have ever made. . . .

We also encourage our suppliers to practice good human relations. Thirty years ago I was visiting stores with Simon Marks, then chairman. We were leaving the Dartford store, which was in the middle of a major rebuilding programme which would take nearly two years. The rain was pouring down. As we got into the car Simon said to me: "I must go to the john." Instead of going back into the store, he went to the building labourer's area where the workers were sitting under a tarpaulin slung over two girders from which the rain was coming down in buckets, drinking mugs of tea, eating thick sandwiches, and looking as miserable as hell. The toilet was a primitive chemical closet.

In the car, Simon said, "You know, Marcus, those fellows will be working on that site for one to two years. They are really working for us; we can't have two different standards."

We met with our main builders, Bovis, to discuss providing decent facilities for all their labour. We agreed with them that on our building sites the first structures to go up would be decent facilities for the building workers—canteen, proper lavatories, showers, and a drying room for clothes.

Bovis does 95 percent of our building. In the last 29 years, they have completed about 400 major jobs for us costing hundreds of millions of pounds. No building has been handed over a day late, and quite a number have been handed over many weeks early. Bovis is profitable, progressive, and held in high esteem.

We enjoy good relations with our customers. We work hard to ensure good service. Our policy of easy exchange of goods or refunds gives our customers confidence. Our customers reward us with loyalty and constructive suggestions for improvement. When we make a mistake, and believe me, we make plenty, then our customers will tell us. They tell us often more in sorrow, not in anger. . . .

But in today's difficult economic conditions, good human relations with staff, suppliers, and customers are not enough. A profitable business cannot progress in isolation from the community in which it works and trades, and many communities in the United Kingdom are in recession with unemployment and inner city decay.

We donate, as do many other companies, substantial sums to medicine, the arts, and worthwhile charities; our staff are involved in supporting local causes. But the responsibilities of a business go further.

In addition to helping financially, we have seconded for periods from six months to two years some of our most capable people to help develop and direct various worthwhile community projects. Their work has been valuable and constructive. At any one time, between 12 and 20 people are seconded. . . .

As I said earlier, this is our centenary year. We decided to celebrate the year by asking each store to choose a community project for which we would give the seed money to get the project off the ground, or in some cases where the projects were small, we would pay for them in their entirety. We set aside, in addition to the normal funds we make available for charity, some £3¹/₂ million for this work. Our store staff have worked enthusiastically in their spare time for these projects and, unasked, have themselves raised several hundred thousand pounds to add to the money we are providing. This reflects the degree of their involvement.

I imagine most of you have read something about the troubles in Northern Ireland. Belfast has seen a great deal of violence. When, some time ago, I was visiting our Belfast store I asked one of the supervisors what they were doing for the centenary. She said that their project was to help provide sheltered housing for people with orthopaedic disabilities who would otherwise have to go into geriatric wards in hospitals.

The company had allocated the store some £27¹/₂ thousand as seed money. She said: "We are going to raise the same amount ourselves." I said: "Have you started?" She said: "Yes; we have been at it for five weeks and the staff have raised £4,000." I said: "How?"—and this was just before Christmas—she said: "Last night we sang carols in the centre of Belfast and raised £700." I said: "Who are we?" She said: "We were 50 percent Catholic and 50 percent Protestant."

I hope I have explained to you some of the reasons which have contributed to our progress. If we managers do not appreciate the value of, and pursue with patience and tenacity, a policy of good human relations at work and constructive involvement in the community, and instead go for the "quick buck," then we must not be surprised if we wake up one morning to find ourselves members of a society that few of us want, where democratic values no longer operate, and there is little freedom. Then we shall have only ourselves to blame.

HUMAN RESOURCES— THE LIMITATION TO HIGH-TECHNOLOGY GROWTH

Ray Stata

To begin our conference, I thought it would be appropriate to explore exactly what we mean by the high-technology industry; to identify some of its characteristics and trends in relation to the overall economy; and to question some of the limitations to growth within it. This discussion will show, I believe, that human resources are, today, the major limitation to growth for many segments of the high-technology industry and will become a significant limitation for other segments as well in the future. I shall conclude by speculating on the strategic, long-term implications of a human-resource limited environment. . . .

DEFINING THE HIGH-TECHNOLOGY INDUSTRY

What do we mean by high technology industry? We called various agencies, private and public, only to learn that fact and opinion on this subject are sparse. The Conference Board, which is regarded as the most comprehensive private business research organization in the country, surprisingly replied that none of its researchers is familiar with the high-technology industry. So before we get too heady about our importance to society, we must realize that high technology is not yet Main Street, U.S.A.

We did find, however, that economists from the Department of Commerce have given this subject some careful thought and have found that high-technology companies share these characteristics:

1. Research and development expenditure as a percentage of value added is greater than ten times non-high-technology companies.
2. The ratio of scientific and engineering manpower in non-research and development functions to production workers is five times greater than non-high-technology companies.

Ray Stata, "Human Resources—The Limitations to High-Technology Growth," summary of the keynote address at the Industrial Marketing Conference on High Technology, American Marketing Association, March 19, 1979. Reprinted with permission.

3. The ratio of skilled to non-skilled workers is 70 percent greater than non-high-technology companies.

This definition appropriately focuses on the knowledge and skills of the workforce as the distinguishing feature of the high-technology industry.

By this definition, three SIC codes represent a concentrated number of high-technology companies—SIC#28-chemicals, including drug companies; SIC#36-electrical equipment, including electronic component companies, and SIC#38-professional and scientific instruments. These SIC categories were used to compile the statistics we shall present later, since this is the data base used most often by researchers in this field, including the important study by Data Resources, Inc., of Lexington, MA, entitled "Technology, Labor, and Economic Potential."

Bear in mind that the data you will see is very crude in that many of the three-digit subcategories of these two-digit industry segments are distinctly low technology, and some of the more "glamorous" high-technology segments are not included at all. For example, office equipment, SIC#357, which includes the fast-growing computer industry, is mysteriously stuck in the category for non-electrical equipment, SIC#35, which is predominantly made up of low-growth, low-technology companies. In many ways, published data on trends in the high-technology industry are misleading because it is so difficult to get meaningful statistics.

ECONOMIC TRENDS

But even with these smoothing effects, high-technology employment, by this definition, is becoming a significant percentage of total manufacturing employment, and an even greater percentage of real manufacturing GNP (Figure 1). While total manufacturing is only 22 percent of total U.S. em-

FIGURE 1.   High Technology as Percentage of Manufacturing

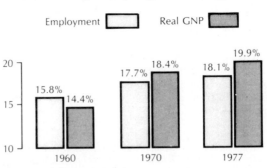

Source: Bureau of Economic Analysis.

FIGURE 2.   Dynamics of High Technology (Annual Growth 1960–77)

	Employment	GNP-Real	Productivity	Prices
High Tech. Mfg.	1.8%	5.7%	3.9%	1.7%
Low Tech. Mfg.	0.5%	2.9%	2.4%	3.6%
Manufacturing	0.9%	3.8%	2.4%	3.1%
U.S. Economy	1.9%	3.5%	1.6%	4.3%

Source: Bureau of Economic Analysis

ployment, we should remember that manufacturing jobs are the cornerstone of our economy, since each primary job in manufacturing supports several additional jobs in service industries and in government.

In looking at the comparative dynamics of the high-technology industry, other important features emerge (Figure 2). For one, high technology is gradually replacing low technology as a source of manufacturing employment growth. Its real GNP growth is substantially ahead of that of the U.S. economy and of the total manufacturing sector. Its productivity is growing at a rate of 3.9 percent versus 1.6 percent for the total economy. And price inflation in high-technology products has been well below that of the total economy as a result of productivity improvements and advances in technology. In fact, some high-technology products like electronic integrated circuits are actually experiencing significant price deflation due to rapid technological progress.

Finally, high-technology products contribute favorably to our trade balance as the technology underlying many of our capital goods products is ahead of other developed countries (Figure 3). For example, the United States is a net importer from Japan of consumer electronic products like radios, TV's and Hi-Fi's; but it is a net exporter to Japan of electronic capital goods like computers and instruments. While high-technology products ac-

FIGURE 3.   Contribution to Trade Balance, 1976

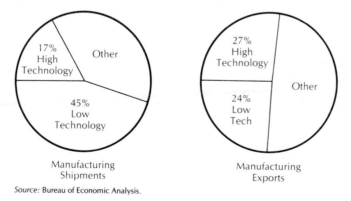

Source: Bureau of Economic Analysis.

FIGURE 4.   Selected Electronics Growth Companies

	Employment	Sales ($M)	Exports As % Sales	Sales Growth (5-Year Avg.)
Texas Instruments	78,571	$2,550	31.3	12.8%
Hewlett Packard	42,000	1,728	47.6	18.2
Digital Equipment	37,500	1,437	38.0	35.8
Intel	10,900	401	33.9	43.7
National Semiconductor	26,500	494	29.0	23.3
Data General	10,830	380	31.2	42.2
Total	206,301	6,990	36.6%	20.6%

count for 17 percent of manufacturing shipments, they account for 27 percent of our manufacturing exports, a significant fraction that is still growing.

These statistics and trends, while impressive, mask the dramatic growth which is occurring in the more vigorous sectors of the high-technology industry (Figure 4). If we look in detail at selected companies in high-growth sectors, we get a more accurate picture of the dynamics of many high-technology companies. For example, Intel has grown from a dead start in 1968 to over $400 million in sales in just ten short years. This is one of the most impressive growth records in the history of industrial development. These high-growth companies are also exporting a significantly higher percentage of their sales than the 17 percent average for the high-technology industry as previously defined.

LIMITATIONS TO HIGH-TECHNOLOGY GROWTH

With this background, I'd like to now explore the limitations to growth of the high-technology industry. A great deal is being said and written about technology as a limitation to growth, and specifically that U.S. companies are falling behind Europe and Japan in technical innovation. It is encouraging to see that at the highest levels of government there is concern for this important issue, and that some effort is under way to steer government policy in a direction that will not handicap our high-technology industry compared to other countries.

While the technology gap between the United States and Japan and Europe continues to narrow, the facts are, at this point, that the United States has retained technical leadership in many important areas. I think the problem in America is not so much that the technology of our leading-edge companies is lagging behind the rest of the world as it is that the redeployment of labor and capital from inherently low-technology, low-productivity industries to high-technology, high-productivity industries is proceeding too slowly and that incentives to apply existing technology to increase labor productivity are inadequate. In any case, I do not believe that technology per se will be a significant limitation to growth of the high-technology industry in the future. This is not to say that we should be complacent about the challenge to our technical leadership, but rather we should acknowledge that there is already a great deal of technology available today in this country and around the world which has yet to be fully exploited.

By the same token, I don't believe market opportunity will be a limitation to growth of the high-technology industry. If anything, the marketplace is suffering from a case of indigestion in its inability to absorb new technology as rapidly as it is being developed. New market opportunities are already opening up at an exciting rate based on the technology we now have in hand and based on the return-on-investment and other benefits which this technology offers the user.

AVAILABILITY OF CAPITAL RESOURCES

Since 1969 there has been serious concern about the availability of capital resources to fund the growth of high-technology industry. While this is still a concern, it can be argued that the tide has turned on national tax policy, as evidenced by the reduction of capital gains tax last year, and by the further initiatives under way to stimulate capital formation. Furthermore, high-technology companies in the high-growth sectors are not very capital-intensive, and, therefore, once they have achieved a profitable mode of operation, they can usually internally generate most of their capital needs. The critical need is to assure an adequate flow of high-risk venture capital to new companies by further reduction of capital gains tax.

I would argue that while all these factors and many others place constraints on growth for some industry segments, the most fundamental and enduring limitation to growth will be the availability of human resources with the knowledge and skills required to maintain the growth potential of this industry.

HUMAN-RESOURCE LIMITATIONS

I cannot speak knowledgeably about other industry segments, but in the electronics industry there is a critical shortage of manpower today. There is a hierarchy of shortages based on the length of post-high-school training which is required as indicated in Figure 5. From time to time, there are shortages of unskilled workers, but this is not a fundamental problem since, in three to six months, workers can be trained for these positions. In the worst case, expansion of production capacity can be moved to pockets of unemployment.

FIGURE 5.   Hierarchy of Manpower Shortages

	Post High School Training
Unskilled Workers	3–6 Months
Junior Paraprofessionals	2–3 Years
Senior Paraprofessionals	3–7 Years
Junior Professionals	5–10 Years
Senior Professionals	10–25 Years

The problem becomes more serious with paraprofessionals like technicians, draftspeople, and computer programmers who generally require two to three years of post-high-school training, plus up to five years of industrial experience to become fully proficient in their skills. But the most critical shortages are professional workers, primarily engineers and managers, where the education, plus on-the-job experience, can take as much as 10 to 25 years to develop a senior-level professional worker. The intensity of professional workers in the high-technology industry is driven home by our own statistics: about one third of our employees hold college degrees, of which more than one half are in science or engineering (Figure 6).

As indicated in Figure 7, the sources for high-technology employment are either graduates from high schools and colleges or transfers from the non-high-technology labor base, which today numbers about 90,000,000. Over time, a gradual employment shift from the non-high to the high-technology sector will occur, but only for job classifications where the retraining requirements are modest.

Certainly it is possible to retrain unskilled workers for employment in the high-technology industry; and it is possible for professionals with

FIGURE 6.   Typical Workforce Profile

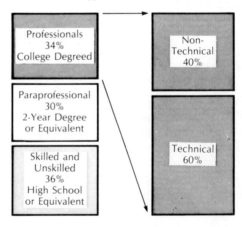

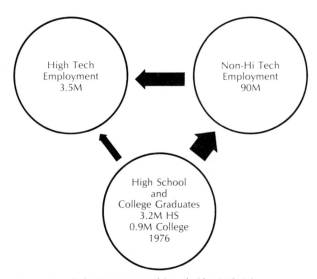

Source: Bureau of Labor Statistics, National Center for Education Statistics.

FIGURE 7. Sources of High Technology Employment

general business skills such as finance, industrial relations, and general administration to apply their prior experience to similar job functions in the high-technology industry. However, it is very difficult for professionals in functions like engineering, marketing, and manufacturing, where specialized technical knowledge is necessary, to make this transition because of the extensive training requirements. Therefore, the primary source of employment for technically oriented professionals is directly from universities. This is where the bottleneck to growth is occurring. Thus, growth in the high-technology industry is limited by the flow of new technical graduates into the workforce.

When we look at the demographics of the United States in Figure 8, we see some disturbing trends regarding the growth of high-technology in-

FIGURE 8. Demographics (Annual Percent Growth)

	Population			Civilian Labor Force		
	Total	18–21	22–24	25–64	Total	16–24	26–64
1960–1970	1.3	4.4	4.3	0.8	1.7	4.4	1.2
1970–1976	0.8	2.2	2.2	1.5	2.3	5.3	1.9
1976–1980	0.6	0.5	2.0	1.7	1.8	4.2	1.9
1980–1985	0.7	− 2.0	0.1	1.7	1.6	− 0.4	2.3
1985–1990	0.6	− 1.2	− 3.0	1.4	1.4	− 1.4	2.2

Source: U.S. Bureau of Census, Bureau of Labor Statistics, Data Resources, Inc., National Center for Education Statistics.

FIGURE 9.   Education of the Labor Force (Annual Percent Growth)

	High School Grads	BA College	BS Eng'g
1960–1970	4.5	7.9	1.6
1970–1976	1.4	2.6	0.8
1976–1980	− 0.4	2.2	11.3
1980–1985	− 2.7	0.1	−0.1

dustry. First, population growth at the college level has already started to decline and will continue to decline for the next decade. This impact has not yet been fully realized in the growth of the civilian labor force because of the increased percentage of women taking jobs. But this can be a deceiving statistic for the high-technology industry, since few women today are trained for technical and managerial positions in this industry.

The significance of these statistics is better summarized in Figure 9 by the expected growth of the labor force by level of education. The expected sharp decline in percentage growth of college graduates after 1980 comes at a time when the high-technology industry will be in full bloom. The uneven growth of engineering graduates is graphically portrayed in Figure 10. College enrollments in science and engineering dropped sharply in 1970 when dramatic cutbacks in defense and space spending, on top of a general recession, threw thousands of engineers out of work and Ph.D.'s ended up driving taxi cabs. Six years later, we started to suffer the results of this debacle, with severe engineering shortages at a time when competition from Japan and Europe was becoming more intense. Engineering enrollments rose

FIGURE 10.   Number of Engineering Graduates Compared to All BA Graduates

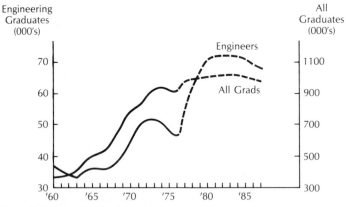

Source: National Center for Education Statistics.

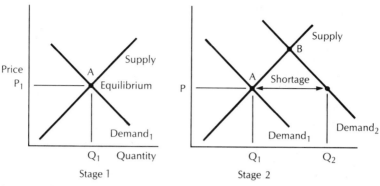

Source: Kenneth Arrow.

FIGURE 11.   Dynamic Shortages

again as career opportunities reappeared, and we are now seeing an unusual growth at this time. But, as predicted here, demographics may soon constrain the growth of engineering graduates.

Apart from demographics, from another point of view, Kenneth Arrow, a noted economist, asserts that there will always be dynamic shortages in high-growth industries. As illustrated in Figure 11, a sudden increase in demand creates a dynamic shortage, since labor prices in the market respond slowly to changes in demand, and supply will not instantly respond even if prices rise. Colleges are constrained to some extent by tenure from shifting teaching resources to respond to changing demand, particularly now that they are under fiscal pressure with an outlook for zero population growth. And in any case, it takes five years on average to graduate an engineer, and another five years of experience to reach professional maturity in high-growth industries. Demand keeps moving out faster than the market forces and the structural constraints can respond, thus creating a continuous dynamic shortage. The longer the training lead time, the more critical the shortage.

Researchers on the subject of engineering manpower trends at M.I.T. reach a different conclusion. They argue that, due to the delay time through the training process, there is an inherent oscillatory or cyclical characteristic to engineering enrollments. This, they say, will lead to a glut of engineers on the market in the early '80's as the current euphoria over employment opportunities will generate more engineers a few years hence than the industry can absorb.

I come down on the side of Kenneth Arrow with the conclusion that, despite the high growth of engineering graduates we are now seeing, unless we have another severe recession, we are in for a prolonged period where demand for professionals, especially technical professionals, will exceed supply.

STRATEGIC IMPLICATIONS

If we assume that human-resource availability will be the limiting factor to growth in at least some segments of the high-technology industry, then what implications will this have on business strategy?

Clearly one implication is that organizational development and the management of human resources will have a greater bearing on success in the future than it has had in the past. Companies must rely more on college recruiting rather than on pirating experienced people to expand their organizations. This, in turn, will put greater emphasis on internal training and career development programs, particularly in smaller firms. We shall also be under pressure to make our experienced professionals more productive by greater investment in supporting personnel and in capital equipment that will automate routine work. For example, justification for buying a $200,000 computerized drafting machine might not be based so much on classical return-on-investment as on improving the productivity of senior design engineers.

Greater emphasis on human resources applies to the management of every function, so that as a sales and marketing manager you will have to broaden your knowledge and skills in human-resource management and focus more of your attention on how to acquire and train the people you need to grow.

SMALL VERSUS LARGE ORGANIZATIONS

Another point is that college graduates are showing a preference for smaller organizations. This reflects a quest for autonomy on the part of young professionals, and a desire to make decisions and to shoulder responsibility early in their careers. They perceive that smaller organizations provide a better environment for delegating responsibility than larger organizations. And, in fact, small, fast-growing companies are so short on experienced managers that they often promote bright young people before they have adequate experience, by conventional standards, and then force-feed their development on the job, often, I might mention, with a high level of success. Other statistics show that smaller companies produce a substantially greater number of technical innovations for the same resources employed than do larger companies.

Taking these factors together, large companies should not discount the ability of small companies to effectively compete in human-resource-limited environment. Small companies can attract perhaps more than their share of good talent, and they tend to use this talent very productively. This suggests that larger, high-technology companies should decentralize their organizations and push decision-making responsibility well down in the structure; that is, they should look and act more like a combination of highly flexible, small companies.

SPECIALIZATION

The degree of industry specialization becomes very sensitive to human-resource availability in a shortage environment as depicted in Figure 12. For example, in the limit if there were only two companies each with only one product design engineer, an optimum business strategy would presumably be to work on totally different products with, therefore, an infinite degree of industry specialization. Whereas as product designers become available without limit, competition between firms intensifies and other factors like channels of distribution and capital-resource availability have a greater influence on the degree of industry specialization.

We see this phenomenon at work in the electronics industry with end-user equipment manufacturers buying certain specialized components and subsystems, which they used to manufacture themselves. Specialization conserves industry engineering resources by sharing engineering investments in component and subsystem building blocks with a large number of end-user equipment manufacturers. Many electronic companies find they are better off investing their scarce engineering resources in the design of the products they sell rather than duplicating the design of standard components and subsystems which they can buy at attractive prices. We also see a proliferation of new companies growing up to serve emerging markets where established companies do not have enough engineering resources to address both their present markets and emerging new ones.

FIGURE 12.   Human Resources Effect on Specialization

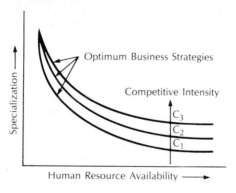

MARKETING VERSUS TECHNOLOGY

Human-resource limitations reemphasize the importance of good strategic marketing decisions. What products and markets will give you the most leverage from your scarce human resources? What new product and new application opportunities can be milked from your existing technology base? How can you broaden the market and customer base for products already designed and in production?

One way to achieve greater leverage on investments in technology is to adapt a worldwide marketing orientation. Many high-technology companies in America do not penetrate foreign markets anywhere near their full potential. There is a tendency to treat export sales as add-on business to domestic operations, rather than to develop policies, strategies, and organizations specifically to optimize foreign market penetration.

While I don't want to down-play the importance of technology development, it can be argued that growth may be more feasible through market development than through technology development when there is a critical shortage of engineers, particularly when the market has not fully absorbed or comprehended the technology which is already available.

Even the more forward-looking high-technology companies that have aggressively developed foreign markets have tended to concentrate their research and development effort in this country. In a human-resource-limited environment, multinational companies should spread their nets to capture engineering and management talent in other developed countries, and to develop and manufacture products in those countries for international export. Perhaps the most attractive feature for business development in Japan is the growing number of well-educated, energetic engineers. We should get used to the fact that the technology gap between America and other developed countries has narrowed and may, in time, vanish altogether. But to move in this direction will require a large change in the thinking of U.S.-based companies and in the structure of their organizations.

GOVERNMENT POLICY

The scenario discussed here suggests certain government policies that would benefit the high-technology industry and, therefore, the U.S. economy as well, due to the higher productivity and export potential for this industry. First, to direct government policy we need to get the facts straight. The true dynamics of the high-technology industry are being masked by the way industry statistics are compiled. We need a much better handle on employment growth rate data, which should be broken down by educational requirements, so that industry and educational institutions can better judge the whole picture. Knowledge-intensive industry is a new phenomenon which is still poorly understood.

Second, we should restore the tax incentives of qualified stock options to attract talent to high-risk, high-growth opportunities. Third, government should, at all costs, avoid a repeat of the disastrous destabilization of critical resource employment, which it induced in 1970 and, to the contrary, should seek measures to absorb temporary oversupply of critical talent should a recession disturb the long-term growth trend. Fourth, while unrelated to human resources, the high-technology industry should urge our government to further reduce capital gains tax so that equity capital is available in America competitive with Germany and Japan. A restoration of tax policy to encourage risk-taking is the single most important step we can take to stimulate technical innovation.

SUMMARY

To summarize, marketing professionals in the high-technology industry must take a very broad view of their role in formulating business strategy. This discussion illustrates how issues like human-resource limitations not normally associated with marketing decisions can have an important influence on your area of responsibility. Hopefully, this information will stimulate you to think more about human-resource issues and how they may affect your business and your career growth in the future.

MATCHING CORPORATE CULTURE
AND BUSINESS STRATEGY

Howard Schwartz   **Stanley M. Davis**

Which are the well-run companies? Are they the star performers so often referred to in articles about good management and organization—GE, GM, IBM, Texas Instruments? Not to mention the Mitsubishis, Sonys, ICIs, Phillipses, and Siemenses of the world? Whatever your list, a discussion of what makes these firms tops will involve notions of their strategic sense, their clear organization, their management systems, and their excellent top people. Even then, a description generally ends up with statements about some vague thing called corporate "style" or "culture." Apparently, the well-run corporations of the world have distinctive cultures that are somehow responsible for their ability to create, implement, and maintain their world leadership positions.

Coca-Cola and Pepsi, Hertz and Avis, Mars and Hershey are direct competitors within their industries. No doubt their strategies differ significantly. No less doubtfully, so do their companies' cultures. All one has to do to get a feel for how the different cultures of competing businesses manifest themselves is to spend a day visiting each. Of course there are patterns in the trivia of variations in dress, jargon, and style—but there is something else going on as well. There are characteristic ways of making decisions, relating to bosses, and choosing people to fill key jobs.

These mundane routines buried deep in companies' cultures (and subcultures) may be the most accurate reflections of why things work the way they do, and of why some firms succeed with their strategies where others fail. And if we can get at the way in which these minutiae determine an organization's ability to create and to carry out strategy—that is, if we can learn how to evaluate corporate culture—we can also learn a great deal about how to manage a large organization through a period of strategic change.

There are many examples of corporate cultures that, though once a source of strength, have become major obstacles to success. In 1978, for instance, AT&T announced that it was making a major strategic shift—from a service-oriented telephone utility to a market-oriented communications

Howard Schwartz and Stanley M. Davis, "Matching Corporate Culture and Business Strategy," reprinted, by permission of the publisher, from Organizational Dynamics, *Summer 1981, © 1981 AMACOM, a division of American Management Associations, New York. All rights reserved.*

business. Chairman J. D. deButts went on intracompany TV to announce to every employee that "we will become a marketing company." To implement this new strategy, AT&T has had to undertake the largest organizational transformation in the history of U.S. industry. One out of every three of the one million jobs in AT&T will be changed. Despite the major changes in structure, in human resources, and in support systems, there is a general consensus both inside and outside AT&T that its greatest task in making its strategy succeed will be its ability to transform the AT&T culture. It will probably be a decade before direct judgments should be made as to its success. In the meantime, however, we are concerned with how to get your hands around an organization's culture.

One man who tried was Walter Spencer, the former president of Sherwin-Williams Company. For six years Spencer tried to turn around a firm that suffered from an overabundance of unprofitable products that could not, it seemed, be cut; from antiquated plant and equipment that could not be written off; and from a deeply entrenched manufacturing bias on the part of the board of directors, who were sitting in the capital-goods-oriented city of Cleveland. Speaking of his attempt to transform Sherwin-Williams from a production-oriented company to a marketing-oriented one, Spencer said, "When you take a 100-year-old company and change the culture of the organization, and try to do that in Cleveland's traditional business setting— well, it takes time. You just have to keep hammering away at everybody." After six years of such "hammering away," Spencer resigned, saying the job was no longer any fun. He had dented but not changed the culture.

Corporate cultures impose powerful influences on the behavior of managers. As the examples given above suggest, a business that is shifting its strategic direction may find its culture a source of strength or of weakness. It is possible to evaluate this elusive aspect of organization that appears to be so intimately linked with strategic success or failure. One can gauge the likely impact an organization's culture will have on the chances for success of future business strategies, and it is the aim of this article to show how to do so.

STRATEGY AND ORGANIZATION

Most people realize intuitively that corporate organizations designed to implement strategy are a lot more than the boxes and lines on an organization chart. Despite this awareness, managers often behave as though organizing a business to execute a new strategy is primarily a question of redrawing the boxes. In such a situation they frequently ask "What is the right structure for dividing and coordinating work?"

Executives are generally aware, however, that a corporation's management systems, and the skills and experience of its people, are as much a part of its organization as its structure. Organizations cannot function without some degree of regularized, formal information flows, policies, procedures, and meetings through which the essential tasks of the business are carried out. Organizations are also built upon the skills, experience, and needs of the people who compose them. It has also become clear that corporations have distinct cultures.

Anthropologist Clyde Kluckhohn has usefully defined culture as "the set of habitual and traditional ways of thinking, feeling, and reacting that are characteristic of the ways a particular society meets its problems at a particular point in time." A corporation's culture, similarly, is reflected in the attitudes and values, the management style, and the problem-solving behavior of its people.

Organizational theorists and executives agree that the best answer to the question, "How should we organize to pursue a particular strategy?" depends on a complex set of trade-offs among structure, systems, people, and culture. No organization will perform well in a competitive environment unless these four dimensions of organization are internally consistent and fit the strategy. While a great deal is known about managing the first three dimensions—structure, systems, and people—there is little more than an intuitive sense about how to manage the fourth dimension of organization—culture—and we will therefore limit ourselves in this article to matching corporate culture and business strategy.

WHAT CORPORATE CULTURE IS
(AND ISN'T)

Most executives with whom we have discussed corporate culture are comfortable with the idea that their companies have such a dimension. They are unsure, however, about what the word means in a business context and what use they could make of a better understanding of their own organization's culture. It was suggested earlier that an understanding of culture might reduce the risk of failure. Before describing how, it is important to clarify what we mean by culture and to illustrate how a company's culture can be usefully understood.

One way to understand culture is to understand what it is not. Many large corporations, for instance, periodically undertake climate surveys to "take the temperature" of their organizations. But climate is not culture. Climate is a measure of whether people's expectations about what it *should* be like to work in an organization are being met. Measurements of climate can be very helpful in pinpointing the causes of poor employee motivation, such as unclear organizational goals, dissatisfaction with compensation, inadequate advancement opportunities, or biased promotion practices. Action to address these sources of dissatisfaction tends to improve motivation.

Improved motivation ought to result in improved performance, and by and large the evidence suggests that it does.

Culture, on the other hand, is a pattern of beliefs and expectations shared by the organization's members. These beliefs and expectations produce norms that powerfully shape the behavior of individuals and groups in the organization. So, while climate measures whether expectations are being met, culture is concerned with the nature of these expectations themselves.

For example, Douglas McGregor's early notions about management style, Theory X and Theory Y, were reflections of two distinct views of life leading to two different managerial cultures. Theory X was based on the belief that employees were inherently unwilling to work, and this led to a set of attitudes and norms that emphasized coercive controls and hierarchy. Theory Y assumed that employees were self-actualizing and produced a culture that emphasized self-control and collaboration. In either case the climate could be "good" or "bad," depending on whether the employee's own view of life fit the prevailing managerial culture.

What climate really measures, then, is the fit between the prevailing culture and the individual values of the employees. If employees have adopted the values of the prevailing culture, the climate is "good." If they have not, the climate is "poor," and motivation and presumably performance suffer. If, for example, the culture includes the belief that individuals should know where they stand, but the performance appraisal process does not allow for this, climate and motivation will very likely suffer.

While climate is often transitory, tactical, and manageable over the relatively short term, culture is usually long-term and strategic. It is very difficult to change. Culture is rooted in deeply held beliefs and values in which individuals hold a substantial investment as the result of some processing or analysis of data about organizational life. (Technically speaking, these beliefs and values are manifestations of the culture, not the culture itself.) These beliefs and values create situational norms that are evidenced in observable behavior. This behavior then becomes the basis for the formation of beliefs and values out of which norms flow. This closed circuit of culture development, which is illustrated in Figure 1, accounts for much of the tenacity that organizational cultures exhibit. In most groups, individuals who violate these cultural norms are pressured to conform and may be ostracized unless norms change to accommodate those who deviate from them.

Culture Reflects What Has Worked in the Past

Recent research by Richard F. Vancil, which was aimed at understanding the behavior of decentralized profit-center managers, suggests that the primary influence on their behavior is top-management behavior, "which, in turn, reflects their [top management's] philosophies of management and

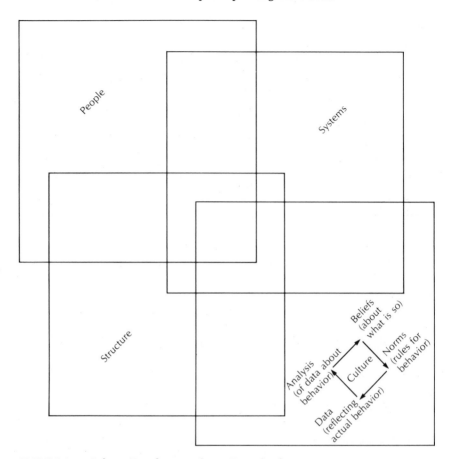

FIGURE 1.   Culture Development in an Organization

style of leadership." While top-management tasks may be similar in most decentralized firms, their approach to these tasks may be quite different. The choices senior managers make about their approach to management tasks, about how they spend their time, and about the structure of their relationships with each other and with their subordinates will "clearly produce different behavior on the part of profit center managers in . . . different firms." Such choices were found to be "the single most important determinant of a profit center manager's perception of his [or her] autonomy."

Anthropologist C. S. Ford has defined culture as "composed of responses which have been accepted because they have met with success." The choices top managers make reflect their view of reality—the values, beliefs, and norms that served them and the company well during their own rise to power. It is these choices that continually reaffirm the corporation's culture and reinforce the expected behavior across the organization.

Many executives have learned the hard way that reaching the top rungs of their organizations does not necessarily confer a license to violate the corporate culture. Studies of small-group behavior tell us that groups tend to choose as leaders those who most embody the norms of the group. One of the dilemmas of leadership in a changing business environment is the need to violate the norms on which the leader's selection was based. Deep resentment and resistance nearly always result.

The former chairman of a large oil corporation, for example, led his company through a major restructuring to prepare it for a world of reduced crude oil margins, less-favorable tax treatment, and the possibility of forced vertical divestiture. Other steps he took included a major commitment to strategic planning, an influx of outside professionals to staff the planning effort, attempts to change marketing from its traditional obsession with volume to a focus on profit contribution, turnover in many key executive posts, and emphasis on diversification outside the energy field.

To many of his former peers, this executive's behavior was an unfathomable violation of the cherished beliefs on which the corporation's culture was based. He realized, however, that the effect of the firm's culture was to place restrictive limits on the strategic options the executive group would consider and to seriously hamper the firm's ability to execute a new strategic direction. Predictably, as soon as he resigned, the company's leadership group returned to the time-tested patterns of action that had served them and the company well in the past.

As this oil executive discovered, culture is capable of blunting or significantly altering the intended impact of even well-thought-out changes in an organization. A lack of fit between culture and planned changes in other aspects of organization may result in the failure of a new measure to take hold. All too often the result is, "We tried but it didn't work the way we thought it would." Something has to give. In this case, either the culture is changed to fit the strategy or the strategy is changed to fit the culture.

MEASURING CULTURAL RISK

Most attempts to define organizational culture leave managers who have tried it at a loss. The usual product is a list of eight or ten phrases describing the informal rules that govern the interaction of management team members. This may appear useful until an attempt is made to judge from the list whether a proposed strategy will find that the culture is amenable to its execution.

Such efforts have been disappointing because managers have had no method for thinking through the relationship between culture and the critical success factors on which strategy is contingent. The way to fathom this relationship is to recognize that the four components of an organization—structure, systems, people, and culture—determine important managerial behavior. They influence the way in which major management tasks are carried out and critical management relationships formed.

An organization's culture can also be described by its management in terms of the way their tasks are typically handled in the context of these key relationships (see Figure 2). Then, once culture and the other organizational dimensions have been defined in similar terms, their compatibility can be systematically assessed.

In Figure 2, each of the lines is to be filled in to describe how a particular task is handled in the context of a particular relationship. The table serves as a checklist and a way to spot interaction between the cultural characteristics of each level of relationship and between the various managerial tasks. The richness of the analysis is particularly useful for identifying the underlying patterns that must be understood in any attempt to change aspects of the culture or in seeking the means to manage around it.

This framework is helpful in assigning meaning to the anecdotes in which much of the data about organizational norms are stored. We have also found it useful to help interpret what we see in management meetings and to analyze records of how executives and managers spend their time. As is true when any management tool is used for the first time, internal support services and/or external consultants are often helpful.

Figure 3 is a simplified presentation of the results of a cultural analysis. Adding across the rows of the table in Figure 2 will provide a composite portrait of how the organization tends to handle particular kinds of tasks. Adding down the columns will portray the way in which each type of relationship is typically structured. For ease of communication, we have displayed only the result of the rows and the columns, not the material in each cell.

The degree of control that managers have over culture is very limited in comparison with the degree of control they have over structure, systems, and people's skills. Indeed, most of the risk surrounding organizational shifts arises from the relative immutability of the organization's culture. Because an organization's current culture is relatively fixed, it is most useful for a manager who wants to effect a strategic change to ask: How compatible with the existing culture are the other organizational elements—structure, systems, and people—through which a shift in strategic direction is to be implemented?

It is then possible to highlight those task/relationship areas where major problems exist. If these problems involve task relationship areas that would be critical to the success of the new strategy, they represent sources of cultural risk that must command major management attention.

FIGURE 2. Corporate Culture Matrix

Tasks	Relationships		
	Companywide	*Boss-Subordinate*	*Peer*	*Interdepartment*
Innovating				
Decision making				
Communicating				
Organizing				
Monitoring				
Appraising and rewarding				

FIGURE 3.   Summary of Cultural Risk Assessment (International Banking Division)

Relationships	Culture Summary
Companywide	Preserve your autonomy. Allow area managers to run the business as long as they meet the profit budget.
Boss-subordinate	Avoid confrontations. Smooth over disagreements. Support the boss.
Peer	Guard information; it is power. Be a gentleman or lady.
Interdepartment	Protect your department's bottom line. Form alliances around specific issues. Guard your turf.

Tasks	Culture Summary
Innovating	Consider it risky. Be a quick second.
Decision making	Handle each deal on its own merits. Gain consensus. Require many sign-offs. Involve the right people. Seize the opportunity.
Communicating	Withhold information to control adversaries. Avoid confrontations. Be a gentleman or lady.
Organizing	Centralize power. Be autocratic.
Monitoring	Meet short-term profit goals.
Appraising and rewarding	Reward the faithful. Choose the best bankers as managers. Seek safe jobs.

DOES THE CULTURE FIT THE STRATEGY?

To illustrate how cultural risks can be identified and managed in an organization, it is useful to look at the strategy and culture of the international banking division of a major money center bank. (This example was developed as a composite of the strategies and cultures of several such banks.) The international division has developed a strategy to grow its off-shore correspondent banking business. Many months were spent in creating a sound, market-based plan.

In the arcane world of international correspondent banking, profits are earned by U.S. multinational banks through the collection and issuance of letters of credit, foreign exchange trading, loans and loan participations, and other banking services provided to foreign banks. Income is taken as fees, interest payments, and as spreads earned on deposit balances.

To succeed in this business, the services of numerous foreign branches must be carefully coordinated with those in New York, Chicago, London, and other global money centers. Operational support for money transfer and other services must be of high quality. Response time to customer inquiries must be short. A high level of calling officer quality and customer contact is needed to add value to what is otherwise a commodity-like service. It is also important to hold costs to a minimum.

Implementation of a new strategic plan in the international division postulated these eight major changes:

STRUCTURE

1. Dedicate an organization to the foreign correspondent banking market. (Previously this market had been managed by each geographic area.)
2. Establish a matrix structure between the new line of business organization and the geographic areas.
3. Place predominant decision-making authority with key correspondent banking personnel rather than leaving it with geographic managers.
4. Use an intergroup team (both correspondent bankers at headquarters and local offices in the field) to improve international money transfer.

SYSTEMS

5. Coordinate closely with other bank operations units.
6. Develop a management information system to measure account profitability.

PEOPLE

7. Increase continuity in client relationships.
8. Attract superior personnel from within the bank to this new line of business organization.

In any industry or company that is implementing major strategic shifts, success depends on successfully combining the culture with changes in organizational structure, management systems, and people to produce desired behavior. Where changes in any of these three aspects of organization are aimed at behavior that is crucial to success, the risk that performance will suffer increases if the culture rejects or alters their impact. Can the proposed strategy be successfully implemented in the international division culture? What are the cultural risks? What is their source?

Figure 3 is a summary of the culture of the international banking division of our composite money center bank. It was actually developed through a series of individual and small group interviews in several such banks. Executives and managers were asked to describe the survival rules (that is, "the way the game is played") as if they were coaching a new member of the organization. The result was a collection of simply stated imperatives that are the norms implicitly accepted by the group. These statements were summarized into patterns that represent the principal shared expectations about behavior, and the summaries were fed back to small groups of managers to develop agreement among them on definitions of the central norms in the culture of the international division.

The categories used, which reflect the language and meanings within the division, were chosen to help the managers organize their impressions. Relationships were defined from each manager's point of view and included those between bosses, subordinates, and peers within the division; between the international banking division and other banking divisions, such as domestic corporate banking; and with the bank's top management.

The resulting summary of the international banking division culture characterized individual area managers as feudal barons. Each had been in place from five to seven years. As long as their profit contribution goals were met, they operated with almost complete autonomy. To preserve that autonomy, their concern for short-term performance was paramount. Planning and decision making were undisciplined, excessively personalized, and focused on each individual deal. Subordinates were highly averse to taking risks. So many people were involved in signing off on a loan decision that it was difficult to hold anyone truly accountable for results.

There was, furthermore, a veneer of mannerliness and colleagueship that inhibited frank and honest confrontations to resolve conflicts in the bank's best interest. Information, jealously guarded, was used to manipulate and control adversaries. Political intrigues abounded, with advancement often going to people most loyal to immediate supervisors. As a result of these cultural aspects of our composite division, innovation was risky and received little support. Anything the area manager decided to address was quickly picked up by subordinates. Opportunism was more important than strategy. Not surprisingly, the organization very quickly fell into second place behind more innovative, effective competitors.

The international division's culture described in this analysis appears on the surface to be an obstacle to the successful implementation of the eight-point correspondent banking program. But it is equally unrealistic either to forge ahead; to launch a difficult, expensive, and time-consuming effort to change the culture; or to abandon the strategy as unworkable. What is needed is a careful analysis to determine the degree and source of cultural risk involved. Then policy makers can make decisions about which specific aspects of culture might be changed and how the strategy might be modified to increase the chances of success.

CULTURAL RISK ASSESSMENT

Each of the eight organizational approaches outlined in the international division's implementation plan is aimed at influencing the tasks and relationships of managers, credit officers, and bank operations personnel. Approaches that run counter to the cultural norms of the international banking division will encounter resistance. Others, more compatible with the culture, will be more readily accepted. Some of the behavior sought is particularly crucial to the success of the strategy. The degree of cultural risk, therefore, depends on the answers to these two questions: How important is each organizational approach to the success of the strategy? How compatible is each approach with the division's current culture?

Significant risks result from organizational approaches that are highly important to the success of the proposed strategy but not compatible with the existing culture. Each organizational approach under consideration was therefore reviewed. The results suggested where the implementation plan

FIGURE 4.   Assessing Cultural Risk

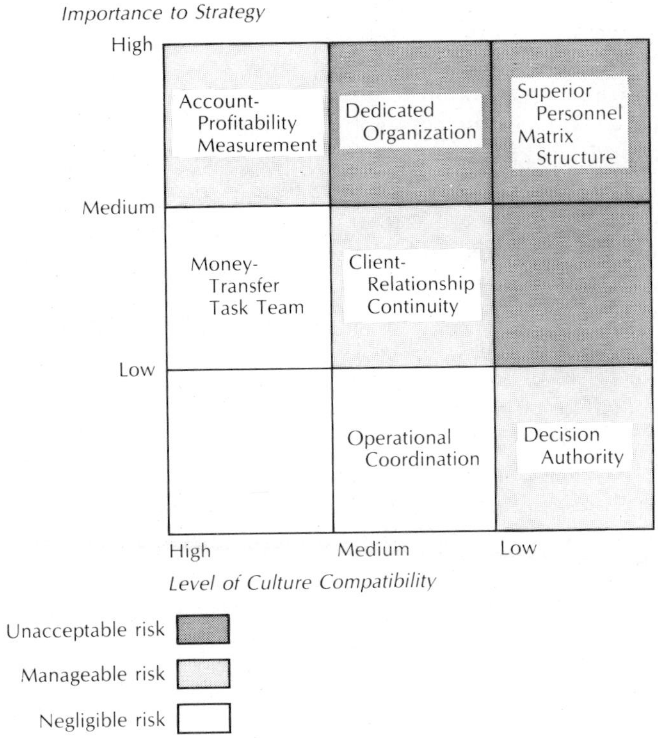

should be changed to manage around the culture, or where efforts to change the culture might be necessary. There are times when it is better to manage around the culture than to attempt to change it, and there are times when the strategy itself should be modified or abandoned.

Figure 4 shows management's judgments about the cultural risks involved in implementing the strategic plan. The proposed matrix organization and the attraction of outstanding personnel were judged to be the most troublesome aspects of the plan. Each was found to be particularly important to the success of the growth strategy objectives, yet each was highly incompatible with the current culture of the banking group.

IMPORTANCE TO STRATEGY

The importance of each organizational approach to strategy is relatively easy to assess if the strategy itself has been well thought through. An organizational approach, such as dedicating an organization to the offshore correspondent banking market, is important to strategy if the intended behavior affects a critical success factor. In this case it is difficult to see how a key competitive edge (that is, closer coordination between foreign branches and domestic headquarters) could otherwise be achieved.

The proposed matrix structure is aimed at achieving a balance between the resource claims of the correspondent banking line of business and the other corporate and personal banking businesses the bank operates in each area. It is essential to the bank's long-term performance that these trade-offs be made with the bank's total interests in mind. Top people must be recruited to gain the credibility necessary to win the cooperation required from other departments in the bank.

In assessing the importance of each organizational approach to strategy, we have found it useful to ask:

1. *What specific behavior is the organizational approach designed to encourage?* (How will key management tasks be affected? How will important relationships be affected?)

2. *How is this behavior linked to critical success factors?* (What specific customer needs or requirements is the behavior intended to satisfy? What competitive advantage will be gained in the marketplace? What impact will such behavior have on costs? What impact will this behavior have on such external factors as government, regulatory agencies, the financial community, public opinion, prospective employees?) The discipline of this approach forces planners and executives to think hard about the relationship between a business plan and the organization designed to carry out that plan.

Cultural Compatibility

The planned matrix structure and the attraction of top people to the correspondent banking business were both judged to have low compatibility with the international division culture. The lack of open resolution of conflict apparent in the culture, combined with the division's customary deal-oriented decision making and the subjectivity with which the reward system operated, made the success of the matrix structure unlikely without major cultural change.

Attracting top people to staff the matrix was a key success factor. In this culture, advancement by association rather than by performance had been the rule. Status and prestige were conferred on those who managed the largest corporate client relationships. Correspondent banking has never been a place to go to get ahead. Turnarounds more often failed than succeeded. In such an environment, what was the likelihood that top talent could be attracted into major jobs to turn around an international correspondent banking business?

To determine the plan's compatibility with the culture, we asked: How much change is involved in key tasks and relationships? How adaptable is the culture? How skilled is the management?

In this example, the amount of change envisioned seemed unrealistic given the current culture. Perhaps if the culture valued adaptability, as in some high-technology firms where organization is continuously forming and reforming, such change could be accommodated. In any case, strong leadership, skilled at managing a complex organization through change, would be necessary. In the bank's case, both adaptability and leadership experienced at managing change were lacking.

The case of the international banking division is not unusual. Many months of study and hundreds of thousands of dollars in consulting fees were spent in devising a tightly woven, well-documented strategy that would be responsive to customer needs, and in making good use of the bank's competitive strengths in a very attractive market. The organization plan fit the strategy, but it did not fit the culture. For that reason it was almost certain to fail, unless adjustments—either to strategy or to culture—were made.

It is not difficult to see why the problem faced by the bank is so common to other firms and industries. In many industries and in many companies, organizational cultures do not value adaptability. Most executives and managers are not particularly skilled or experienced at managing complex change. The cultural risks may be significant even where the changes contemplated do not represent an overwhelming challenge to the existing culture. A culture that values the status quo over adaptability, as most do, and that is led by executives and managers who have limited experience with strategic change, may find even modest change deceptively difficult.

CULTURAL RISK CAN BE MANAGED

The case of the international banking division illustrated how a cultural risk analysis can help management pinpoint where the implemention of a proposed strategy is likely to encounter serious cultural difficulties. One or more of the organizational approaches planned may fall into the unacceptable risk zone shown in Figure 4. If so, the options available to reduce the risks to manageable proportions should be reviewed. Anything that makes the implementation plan more compatible with the culture, or reduces the strategic significance of the behavior sought, tends to reduce cultural risk. Depending on the strategy chosen, the choices open include the following: (1) Ignore the culture; (2) manage around the culture by changing the implementation plan; (3) try to change the culture to fit the strategy; and (4) change the strategy to fit the culture, perhaps by reducing performance expectations.

Q.   Can the impact of a company's culture be safely ignored?

A.   The position taken to preserve established ways of doing business is, nearly always, to maintain the status quo. We have argued that culture can seldom be ignored when making informed management decisions.

Q.   Should ways be sought to manage around the culture?

A.   In certain circumstances, yes. Consider, for example, a multibillion-dollar industry leader facing several major threats to its record of outstanding growth and profitability. A study is launched to consider restructuring around major markets. After formally assessing the cultural risks of such a move, the proposal is rejected as too radical and too inconsistent with the company's functional culture to warrant the risk. As a positive alternative, a major increase in planning and coordination personnel is begun.

   To further illustrate the action implications of managing around a firm's culture, Figure 5 outlines four typical strategies that companies might pursue and the "right" organizational approaches to implement them. The third column summarizes a number of central aspects of the cultures of each of four companies. In each case none of the "right" organizational approaches is compatible with the company's culture. In the fourth column

FIGURE 5. How to Manage around Company Culture

	Strategy	"Right" Approach	Cultural Barriers	Alternative Approaches
Company A	Diversify product and market	Divisionalize	Centralized power One-man rule Functional focus Hierarchical structure	Use business teams Use explicit strategic planning Change business measures
Company B	Focus marketing on most profitable segments	Fine tune reward system Adjust management-information system	Diffused power Highly individualized operations Relationship-oriented managers	Dedicate full-time personnel to each key market
Company C	Extend technology to new markets	Set up matrix organization	Multiple power centers Functional focus	Use program coordinators Set up planning committees Get top management more involved
Company D	Withdraw gradually from declining market and maximize cash throw-offs	Focus organization specifically Fine-tune rewards Ensure top-management visibility	New-business driven Innovators rewarded State-of-the-art operation	Sell out

alternative organizational approaches that are more compatible with its culture are suggested to accomplish the same ends for each firm.

Managers familiar with the situation of each case, of course, are best equipped to determine the most appropriate options. Generally speaking, organization is aimed at achieving an appropriate degree of specialization, coordination, and motivation. A limited number of devices are available to achieve each objective, but in each case there is likely to be more flexibility than we often allow ourselves to see. Thinking of an organization as four components—structure, systems, people, and culture—helps keep the focus on the results sought rather than on the means chosen to get there. It is thus possible for corporations to evolve unique approaches to management processes. They meet competitive challenges by finding more culturally compatible ways to implement their strategies.

Q.   Should an attempt be made to change the culture to fit the strategy?

A.   Although extremely difficult to accomplish, culture can, and in some instances must, be changed. However, this is a lengthy process requiring considerable resources, and should not be entered into lightly. There are three prerequisites for changing a culture. First of all, the strategy and all its elements must be explicitly stated. Second, the current culture must be analyzed and made tangible. Finally, the strategy must be reviewed in the context of the culture to determine where the risks are.

An organization's culture is best altered by gradually reducing the perceived differences between current norms and the new behavior, increasing the value that the culture places on adaptability, and enhancing the ability of the managers involved to effect the desired change. There are several interrelated management techniques utilized in changing the culture. However, all steps must be prefaced by strong top leadership creating the pressure for change coupled with new top-management behavior that sets the example. It is also necessary to have a united front at the top for the sake of sending consistent messages to other managers. The pivotal word is commitment—the commitment to initiate the cultural change and the staying power to see it through.

Managers cannot be expected to change the manner in which they approach their tasks and relationships unless they are fully aware of the behavior required to get things done in the new culture, as well as to enhance their development and advancement in the firm. In short, they must know how to behave and be rewarded for behaving properly. It may be stating the obvious to say that the culture change should be coordinated with other planned internal changes in management systems and organization structure. The result will be mutual and positive reinforcement of the overall strategic change.

The company's management information and compensation systems are valuable tools in effecting change, particularly when used in conjunction with an intensive management education program. The latter both stimulates the managers to change and gives them the tools to facilitate the change in culture. It is also useful to conduct pilot programs for implementing key areas of the new strategy under controlled conditions in an effort to create an environment of success and enhance the acceptance of the new culture.

In all these activities, it is important to set priorities that focus on issues that are strategically significant, while concentrating on those elements of the culture where change is important to success. In fact, it may not be desirable to totally change the culture—only those parts of it that demonstrate high cultural risk.

Q. Should strategy be changed to one that is more compatible with the existing culture?

A. A good example of this occurs when two organizations with distinctly different cultures merge. The results may fall far short of expectations. The Rockwell-North American merger in 1968 was sought by both firms for its synergistic potential. Rockwell, looking for new technologies and new products for commercial markets, saw North American as a place where "scientific longhairs" threw away ideas every day that could be useful to Rockwell. North American, in turn, was attracted to Rockwell's commercial manufacturing and marketing muscle.

Four years after the merger, some markets failed to develop as expected, and there were also problems in bridging the two cultures. As then-CEO Robert Anderson lamented, the aerospace people weren't used to commercial problems. "We kept beating them on the head to diversify, but every time they'd try it, they'd spend a lot of money on something that, when all is said and done, there was no market for, or they overdesigned for the market." The depth of the culture problem was foreshadowed by North American President John Atwood, who saw opportunity for improvement but felt that none of it would do any good unless they continued their basic line of business: aerospace engineering. Rockwell's company culture looked at the world as a rough-and-tumble place where profit margins dominate decision making. North American's environment was more noble. Some 60 well-paid Ph.D.s, for example, spent only 20 percent of their time on company business and were free to devote the rest as they chose to basic research. This was not compatible with Rockwell's obsession about controlling costs and margins.

Over a decade has passed since the merger, and Rockwell continues to have problems with its strategy of capitalizing on North American's scientific strengths to develop important new commercial businesses. Put simply, the poor cultural fit of these two firms has restricted their ability to implement the most desirable strategy for the combined firms.

A strategy in serious cultural trouble is likely to require some combination of the three types of actions—that is, manage around the culture, change the culture, and modify the strategy—to bring cultural risk into the manageable zone. Any business decision involves a risk/reward trade-off. Cultural risk analysis is a means to clarify organizational risks that frequently go unmanaged and result in unanticipated problems.

A Top-Management Perspective

We have discussed the management of cultural risk from the viewpoint of the general manager of a single business unit. The manager of a portfolio of businesses, such as a group executive in charge of a number of businesses or the chief executive officer managing an entire corporation through a period of strategic redirection, can also use a cultural risk analysis to identify priorities for future change. These executives need to know:

- How much cultural risk is there in my portfolio of businesses, each with its own strategy and approach to implementation?
- How is this risk spread across my businesses?
- What are the specific sources of cultural risk, and do any patterns emerge across my portfolio?
- If too many important business units are at significant cultural risk, is the total corporate strategy endangered?

To answer these questions, a group executive or CEO must know how many business units in the group or corporation are faced with unacceptable cultural risk. The source of such risk anywhere within the corporation must be understood; so must the potential impact on corporate performance.

So far, corporate culture has been discussed in a post-strategy-formulation context. However, it is the perceptive manager who elects to address the issue of culture before it becomes a barrier to making strategy happen. There are several areas in which cultural analysis at the front-end can pay dividends later.

- **Formulating Strategy.**   Strategies are built on management's assumptions about many external factors. But a corporation's culture filters top management's perspective, often limiting the strategic options they are prepared to consider seriously. Defining the central values of a company's culture can remove old taboos that have unnecessarily constrained past strategic decision making.

● **Competitive Analysis.** As culture conditions the direction of a company's strategic choices, a competitor's own culture conditions its strategic decisions and the effectiveness of their implementation. Understanding a competitor's corporate culture can provide useful clues to how that firm will behave in the competitive environment.

● **Managing Cultural Formation.** Rapidly growing companies, such as high-technology firms, often find that the ideals and values of the founding group or individual are lost as the culture becomes institutionalized through formalized organizational structures, reporting systems, and controls. Managing the process of cultural formation in relationship to the more tangible aspects of organization can help preserve the original driving force of the company.

● **Merger Planning.** The failure to successfully integrate the disparate cultures of merging companies, as in the previously cited North American-Rockwell example, is often the cause of considerable problems in turnover and productivity. Early definition of culture in both companies and the identification of cultural compatibility and cultural risk facilitate a smoother transitional period and the realization of the desired synergy.

● **Installing a Planning System.** Experience demonstrates that there is a long lead time (often four to five years) in achieving good results from a formal planning system. One reason is the often dramatic change in how managers are required to approach their tasks and relationships. This change is frequently very stressful and, therefore, a natural inhibiting factor. Considering culture's role in planning can shorten the installation process to two or three years.

HOW TO PROCEED

It has been clearly demonstrated that every corporation has a culture (which often includes several subcultures) that exerts powerful influences on the behavior of managers. For better or worse, a corporate culture has a major impact on a company's ability to carry out objectives and plans, especially when a company is shifting its strategic direction. Well-run corporations have distinctive cultures that are somehow responsible for their ability to create, implement, and maintain their leadership positions. Awareness and agreement within the company about the culture phenomenon and its effect is a vital point of departure for dealing with it. Although getting one's hands around a company's culture is like putting one's hands into a cloud, there is a methodology for capturing the effects of culture and enabling management to deal with it more effectively.

Step 1:   Define the relevant culture and subcultures in the organization. Use individual and small-group meetings. Develop a list of simply stated beliefs about "the way it is" in the organization and of current imperatives for how to behave. Feed these back until there is a consensus about the central norms in the culture.

Step 2:   Organize these statements about the firm's culture in terms of managers' tasks and their key relationships. This procedure is spelled out in Figures 2 and 3; it provides a matrix of tasks and relationships that will enable the evaluator to translate an undifferentiated list of culture traits into a tool for pinpointing the specific traits that place the business strategy at risk.

Step 3:   Assess the risk that the company's culture presents to the realization of the planned strategic effort. This is done by first determining the importance of the intended organizational approaches and then determining their compatibility with the intended strategy. The procedure is illustrated in Figure 4; it enables the evaluator to differentiate the risks of the corporate culture into three categories: unacceptable risk, manageable risk, and negligible risk.

Step 4:   Identify and focus on those specific aspects of the company's culture that are both highly important to strategic success and incompatible with the organizational approaches that are planned. It will then be possible to develop alternative organizational approaches that better fit the existing culture, as well as to design planned programs to change those aspects of culture that are the source of the problem. The analysis will at this point be moving into areas that are beyond the scope of this article; it will have moved from an analysis of cultural risk to the first steps in creating a new and better-matching culture for the future business.

To match your corporate culture and business strategy, something like the procedures outlined above should become a part of the corporation's strategic planning process. Remember, these steps can be taken in as sophisticated, or in as informal, a manner as you desire. External consultants or internal staff support may be used, or the relevant executive from CEO on down may undertake these steps directly and informally. It has been our experience that baseline descriptions of the important aspects of culture, especially in major business units expected to make significant shifts in strategy, can be prepared by line managers with the help of strategic planning and human resources staff. An advantage of the approach outlined here is to provide a more effective way to integrate human resources perspectives into the strategy formulation process. Over the last decade many firms have acknowledged that plans are frequently unrealistic because of the inability of the people to effectively execute them. Cultural risk analysis can help surface "people problems" before a strategy is implemented, expanding the options for dealing with the most important issues.

Strategic plan reviews should include an explicit assessment of the implementation problems likely to be encountered and a discussion of the options to be considered for their management. Finally, the results should be summarized so that group executives and CEOs can direct their attention to the most strategically significant cultural risks across their portfolios of businesses. Appropriate action to manage around the culture or to change it would then be determined.

Changing a culture is a complex, long-term undertaking that involves coordinated efforts by top leadership to change their own behavior and the signals they send to their subordinates and others in the organization. Such changes must be reinforced by shifts in management processes, information and reward systems, reporting relationships, and people's skills. Major changes in management personnel, including adding outsiders as a source of new skills and new cultural patterns, are often necessary. Massive management education may be required. A cultural risk analysis helps identify the need for such costly and difficult decisions and provides a practical way to evaluate cultural change options against possible changes in the strategy to create a better match with the existing culture.

SELECTED BIBLIOGRAPHY

A number of authors have recognized that organizations do in fact have cultures. Several have focused on identifying the elements that should be included in a definition of organizational culture. Andrew M. Pettigrew provides a useful compendium of these approaches in his article "On Studying Organizational Cultures" (*Administrative Science Quarterly*, December 1979). The recent work of William G. Ouchi, *Theory Z* (Addison-Wesley, 1981) describes a Japanese-oriented management philosophy as a better model for organizational cultures in U.S. businesses. Douglas McGregor's *The Human Side of Enterprise* (McGraw-Hill, 1960) describes the roots of the current U.S. model.

The difficulty of changing an organization's culture and one way of systematically approaching the task is described by Stan Silverzweig and Robert F. Allen in "Changing the Corporate Culture" (*Sloan Management Review*, Spring 1976). The decisive impact that culture can have on managerial behavior and business performance is discussed by Richard F. Vancil in *Decentralization: Ambiguity by Design* (Dow Jones-Irwin, 1978).

Issues involving culture are frequently reported in the business press, although the articles may not specifically refer to culture as the problem. Examples include those we cite in the text: For the North American-Rockwell merger, see

"North American Tries to Advance Under Fire," *Business Week*, June 3, 1967, and "Forget the Magic Mergers," *Forbes*, July 15, 1972; for the AT&T example, see Bro Uttal's "Selling Is No Longer Mickey Mouse at AT&T," *Fortune*, July 17, 1978; and for the Sherwin-Williams example, see Harold Seneker's "Why CEOs Pop Pills (And Sometimes Quit)," *Fortune*, July 12, 1978.

Finally, an excellent description of a major corporation's culture from the viewpoint of a former insider is provided in *On a Clear Day You Can See General Motors*, by J. Patrick Wright (Avon, 1980).

CORPORATE STRATEGY:
THE ESSENTIAL INTANGIBLES

Kenneth R. Andrews

I.

I am probably more honored than qualified to have the last word at a conference on a most important subject in a most sophisticated company. The last time I spoke in New York on strategic planning (some years ago) I had to reply to the assigned question, "What's new in corporate strategy?" with a disappointing "Not such a hell of a lot." I had occasion to refer then to the "short and unhappy life of the long-range planner." I am glad to see that you have achieved considerable longevity and security, and have increased enormously in number, as planning has become strategic in mystique rather than merely long in range. The imminent rise of your function was even then evident, for one or two of the members of the audience subsequently became chief executive officers of their companies, probably not as a direct consequence of being known to have heard my address.

Planning in that remote era consisted largely of extrapolating forward the previous year's operating results, calculating the discrepancy between forecast results and an arbitrarily chosen growth rate, and looking at acquisition possibilities to plug the gap. Such activity seems now mechanistic, and hardly at all related to the formulation and execution of a comprehensive and durable corporate strategy. Planning was at least becoming accepted as somehow necessary, for however foreign to the conduct of public affairs, it was seen as reducing uncertainty in business, providing a means for evaluating managers, and above all underscoring diversification as the basis for growth.

Times have changed, but problems remain. The recent history of strategic planning reveals a ballooning of interest in the tools of analysis, disillusion with what they have produced, and a wish for something more. Simple arithmetic projections of the future of existing businesses have been replaced long since by portfolio analysis, industry and competitive analysis, scenario planning, and reference to cross-sectional databases like PIMS and PICA. The Boston Consulting Group bloomed and developed partners who left it to found a number of competing firms (now referred to in the industry

Kenneth R. Andrews, "Corporate Strategy: The Essential Intangibles." These remarks were delivered by Professor Andrews at the 1983 Strategic Planning Conference of The Conference Board at the Waldorf Astoria in New York on March 22, 1983. Reprinted with permission.

as "strategy boutiques"), popularized the two-by-two matrix, elevated high market share and growing markets to compelling dignity. PIMS made possible a comparison of policy and results and supported portfolio analysis with the firm assertion that the parallelism between market share and profitability was to be interpreted as cause and effect.

Industry and competitive analysis, developed brilliantly by my young colleague Michael Porter, became another popular mode of appraising the future evolution of an industry and the competitive position in it of one's own company. Scenario planning, developed to an impressive art form by Royal Dutch-Shell, has taken the old "best-worst-and-most-probable case" projections into two fully integrated but contrasted concepts of the future. Scanning the environment, to be sure, had long been established in the policy group of the Harvard Business School as the conceptual starting point in articulating a conscious pattern of objectives and policies that would shape a company's present activities toward future superiority in competition. I suppose it is unbecoming of a member of that group, as I am, to find fault with new forms of environmental analysis.

Simultaneously, of course, the development of quantitative analysis, decision theory, and unlimited computational capacity made possible the generation of quick numbers around what-if modulated questions to make strategic choice appear to be less intuitive. Theory-dominated business schools became more and more quantitative in their instruction (and many of their best students, by the way, went to strategy consulting firms). The development and use of mathematical models, alas, require suppression of the situationally unique and adoption of simplifying assumptions. Inherent in this simplification is the tacit, if not religious, adherence to profit maximization as the single goal of business enterprise and to the efficient market hypothesis that makes share price the accurate present value of the company's future earning stream. The alleged sharing of information that makes the market efficient does not enter the realm (except for the Wall Street reputation of top management) of implementation, which has as its attendants will, desire, and leadership.

Planning has flourished under this proliferation of analysis, quantification, and mathematical modeling. It is now fully equipped with technique. But finally, as with all enthusiasms that sweep the management community, a backlash has developed which may reclarify the meaning and role of strategy, the fashionable word on every tongue. The term has been so narrowed by the ready applicability of analytical technique to the choice of products and markets that the meaning of *corporate strategy* has been submerged. In the meantime, the incrementalists, who believe that planning is neither possible nor constructive, have been encouraged to redeclare themselves in academia ("Organizations don't have goals; only people do") and in business ("I don't want a strategy on Wednesday that I can't change on Friday").

There is something to be said, I must admit, for the owlish adherents to the primacy of incrementalism and administrative process. Repelled by the best and brightest analysts, they assert the wisdom of the practitioner and believe that an organization, properly nurtured, can lay out like a snail the path of its own progress. So it can, but the path is visible only behind the snail. Those who believe that life is too uncertain to permit planning and that purpose must remain mostly intuitive, are a kind of Greek chorus, keeping the rest of us honest while they hymn their classic cop-out.

The current disillusion is better founded than the defeatism of the muddlers-through. It arises in the excesses of quantification (which applies, after all, only to some aspects of management problems), in the perennial quest for false certainty in a truly and permanently uncertain world, and in the rejection of a definition of corporate strategy that encompasses non-economic and unquantifiable goals. (I will come back in a minute to what I mean by that.)

Let me risk your irritation by referring to points at which, in inexperienced hands, strategic planning has gone wrong. First is the once universal and now residually influential choice of an annually compounded growth rate as the primary goal regardless of foreseeable external conditions and internal capabilities. A compulsory and regular target percentage for volume, typically unchanged as the base enlarges, seems to be as primitive and nondirectional as is setting profit at a level unrelated to reasonable foreseeable achievement. To consider profit as *purpose* rather than necessary *outcome* leads to disrupting the normal course of future investment and product development. It entails bowing to the necessity for quarter-by-quarter increases, a tyranny unknown in the rest of the capitalist world.

In naive hands, portfolio analysis and competitive analysis lead to automatic "strategies," like divestment of dogs, milking of cash cows, massive dispersed investment in question marks, and diversification into growing industries. It leads also to exit from such "unpromising" or "declining" industries as those in which the company's history and capability once lay, providing thousands and tens of thousands of jobs.

At its crudest, this consideration of the present and future status of individual businesses presumed them unrelated to a unitary corporate strategy. It implied that the corporation is a collection of separate businesses. It assumed that the institution giving them temporary harbor had no continuing responsibility to its own integrity or to our economic, political, and social system or any special capability to make some strategic choices more effective than others. Such a corporation becomes permeated by lack of commitment, distrust of fickle leadership, by cynicism, and self-defeating mediocrity.

The domination of strategic planning by overriding growth goals, together with a strategically irrelevant joy of combat, has taken once comprehensible institutions into a crazy-quilt pattern of acquisitions now often being divested or written off. The ultimate development is the hostile take-over, solemnly defended by free-market economists as promoting efficiency of management. Lammont DuPont Copeland's famous deprecation of conglomerate acquisitions ("Running a conglomerate is a job for management geniuses, not for ordinary mortals like us at Du Pont") has perhaps been modified by successors several times removed. At any rate, they have achieved a strikingly invisible synergy and visible debt by acquiring Conoco in a complex contest not yet recognized as being a strategic coup. Such auxiliary weaponry as golden parachutes, like the general excesses of executive compensation in which too much is regularly paid for strategically defective performance, may really be unimportant. They sour the attitudes, however, of company members and observant society toward the quality of strategic decision offered to the enterprises whose future performance must add up to our economic health and ability to compete in world markets. Strategic planning, in the grip of its current conventions, may have completed the distraction of management from its primary tasks.

If we put aside the quick-answer strategies following automatically from the new analytical techniques, then we discover that the unlimited multiplication of strategic alternatives, fed by exhaustive consideration of future external possibilities, leads to increased uncertainty rather than less. Once the array is made available, prolonged debate ensues, which when ended by edict leaves residual discontent among the champions of lost causes. Analysts of PIMS data tell us that it takes seven years or more to achieve success in a new venture or product line and that massive investment in one to achieve market share is better than modest investment in several new products. But which single basket merits all our eggs? Statistically significant but anonymous experience does not answer the question that must be answered: Which path will we take? The irresolution that follows the identification of alternatives, each of which picks up its advocates, tilts the confused relation between short-term and long-term results (the resolution of which may be the most important component of strategic decision) irretrievably toward the short term.

In such situations it becomes brilliantly clear that we need criteria for choice commanding enough to still the arguments over relative net present values of investments made plausible by projected growth of markets. Meanwhile, critics of business, especially economists and political scientists, find the present plight of American business to be the proper object of national industrial policy, which when once formulated will influence or preempt the strategic planning of autonomous corporations. One monster or another lies in wait for the irresolute.

Whatever else may be said about the recent progress of strategic planning, the tools of analysis recently embraced have turned the architects of strategic decision (that's you guys, unisexually speaking!) away from your own companies. You have acquired the habit of looking outside the firm toward ostensibly greener pastures and conventionally defined new industries rather than to the aspirations and capabilities of your organization and its members. *In defiance of these intangibles, no victories can be achieved.* The generation of strategic alternatives has produced many paper flowers, but criteria for picking one (other than the uncertain projected financial results theoretically available) have not been fully developed, despite their closeness at hand.

So too the attention to the formulation of corporate strategy has far outrun that given to implementation. The importance and difficulty of institutionalizing corporate purpose, the essence of leadership, elude some strategic planners, especially those without line experience. They escape also many business school professors, who increasingly sidestep the quantifiably intractable problems of administration (which yield only to clinical research) to undertake analytical activities in which they are more comfortable.

II.

Rather than cast out strategic planning or let it wither away, a simpler and more productive move is possible. Strategic planning, I have said, has been distracted by the development of analytical techniques away from the needs and capabilities of the business and away from implementation to generating alternatives only theoretically available. But it lies within the capability of intelligent and thoughtful people to push strategic planning resolutely into its next phase of development. This must be greater emphasis on planning the identification, extension, and applicability of the unique capability of the company and its special strengths in competition. If the quality of a company's strategy cannot be known until it has been in effect for some time, all of us who direct and plan are in the hands of our organizations, which can be led but which have needs, power, and stubbornness of their own. It follows also that the implementation of strategy, its predictable problems, requirements, and feasibility must be planned in advance, not left to improvisation later. (Already, in lieu of action, one can hear implementation ringing like a bell in the rhetoric of the modish. Consulting firms, which usually have never claimed any competence beyond their final reports, now are available for extended assignments in advising management how to manage the programs recommended. I predict that soon "implementation" will be a term as carelessly used as is "strategy." We should not be repelled by this development, for fads are ultimately cooled by common sense.)

Neither portfolio nor competitive analysis acknowledges that people populate organizations. The product of their projections is unprocessed by problems of motivation, will, and desire, except as generalized in economics and game theory. Human energy, creativity, productivity, and determination cannot be precisely measured by (to coin a phrase) discounted human achievement analysis (DHAA). No excuse can be derived from that inconvenience, however, for ignoring their crucial contribution both to the successful execution of strategy and to the generation of continuous innovation more successfully engendered by experience than by analysis.

That quantitative analysis, riddled as it is by unseen qualitative assumptions, characteristically drives out unquantifiable judgment is a simple breakdown of information, intelligence, and maturity. A comprehensive definition of corporate strategy, incorporating quantitative and qualitative components of business decision, has been at the heart of such work in the academic field of "Business Policy" (now called often "Strategic Management") for 20 years. As long ago as 1965, I ventured to describe in widely published and uncontested form corporate strategy as a pattern of purpose and policy that began with, but did not end in the definition of a company's business in product/market terms. The inquiry my colleagues and I had for years made into the experience of companies grappling with opportunity had convinced us that formulation and implementation were equally important and that they were inextricably interrelated.[1]

In our simple definition, which assumes power only when applied in detail to a single company, the range of all that a company might do and the ordering of objectively attractive opportunities are drastically affected by considering what it is capable of doing. The linking of opportunity with resources, either in hand or realistically attainable, and with the distinctive competence that lurks somewhere in every company, however humdrum, is the first step away from such distorted response to opportunity as entering the computer business or office information services, because they promise enormous growth.

But a strategically managed company has not only defined its business by identifying the products and markets it is best equipped to serve in some way different from and better than its competition. Its sense of purpose must extend to the kind of human institution it is to be, for the kind of implementation we have to have to compete successfully means that the members of our organizations not only know and accept the company's economic strategy but see it embedded in a context of relationships satisfying their own needs, promising reward for their achievement, and stimulating their own development to greater capability. Since people, executives not excluded, do best what they want to do, however highly paid, individual and corporate values should be allowed to condition choice. If "people are our most important asset," as we hear ad nauseam, we should acknowledge that corporate purpose—at the heart of a full-bod-

---

[1]The first statement appeared in Learned, Christensen, Andrews, and Guth, *Business Policy: Text and Cases* (Homewood, Ill.: Richard D. Irwin, 1965). *The Concept of Corporate Strategy* (Dow Jones-Irwin, 1981) is a more convenient and up-to-date version.

ied concept of strategy—must attract not only their consent but their commitment, their loyalty, their cooperation, their energy. We must be prepared to make some sacrifices in scope for effective performance. We must purposely invest in implementation, as we do in products. The principal new contribution that planning can make to implementation is, incidentally, continuity of employment. Planning can make continuous employment feasible. The surface of this enormous challenge has not even been scratched by the limited analysis so far developed. In the process of extending planning to human capability we have to acknowledge that employees are no more solely economic persons bargaining their work for pay than the corporation is solely a profit-maximizing economic unit.

If we turn our attention to what society expects of the corporation—especially the large publicly held institution—we are forced to extend our intentions beyond our employees to other communities. We hear daily the rhetoric responsive to this idea. Piety, good conscience, and even good works in ascending order assert that the company has responsibilities not only to shareholders, but to its employees (yes indeed, in terms of work satisfaction or motivation for the sake of successful performance), to its customers (yes indeed, in terms of quality, service, and price for the sake of sales), and to its communities (uh-huh, for somewhat confused but persistent reasons). Fully developed strategy, individualizing a company and equipping it to accomplish what planners recommend, will go beyond the clichés of corporate responsibility to specific objectives and programs that demonstrate the depth, durability, and comprehensiveness of corporate purpose. Goals in this realm should be as concrete and carefully defined as developing experience makes possible; they should be consistently related to economic strategy.

It is not appropriate here to single out companies that in their behavior, if not in so many words, acknowledge that their purpose is as much to maintain and develop a cooperative and creative organization, to foster effective execution, in short, as it is to plan and to measure performance against plan. A number of such companies are represented in this room; their representatives may be very diffident about discussing the intangible but centrally important aspects of strategic planning. I am trying to get these intangibles back on the table, stripped of paternalistic clichés and sentimentalism and related to organization purpose. I would like them addressed in individual companies in terms more bold than bland and with less fear of giving offense.

As you see then, I am concerned about how much attention fully developed and sophisticated strategic planning (especially in staff departments) gives to the identification of special capability and the resolution of what a company can do in relation to what it might do. What kind of exploration is made of the appeal of new strategic alternatives to the R&D people, the regional sales managers, the human resources people? You can't ask the employees of a steel company whether it should go out of the carbon steel business, but the kind of wage and work rule concessions that make survival possible have to be discussed before liquidation becomes the proper strategy. In our new recognition of the value of product quality, how much attention do we give to the quality of purpose and the values relevant to its appraisal?

Bringing the intangibles of implementation into strategic planning may blur the distinction between strategic planning and management, but how else do you strengthen the linkages you discussed this morning? The interpenetration of formulation and implementation is indispensable to the choice of direction, to determining the future of the company, and to achieving the goals that a combination of market opportunity, distinctive competence, will, desire, and ethical intention makes appropriate. Expanding the purview of planning with these intangibles opens up new opportunities for major innovation, even in traditional companies and industries. If a strategy is embraced that renews dedication to segments of a market appropriate to a company's developed competence, then planning can be extended to the organization structure, the coordination processes and relationships within the structure, the administrative systems and control, and even to the kind of leadership likely to move the sales force, manufacturing group, or research and development laboratories to new levels of accomplishment. Focused strategies permit lean organizations to develop clout in sharply defined markets.

The influence a staff planning group can have in the line management of a large organization will increase as more attention is given to looking inside the organization for new opportunity. A strategic planning group may recognize the opportunity for an expanded services business in the success of a cost center maintaining one set of hardware. Another may see that the implementation of high-quality special application in an industrial products company faced with the decline of its traditional customer industry depends on a reorganized and augmented marketing effort to search out parallel applications in other industries. A third may see that while its company's business in a single major structural product sold to heavy contractors declines, it is located and equipped to establish a supply center business making available to those contractors everything they need in their kind of construction. The strategic planning group that does this kind of thing may not be shaking the world, but it is making a contribution that will be recognized and eventually seen as essential. It is the essence of survival and adaptation as our traditional industries stagger under the load of obsolete conventional strategy and cost structures that new opportunities be found in old undertakings via product differentiation and cost reduction.

As a country, we face a crisis of economic stagnation that hindsight shows is in part our own fault. The neglect of the basic everyday necessities of good management by a corporate leadership competing in rates of growth rather than in quality, price, and service seems now indefensible. That power over the future lies in steadiness of purpose, rather than, for example, in unrelated diversification, becomes more and more clear. Unplanned adversity may be the ultimate clarifier. In its light we can see that purpose to be effective must be committed to. The likelihood of achieving commitment and the availability of the leadership to get it are more important, if less measurable, in planning a company's future than calculations of market opportunity. These are among those unarguable ideas that get shoved aside by the momentum of conventional thinking and the tyranny of the short term. Such management imperatives are ignored by financial analysts who, like some corporate financial officers, march to a different drummer in diverting their companies from their organically suitable destinies.

It is part of the *comprehensive* concept of strategy—the idea whose time may finally be now—that the leader of a company or of any organization unit must be dedicated to the durable core of a company's character and strategy while encouraging innovations in product and organization that will bring about or respond to the changes taking place in its surroundings. The quality of leadership is to be appraised not only in terms of quantitative results but in less tangible but equally observable terms of character and interest in the needs of other people. If companies are to be strategically managed, executives are called upon to dramatize organization purpose and performance, establish the level of quality expected in every aspect of performance, and demonstrate that they themselves are doing what they wish their juniors to do—devoting their power to causes they know are worth serving.

When you leave this large congress of planners, take a new look at how implementation can be more firmly incorporated into strategic planning. Look at the capability of your own company as a principal source of its future growth. Imagine competitive advantage as the product of originality and uniqueness in defining markets and of consistent superiority in performance. What you are determines what you can be.

MATCHING HUMAN RESOURCES TO STRATEGIES

Donald W. Meals   **John W. Rogers Jr.**

A company whose business has always been the steel industry diversifies by acquiring a printing company. Should the benefits package of the parent, a member of the mature and highly-unionized steel industry, be extended to the printing industry where benefits are not traditionally as generous? A textile firm whose traditional business has been stable for years finds that its fabric processing division is growing very rapidly and holds a strong position in an expanded market created by the use of new synthetic fibers. Are the firm's traditional criteria for selecting, promoting, and compensating executives appropriate to the management of this growing sector? The management of a company that has grown rapidly for ten years decides that the firm has attained an optimum size and that future growth should be limited and highly selective. Do the personnel policies in recruitment, training, compensation, and management succession still fit a company that will now experience slower growth?

These examples all illustrate the problem of matching human resources to business strategies. In the modern corporation it is accepted that effective organization is not only a precondition for the successful implementation of strategy, but should also be a reflection of strategy. In addition, most managers agree that people are the single most important factor in creating an effective organization and in determining the success with which strategy is implemented. The management of the corporation's human resources—attracting and retaining the right people, motivating them and rewarding them for good performance, designing appropriate training programs, planning for the replacement of key people and skills—thus becomes fundamental to the implementation of the corporation's strategy.

While these principles are not in dispute, both practical managers and academic commentators have been slow to adapt them to the portfolio concepts of managing diverse corporate activities. Whereas the theme of personnel management has typically been to develop uniform policies and procedures, the portfolio concept of strategy formulation maintains that, just as capital requirements differ according to the strategic posture of the business unit, so do human resource requirements. Implicit in the view of

Donald W. Meals and John W. Rogers, Jr., "Matching Human Resources to Strategies," Planning Review, *September/October 1980. Reprinted with permission.*

the corporation as a portfolio of diverse business assets is the concept that human resource systems must be congruent with the strategy of the business unit they are meant to support, even if this leads to considerable variation in programs across the corporation. A business unit positioned in a growth industry, where the strategy calls for investment, risk-taking, and aggressive pursuit of market share, will need quite different kinds of people and will manage them quite differently than a business unit positioned in a mature or aging industry where the strategy calls for maximum return on assets. In the diversified corporation, therefore, the challenge for human resource professionals becomes one of designing systems that will support a diversity of business unit strategies without losing sight of overall corporate objectives and the need for a certain equity across the spectrum of the corporation's activities.

As we have observed, strategic planners identify changes in the management systems needed to support a new strategy; we find that they do make distinctions between appropriate and inappropriate components of their management system. All too often, however, those charged directly with the management of human resources are excluded from both the process of strategy formulation and its implementation. The result is a lack of focus on one of the most fruitful areas for the differentiation of management systems. Our purpose in this article is to illustrate the need for a differentiation in human resource systems that might allow for more effective human resource support of particular strategies, and to focus attention on the implications of differentiated human resource systems.

COMPENSATION

Compensation is a key element in the implementation of strategy at the level of both the corporation and the individual business unit. A compensation system is a set of related rewards and signals that has a direct effect on employee behavior. In its ability to mold behavior in the organization by determining how much people are paid, in what form, and according to what criteria, a compensation program that is congruent with strategic objectives becomes a cornerstone of a successful management system. Conversely, a compensation program that does not give rewards and signals consistent with the objectives of the business can be a major impediment to the attainment of those strategic objectives.

Both the academic literature on compensation and the compensation programs of most companies tend to focus on general principles that can be applied to a wide range of organizations and across all divisions of a diversified company. They typically devote little attention to the different strategic postures of different business units within the same organization. Specifically, in developing incentive programs, particularly in executive compensation where the impact on strategy is greatest, bonuses and other incentives are normally tied to measures of annual profitability, usually earnings per share, without regard to either the long-term strategic objectives of the corporation, or the differing needs of individual business units.

Considerable evidence points to the conclusion that such a basic measure of executive performance as short-term increase in earnings may be quite inappropriate to attainment of the long-term strategic objectives of the corporation.[1] At the level of the individual business unit, general principles of compensation, particularly executive compensation, may need to be substantially modified and varied if they are to reward behavior that is consistent with the strategic posture of the business unit.

Bonuses and other forms of incentive compensation motivate executives to achieve ever higher earnings per share. The annual *Business Week* survey of major corporations shows that bonuses for the top three executives of major corporations are closely tied to the previous year's reported earnings. In a profitable year, like 1976, bonuses can double the executives base salary. Usually the extra pay is also highly leveraged; once earnings reach an acceptable performance level, bonuses escalate rapidly. *Business Week* reported that in 1976 executive salaries increased 14.7 percent, while bonuses increased 67.1 percent over 1975.[2] At the division level, bonuses are also generally awarded on increase of short-term profitability or profit improvement. The drive to produce short-term results, however, may influence management to forego investment in capital equipment and R&D that would benefit the corporation several years hence even more than would improved earnings next year. Even in firms having sophisticated capital budgeting techniques, executive compensation may be tied to the bottom line on a conventional income statement. At the extreme, there undoubtedly are managers who are being awarded more compensation and promoted up the executive ladder in return for increased reported earnings when in reality they are running an operation that, in real terms, is dissipating its capital.

The limitations of rewarding managers on the basis of their contribution to earnings are also evident. Just as the capital requirements of a business are different at each stage in its development, so are the measure of executive performance and reward. In an embryonic business, costs and immediate profitability are less important than gaining market share, product quality measures, or improvement of delivery schedules. Managers of a business in the growth phase would be expected to concentrate much of their effort and, in turn, be judged on building an effective organization so that orderly growth can continue. A willingness to take calculated risks is

---

[1]This is a major issue in business policy for a number of persons. See, for example, Alfred Rappaport, "Executive Incentives vs. Corporate Growth," *Harvard Business Review,* July–August, 1978; Rolf H. Wild, *Management by Compulsion,* New York, 1978.

[2]*Business Week,* May 23, 1977, p. 48.

usually crucial in the successful management of embryonic and growth businesses, and this is not a quality normally fostered by an emphasis on short-term bottom line gains. In the mature phase of the business life cycle, where critical administration is a key management trait, executives might be judged on their contributions in such areas as preventive labor relations or externalities like government and consumer relations, in addition to bottom line performance. Finally, in an aging business where the criteria of performance are maximum return of cash to the corporation, control of costs, maximization of profits, and avoidance of risk, executive reward keyed to annual profitability might be entirely appropriate.

Given these quite different measures of performance at different stages in the life of a business, it becomes supremely important that an executive compensation program reflect and reinforce the strategies appropriate to a particular business posture. It would, for example, be inconsistent for a compensation program in an embryonic business to penalize risk-taking and investment in favor of immediate higher reported earnings. In the aging business, on the other hand, where the emphasis is likely to be on milking cash from existing products, short-term measures of performance are probably quite appropriate. What is important is that criteria used in setting executive compensation flow from the strategic objectives of the enterprise can be used to reward behavior that is congruent with these objectives.

BENEFITS

Employee fringe benefits are the area of personnel management most typically treated on a corporate basis without regard to differing divisional or business unit postures and objectives. There are a number of reasons for this: the legislation pertaining to the treatment of qualified benefit plans, difficulties in transferring staff between units of the corporation, and general considerations of corporate equity. Nevertheless, with fringe benefits representing the most rapidly increasing personnel cost, there are equally compelling reasons to differentiate between both the level and kind of benefits offered to business units within a single corporation. For example, a company might have a generous benefits package based on union pressure and the competitive situation in the industry where its principal business is located. However, if the company were to expand into an industry with a different competitive structure or perhaps weaker unions, there is no reason why it should transfer the full package to its new unit and, in the process, hobble it with unnecessary costs. The same differentiation might also be based on the business posture of the unit. For example, the benefits package appropriate to a business in the invest/grow/increase market share phase might be significantly different from business units in either the mature or harvest/divest phases of development. Building flexibility into the total cost level, as well as the elements of the package, can make benefit planning a tool in the implementation of strategy.

To date, most companies that have experimented with variable benefit programs have used a form of the cafeteria approach whereby individual employees are given the option of choosing the specific benefits they want from a selection offered by the company. A point system of valuation sets the upper limit of the total package that any individual employee is allowed. A few companies, most notably American Can Corporation, have seized on this variable benefits approach as a tool in wider corporate planning and in the implementation of strategy.[3] Going back to the assumption that using the right people and motivating them properly is what makes a strategy work, they have designed variable benefit programs appropriate to the competitive needs of different businesses within the corporation's portfolio. In doing this, the system of allocating points to each company-paid element in the benefit package can be expanded so that different business units are allowed a different total number of points per employee. Normally, there is a core level of company-paid benefits which the corporation provides in all divisions, supplemented by either additional benefits or higher levels of company contributions in selecting divisions. In this way, the actuarial advantages of using corporate benefits programs can be combined with the need to differentiate between the cost of structures, competitive needs, and strategic objectives of different business units.

TRAINING

It is sometimes difficult to determine just why various kinds of training and education are made available to employees. Some training programs appear to reflect only a general conviction that it is good to know more. Others seem to provide educational benefits as part of a package of things given to maintain a competitive position in the labor market. In some instances, training is offered as a reward for diligence or because it is the participant's turn. When training is thus justified by the promise of some general benefit, the activity is detached from strategic considerations. It is almost universally ignored as a means of making a strategy effective. One example is the following:

> The Steigmeir Manufacturing Company recognized that its line of high pressure pumps was well positioned in an expanding market. The growth strategy it adopted called for considerable capital investment along with a major expansion of its workforce, many of whom were high grade technicians. Meanwhile, a re-

[3]*Dun's Review*, September, 1978.

cently acquired division producing cast iron pipe was recognized as unlikely to grow. A strategy consistent with its aging strategic posture anticipated level or declining markets with opportunities to capture some of the cash needed to expand the staff and facilities planned for pump production. But, the pair of symbiotic strategies fell short of their objectives. One of the reasons was a single training program for both strategies that supported neither of them effectively.

Located near a university center and influenced by the founder who became a trustee of the engineering college in his later years, Steigmeir Manufacturing had developed very liberal educational benefits. At first the engineering staff were reimbursed for college credit courses. As margins and volume improved, entitlement expanded to cover seminars and several in-plant courses responding to an annual survey of employee preferences. Five years ago when the subsidiary was acquired just before the founder died, it was announced that all fringe benefits including training and education programs would be extended to the new member of the Steigmeir family. There were no changes in the training and educational policy when several years later the strategic business plans for both were being implemented.

When interest rates peaked and the cash cow produced less than the expected funds for new pump production facilities, the education and training programs fell prey to a cost cutting attack. The programs were slashed for both pump and pipe as the following came to light.

- Profitability of the pipe operation was less than expected. This was attributed, in part, to the fact that training costs had increased as had costly interruptions for the newly budgeted seminars and training programs.
- Few of the pump personnel who had taken advantage of the liberal education benefits had acquired the skills needed by the expansion program. The job-related criterion, loosely applied, failed to provide more than a few individuals with the qualifications needed to operate the more sophisticated technology of the expanded production facility.

The training and education budget was cut drastically. The more serious consequence was a discredited training department and costly reliance on recruiting to fill expansion needs and cope with increased turnover among pipe production personnel.

How could the situation have been made more favorable for the pair of related strategies? First, it is obvious that Steigmeir had failed to link training and education activities to its business strategies, except in a very general way. Once the growth posture of the pump operation had been recognized, a staffing plan could have revealed what skills were needed to accomplish that plan. A small but highly specific set of training programs could have upgraded key personnel, reduced recruiting, and very probably improved morale. Training would have been recognized as contributing directly to profitability rather than as a benefit offered the employees. Meanwhile, the pipe operation would have been found to have few requirements for new skills. Relatively little training effort was needed; costs could have been held down to generate the capital for expanding the pump operation.

Even if some of the liberal educational support had been continued, the emphasis on strategic skills would have helped communicate to employees and supervisors the relevance of training to strategies.

More companies, we believe, will find it desirable to look on training as an investment. When they do so as part of the hard work associated with implementing strategies, distinctions between training programs that support different strategies will become apparent. A growth industry environment will usually justify more investment in training than that seen as appropriate for either an embryonic or aging environment. In each environment, however, training will be challenged to demonstrate that it produces results that contribute to the business strategy. Answers are likely to be fairly flaccid if the training director does not understand the strategy and cannot relate training results to the objectives and programs associated with it.

PERFORMANCE ASSESSMENT

Like training, the assessment of employee performance frequently serves a variety of purposes. Rarely are these purposes defined in terms of the strategy they should be supporting. Consequently, distinction between assessment systems based on associated strategies is reasonably rare. The advantages inherent in differentiating assessment systems among strategies are apparent in the Steigmeir case introduced above.

> The Personnel Department of Steigmeir was proud of its performance assessment system. Initiated ten years ago when the current director was new to the company, it called for annual reviews of each employee by his immediate supervisor. Achievements during the past year were carefully noted and evaluated for their contributions to the output of the division. The fact that there were few complaints, until recently, about wage and salary increases was attributed to the fact that they were known to be based on the well administered assessment system. It was not until the Steigmeir Board of Directors insisted on a 10% cut in the staff of the Pump Division that vigorous criticism of the assessment system erupted.
>
> - In the pipe operation the management and workers alike regarded the assessment forms as highly useful. The practice of identifying achievements during each year was well supported but not the evaluation of them in terms of corporate profits. The more vocal employees argued that their achievements should be related to division margin. They were, of course, seeking to avoid the anticipated slowdown in the rate of wage and salary increases occasioned by the Pump Division's development of new production facilities.
> - Managers and supervisors in the Pump Division argued against the attention paid to yearly results. They urged revisions to the assessment system that would credit contributions to long-term growth. The argument was convincing in light of the ongoing development of new production capacity, new products, and new markets.

- The Personnel Department found itself not only faced with open criticism of its assessment system but the sudden realization that it offered little information that could be used to form a list of candidates for out-placement. Although each employee's record contained extensive data on annual achievements, there was no direct basis for determining which employees were most likely to contribute to the future growth of the Pump Division.

To accommodate the concerns about the assessment system coming from the Pipe Division seems simple enough; not so for the pump operation. Failure to focus on the potential for future contributions in evaluating employees could not be accomplished retroactively. The assessment system had not been designed to support a business in a growth industry where the selection of the best staff to play key roles in future expansion is essential for success. Moreover, the lesson this failure taught carried with it another problem. If future potential were to be evaluated in the Pump Division, would such data be equally appropriate for those in the Pipe Division? We think not. Here the strategy does not look toward future growth; does not call for the identification of staff to accomplish growth. Assessment of annual contributions to margin identifies high producers and encourages behavior that has a short-term payoff.

Again, a technique for managing human resources is not equally appropriate for several different strategies. Assessment systems, like training programs and compensation policies, need to be linked to strategies. The problem is not so much that of devising acceptable ways of doing so but of getting the human resource manager familiar enough with the prevailing strategy to use assessment tools creatively and supportively.

MATCHING MANAGERS TO STRATEGIES

The view that there is one best way to organize and manage an enterprise is no longer widely held by those writing in management literature. The trait approach to identifying managers, popular in the 1940s and 1950s, has been set aside. Both are being replaced by approaches that place primary emphasis on situation requirements. The successful manager is currently seen as modifying his style to fit the differing demands of different situations. That is, the effective manager does not consistently manifest a particular set of traits or skills. As Skinner and Sasser have observed: ". . . one cardinal imperative of life as a manager is the necessity to perceive differences . . . differences between one situation and another, differences between people, circumstances, motives, assumptions, and physical and technological realities."[4] We would add to the top of this list differences between strategies.

[4]Skinner, Eickham and W. Earl Sasser, "Managers with Impact: Versatile and Inconsistent," *Harvard Business Review*, November–December, 1977, p. 143.

Along with recognition of the importance of situations in determining the demands on the manager has come an interest in the management skills different situations require. Having recognized that the level of the position the manager occupies helps determine the relative importance of skills that are critical for his success, Katz has suggested that executives should be chosen "on the basis of their possession of the requisite skills for the specific level of responsibility involved."[5]

A similar point of view is advocated by Adizes[6] who considers mismanagement as a lack of congruence between the roles managers are skillful in playing and situations which present different levels of demand for each of these roles. Woodward, reporting on research results obtained in British companies in the 1950s, observes that in successful firms management practices were largely a function of the production technology.[7] The work of Fiedler and others related to work-group situations and leadership styles suggests variations that are effective in each.[8] The geographic, cultural, labor organization and other features of the immediate environment of the business unit also present situations calling for adaptations that are sometimes recognized, sometimes not. Thus, close and consistent attention to the situation in determining what the effective manager must deliver is in order, if not long overdue. Once recognized in light of current interests in business strategies, the situational approach to management invites interest in matching management skills to the need for various combinations of skills required to carry out programs based on different strategies.

Widespread experience with the implementation of strategies will soon reveal situational requirements associated with various strategies. Examinations of needed management system changes identified by strategic planners as they begin to put a selected strategy in operation are beginning to suggest some important considerations. For example, the manager of a new enterprise positioned in an embryonic industry will need to recognize and accept risks his counterpart responsible for an established business in a mature industry should avoid. Skills needed to exercise sharply focused control over production and costs are in greater demand among businesses operating in aging industries than in those leading businesses in growth situations. The latter would appear to call for skills, interests, and values that support a long-range perspective and activities that integrate growing resources. In our example, Steigmeir should give responsibility for pumps to a different kind of manager than the one it makes accountable for its pipe

[5]Katz, Robert L., "Skills of an Effective Administrator," *Harvard Business Review*, November–December, 1977, p. 98.

[6]Adizes, Ichak, "Mismanagement Styles," *California Management Review*, Winter, 1976.

[7]Lutherans, Fred, "The Contingency Theory of Management," *Business Horizons*, June, 1973, p. 70.

[8]Michael, Stephen R., "The Contingency Manager: Doing What Comes Naturally," *Management Review*, November, 1976, p. 25.

operation. At the very least, the two managers must recognize the demands these different situations present and be able to apply or quickly develop the skills and approaches their respective situations require. Failure to do so could lead to the difficult problem of untangling the causes for the failure of a fully appropriate strategy.

We see the recognition of different demands on managers by different strategies as an extension of the growing regard for a situational approach to management. Attention to the matching of management skills and the demands on managers presented by different strategic situations is likely to be an essential feature of the important process of making strategies succeed.

THE IMPACT ON HUMAN RESOURCE MANAGEMENT

It is one thing to identify a principle that, on logical grounds, should guide adjustments in human resource management to the growing commitment to strategic planning. It is a different challenge to speculate usefully about shifts in skills and priorities needed to cope with the strategic planner's relentless pursuit of sharply focused programs. Yet, it is the ability to anticipate change that is often most helpful. We suggest, therefore, some changes in human resource management that seem likely.

• **Management Initiatives.** As planners turn to the tough task of strategy implementation, human resources will be recognized as having a critical influence on success. The search for ways to manage a strategy will result in a call for human resource policies and practices that support it fully. Unlike demands such as unionization and Equal Employment Opportunities, which have shaped the personnel function in the past, the source of the initiative is within the organization. It will be the chief executive officer (CEO), business unit manager, and the planner who seek adjustments in the management of human resources as part of a restructuring of management systems enabling them to support strategies. In fact, several large corporations have recently begun a systematic search for different patterns of human resource management that fit business units having different strategic postures. One CEO drafted a separate Human Resource Strategy and then asked his personnel manager to implement it. We believe there will be many more instances of top-down demands that the personnel department help make strategies work. To the extent that the growing seriousness continues about making strategies succeed, the resulting challenges from management will alter the personnel function as it attempts to cope with them or, better yet, anticipate a more active role in business planning.

● **Tailored Personnel Programs.**   It seems likely that within a few years human resource specialists will respond to the challenges of strategic plan implementers. Programs will be devised that treat training, assessment, career planning, etc. differently as they are made to contribute to different strategies. Before long it will not be uncommon to find diversity rather than uniformity in personnel programs across the varied business units in the corporation. An early indicator is the development of flexible benefits at American Can where the challenge of diversity has resulted in diverse rather than uniform benefits.

● **Changes in the Corporate Human Resource Function.**   One need only visualize a corporation with several sets of human resource programs, each tailored to a business unit, to anticipate changes at the corporate level. With one unit in an embryonic industry vigorously supporting career development and another in an aging industry giving it little attention, what involvement, if any, is appropriate at the corporate level? Will limits to diversity have to be set, administered, and adjusted from time to time? Is it likely that a human resource strategy will become a part of the corporate strategy? The answers to all these questions, we believe, will eventually be affirmative. When the questions are asked will depend on how quickly tailored human resource programs are devised to help strategies succeed. Once this development unfolds and corporate strategic planning becomes as prevalent as it is today at the business unit level, new challenges will be apparent and new demands on the human resource system will emerge at the corporate level.

● **Changes in the Human Resources Staff Orientation.**   It is clear that the alignment of personnel programs with strategies calls for new dimension to the human resource function. If human resource considerations play a central role in planning, the personnel department will need planning skills. If human resources are truly a part of the business, the personnel department will need a solid business orientation. If developing and using human resources is a top management concern, the personnel staff will need a management orientation. All this seems reasonably obvious with or without the emphasis about to be given to the implementation of strategies. Given the orientation toward service, administration, and external-legal demands, however, the obvious may be difficult to perceive. Perhaps the failure, thus far, of so many personnel professionals to be thoroughly tuned to business matters accounts for their lack of participation in the tough process of pounding out a new strategy. To the image of the house humanist must be added a practical business orientation backed up by much more knowledge of finance, markets, and technology than is usually the case. For one thing, the personnel staff can begin to learn about strategic planning. Those who do so soon and learn to participate effectively as managers of the most important of all resources will have joined the club. This is what the best general managers have wanted all along—a new brand of humanism that helps match the performance of people to plans.

THE TURNING POINT
IN HUMAN RESOURCES MANAGEMENT

David J. McLaughlin

In 1959, on a fall day much like this one, I arrived in New York City to offer myself to American business. I'd hedged my career plans by taking dual degrees. Not having very good career counseling, my degrees were in Ancient Greek and American Literature.

I had no earthly notion of how business could use a young man who was both a budding expert on the novels of Stephen Crane and a fair translator of the Iliad. But to my astonishment a consensus quickly emerged. I received four job offers (from Mobil Oil, Union Carbide, Bell Labs, and American Airlines). I have used their products and services out of gratitude ever since.

All of these wise large corporations had the same vision—I should be in personnel.

We called the field "personnel management" 24 years ago, until the behavioral wave of the 1960s introduced the concept of deeper interpersonal relations in all facets of American society. For a while, along with more open sexual relations, companies felt they must have "relationships" with their employees . . . and so "personnel management" became "employee relations."

Now, of course, the popular term is "human resources"—usually with "management" tagged on to the functional title, since these are serious times.

Actually the issue of whether the people who work in our corporations are "resources" may be one of the subtle issues of this conference. The typical chairman's statement that "our people are our most important asset" is one of the most overworked cliches in American industry. Most companies still view employees as resources, in the minerals derivative of that term: assets to be mined (recruited), assets to be processed (trained and organized, to add value), assets to be stored (retained) and disposed of (laid off, terminated, or retired). Of course, we talk a great deal about developing people, but then we savage the training budgets in economic downturns, as American industry did in 1981 and 1982, quite unlike the pattern in Europe and Japan. We talk about motivation a lot, but mostly when we are

David J. McLaughlin, "The Turning Point in Human Resources Management," speech given on October 31, 1983, at the Hay Report Conference at the Waldorf Astoria in New York. Reprinted with permission.

giving out money, and especially when the board is being asked to adopt a new executive incentive plan.

A WATERSHED PERIOD

Now . . . we are at a watershed in the management of our "human resources." It is clear that we need to fundamentally rethink some of the outmoded concepts and tools of personnel management. . . . Employee attitudes have deteriorated at all levels. Satisfaction with pay and benefits is at the lowest level it has been in years. Professionals—and even middle and upper management—feel less informed. Job security has deteriorioated. Worst of all, people's feelings about their company as a place to work are at an eight-year low.

Surely some of these adverse trends can be explained, in part, by the severity of the recent recession. All of the economic data that terrifies employees—layoff rates, unemployment trends, business failure statistics, plant closings—have been, and most still are—at the highest levels since the great depression.

But . . . the waves of change buffeting us predate the recent recession, and will continue to affect us for the rest of this century. My friend Jim O'Toole of USC contends that the combination of technological and demographic changes, along with massive sectoral shifts, have created a period of disequilibrium akin to the industrial revolution. The U.S. auto industry has suffered earlier and deeper than most—buffeted by the combination of government regulation, foreign competition, changing consumer tastes, and technological advancement. Unfortunately for our economy, the auto sector, with all of its suppliers and dealers—accounted for some 25 percent of our GNP. I find it symbolic and somewhat scary that this seminal industry had about as many manufacturers in its peak early years (about 250, in 1908)—as the infant personal computer manufacturing industry has today. Let me assure you that it will *not* take several decades for this new vibrant "high tech" sector to shake out to a handful of dominant firms.

Speed. This is perhaps the most awesome factor in the challenge we face. The combination of accelerating technological change and worldwide competition has decreased the margin for error and compressed the window time available for us to respond. If the U.S. automotive industry had progressed with the same rate of technological advancement and improved cost effectiveness of the computer industry since the first Univac, you could buy a Rolls Royce today for $2.75 and it could run 3 million miles on a gallon of gas.

Now . . . the business imperatives that are forcing companies to redeploy their assets are occurring when we are experiencing the most profound demographic shifts. At a time when there will be 40 to 50 percent fewer promotional opportunities in the average large company, there will be double the number of workers in the critical 35 to 45 age bracket. The composition of the work force has also changed. Women now constitute 43.5 percent of the civilian labor force. By the turn of the century, that will increase to over half. Nine out of 10 married women will work.

Is it any wonder that employee attitudes are "heading south"—even those of "managers" who we sometimes forget are employees? It's clear, of course, that some companies are enjoying rapid growth. And significantly, there are things these growing companies can teach us about the management of people. . . . Rapidly growing companies are more egalitarian than hierarchical, and emphasize development more than control—companies like Intel Corporation. One of the Intel founders and the current President Andrew S. Grove was asked recently whether their emphasis on egalitarianism wasn't "so much affectation." His answer was "it's not affectation but a matter of survival". . . .

But growth companies mature. A recent study by a prestigious group of middle-sized high-growth businesses found that only about one out of 10 of their members were able to sustain extraordinary growth (of over 35 percent) for 10 years. In today's economic era, some growth businesses are just shooting stars. (Witness the short odyssey of Osborne Computer from . . . new venture in 1981, to $100 million dollar "high flyer" in 1982, to Chapter 11 in September of 1983). . . .

Among both fast growing and more mature companies, study after study shows that employee attitudes are deteriorating. Employees feel there is massive duplication of effort and a lack of clarity on how their job performance is judged. Other employee survey statistics show a relative decline in the importance of work in people's lives and a widespread belief by employees that they are not being utilized to anything near their capacity during the time they do work. For instance, a study by H. Walbauk found that people use only about 44 percent of their abilities on their job. A study in the late 70's by Berg and Associates found that 54 percent of employees felt they could work much harder than they do. A more recent study, by the Public Agenda Foundation, found that fewer than one in four workers (23 percent) felt they were working as hard as they could at their jobs, even though over half claimed they had a strong work ethic. The evidence is all around us. On any given day more than five *million* workers report absent. Mike showed you data that underscored the challenge we have in the motivation of the young professionals who will be so central to our future in a more technologically intensive, information-based economy. In 1960, management turnover for college graduates five years out of school was 10 percent—today close to half of new professional-level hires will quit within five years. E. I. Steinberg's research shows that white collar/professional mobility has increased pretty steadily—despite economic recessions.

Now there are those who seem to have concluded that tough times, particularly the threat of unemployment, will whip the U.S. workforce into shape and restore the good old Protestant work ethic. More companies are choosing to operate despite strikes—Phelps Dodge and Whirlpool Corporation, for example. A few companies—like Continental Airlines, which declared bankruptcy . . . with the avowed objective of "winning $100 million in cost savings from its unions"—are practicing an extreme form of confrontation.

Clearly, tough times have increased management leverage. But this is a short-term phenomenon. The era when U.S. management could fire or lay off nonunion employees at will, with minimal costs, is rapidly disappearing. Plant closing and other job-security legislation has already been enacted or proposed in several states and even a few cities. A House labor subcommittee has a plant closing bill requiring notice and special worker aid in the Legislative hopper. But perhaps more significantly, we can't ignore the experience of those hundreds of pacesetter, successful companies, who are forging new links with their employees to address the complex challenges of the 1980s. These leaders recognize that executives and their workers are "in it together," and that they must depend on people for the productivity improvements and innovation required to grow and survive in a time of massive change.

Now I would like . . . to reflect with you on the nature of the personnel management challenge facing all companies, and share some concepts and specific company experiences in managing personnel during this quite evolutionary era.

It is clear that the nature of the challenges facing us require a fundamentally different approach to personnel management. Back in 1970, Mason Haire decried the pervasive tendency of personnel practitioners to come up with programmatic solutions to complex challenges. Sadly, our field has been dominated by a quick-fix mentality and a fascination with gimmicks and so-called "new" approaches from T groups, to management grids, to MBO programs, and yes, to quality circles. We have thrown new programs and money at problems all too readily, and been all too anxious to justify these with a prompt reference to other companies' practices. To a disturbing degree, personnel professionals have become administrators. If you talk to the young people at the ASPA, ASTD, and ACA conventions, many sound like accountants or industrial engineers.

It is clear to me that the nature of the challenges most businesses face will require a different context for personnel management, and a rather awesome set of multidisciplinary skills.

SIX CHALLENGES

In my opinion, we face six complex, related challenges.

First, we must learn to manage employee expectations in an era of slower growth. Like many of the personnel challenges of this decade, this one involves a paradox. On the one hand, more people than ever before are trying to better themselves. Interest in personal financial matters is at an all-time high. Employees are intent on making up ground they feel they lost in the high inflation era of the 1970s. But opportunities for rapid promotion have slowed. Employees know intuitively what many studies have shown—that as much as two-thirds of the income growth of top professionals and managers come from promotions. And our culture as well as most companies' values put a premium on "getting ahead."

A second challenge both complicates the response to the management of expectations, and helps answer it. *We must improve our capacity to develop employees.* The 1980s and 1990s promise to accelerate the amount of knowledge and skill required in business. By the time the average young college graduate entering the work force this year will be in middle management, the amount of knowledge available will have increased *fourfold.* Over the rest of this century, over half the job content of all positions will change, at least a third of existing types of jobs will disappear. For example, . . . the personal computer is revolutionizing middle management jobs. . . . Today it is estimated that 4 to 5 percent of managers have personal computers (9 to 10 percent if you include dumb terminals), but this will grow to over 60 percent by 1990. Beyond the obvious training challenge stemming from massive technological change and simplification of management structures, study after study has shown that most employees do want to be developed. The concern about job security (at a time when technological obsolescence is a threat at all levels) will increase the pressure for more training. . . .

Third, we must close the widening communication gap in an era when the pace of change is accelerating, and we are going to have to ask more of people. . . . This isn't a programmatic problem requiring more employee newsletters and the like. Employees prefer to get information directly from their supervisors and top management. Technology will help. Most companies that rank higher in communication effectiveness are utilizing video technology. But fundamentally, effective communication requires treating employees as partners; it requires an environment of trust. There is a fascinating example of this being played out in the airline industry.

A fourth challenge facing American industry *is the need to nurture innovation and an entrepreneurial spirit.* This affects all levels of the work force, and we have made a start at this with the quality circle movement (several decades after it was developed by an American and applied extensively in Japan). But even today I note that for every suggestion put forth by American auto workers at GM, 18 are being offered at Toyota. And the Japanese act on over 90 percent compared to some 25 percent in the giant U.S. auto company. Fostering an entrepreneurial spirit requires innovative new approaches to organization and reward. Look at what IBM did to develop its successful personal computer. It set up a separate entity in a nondescript building in Boca Raton, Florida, in 1980 totally removed from Armonk. Remarkably, for the first time in IBM's history they did not insist the new venture team utilize proprietary IBM technology. IBM now has over a dozen such new venture groups in place. . . .

A fifth challenge facing all companies *is to control people costs and improve the cost effectiveness of compensation expenditure.* While the era of the fringe binge and automatic increase is over, and a few years of 4 to 5 percent inflation will enable companies to reinstall pay for performance and merit pay concepts, every study I have seen suggests that the average costs of salaries and benefits will continue to increase at a minimum rate of 6 percent. This will double average compensation again by 1994–1995. Some industries face an almost impossible dilemma. The average compensation cost in the major U.S. trunk carriers is $42,000, almost double the average of $22,000 in the upstart nonunion competition. People costs as a percent of total operating expenses in beleaguered Eastern Airlines is 37 percent, while it is only 20 percent in a fledgling enterprise like Peoples Express.

Sixth, a challenge related to cost containment is *the critical need for sustained improvement in our productivity.* Let's not be misled by the simplistic measures of productivity that always improve during an economic recovery. Sure, productivity improved in the 1982–83 period, as companies showed great restraint in restaffing. But one must take a long-term perspective on this. We need to learn from what happened to our basic industries, where productivity improvement noticeably trailed other countries. Bill Denning, of Quality Circle fame, estimates it will take *another 30 years* for our auto industry to reach productivity parity with the Japanese!

Make no mistake—over the next few decades the productivity improvement challenge will increasingly involve salaried personnel, who increasingly make up the bulk of the work force. Even in the manufacturing sector, nonproduction workers have increased from about 15 percent of the work force in 1950 to about 35 percent today. Technological change and the increasing dominance of the service and information sectors will accelerate that trend.

Part of the answer to this challenge will come from increased capital expenditures for salaried employees. It has been estimated that in 1980, the average company had $800 invested in equipment per salaried worker. This was about one-third the level invested in equipment for production workers. This per capita investment is projected to increase three to fourfold over the next 7 to 8 years, and by 1990 we may reach a capital investment parity between production and "staff" personnel. Leader companies on the productivity front, like TRW, are finding that space arrangements and the design of chairs can also effect productivity—they achieved a 39 percent productivity improvement with programmers recently in a controversial space/equipment redesign. The National Institute for Occupational Safety and Health reports a 25 percent gain in keypunch and word processor productivity in an ergonomically designed environment. But capital investment, and workplace redesign, while it is a primary source of productivity improvement, will not provide the whole answer. Although the economists and productivity experts don't agree on the precise proportions, most conclude that a minimum of a third of productivity improvement must come from the softer areas such as greater employee involvement. Many feel that better trained and motivated employees will have to account for over half of productivity improvement.

NEW DIRECTIONS

Now, in reflecting on these complex, related challenges, it becomes obvious that there are no simple, universal remedies. No "quick fixes" here. One of the biggest contributions George Gordon has made in his ongoing research is to document how the management climate and mix of personnel required varies by industry and company type. While some of the insights popularized in such works as *Search For Excellence* have broad applicability, they rely heavily on experience drawn from high-technology and consumer product firms. And even within those companies, approaches are distinctive.

Perhaps the biggest challenge for personnel practitioners is to resist the temptation to rely on "competitive practice" for anything more than a directional clue. Unfortunately we have saddled our cost structures with too many "good" programs—programs like dental insurance—that were justified by references to other firms.

It is also true that the right response to these challenges rarely comes from a single program. If there is one valid generalization about effective people management in leading companies, it is that the approach is comprehensive (involving policies, programs, and that most convincing of all change agents, management action); that it is tailored (to distinctive employee groups and units); and that it is sustained over years.

However, there are several aspects of people management where I see evidence of fresh thinking and some early successes. Let's look at them.

#1. A Strategic Focus

First, leader companies are beginning to approach personnel management strategically. Recently I saw a fascinating study that compared the personnel department emphasis of 24 high-performing billion-dollar companies in 11 industries with paired "average performing" competitors. The research showed that 54 percent of the HR executives in the high-performance firms saw their role as primarily *strategic,* participating in the formation and implementation business strategy. Only 10 percent of personnel heads in the average performers emphasized strategy—to them their job was primarily administrative.

For three years now, I have had the privilege of meeting each fall for three days with the senior personnel executives in a group of some 30 multibillion-dollar companies, most of whom rank among the 100 largest U.S. firms. The highest priority in this group of leader companies is to develop concepts, databases, and methodological tools that permit them to participate in the strategic and long range planning processes of their firms. They are integrating payroll and personnel information systems, and developing better productivity and turnover measures. They are addressing future personnel requirements in a more sophisticated way than extrapolated headcount forecasts based on historical ratios. They are using delphi techniques and other approaches to spot areas of likely legislation that will affect people cost or hamper flexibility of using employees. They are taking steps to cope with supply/demand imbalances (such as the shortage of some 110,000 electrical and computer sciences engineers over the next five years, noted in a recent American Electronics Association forecast).

I find it significant that in most of these firms, the personnel management decisions and plans are not "staff" activities at all, although better data and tools are being developed within the personnel departments. Rather, most of these executives sit on the top policy councils where the focus is on broad business decisions that stem from major corporate strategies: divestiture plans, acquisitions, or new product developments. One example of the kind of strategic personnel thinking that will characterize the 1980s in leader companies is IBM's decision to farm out the development of software for the personal computer to outside small vendors and their own employees. This was a strategic personnel decision!

In my opinion, we are going to see more of this kind of strategic personnel planning, where the approach of other firms is often irrelevant, and the correct answers involve putting the work process in an entirely new context. This will involve greater use of joint ventures, the use of subcontractors (this is a major trend in the auto industry), greater use of part time personnel, and so on. One of the large companies I meet with each year—a multibillion-dollar high technology company—has developed an elaborate "ring strategy" involving subcontractors, temporary personnel, early retirement and outplacement programs—some dozen integrated programs in all. This not only gives them greater flexibility in staffing, but also enables them to protect their core work force in a period of greater uncertainty. This, incidentally, copies a page from the Japanese book. As you probably know, the much-publicized "lifetime employment" in Japan only extends to about 25 percent of their work force.

#2. Improved Selection and Retention

Another frontier area closely related to strategic personnel planning is the growing recognition on the part of sophisticated companies that they need to insure a better employee company and employee-job fit. The recruiting and placement function is among the oldest in industry, and the largely pragmatic/experience-based approaches to selection haven't changed in decades. Most companies have very workable processes for hiring the best people available and good correlation with the success requirements for initial job. But leader companies have developed more elaborate profiles—some of them fact-based, some built around company culture and lore. They identify, with uncanny success, the type of personnel appropriate to their institutions.

In all honesty though, an avalanche of federal and state legislation, pressure on the equal employment opportunity front, and economic gyrations of the last decade have introduced other considerations into the equation. In an era where there will be slower growth and more need to provide job security, I sense a fundamental examination is starting.

Companies are beginning to become more explicit and more careful about probationary periods, and much more conscious of when they effectively grant "tenure."

In the large multidivisional companies—most of whom are in the early stages of asset redeployment—companywide personnel policies often make less sense than ever. Unless I am reading the situation wrong, there will be a growing movement within industry to focus more on the individual work unit and business entity—in everything from compensation systems to the management of employee mix and career pathing.

We are going to see an exponential increase in data available—on everything from reference checking to the facilitation of spouse employment at the time of transfers, to improve correlation of functional/job family performance with both employee backgrounds *and* motivational/value profiles. We are going to tap psychological and sociological research more effectively.

#3. New Approaches to Employee Appraisals

Another area where I see progress being made is in the area of personnel appraisal. Better appraisal is urgently needed, since it feeds into human resource planning and is at the heart of the productivity improvement challenge. Here again, there is no simple programmatic solution. There is overwhelming evidence that there is no appraisal program, no specific technique and approach, that works universally.

One of our clients, a giant manufacturer who ranks among the top 10 companies in the U.S., did an exhaustive study of the different appraisal systems in effect in their 100-plus business units (some of these, incidentally, were deliberately installed to test alternative approaches). The results of an extensive year-long study that involved employee and supervisor attitude surveys, pay/advancement correlations of appraisals, were revealing but not unexpected. The first two conclusions didn't surprise them, although the universality of the response did. First, no one liked the current appraisal systems—employees felt that their performance wasn't being assessed properly, supervisors hated the processes and felt inadequate in making the appraisals, and top executives didn't believe the end results. Second, *there was no substantive correlation* between the results achieved and the particular appraisal system being used—from MBO systems, to forced ranking comparative processes, to old-fashioned trait appraisals. The third finding was the most fascinating of all: consistently employees said, "Don't take them away, in fact we want more feedback on performance."

Now what are the implications of this? For one thing, we have to get off this obsession with programs. Yes, techniques like MBO processes can be helpful within certain types of companies, and at certain professional levels . . . but they are also very time-consuming, and they can bog down strategic vitality. For example, Texas Instruments is one of the companies who applied MBO type processes extensively. Yet over the years what initially was a useful process became a paperwork mill in many units. Now the elaborate TI planning system [called OST—for *objectives, strategies,* and *tactics*] is being simplified and refocussed, as this leader company responds to a new competitive environment that has driven it to its first quarterly loss in its history.

Leader companies are beginning to grapple with the appraisal reality.

First, appraisals—formal or informal, separated from or linked with pay action—need to reinforce the positive. There will never be a bell-shaped curve of individual self-assessment. In fact, the research shows people almost universally rate themselves in the upper quartile. As Tom Peters cited in his book, successful companies design appraisal processes where most people can win.

Second, there is pretty clear evidence that we need to give feedback on performance more proximate to the event. And this feedback should be based around specific incidents rather than just global patterns. I recommend the work that Harry Levinson has been doing in this area. Companies like Bristol Myers are in the early stages of applying his concepts and findings.

Third, we have to face up to the reality that the immediate supervisor often is the weak link in the appraisal chain. This fact implies a complex training challenge. Some innovative work is being done here—again not surprisingly using computer-based approaches. A group of psychologists on the West Coast have developed an elaborate software program that enables a company to introduce specific responsibility and performance data on an individual into the system. Then the supervisor and employee separately go through an elaborate q&a routine, to build up better insight (in a nonthreatening context) about the underlying facts. While this is still in an experimental stage, the early results are promising.

Now there is a big dilemma in all this—one more among the many paradoxes that characterize the personnel management challenge. The harsh fact is that most employees don't feel they are adequately paid for performance. The three-year Public Agenda Foundation study I cited earlier found that 73 percent of the workers (at all levels) felt that "the quality and amount of effort that they put into their jobs had very little to do with how much they were paid."

Frankly, ladies and gentlemen, I believe that the leadership of American industry—and yes, we large consulting firms have to take part of the blame—have contributed to this perception by largely failing to tie *top management* pay to performance. In 1981 Hay updated Harvard professor K. R. Murthy's pioneering study of strategy and pay and found that even when you used a long time frame and looked at total compensation, less than one company out of three showed any correlation of executive reward and relative corporate performance within their industry. Too bad we can't get at this concept as simply as baseball immortal Babe Ruth did back in 1930. When asked how he could justify making more money than President Herbert Hoover, Babe said, "Why shouldn't I? I had a better year." And he was right.

I think the move to golden parachutes has been one of the most destructive trends of recent years—a phenomenon that I am happy to report is abating. But the payouts reported in a few isolated instances—at Norton Simon recently, for example—have created exactly the wrong message. To the average worker, it looks like the top management knows only two compensation terms—more and up—and they are protecting themselves to insure pay despite performance.

I can't present you with all of the hard data I'd like, but the information I have seen suggests that the pay differentials—particularly in base salaries—are lower from top to bottom in leader companies with sustained performance record, and that the extras for key personnel are in true performance-based, long-term incentives.

#4. The Training and Development Process

Another fertile area for innovation in personnel management is in the training and development processes. American industry spends an incredible sum on training—the Hope Report put the figure at $30 billion a year. Yet the professionals in our Conference and Training Division tell me that less than one company in a hundred has an effective system for measuring the impact and value of its training courses. I might say too, that with the increasing employee interest in development and the more rapid job obsolescence, there is a potential cost exposure that could rival runaway medical costs as an issue. Our surveys show that while over 90 percent of companies have some form of tuition refund program, currently less than 5 percent of employees utilize them. These numbers are going to increase, as will the contractual obligation to retain displaced workers. . . .

#5. Managing Cultural Change

The seminal work of Tom Peters and Bob Waterman has helped all of us realize that "the dominance and coherence of culture is an essential quality in the excellent company." Helping manage culture is a central HR mission. This includes all types of cultural change—changes in functional emphasis because of new strategies and marketplace pressures, and changes in performance orientation and management values. Of course, the massive, decade-long struggle of AT&T to create a more competitive, market-oriented culture has been in the news for some time. Other examples abound in some of the most successful large enterprises. . . .

Two things should be evident from this conference. There *are* tools available to profile management climate and culture, and these tools will continue to get better. We have an extensive effort underway to expand our data banks and add additional strategic change factors to our measurement tools. Second, personnel policies and practices are frequently *at the heart* of the reaffirmation or modification of existing values. Personnel policies, along with shifts in organization structure, represent major agents of change. Increasingly, we are finding it mandatory to build in diagnostics of climate into the initial stages of our work (in human resource planning or incentive plan development, for example).

Anyone who doubts the central role of personnel policies and plans in managing change in the 1980s should study the research findings of Yale Professor Rosabeth Moss Kanter (author of *The Change Masters*). She has found that "changes in an organization's human systems are its innovation-enabling mechanisms" and that failure to change "neighboring systems . . . such as selection systems, and reward systems" have doomed many quality of work life programs.

THE CHANGING ROLE OF PERSONNEL

Of course, all of this adds up to a very different role for personnel professionals, and the evidence of the changes abounds. I'd estimate that over a third of the senior human resource executives in the top 1000 companies are new to their jobs in the last five years. That includes such leader companies as Bank of America, Coca-Cola, and Consolidated Foods. These new men and women are, by and large, generalists with strong planning skills, and a bottom-line orientation. The human resource field is becoming less administrative and more strategic.

But we have a long way to go to develop the multidisciplinary talent pools necessary to deal with the types of issues we touched on today. Part of what is required is a greater financial orientation and the analytical skills to take on the difficult task of managing the cost of people. . . .

The main thing to realize is that we are going to have to build a better contextual framework for the management of people in the turbulent 80s.

All of the research suggests that personnel is going to have to shift away from its control orientation. It must work to help top management reexamine traditional beliefs—beliefs about hierarchy, and power distribution, and the real sources of employee satisfaction. . . .

Let's not get bogged down in the technical aspects of personnel management. Our failures may occasionally stem from noncompliance with the growing body of laws governing employee relations. But that does not represent our major problem. Nor is the need for legal compliance more than a transitional rationale for a stronger personnel function. Let's not focus excessively on what other companies do, even though you will continue to get asked that question by top management. The practices of others rarely point you toward the right answer. Do let's have the courage to think deeply about our beliefs and approaches. I am reminded of that quote from humorist Josh Billings over a century ago, "It ain't what a man don't know that makes him a fool, but what he does know that ain't so." Our biggest failure of all will come from our lack of courage to seize the initiative and create a framework that will contribute to economic viability of our organizations and tap the potential of our people.

Clearly your employees are assets and resources. But they also have aspirations and fears and deep human desires that raw material and machinery do not possess. Remember Herzberg's admonition to employers. He said, "Their task is not to motivate people to get them to achieve; they should provide opportunities for people to achieve, so they will become motivated."

We need to find a way to integrate sociological and psychological insights with systems and discipline. Failure to do so limited the behavioralists of the 1960s. The brilliant work by Harvard professors Paul Lawrence and David Dyer (*Renewing American Industry*) outlines the successful ingredients in the "readaptive" process for American industry. They show, with example after example, how this requires *both* efficiency and innovation, and how employee involvement is essential. They concluded that "a balanced mix of clan (identification with a social entity, à la Japanese cooperation), market mechanisms, and *bureaucratic* human resource processes are essential to achieving adaptive outcomes." . . .

Personally I am excited about the future. I am glad that a few large companies saw something in me that pointed a young academic toward personnel management. I think this field is going to be the most exciting, innovative aspect of business management for the rest of this century.

It is exciting, not only because of the magnitude of the challenge . . . and of the new program approaches and information sources that are emerging. To me it's exciting even more because we have the opportunity— and I believe the need—to re-examine the context and basic principles of people motivation and management, and then forge approaches that will improve our bottom-line performance and our worldwide competitive edge. . . .

Part III

The HR Function Itself—
Purpose and Mission,
Role and Orientation

The five selections in Part III provide the reader with useful perspectives on the personnel function, its role, and the requirements for effective leadership and success in the future. Written by line managers (including two company presidents), personnel heads and academicians, these articles state well how senior management views or wants to view the human resource function. One finds a developing consensus that will be beneficial to both human resources practitioners and line managers.

James A. Henderson, author of "What the Chief Executive Expects of the Personnel Function," is especially well-qualified to write on this topic, for he is one of the very small number of personnel vice-presidents in the United States to become president of his company, Cummins Engine. Although he writes that his views on the subject have not changed since he moved from personnel into general management, he states that his "sense of urgency has." After first discussing the likely environment for the foreseeable future and then delineating a partnership role for personnel with top management, he states that personnel departments must prepare for an era of hiring fewer, better employees.

In "Conversation with Edson W. Spencer and Fosten A. Boyle," a wide-ranging interview with the chairman and employee relations vice-president at Honeywell, the CEO discusses his close working relationship with the employee relations officer. Top management expects the human resources manager to be a "doer," to create programs that have payoffs for the company. In a company that faces a shortage of qualified employees in the coming years, it is an essential part of the task of the employee relations head to sit in on all strategic-planning and operations-planning meetings, raising questions about human resources issues.

Robert H. Murphy, vice-president for organization and management resources at Rockwell International, also sees the human resources officer as "a catalyst and leader in effective management of the corporation's most precious resources" ("A Line Manager's View of the Human Resources Role"). Murphy offers seven essential characteristics for the human resources professional of the eighties. He also outlines a complete planning process for human resource managers, including a strategic business support plan, a professional development program, a human resources advisory board, and executive reviews.

Walton E. Burdick, personnel vice-president for IBM, is one of the most highly regarded personnel professionals in the nation. A graduate of the Cornell School of Industrial and Labor Relations, he advanced rapidly within IBM. Besides being an influential member of IBM's senior management, he also gives much of himself to the advancement of the personnel profession. In an address ("Impact/Influence: Defining and Charting a Course for Personnel Vitality") to personnel administrators given in 1976, he argues that a number of events have made "personnel the critical business activity of the final quarter of this century." He speaks of a much more proactive personnel role within the corporation and within society. Walt Burdick's commitment to improving personnel professionalism is evident from his words and actions.

In "Organizing and Staffing the Personnel Function," Dean Henry Morgan and I focus on personnel's new, more active role and how to organize and staff to get the job done as effectively and efficiently as possible. Asserting that personnel's principal activities consist of four essential roles—policy, service, review, and innovation—we say where in the organization we believe each of these roles should be performed. We, too, speak of the need for staff development and for more professional development opportunities and programs.

Taken together, the readings in this section should provide greater insight into the personnel function and its changing role. The reader should also learn what personal and career issues are involved in choosing the field of human resources as a profession.

WHAT THE CHIEF EXECUTIVE EXPECTS OF THE PERSONNEL FUNCTION

J. A. Henderson

I have been on both sides of the question: "What does the chief executive officer expect from the personnel function?" My views on the subject have not changed since I moved from personnel into general management, but my sense of urgency has. I think the future poses some new and more difficult challenges that relate directly to those expectations. But perhaps some history is necessary to put the future into proper perspective.

After four or five years of adjustment and changeover from the wartime production of World War II, our country entered a prolonged period of business prosperity that may one day be known as the Golden Age of Business. For roughly 20 years, from 1950 to 1970, the climate for business in this country was unusually good.

Let's look at some of the major factors. First, the economic environment was relatively stable although there were some ups and downs in the '50s. The economy was characterized by a generally high rate of real economic growth and, of particular importance, virtually no inflation. This, in turn, led to nearly full employment, uninterrupted annual gains in disposable income and, therefore, a rising consumer affluence and confidence.

Second, this economic climate meant that corporations looked forward to generally rising demand and growth. International growth opportunities added to domestic prosperity. Profit margins and cash flow were relatively high and expansion could be financed while maintaining reasonable debt levels. The stock market reflected these business conditions and generally was in a rising mode. Many people were beneficiaries of this trend, which, in turn, led to even more consumer affluence.

The political and social environment was also favorable. Businessmen were generally accepted as leaders, the best problem-solvers of our society and as people to be trusted.

Finally, the people in our businesses and in the society by and large

James A. Henderson, "What the Chief Executive Expects of the Personnel Function," reprinted from the May 1977 issue of The Personnel Administrator, copyright 1977, The American Society for Personnel Administration, 606 North Washington Street, Alexandria, VA 22314.

believed in hard work and security. The older people of the working group had experienced the great depression of the '30s first-hand. That depression left its mark in terms of an overriding concern for savings, for security and a good job.

The younger working generation in the '50s and '60s had experienced World War II and, as a result, were part of the greatest effort of all time—to defeat the Axis. Out of that effort came a faith and pride in our country. Since most had firsthand experience with the military establishment, they were conditioned to accept a big organization geared to achieve national objectives. So the society and the workforce were, in general, ready to accept the leadership of business management.

Near the end of this 20-year period, however, trends began which have culminated in making the '70s rather confusing and unpredictable. One of the most dramatic changes came about in the people environment. Young adults in the late '60s had a far different view of our society than did their elders. The waves of protest touched off by the Watts Ghetto riots in 1965 and later against the Viet Nam War set the tone of confrontation and open revolt against many of our institutions.

These youngsters were a product of the best educational system in the world. Although there were certainly a handful of radicals, in retrospect these young people were impressive. Their education had taught them to question the institutions of our society and the values that older people accepted. They placed human values above material ones and felt that major change must be made in most of our institutions.

Business leadership, in particular, did not come off well in their eyes. They saw rivers and air polluted, an industrial community that ignored the black, the Mexican-American, the Indian and even the female. Business had become complacent about the way it served the customer—unreasonably high prices and, in some cases, inferior or even dangerous products.

Unfortunately, business leadership did not respond well, perhaps because the young people often used confrontation as a tactic. Real communication never took place. These young people soon convinced enough of their elders that the credibility of business leadership declined rapidly and the role of the businessman as a leader and respected citizen diminished. The consumer revolt was on.

Although there were attempts, business as a whole did not police itself and it was inevitable that the government would be drawn into the picture in response to voter pressure. More regulatory agencies and Congressional committees were formed. The social/political environment changed greatly in just a few years.

Simultaneously, we experienced major changes in our economy. In 1969 and 1970, the economy experienced its first recession in nine years, rebounded to very strong growth in 1972 and 1973 and then spiraled into recession. Basic inflationary trends were set off which have not yet been arrested.

These wide swings in the economy in the face of inflationary pressures were very difficult for business to handle. Planning was particularly perplexing. I think most of us believed that this uncertain period was temporary, that long-term and favorable business conditions would resume and, therefore, planning for expansion continued, despite the lower profit margins from inflation. Since this investment in fixed assets and working capital could not be financed out of cash flow from operations, funds were borrowed.

The result has been that the nation's industry has undergone a major and significant change in its capital structure. The efforts of the Federal Reserve System to combat inflation and offset larger and larger federal budget deficits resulted in restricted credit availability and a dramatic increase in interest rates. In 1965, the prime interest rate was four-and-a-half percent while in 1973 it reached 12 percent.

After several years of this instability, I think we can piece together a clearer picture of what we face in the future. We can expect periodic recessions along with periods of moderate growth. The upward and onward growth rates of the '60s are a thing of the past. Unfortunately, we also appear to have institutionalized inflation and unemployment in our economy. Higher unemployment will slow the rate of economic growth in time of prosperity and inflation will continue to keep corporate profit margins under severe pressure. The energy crisis will continue to keep the inflationary pressure with us.

Therefore, the corporation, already at a very high debt level, will have difficulty in affording capital investment to modernize plants and equipment and invest in new technology. Overcapacity which has resulted from the heavy investment of the '60s and early '70s will be with us for some time, making it difficult to raise prices to preserve margins. The profit squeeze will continue.

We can expect little relief from government in the form of reduced regulation or reduced taxes. In fact, governmental pressures are likely to go in the other direction. The regulatory commissions are still at work but under increasing attack from all sides. There is a trend toward ever-increasing use of the judicial branch as a final arbitrator of all complaints and this slows the process of government. The outlook is likely for increasing government involvement in business rather than less, at least until business succeeds in establishing some credibility in the eyes of society.

If this is the environment of the future, it means a whole new orientation for business.

For many companies, the focus must shift from growth to survival. Business leadership, in general, faces a major task of getting its financial structure in shape. This can only happen if we make major gains in internal efficiency and productivity and this is largely a job of cost cutting. We can expect no outside help. If we cannot do it ourselves, then our country may face a combination of decline in our standard of living and fundamental changes in our economic and social system.

I feel it is imperative that we make those changes ourselves. Where business has turned to government or government has intervened, the results are not impressive. Unfortunately, the period of the '50s and '60s have made the task of cutting costs more difficult. Those of us who managed in this period have not been trained in such an effort nor are we experienced. Growth has helped us hide inefficiency and tolerate high overhead.

I think it is very important that we understand how we got to this point in order to comprehend the changed emphasis of both top management and the personnel department. I have always viewed top management and the personnel function as a partnership. Management is, after all, people. At Cummins the personnel head has always reported to the senior operating officer and has been a part of all major decisions. He is one of our most important officers and is paid accordingly. I believe this will be the only way a company can operate effectively in the future. The personnel head must be one of the very best people in the company—confident, courageous, warm and perceptive.

The job ahead for both top management and the personnel department can be summed up very simply as: fewer people, better people and leadership. That is, fewer people to do a given amount of work, thereby increasing productivity and ultimately cash flow. Better people, in order to cope successfully with a less favorable environment and find new ways to do the job, and leadership, in order to make major change in the way we do business. Management can be static; leadership is making change.

I'd like to examine these points and the role personnel plays in each. First, fewer people. When you run a five year or longer projection of cash flows in an inflationary environment, you realize that each single person is a very costly asset. If manpower can be held or reduced, margins increase very sharply in such a projection.

I'm not referring only to direct labor. In staff groups, salary and wages account for a very high percentage of the total cost of that department. In an inflationary environment, that cost escalates rapidly. A young executive making $20,000 today, will be making $52,000 in 10 years if he or she receives a 10 percent increase per year. If inflation is five to eight percent, then two to five percent per year for merit or promotion would not be unrealistic *under past standards.*

We have built such expectations during the '60s. Our people say they expect to stay even with inflation *and* make gains. There seems to be a feeling that "we have a *right* to our compensation growth." The fact is, most likely we cannot sustain such a high level of individual compensation growth in future years. Certainly we will be unable to do so unless we can increase productivity. But I can conceive of a highly productive organization with a relatively few (by past standards) well trained, highly flexible, and therefore, well paid people.

There is not only the direct wage or salary increase; union pressures have brought a very high level of fringe benefits for both hourly and salaried people. I can remember in 1964 using a figure of 17 percent of direct labor for fringe benefits and in 1975 we used 33 percent. There is talk in some companies of 50 percent in the near future. The amount of worry and administrative and overhead costs concerned with fringe benefits are much higher than for direct labor, as we all know. Most of these benefit systems are patchwork which have grown from the process of collective bargaining over the golden years and need overall re-examination. Changes will be difficult in the bargaining process, of course.

I personally had a rude awakening when we were asked to project our pension costs in the future. In 1970 we paid approximately $2 million a year and in 1975, after negotiations, it was $10 million. We then projected pension costs for 20 years. We made a modest inflationary assumption of five percent and a benefit level which only stayed even with inflation. Most important, we held our growth and headcount level at *no* additional people. In 1995, the pension cost of the corporation at these modest assumptions will be $42 million, 20 times as great as 1970 and virtually equal to our before tax profits of 1974.

When you look at this escalation in cost, you can't help but reach the conclusion that a commitment to hiring a single person is a commitment to greatly increased costs. Each opening must be critically examined with a return of investment justification. We can no longer regard people as a relatively inexpensive and therefore expendable asset as we have.

Second, we must take a fundamental look at organizational concepts that have long been accepted. American business was one of the first to break the job down into its simplest elements under the influence of Frederick Taylor. This happened at a time of rapid industrial growth and was particularly suited to the growth of our society at the time. Many of the people entering our workforce were immigrants who did not handle the language well. A very simplified job which they could understand and which they were grateful to have was an obvious solution. But, it has also built a massive overhead in the form of staff support and a military hierarchy-type structure. Setters, inspectors, engineers, salvage men, material expeditors, maintenance men and a seemingly endless group of other specialists have been built in as support—as well as several layers of management. This factory-type organization influences organization throughout industry—even in staff groups.

We are all familiar with the work of the behavioral scientists. Some very important concepts—that are really quite logical—have been agreed upon:

- Most people are able and willing to do more than they have been asked to do.
- Achievement, recognition for that achievement, the work itself and the responsibility and opportunity for personal growth that the work offers are most important.
- Identification with the goals and success of an organization is important.

Several experimental operations are underway—we have some in Cummins. They show promise of operating with far less supervision and overhead and at equal levels of quality and output. They also are looked upon with suspicion. In part, this is because some over-zealous behavioral scientists and their followers got caught up in the jargon, sold the concept as a way to increase employee happiness and turned busy managers off. Probably more important, they threaten, because the traditional role of the supervisor to the people is dramatically changed.

There is definitely promise in these organizational efforts of far more productivity and effectiveness than American business has achieved to date. The task of applying these to established plants and staff groups will be very difficult, but now also very vital, as business seeks higher productivity to do the same work with fewer people, or more work with the same people. . . .

If we are to hold or reduce manpower, then what things must the personnel department do? First, it must perform a greatly expanded manpower planning and organization analysis function. It must thoroughly understand all aspects of the business and how it operates. It must be able to spot situations where there is excessive overhead, ill-designed job content, overlap of responsibility, lack of proper motivation, opportunity to combine functions and the like, and have the credibility to convince line managers to investigate these areas. This is an action concept rather than one of pure reaction.

Second, the personnel department must become expert in solving the problems of organization re-design that eliminate needless overhead and become the change agent or expert. Implied in this is the ability to effect major change *and* solve the people problems.

Finally, it must be numbers-oriented. It must project future costs and reduce them by straightening out and cost-reducing overlapping benefit schemes. If we are to reduce people, it must be largely by attrition. Personnel must project and plan attrition levels and devise new compensation methods—such as early retirement—to increase it and it must measure productivity in new ways and project what a corporation can afford in compensation as it relates to this productivity.

In addition to fewer people, we identified *better people* as a need for the corporation.

Peter Drucker has said that people now must work "smarter, not harder". The companies that have the ablest people at all levels, and working in the proper environment, will cope best with the future because personal creativity, willing effort and the capacity for innovation will be the highest order.

Again, the '50s and '60s did not prepare us for this effort. Business was good. We could afford to hire and promote persons of relatively *limited* ability to innovate or manage people effectively—and we often did. Seniority and loyalty counted more than they should have. Also, too often we put up with individual behavior which should not have been tolerated. It is still far too easy for an able person in a major U.S. corporation to get crossways with an arbitrary boss who has perhaps been threatened and find him or herself sidetracked or even fired.

Corporations have used the percentage of projected growth as the percent of people to add in the past. In too many cases this has produced far too great a growth in people—and produced bureaucracy which slows decision-making and dulls innovation. Organizations have lost their warmth and sense of community. There is little personal attention or interest in the individual. The sense of belonging people felt in small organizations is missing. Supervisors carry their worries in their sleeve—and don't interact with their people.

For the most part, we have not yet tapped minority or female sources of talent as we should. There is, of course, now federal legislation to give impetus to this effort—but we have allowed ourselves to become cut off from these sources of talent—and missed an opportunity to broaden and enrich our management teams. . . .

Again, better people are required at *all levels*. If business conditions warrant hiring into our shop or clerical forces, then the same care should go into their selection as for managerial level people. This has been overlooked, but organization changes will require able people there, too.

The role of the personnel department in attracting and holding better people is again an active one. First, it must re-define and re-examine hiring standards for all sources of people, shop, office and salaried, and maintain an active search for talent at all of these levels—including minorities and women.

Second, it must make sure it understands the capabilities, situation and feelings of each *individual* in the organization. The emphasis is upon the individual and not the organization. This is a big order and if problems are encountered—personnel must have the clout to force action.

Third, the personnel department must have a role in selection, both hiring and promotion, and then have the objectivity and courage to recommend employment or advancement for those able individuals who might not be selected by popular vote of the high seniority people.

Finally, the personnel department should be developing salary and compensation systems which allow for organization change. In the successful corporations, we will see smaller, flatter organizations with more highly trained, capable people in both the office and shop—and we must compensate those taking on increased responsibility. Job evaluation systems must be capable of rewarding innovation and flexibility rather than seniority, working conditions or number of people supervised.

The final area which we identified for the future was leadership. Here, we are talking about top management—but there is a vital role for personnel, too.

There are several aspects to leadership that I would like to mention. I want to emphasize that I am not talking only about company presidents—but leaders of units within a company, too—in other words, the key management members.

First, we have discussed the decline in business credibility. I was at a Board Meeting recently when a statement by a major company head was quoted and none of the persons at the table, all of whom were businessmen, believed it. This lack of credibility is particularly obvious in relation to government. Too often our business spokesmen take a position in opposition to *all* government regulation or *all* social programs or put the blame for business problems at the government's doorstep. This does not ring true to the reader or listener and is not the way business decisions are made. We consider facts and alternatives and select the most practical course of action. Business decisions aren't made from an ideological base. It appears that too often our business leaders are not at home in the world of ideas and cannot relate to the society as a whole on which they are dependent for the ultimate success of their companies.

A second aspect of leadership is the moral or ethical tone that key members of management set for their organizations. What appears to be concern only for business or personal success, no matter what the means, has surfaced in recent years in a number of companies. The leadership we require must be of the highest personal integrity, genuinely concerned about each person in the company, intolerant of bureaucracy and have a healthy suspicion of the chain of command. Quality, integrity, openness and a capacity to relate to and to *listen to* customers, to employees, to society, to government, are vital.

Finally, of course, the key to the future will be the capability to effect the changes we have discussed. A leader who makes change effectively must gain organization acceptance and change the concept which the organization has of what is acceptable performance and what, indeed, it is possible to accomplish. The leader has a sensitive job of selecting goals and objectives that stretch and require innovation and hard work, but which are achievable and within the capability of the organization. The ultimate goals must be accepted by the organization or the result is that the organization will reject it—either by inaction or perhaps by departing. The leader must give direction, achieve commitment and impart confidence and spirit. He or she must work to re-establish the sense of community, of shared goals, of everyone having a part in success.

The role of the personnel department in the process of leadership is vital. First, there is the rare but occasional opportunity to vote in the selection of corporate leadership, or key management personnel. Be prepared. You are helping to select your own leadership. An understanding of how a prospective officer or management member conducts himself or herself in a variety of situations, not just business, is vital. How is he or she perceived by peers, subordinates, the community? Is there a basic moral guidance system in the prospective leader? Is he or she concerned about people and willing to try new ideas?

Second, the personnel head should be a close advisor in the process of change. The personnel head must provide guidance as to whether the change is accepted—is too fast or too slow. He or she must sense attitudes and how to make the leadership more effective. This input is absolutely vital to the chief executive and to key management members, who are inevitably isolated.

The business environment has changed and the future is not favorable by past standards. A large number of companies have a major task to get their financial structures in shape and all companies must look very hard at their productivity and, therefore, their people. In general, a tougher, more complete leadership job must be done. The environment will be difficult, but in some ways, more predictable. Three areas—fewer people, better people and leadership—are vital for the future of business.

I am a firm believer in a partnership between personnel and the top manager. The personnel director must tread the delicate line of maintaining close contact with top management and with the people. In many ways what I've described is not new. Personnel people have advocated much of this for years. However, as we have seen, it simply wasn't vital to business success in the past. Now it is. I predict far more top management interest and concern. The time spent on people matters has already risen dramatically in our company and I expect that trend to continue.

CONVERSATION WITH EDSON W. SPENCER AND FOSTEN A. BOYLE

The year 1983 marks the 100th anniversary of the invention of an automatic temperature controller by A. M. Butz of Minneapolis. William R. Sweatt, some years later, salvaged the small firm that originally produced the heat regulators, nurtured and expanded it, then passed it on to his sons Harold W. and Charles B. Under the leadership of the Sweatts, whose Minneapolis Heat Regulator Company merged with Mark C. Honeywell's Heating Specialties Company in 1927, the corporation flourished. Known as Honeywell Inc., by 1982 its revenue had grown to $5.5 billion and its workforce to more than 94,100 employees worldwide. . . .

In its growth and diversification—by merger, acquisition, and internal expansion—Honeywell's history is an American classic. Harold W. Sweatt, during his tenure as chairman of the board, described his business philosophy as follows:

> While I always want to strive for perfection and never want to be satisfied with less if I had to choose, I would prefer to settle for a little less perfection today and a little more imagination for tomorrow—recognizing that in pushing this spirit of restlessness we are bound to make more mistakes and sacrifice some immediate gains.
>
> Whatever else we may do, we must strive always to keep it fully alive—this spirit of restlessness. If we do this, if we refuse to become satisfied and content with the status quo and always strive to do better and, in the process, do a little more imagining for tomorrow—we will preserve one of our most priceless and fundamental possessions.

Tradition remains a powerful force in shaping Honeywell's culture. Edson W. Spencer, chief executive officer since 1974 and chairman since 1978, is dedicated to maintaining the restless spirit. During his term at the helm, Honeywell has continued to be an innovative, growing company with imaginative yet sound management practices.

In this interview with Noel Tichy, associate professor of organizational behavior at the University of Michigan's Graduate School of Business Administration, . . . Spencer and one of the officers who report directly to

"Conversation with Edson W. Spencer and Fosten A. Boyle," reprinted, by permission of the publisher, from Organizational Dynamics, *Spring 1983, © 1983 by AMACOM Periodicals Division, American Management Associations, New York. All rights reserved.*

him, Fosten A. Boyle, vice-president of employee relations, candidly discuss how this diversified multinational corporation approaches the future, especially the management and development of its people. They describe how Honeywell is grooming tomorrow's leaders and how human resources management philosophy and practice throughout the company are supporting the corporate business strategy.

Tichy: I would like to start with a general discussion of Honeywell's environment in the 1980s. How do you two see the business environment that Honeywell and other U.S. organizations face in this decade?

Spencer: I would say that the whole world is going through a rather prolonged period of economic readjustment, which comes out of this recent period of excess—excess credit, excess growth, and excess inflation—and it's going to take some time to wind that down. That means that companies like ours will be going through periods of slow growth rates in the 1980s and 1990s. We may have some brief periods of high-growth rates with high inflation, but it's going to be, I think, a rather more gradual growth in the economy because people are going to conserve their capital a little better and borrow a little less than in the past. That means a much more competitive economy: it means having the personnel who can adjust to a much more competitive, slower-growth economy overall. It also means being sharp and looking in the places where you can grow faster than the total economy grows. But we have to recognize that it will be a more competitive, more difficult business environment in the next 20 years than it has been in the last 20. The second absolutely critical thing is that since Europe and Japan have become so strong in the world economy, we can no longer just view our competitors as those across the street. We are now truly in a society in which consumers are demanding the best product at the best price and "made in the United States of America" is not necessarily something they are going to buy on that basis alone. They are going to buy because they want a product, wherever it comes from. So that means we must deal with more extensive worldwide competition than we have had in the past.
. . .

Tichy: It sounds as if you assume that . . . [Honeywell will compete increasingly in international markets.] Let's look specifically at some of the people implications at the senior executive level and then on down through the organization. What are the important people issues that Honeywell should consider?

Spencer: Let me start down lower in the organization because it fits our story. About six years ago, we senior managers sat back and said: "What kind of people are we going to need in the 1980s and 1990s to manage this business? What are we going to have to do to attract them? What kind of motivation and desires are they going to have? What differences are there between their motivations and the motivations that we all have?" We are all products of World War II, the job boom, and the years immediately after that, when getting work was fairly easy. Most of us in senior management are in our mid-40s and 50s. And we suddenly realized that the people we will need are, first, going to have to be trained differently; they will have backgrounds in computer science, mathematics, and engineering. And we'll need a whole new raft of skills to deal with the type of products in our high-technology business.

The second thing we realized is that we are going to shovel a lot of software. We are moving from a hardware to software company. We're moving from an electromechanical or mechanical type of product to an electronic product. We're moving throughout the whole business into computer- or microprocessor-driven systems with all the software implications that go with it. So we will require very different skills. The old skills of the mechanical engineer, assembly-line worker, and tool-and-die maker are always going to be there, but they are going to be less important in the total picture. Well, then, suddenly somebody said "Gee, you know those people we're going to have to recruit are like our kids, more college-educated, having more finely tuned skills, probably brighter, and with many more women competing for top jobs." Then we considered what our kids are interested in: They're much more mobile, for example; they may have less loyalty to companies and more loyalty to the quality of life that they want to live. They may want to live in the Southwest or the mountains and less in the industrial heartland of the country. So we decided that we'd better start changing the way we deal with people in the company—otherwise we wouldn't be able to attract them and keep them because their desires and motivations are so different from ours were when we were their age.

Boyle: I think we're going to have a difficult time in the 1980s getting the kind of people that Ed is talking about—that is, people who will really make a contribution in a more competitive, world-based economy. This is because if you look, for example, at electrical engineers—one of the prime technical skills we need—I think about 14,000 electrical engineers graduated in 1969. Then the number of electrical engineer graduates actually went down in the early 1970s, and this past year the number rose back to about 14,000. So we are dealing with a static supply—and with the end of the baby boom hitting the colleges, in a few years we will be fighting over not a static supply, but a decreased supply.

Spencer: The implication is that we will need a growth business that is going to grow faster than the slow-moving averages I talked about, so Honeywell looks like a place where there is opportunity. But we are also going to have to be a place where people are going to want to work, where people will like their work, and where they will want to come and stay with us.

Tichy: On this dimension, one of the comparisons you hear a lot in Honeywell is with such companies as Hewlett Packard. Are you going to have to compete with such companies for those young people?

Spencer: I would say that Hewlett Packard is one of a number of companies—there are many—that are younger than ours. We have an old culture; we are 100 years old. A lot of the companies we will be competing with have grown up in the last 20 or 30 years, and they've had the advantage of starting from zero and going up.

Tichy: Why is it better or easier for them not to have the hundred-year-old culture?

Spencer: It's not better—just different. We still have the traditions of senior managers who preceded Foss and me. They have greater difficulty adjusting than perhaps we do. We have an old family heritage that we have had to come out of and over the last 15 to 20 years we have had to build a new, professionally managed business. And, you know, you don't do those things overnight.

Boyle: You mentioned Hewlett Packard as an example of newer electronic-type companies, but we do have similar traits in our philosophy of management and our people orientation. We tend to recruit for entry-level jobs, train, develop, and promote from within. Even in the high-growth mode we've been in, we have been able to maintain that kind of culture. We are stressing teamwork and long-term employment.

  I'm not knocking other industries but if you take the banking industry, particularly commercial banking, it seems to be very competitive without much teamwork. The compensation systems, for example, seem to support the philosophy that you may not be there in a couple of years. I think those are the sorts of traits that we have avoided.

Spencer: Take the case of Silicon Valley. We've had to adjust from a somewhat more traditional, conservative, upper midwestern way of running a business to compete for personnel with such Silicon-Valley businesses as Hewlett Packard, National Semiconductor, and Intel. Therefore, we have to swing a little bit harder and produce more quickly and faster than we are accustomed to in Minnesota, where it's more conservative.

Tichy: I assume the pressure gets put on the management at the next level above that semiconductor group. How do they have to begin to change, or how do they become different, as you begin to pump different people into the semiconductor divisions?

Spencer: Obviously, the people who run the semiconductor divisions for us have to deal with the semiconductor world. But their bosses, who probably aren't products of the semiconductor world, have had to learn how to do things in that world and be willing to adapt and be flexible and to adjust to different reward schemes, different life styles and so on, and I think they've done it rather well.

Tichy: If you start moving up the ladder and you start thinking of executives who can manage Honeywell in the future, are they going to be different—given the world view you have—and if so, how?

Spencer: Well, I think obviously they are going to have to be able to cope with the technology changes. They are going to have to cope with a higher speed of change in technology, product, competition, and marketing than perhaps most of us did in our younger days. They are going to have to cope with this different motivation of the younger people they will be hiring in the 1990s and the next century. They're going to have to be able to deal with a global competitive environment. And I think it requires a broader-gauge person who is trained in a broader way perhaps than a lot of our managers of this decade and the previous two decades.

Tichy: Do you see it changing, or are you in the process of changing the way in which you develop senior managers over the next decade?

Boyle: We have worked hard on development strategy over the last three years. In a company as big as Honeywell, you can run almost any kind of development program two or three times a year and get 25 people to come to it. But we try to match our development strategy with the training constituencies at various levels in the organization. We put together a model in which we split the workforce into five levels, starting with nonsupervisors and going all the way up to vice-president; within each level there are four stages of development. We compare development programs with this model to see where the duplications are, where the gaps are and, in general, to take a more strategic approach to our development efforts. That leads to a core curriculum of courses and a supporting curriculum for all management levels. We have also brought a new corporate conference center on line to assist in our development efforts. Now development, from my perspective, takes place about 80 percent on the job, 10 percent through the coaching and mentoring of one's supervisors or peers, and probably 10 percent in a classroom setting. However, classroom training is a powerful catalyst. I think classroom training sets a tone and pulls the other development efforts together. We are doing some further study in terms of job development and relationship development and the way in which we might put that down on paper and communicate it to the organization. We're still looking at how to develop people more effectively and efficiently and how to get the best leverage for the dollar that is spent. But we still have a lot of work to do on this.

Spencer: Let me expand on Foss's answer with a couple of specific examples of what we are doing to add meaning in this area. We established a human resources department four years ago. Until that time Foss had had a fairly typical personnel career—labor relations, compensation, division personnel involvement, corporate staff work, and so on. At that time the corporate personnel department became the corporate employee relations department, obviously symbolic of a change in attitude toward the function. Though it didn't change a lot of things internally, it was a signal to people. Then Foss went from that very traditional personnel development plan to become the first director of the human resources department. It was a training place where Foss could expand his scope and understanding of this whole process of developing people. That's what we all felt the company had to do and, of course, he moved from there into corporate vice-president of employee relations, reporting directly to me.

Tichy: That was part of this whole plan to focus more attention on human resources?

Spencer: Right. The human resources department became the vehicle for implementing the kind of concept that we evolved—the change in motivation and the openness in dealing with people.

Tichy: How do you make this happen? Is it those on the line that make this happen? A struggle in many organizations and perhaps in Honeywell is getting the line's cooperation. This is a significant part of their job. How is this transition happening at Honeywell, and what are some of the successes and problems you still have to overcome?

Spencer: I think it depends on the attitude that is created by those of us in senior management and whether the chief executive can maintain a non-political, open, easy environment between himself and the people who work for him. Those who work for him who are smart and observant and who agree on the concepts (if they disagree, differences are talked out) are going to transmit that in the way they deal with the people who report to them, and it's going to go on down through the organization that way. It's probably a lot easier for a 40-year-old executive to do that than it is for a 60-year-old executive. And there are some of our senior management who struggle with this, but recognize it and push it in their organizations. There are others, though, who just can't adapt to it, so the process doesn't go at the same rate of speed throughout the whole organization; I think it's fair to say that in some of our divisions and groups, it moves rather slowly. There is still a tendency to be too authoritarian, to be too protective of one's turf. And we just have to find ways to break that down.

Tichy: How do you monitor or manage that?

Spencer: I guess I don't monitor it. The chief executive of this company doesn't monitor. He knows his people very well; he's talking to them and travels among them frequently. All of us travel a lot and get our hands directly on the operations. We have a pretty darn good feel of where it's working and where it isn't; the communications in this company are pretty good. I think we in senior management can see rather quickly where more change is needed and work with those people to help improve their attitude toward this new managing style and try to implement it a little bit better.

Boyle: I think we have to keep in mind that, first of all, changes in an organization's climate and culture are long-term, and they do take a long time to develop. People really measure you in terms of what your actions are and what you do, not what you say, so senior management has to set the tone. In a larger organization there are some symbols that you use. Ed developed some principles, both an operating set of principles and then later an employee relations set of principles. We have been trying to disseminate these widely over time. In addition, we have undertaken some special things in the last two or three years. Jim Renier (current vice-chairman, former president at Honeywell Control Systems) and his staff have taken up the subject of management climate and culture, looking at what we are now and what we should do about it. Then some of his bigger groups took up the same issue themselves, so there have been some special efforts like that. But change comes through people viewing how people manage the business and what they stand for; that's how you implant a strong culture into the line. In some cases, a true change in climate will require the replacement of the managers involved.

Tichy: Are you beginning to hold people more accountable at senior levels for their ability to develop people?

Boyle: We hold them accountable, but I'm not sure we hold them any more accountable today than we did ten years ago. It's just that we're looking for different results from them because we're looking for a different approach to management, perhaps, than we did ten years ago. We still have what we started in 1969, high talent reviews and review of EEO results and promotions. We do this in great detail, all the way up to the top of the company.

Tichy: Does the development review process provide a vehicle for changing Honeywell's culture?

Spencer: Whereas I might work out problems almost daily with the people who work for me—we interact all of the time—the development review process lies in the way in which the chief executive and the employee relations vice-president and the vice-president in executive development get their hands on a broader perspective and can ask lower-level people directly what they are doing.

Tichy: How does the development review process relate to the strategic planning process at Honeywell?

Boyle: Well, our strategic planning process involves a mid-year review that is essentially a five-year look at marketing, research and development, and strategic sorts of issues. Then we have a year-end review, which is a three-year financial plan that really turns more into next year's financial plan. All of the divisions come forward to corporate twice a year.

The development review is not part of these strategic reviews. Now we have a human resources planning process that we are pushing very hard to support the divisional employee relations departments. We want the divisional employee relations director to be a full member of the general managers' team and help in developing the strategic reviews. Any significant human resources issues that fall out of that planning process should be brought forth to corporate management at the time of the strategic review. The development reviews take place division by division; we roll up division reviews in the first quarter and then group reviews by midyear and then go on to corporate reviews. Ed finally takes them to the personnel committee of the board in September. So the two processes are not together. Now, certainly, some companies will argue that's wrong. I think if we were to submerge the development process into the strategic-planning process we would lose some of the people-evaluation aspects that we get by separating them.

Spencer: On the other hand, they come at the same time of the year, so that at the same time I'm reviewing a long-range strategic plan for all of these operating units in the business. I'm also going through the personnel-development plan and it's very easy to see if the two are out of sync.

Tichy: So when you're going through the strategic plans you're conscious of the manager's plan for people resources? Then, if the manager's business plans are out of sync, you will do something about it or raise questions?

Spencer: Oh sure—for example, ten years ago a great deal of interest suddenly arose throughout the organization in developing the type of people who can use integrated circuits in our products. Answers to questions we asked in the talent reviews made it apparent that we didn't have enough integrated-circuit designers in the company. So we started a crash program to go out and train and hire integrated-circuit designers.

Tichy: Do you see more linkages between the business strategic-planning process and the talent-review process in the future—or are you satisfied with the way they are positioned now, looking ahead over the next five years?

Spencer: I'm very satisfied. The two processes are complementary: We use the talent reviews to raise questions that come out of the strategy reviews to be sure we've got the people we need. Then, in the strategy reviews, we make sure we ask the question, "Have you got the people to do that?" We get a *yes* or *no* and then see that any needs are addressed accordingly in the talent-review process.

Boyle: I think that if top management and management at all levels consciously make the linkage, it works fine. You have the best of both worlds.

Spencer: There is another thing that helps it work. Foss, as the vice-president of employee relations, sits in on all the strategic-planning meetings and all of the operations-planning meetings. It's his job, really, to remind me if there are places that, in his opinion, we are not doing what we should be doing.

Boyle: That is a significant advantage over the way we were organized before. It was very hard to ask the vice-president of employee relations to have a strategic orientation about some of these things and make sure we were covering the bases when, in fact, the vice-president was not involved in the reviews.

Tichy: Let me raise an issue—the role of staff and line, especially in the human resources area. I guess at one end of the spectrum might be the view that staff is not to be seen; they're overhead; they'll get in the way. At the other end of the spectrum is the view that they're an integral part of the management team who should be actively involved. Which is it at Honeywell?

Boyle: I think we've made some progress on the line-versus-staff issue. I think effective companies have to operate as a team. I don't think the staff should lose sight of the role that is essentially to support operating management to get the job done. On the other hand, I suppose, Honeywell is like any other company; I've been in situations where I felt certain portions of the company regarded the staff as a necessary evil rather than a productive portion of managing the business. But I do think we've made some progress. It's because of the signals that we have had at the top, where the use of the staff is different than it was before. We have been able to upgrade our staff. After all, you have to bring something to the party before you're really accepted, and we have made some progress on that.

Spencer: Hopefully, everybody in the organization and line management observes that Foss sits with me in all of these meetings and is part of our monthly management committee, and therefore would look on their own employee relations director as having the same relationship with them as Foss has with me. And I think in most parts of the company it works that way. Where it doesn't work that way, many times it's not the organization's fault; it's because you don't have a good enough person or the right fit between the line manager and the staff manager.

Tichy: One of the comparisons I've heard made in Honeywell is between the financial staff and other staffs. The financial staff is characterized as a positive strong force. It's seen as having more of a team relationship with the line than, for example, employee relations. How do you see this?

Spencer: The objective is to have all of our corporate staff departments function the way the financial department has for a very long time, and our corporate controller has been in that job or a job very similar to it since 1969. He had also been a controller in many different operating units in the business before that. A lot of the people in the controller's departments are people he brought in, trained, and moved around. The objective, though, and we're doing this in employee relations increasingly, is that every employee relations director in a line-operating unit of the company should realize that his promotion depends on two things. First, and most important, is satisfying his boss—doing the right things and meeting objectives that he and his boss agree on. When the time comes for promotion, we're going to see that every person also has to be approved by the corporate vice-president of employee relations so that he has his hand into the overall quality, development, and the training of the employee relations department. . . .

Tichy: . . . How do you look at the challenge of developing an employee relations function that can take on some of these new tasks and think more in business terms than had been historically true for employee relations people?

Boyle: That is a challenge. Employee relations, looking back over 20 years, has changed a great deal. It used to be labor relations as the king of the hill, but the labor movement is in trouble. Our company is now more generally made up of salaried technicians, engineers, and so forth. Labor relations is still important, but many other factors have come into the picture. The field is changing as a result of all kinds of legislation passed over the last 20 years. ERISA legislation, EEO legislation, OSHA legislation, and so on have had an impact on employee relations. Practitioners have to be aware of this legislation and know how to effectively deal with the issues created by it. More change is occurring as we face this whole area of motivation and culture, and how you get people involved in changing management styles. It is a different sort of thing; it's much more psychologically based and it requires different kinds of skills. To some degree I think we have to bring new people into employee relations. We have done that at various levels in Honeywell over the last few years, although we're still developing and promoting from within as our main course of action. However, there are certain departments in which we do need specialists who can provide assistance to divisions. We can't afford specialist expertise everywhere, so one role of corporate is to provide some special expertise not present in the divisions.
. . .

Tichy: Let me ask a kind of philosophical question: That is, where on the spectrum you would place yourself in terms of viewing human assets as fixed-versus-variable assets. Some corporations prefer one over the other. For example, IBM makes a big thing of full employment and thus treats the people more as fixed assets. Where do you come out on that?

Spencer: My immediate reaction is that all people are variable assets because they change, and move around, and get promoted; they are not anchored in cement. They are all variable assets to be dealt with accordingly, as they can be changed and developed and promoted and moved.

Tichy: What about laid off?

Spencer: My attitude toward that is very clearly that a company has to do what is needed to be competitive; if it has to reduce employment to be competitive, or if it has to reduce old skills that can't be retrained and hire new skills, it must have the freedom to do that. Even IBM has had lay-offs and early retirements. I don't know of any American company that's immune. It would be marvelous to say we have fixed, full long-term employment, and nobody is ever out of a job. But if we are comparing our situation with Japan, we must take into account the fact that Japanese companies have a very large number of young women who are temporary workers and can be laid off, and companies also have a great ability to off-load their unemployment on their subcontractors. It's not quite what the propaganda makes you think it is.

Boyle: I don't think we do anybody a service if we have a policy that doesn't permit us to react to the business situation. However, we are trying to involve more of our employees in managing the business and we're asking them to share the objectives that we have. The more we do that, the more employees will say to us, "Well, you may have to lay off people, but you should not look at it as the only or the first way to cut costs." We have had some layoffs, but I'm hopeful that as the business goes up we can introduce some buffers that will lessen the impact of layoffs in another down cycle. It's going to take some time and some thought.

Tichy: *The Wall Street Journal* this morning (November 3, 1982) discusses the layoff of 1800 people on the computer side of Honeywell. How do you face that kind of difficult situation and minimize the damage to those who stay in the organization? It is happening right now.

Spencer: One thing to do is to look at each one of those people as an individual and try to recognize his or her other strengths and weaknesses and find other places in the division where they can be placed. That's the first thing. The second thing is to transfer them to jobs in other parts of the company. And the third thing you do is to help them find opportunities with other companies.

Boyle: I think what we also try to do is be as candid as we can in terms of why we have to take the action and the numbers of people involved, and to provide the best outplacement help possible.

Spencer: But you know the thing that I think we should never lose sight of, in any business, is that our success as a company is going to depend on our ability to be competitive and make profits, to grow and expand the business, and to offer more employment opportunities. Therefore, if from time to time we get soft, we get fat, we get lazy, we get noncompetitive, or we have market conditions that turn against us, then we have to take action to bring the costs and number of people in line.

Tichy: In Europe they have legislation that changes the degrees of freedom in terms of doing that. How would you deal with that whole issue of employment—the role of private sector versus government? Coming from Michigan I constantly wonder about that issue, and what happens to the auto industry where several hundred thousand hard-working souls are permanently out of jobs. Who does what with those people?

Spencer: First, talking about the problem of maintaining employment levels outside of the United States, in most countries that I am familiar with you *can* reduce your payroll. It's just that there are legislative costs of doing it as opposed to the negotiated costs of doing it in this country. Where you are involved heavily with the government, my experience has been that it's very difficult, but if the facts are laid on the table you can get the support of the government to go ahead to adjust your workforce to the size you need to be competitive in the business. It's a lot tougher, it takes longer, and it costs more outside the United States than it does in the States.

Tichy: Taking a more philosophical, societal view, what are your thoughts about how that problem should get managed or will get managed in the United States?

Spencer: I've been observing and reading more about people, paying more attention to the issue of structural unemployment, and I think that in this country and in western Europe we are going through a dramatic change in the skills that society needs in the future. It gets back to the question that we discussed much earlier about what kind of people we need in Honeywell in the 1980s and 1990s. Unfortunately for a lot of people who have devoted their careers to working hard on the assembly lines in automobile factories, the steel mills, and the mines in northern Minnesota, there is going to be less of a demand for those kinds of skills and that kind of experience.

That places a great responsibility on society and on government to try to find ways to retrain those people, to provide unemployment compensation for those people, and to assist those people in moving to other parts of the country. In a large, diverse country like ours, it's a difficult problem. The Japanese have handled this problem very well because although they at one time dominated the world export market for textiles, now they are a huge importer of textiles. A lot of their textile workers were moved into shipbuilding and the steel mills. As those industries become more mature, a lot of people are beginning to move into automobiles and into electronics. One of the things that really tells the tale is this: I read an article in the Japanese newspaper recently about how the automobile industry in Japan is not going to be competitive in the later part of the decade on a world basis and therefore they had better begin to think now about what type of opportunities can be created in the later part of the decade for automobile workers who will no longer be needed on the assembly lines.

Tichy: Does this create a societal problem for Japan?

Spencer: Yes. But being homogeneous, and having that strong link between business, education, and government, they're better able to handle the problems and work toward common objectives to solve those difficulties than we are in our diffuse and large society. . . .

Tichy: Let me get back to the challenges of the 1980s. If you look at the world you have laid out for Honeywell, and the kind of environment you are going to be struggling with, what are the major people-related challenges or hurdles that you see out in front of you?

Spencer: I think one of the most critical things we have to do within this company is to develop opportunities in the upper levels of management for minority Americans and female Americans. All of our statistics on equal employment are very, very good in a statistical sense, but we have not done as good a job as we should in getting these people into the upper levels of management. Why do I say that's a responsibility that we look upon as a challenge? First of all, because in a societal framework, it's a necessary thing, but also because there is a lot of skill there. You have got to take those people who have just as much skill as white males because we are going to need those skills in the future, and there is a whole resource out there in female employees and minority employees that we can tap to fill the needs of the future. So that's one challenge that I see out in front of us that has both a self-serving motive and a societal motive to it.

Boyle: I mentioned earlier the availability of technical people. Recruiting the right kind of technical people in sufficient numbers will be a challenge.

Spencer: There is a third area of challenge that I see in front of us. Increasingly, this competitive world needs a very productive workforce. As you know, productivity has been a theme in the company. It relates again to the attraction and the motivation of the type of intelligent people that we are going to need to run this business. But we have to work on the sharing of objectives, the quality circles or quality of work life movement at lower levels in the organization, the openness of communication between all levels of people in the business from the top management on down because that is what I think is the key to creating more productive companies. Productivity, like quality, is an attitude, and there are lots of tools you use to get productivity and to enhance the attitude of people toward wanting to do their job better. You have to create an atmosphere in which people can say, "Yes, I do want to do my job better and here's the way I can do it. I'll go tell my boss about it."

Tichy: Staying on that theme, one observation I have in looking at Honeywell is that there is probably as much innovative, people-oriented activity going on in Honeywell in terms of quality circles, development, and programs addressing these very issues as there is in any other company in the United States. One worry I have in looking at all of this activity is whether it will get institutionalized five years from now. Will it have been looked back on as an interesting time when a lot of activity went on, such as 700 quality circles, but which somehow all faded away? The question that I have is, how do you ensure that it all becomes a way of operating rather than a bunch of programs?

Spencer: I think there's a risk at the lowest level of the quality circle that it can fade away because people are getting kind of tired of it; they have run out of things to talk about. What you have to do on that level is to rejuvenate it every once in a while. If you find that it is running out of gas in some part of the company, you go back in and rejuvenate it. New ideas come from new people who are involved. This can be done, and I think it will be done.
   I don't think the company is going to change the approach to the whole subject of productivity and quality and getting the people involved in things. That's becoming too much ingrained in the way we do our business. Unless they add a new chief executive who felt very differently about this than I do, and hence the people who work for him feel differently than those who work for me, I don't think that is going to change. Again, we go back to the first thing we talked about: the driving force to keep it from changing is probably not the chief executive or upper management—it's the driving force of the type of people we've got to have in this business and what they want to do to stay working productively at Honeywell.

Boyle: We talked about the workforce as being brighter and better educated. Their expectations haven't changed in any revolutionary sense, but they have been changing and the expectations of the new managers are different from those of the old ones and they wouldn't want to manage people in the old way. I recognize what you are saying. I think there are a couple of things that could make it fade away, and one would obviously be a leadership change at the top. Now you're seeing a lot of activity because of the demonstrated commitment of the corporation starting at the top and working down. There probably is too much activity in some areas—too much of it being of a program nature, but I don't think that's adverse. I think if it's important to the company and important to the people up and down the line who work for the company, then it will become institutionalized. I think we are on the right track.

Spencer: There is a risk in going too far; as I have said many times, don't ever forget who the boss is. I don't mean just me—I mean all the way down the line—because you have to make decisions to get things done, and consensus and group discussions are fine but somebody has got to say every once in a while, this is what we are going to do. Let me just say I don't want anybody to think that I'm not attentive to the need to run the business in that way, so I remind people about it every once in a while.

Tichy: On the issue of institutionalizing things, is there an effort being made to examine the kind of personnel systems that support the organization similar to the way you are selecting people, developing them, appraising them, rewarding them, that may need modifications with this new kind of workforce and this new focus on productivity?

Boyle: Yes, we're thinking about some of those things. In fact, this year we have a couple of gain-sharing pilot plans in the reward area that we started. I think that in a large, decentralized company you have the luxury, if you will, to try certain things. In a big company I don't think you want to change reward systems without some analysis and testing. In terms of development, I think I've covered the kind of things that we are trying to do to tie the development systems into our efforts in quality-of-work-life and productivity themes.

Tichy: How about appraising people? Is the quality-of-work-life effort, and the attention paid to those issues becoming a part of the formal appraisal?

Boyle: I wouldn't say it's part of the appraisal process. We have all kinds of different appraisal systems, but I think it's done more indirectly than directly if you get right down to it.

Tichy: Is that something that should or will be happening more, as you look out over the next few years?

Boyle: I think that if you look at what's happening and what we are trying to do, this will come kind of naturally. People will get appraised and rewarded for elements such as how they are involving the workforce in managing the business, because that will just become a natural part of the appraisal criteria. Ed, what do you think? Do you anticipate or think it's desirable or not to begin to build that into the formal appraisal process?

Spencer: It's hard to put a quantitative number on those kinds of things. I don't want people to be evaluated on how many quality circles they have, because you get a lot of quality circles and no quality. But I do think we evaluate people on a subjective set of goals and objectives as well as on things like affirmative action, community involvement, and long-term development of management talent, and this is one very good way. Certainly it ought to be in the objectives, because then it becomes a talking point between the boss and the employee and at least when they go through the appraisal process, they bring that subject up and they focus on what progress is being made.

Tichy: Let me end by asking each of you to discuss your leadership roles. Given the challenges and the things that you say Honeywell needs to accomplish over the next few years, how do you view your own leadership roles on people issues?

Spencer: I think the chief executive should take very seriously how he can raise his own attitudes and his own relationships—not only to those who report directly to him but to those who see him or hear about how he gets along. I frankly am sometimes surprised at the influence the chief executive can have on an organization. It's a great deal more than people write about. Most of us, very humbly don't wish to acknowledge that fact, but nonetheless the chief executive's tone, his integrity, his standards, his way of dealing with people, his focusing on things that are important or not important can have a profound impact on the rest of the organization. What I am saying is that the way the chief executive and senior managers of the company conduct themselves as individuals has a more profound impact on how other people in the company conduct *themselves* than anything else that happens. When people don't fit that culture, either they shouldn't come in the first place, or they will find they are not welcome.

Tichy: How does that consciousness then translate into some things that you may specifically do or not do?

Spencer: Well, let me take a little thing that I think is very important. I didn't start this at Honeywell; I obviously learned it from the people who went before me—two generations of managers before me. That is, going to other people's offices when you want to ask questions rather than calling everybody to come to your own office, and doing things orally rather than asking for memos and then writing memos back. Those are little things but it requires a personal contact to work in that way—and that, in turn, can have impact on this whole subject that we are talking about.

Boyle: I think that one of the leadership goals for corporate employee relations is to be looking at those things out in the longer range that will have an impact on the organization and at least suggest to management that we ought to examine these areas. If we make decisions not to do them, fine, but we definitely need a long-range, strategic orientation in our work. The other thing we need is an orientation that something can get done. A lot of times staff departments say management won't buy that, or that's not going to happen. I think it's important for those in leadership positions in employee relations to be doers, to be able to say either we are not going to do that and forget about talking about it, or work on those things that have possibilities. You want to work on the things that have payoffs for the organization.

Tichy: Is part of your role that of being devil's advocate for senior managers on things you see regarding people?

Boyle: I'm sometimes a devil's advocate when I press Ed on employee relations matters. For example, his view is different from mine on the expansion of the bonus programs that we have. Yet he is willing to listen to a proposal this year to examine the subject further, and we had some examination of these issues last year. In this position you have to be a devil's advocate.

Tichy: Ed, is that how you see Foss's job?

Spencer: Yes, sir, absolutely.

Tichy: Which, if I understand, must be an historical shift in terms of the role that employee relations has played.

Spencer: The role has been expected of employee relations but I think different chief executives relate differently to the department, and perhaps because I'm so conscious of employee relations needs today as being different from those of the past, it may be a more important department in my mind than it was in those of my predecessors to whom it was a labor relations and compensation department. It's an evolution that is going on in most companies. . . .

A LINE MANAGER'S VIEW
OF THE HUMAN RESOURCE ROLE

Robert H. Murphy

It has been 20 years since I first entered this field which we now call human resources. Back then it was termed "personnel." I certainly like "human resources" or "human resources management" better as describing where the profession stands today . . . a catalyst and leader in effective management of the corporation's most precious resource. And it better reflects the many challenges which will face us tomorrow.

Human resources excellence and positioning the function for a more proactive role in running the business are the keys to approaching the subject I am to discuss tonight—"A Line Manager's View of the Human Resource Role."

To set the stage, let's take a brief look at some of the factors that are driving change in organizations and their employees, and hence the role of the human resources function.

For starters, we are making the transition more and more to a global economy. At Rockwell, we project that the international sector will be one of the fastest growing parts of our company during our current five-year strategic planning period.

Yet, the world is changing rapidly, and both the politics and the economics of world trade are on a fast track. There are factors shaping the international environment which are important:

- A population explosion in the underdeveloped nations.
- Fierce competition for available markets among the developed nations . . . automotive, semiconductors, and computers are certainly on our minds these days.
- Increased United States dependence on imported raw materials.

On top of this, profound changes are taking place in the relationships between employers and employees. In all probability, the 1980s will become known as "the decade of the employee." Their agenda is far broader than wages and hours. Profit-sharing, a say in management, controls on plant

Robert H. Murphy, "A Line Manager's View of the Human Resources Role," address at the Business Week Human Resource Conference, New York, May 19, 1982. Reprinted with permission.

closings, recognition of employees as individuals, and improved security are all topics we will be confronting in the years immediately ahead.

Then there is the challenge of productivity. All of our companies' futures depend on productivity improvement, and our country's position as a world leader and supplier of products and service depends on it.

Finally, there is the impact of technology and communication. We are just beginning to see the changes that electronics and automation will bring to the way we work, what we do, and the kinds of employees our companies will need. Taken together, these developments definitely portend lively times ahead for those concerned with human resources management.

To seize this opportunity, however, will require that we transform the function to a broader role than we have known in the past. For the past two or more decades, the function has involved itself primarily in processing forms, maintaining records, developing policies and procedures in response to government regulations, hiring employees, administering compensation and benefit plans, and negotiating and administering labor contracts. These are important matters that we need to continue doing well.

However, the personnel function has typically been a reactor to change, not always an initiator of change. Consequently, managements have tended to view the "personnel" function as an administrative necessity, something you need to have around but not where you turn for counsel of matters dealing with the profitability, future direction, or strategic management of the business.

However, the human element, in all probability, represents the major difference between our companies' winning and losing, particularly when you consider that your competition can buy the same equipment, materials, and facilities you can.

What is needed is not a narrow perspective on the disciplines of the human resource function, but a new and broader perspective that focuses the total resources of the function on issues key to the achievement of the goals of the business.

Those are pretty high flying words. The challenge is to develop a cadre of human resource *business* leaders and *new standards* of human resource excellence.

There are companies that have made measurable progress in this direction, and tonight I would like to describe some of Rockwell's thinking and approaches to the subject, with this important qualifier: We aren't totally there yet! But we are turning ourselves inside out to be a major factor in the growth and performance of our businesses, and our top management is giving us encouragement and support—and their expectations are high.

Let me start by offering you what we believe are seven success factors or characteristics for the human resources professional of the '80s to fully succeed.

First, he or she must be a planner and plan interpreter.

We guide, target, and measure our businesses by plans. In most of our companies, there is a strategic business plan—a long-range road map of the internal and external factors which will affect the business and what we will do about them to win against the best of competition. There is also an annual operating plan, a one- or two-year set of specifics, including the planned levels of sales, profits, capital spending, and strategic milestones.

Probably the single most important step a human resource officer can take toward gaining a broad perspective of the business needs and plan is to become a part of the strategic planning process. We have developed a process at Rockwell for integrating the human resources function into the strategic planning process, which I will share with you shortly.

The second characteristic required is business perspective and judgment.

Business perspective and judgment must be based on understanding the foundation of how a business is run and why certain strategies are pursued. Coupled with that is the requirement to never lose sight of the bottom-line contribution of the human resources function in all actions. After all, the general manager is living and breathing bottom line.

Many of us have witnessed personnel functions requesting an upgrading of salaries and benefits just because it's "something many forward-looking companies are doing." Human resources recommendations without pros and cons on the impact of the greater expense versus how it will improve the business or increase productivity should be considered unacceptable.

Further, if the strategic plan requires a level of employment which will cost more than the business can sustain, the first person to spot the problem and offer a solution should be the human resources executive. Let me be even more specific with a real life example.

Last year, we were reviewing the strategic business plan for one of our major divisions. We noted that if we took the manpower projections and associated payroll costs over the next five years at face value, coupled with an analysis of our projected sales and materials costs, the margins of the division, which were at very acceptable levels, would be in a negative position by 1985.

Needless to say, the division was asked to rethink and replan their human resources utilization. They came back with a strategy to accomplish their business objectives with 17 percent less people required and increased margins.

The third characteristic is being a leader and manager.

"Leader" is one of those words that tends to be used in ways that blur the distinction of meaning. The human resources professional must be "out front" and the first member of a general manager's team to identify issues that affect the work force and then to put actions in motion for effective resolution . . . that's leadership.

But he or she also needs to be a leader in the sense that General Dwight Eisenhower used to illustrate with a piece of string. He would lay the string on a table, then point out that if you *pushed* it, it would go nowhere. But *pull* the string and it would go in any desired direction.

The fourth success factor is being "a proactive problem solver and innovator."

This characteristic goes to the very heart of what a general manager is looking for in his human resources professionals—not reacting to problems that are already taking the general manager's time, but anticipating those conditions and the development of solutions; in other words, getting ahead of the curve.

Fifth, being an internal consultant.

An effective internal consultant is one who can assist the general manager in strategically managing change. The human resources professional should be a nonaligned, knowledgeable sounding board and change agent for management. The question *is not,* should we change?—but how, . . . in what direction, and at what speed?

No matter how capable an executive is, his or her effectiveness from a consulting standpoint can often hinge on other factors, such as access to the top team.

Because we feel so strongly about the consulting role of the human resources officer, Rockwell has taken action to establish a structural norm for major business units, which requires that the human resources function report directly to the general manager—in other words, the top leader. Further, we are filling those top human resources posts with individuals who have the business knowledge and background to effectively perform the internal consulting role.

This role should not *only* be one of consulting on sensitive people issues, but also on the subjects of positioning the organization to support business strategy, and shaping the management process used to direct, control, and grow the business.

In addition to the professional and business qualifications, *the sixth success factor* **is** *a high level of personal qualifications.*

Integrity is first on the list. You are dealing with decisions which affect the basic livelihood of individuals and their families. There must be no doubt in the minds of your boss, your peers, or your staff as to the basis of the decisions and recommendations you are acting upon.

And, finally, communication skills. This is an area where many otherwise talented human resources professionals can fall short. Yet, this is the vehicle whereby we obtain support for most of what we do. And in an environment where time is always at a premium and a thousand other subjects are clamoring for management attention, we must learn to communicate in terms that our general managers can quickly grasp and easily relate to the bottom line of the business.

Last, **but perhaps first in a chronological sense, is the fact that a human resources pro** *must know the broad aspects of his profession.*

The body of specific knowledge needed to develop company policies, perform analytical management studies, and keep up with government regulations and changing social conditions is expanding rapidly. This requires the human resources professional to be extremely well-versed on all social, economic, political, and international issues.

Therefore, I believe the successful human resources executive of the '80s must not only know the functional specialties in some depth, but must have the ability to anticipate and integrate new developments across all business disciplines. For example, Stanford Research Institute tells us that by 1990 about 35 percent of the population and well over 50 percent of the work force will consist of what is termed "new values" group. This group stresses personal values above traditional or economic values. Diversity, direct experience, and social well-being are the things of importance to this group.

How do you bring together this growing portion of the population with the corporate culture and style and then mesh it with the corporate need for improved productivity? At Rockwell, the human resources function is taking a lead in introducing a sweepingly different approach to conceiving, designing, staffing, and operating four new plants. We think this approach holds promise of beginning to blend these emerging human trends with corporate goals.

These plants are planned and designed to jointly optimize both the technical and human dimensions. Decisions are made at the lowest practical level, and joint management/employee problem-solving is a way of life in the plants. The management group which will run the plant is involved in the management planning and plant design process at a very early stage and sometimes even before the plant is built. For example, supervisors participate in establishing the layout of machinery, equipment, and support systems, as well as the pay and progression systems which they will administer. It becomes "their" system, not the human resources department's. Thus far, results achieved with this approach have exceeded our expectations and goals.

Now that you have seen and heard about what we believe to be the seven success factors for the human resources executive of the 1980s, you are probably asking, "Well, *if* I accept this, where do I start?"

As a first step, I would suggest a hard examination of the current strengths and weaknesses of the human resources function in your company. Based on that analysis, coupled with a vision of how you want to see the function perform, there will emerge many issues that you will want to address to upgrade and improve the performance of the function.

We did essentially this same thing at Rockwell, and I would like to share with you some major actions we have taken to refocus our human resources function and become a more vital element of the business team.

HUMAN RESOURCES STRATEGIC BUSINESS SUPPORT PLAN

As you recall, the first success factor calls for improving human resources skills and involvement in the overall business planning process. Working with our corporate strategic planning staff, we modified the corporation's strategic planning guidelines to define *how the human resources function should be involved in the upfront planning with our general managers.*

Further, we reached agreement with our senior-line human resources officer to prepare human resources strategic plans for all 130 business segments—plans that link into and support each business segment's strategic plan. The planning is a "bottoms up" process, with the corporation providing planning assumptions, principles, guidelines, and broad corporate human resource objectives for guiding our corporation's growth and development.

The business support plan includes:

- Development of strategies with accompanying action plans for implementation and integration with strategies of other functions;
- A measurement system. This means:
  - Measurement of performance of the human resources function,
  - Measurement of performance of all managers against their stated human resource objectives, and
  - Development of a human resource performance increment in the system by which all managers' compensation is established.

HUMAN RESOURCES
PROFESSIONALS DEVELOPMENT PROGRAM

A second major initiative taken to help the Rockwell Human Resources Professionals become the catalyst for major change, develop their leadership qualities, and better understand how they can link closer to the needs of a general manager, was the establishment of a professional development program for the top 100 human resources professionals throughout the company. This is an intensive five-day session conducted off-site at a conference-type setting. The emphasis is on strategic planning, the macro issues facing Rockwell, and the ways in which the human resources role must change to help in shaping the future of our business.

An additional element helps attendees understand the financial goals which their bosses must meet, and their role in strategic planning to help position their business vis-à-vis their competition. The seven success factors I discussed earlier are defined and studied: they are *our standard for excellence for our human resources professionals.*

We have put 73 of our top 100 human resources professionals through this development program. Already we can see payoff in improved quality of plan and performance. It has also given a clear signal to the human resources people and their general managers that top management is taking human resources management seriously.

HUMAN RESOURCES ADVISORY BOARD

Another approach we have taken to provide leadership in changing the thrust and direction of the human resource function is the establishment of a Human Resource Advisory Board. This board serves as the corporation's senior advisory body on human resources strategic issues and functional excellence. Board members consist of the top eight human resources executives in the corporation, both corporate and line.

The board meets quarterly and is responsible for providing overall leadership to the function by:

- Reviewing and setting broad companywide human resource objectives, and
- Assuring excellence in all aspects of human resources functional performance throughout the corporation.

We also see the board as an early warning system for major human resources issues. From time to time we create subcommittees made up of high talent professionals down in the organization to investigate and recommend courses of action on selected issues. This also gives the board the opportunity to personally see some of our future human resources leaders in action.

HUMAN RESOURCES EXECUTIVE REVIEWS

We also established semiannual human resources career reviews. During these reviews by the same top eight human resources leaders, the strengths and weaknesses of the corporation's top 100 human resources professionals are considered, along with their career paths and potential next position. In addition, we openly discuss what we consider to be the strengths and weaknesses of the human resources function in total, and collectively establish plans to overcome identified shortcomings.

To date, we have experienced good results:

- Better interdivisional movement of our people,
- Higher morale among the human resource members now that their careers are getting increased attention and action,
- Better matching of our human resource professionals to the issues/needs of the business—and increased focus on areas requiring strengthening, and
- Most importantly . . . improved performance and stature of the function.

Regardless of the size of your organization, some variation on this approach is highly recommended.

In summary then, we have taken a number of significant *initial* steps to bring the human resources function to a level where it will provide the type of support that line managers want, that line managers need, and that line managers have the right to expect now and in the future.

IMPACT/INFLUENCE: DEFINING AND CHARTING A COURSE FOR PERSONNEL VITALITY

Walton E. Burdick

I want to speak with you today on the subject of the *impact* and *influence* of the personnel profession. Most of us no doubt consider ourselves professionals in the field—knowledgeable people who can make a solid contribution to our companies. But where is the personnel pro who hasn't heard of the function being referred to as the "social director" or the "filing cabinet king"—and those are the polite names.

There's a way to tell which of the two names—bureaucrat or professional—fits your department. Do you have a meaningful influence on your company's thinking? Not just its attitude about people, pay, or equal opportunity, but the *total* management philosophy of your companies? How often do you make proposals to your upper management? What percent of top management considerations center around personnel issues? Does your organization—personnel—have frequent impact on line management actions: labor relations strategy, manpower resource planning, or executive selection? Are you in the inner circle? Do you win your share of the showdowns with the chief financial officers? Do you and your organization have the professional respect of your top executives? If you can say yes to those questions, then your company has a professional personnel organization.

Increasingly, the personnel function is taking its place in the sun of the corporate world, and also in the perception of the public. A recent piece in *Fortune* magazine called us the "new heroes." Professor Foulkes, in the *Harvard Business Review*, emphasized recently the importance of personnel, when he called for "an increasing strategic role for the personnel function." An article last year in *Dun's Review* noted that several corporate chief executives had been personnel directors prior to their elevation, and that the experience had been a major factor in their selection for the top.

What brought about this improved view of personnel? I believe a number of influences have combined to increase the appreciation of what personnel can contribute to a successful organization:

Walton E. Burdick, "Impact/Influence: Defining and Charting a Course for Personnel Vitality," keynote address at the National Annual Meeting of the American Society for Personnel Administrators in San Diego, California, June 2, 1976. Reprinted with permission.

- Shorter and more extreme economic fluctuations, with inflation and recession *worldwide* problems.
- The growing recognition of the *cost* and *value* of human resources. Management has always said that "people are our most important asset." They're beginning to recognize the fundamental truth of that statement.
- Changing values in the work force reflected by such things as a growing employee interest in and demand for noneconomic items: leisure time; flexible hours; safety and health; job interest; corporate social responsibility; etc.
- And, most important, better, more professional people are entering the personnel function, which has improved the quality of our contributions.

I'm not sure that any one of those influences, taken alone, would have trained any spotlights on personnel. *But taken together, they have made personnel the critical business activity of the final quarter of this century.*

Now, that's quite a turn of events. Think back. The forces that built American enterprise and for decades drove it forward were entrepreneurial energy and technical genius. We have had the age of the engineer and inventor king. The age when the great financiers marshalled the resources to capitalize on the talents of the Thomas Edisons, the Eli Whitneys, and Henry Fords.

I believe that the forces that built industry, the energy and the genius of individuals, are still critically important. But lately it's become obvious to me that the issues of the remainder of the twentieth century will be human resources. We are entering a new era, and the key members of management will be professional personnel people. Their contributions to continued corporate progress will be as significant in the future as were those of the inventory, the market genius, the great financier, in the past.

Let's take a look at how the various influences I mentioned have affected personnel and heightened the importance of the profession.

In the past five or six years we've managed through a severe economic period. We've already had two recessions in this decade—the last one the worst since the thirties, and characterized by all the things you hate to see happen in an economy:

- Sharply declining GNP
- Reduced real personal incomes
- Layoffs and high unemployment
- Very high inflation rates
- Lower productivity
- And, perhaps unique to this decade, interest rates and prices did not respond to reduced demand, but continued climbing well into the recession. And that has led some to speculation that periods of boom and bust may be structural—that is, built into the system

No single country's economy operates independently of the work economy. Economic programs and problems do not recognize and respect geographic boundaries and national borders. And the recession we've recently experienced was worldwide, and, therefore, uniquely severe.

The reaction to recession of most businesses, and the responsibility of personnel, was to *plan resources*, especially in the labor area, *much more carefully*.

Review for a moment the steps you took, and then ask yourself:

- Is there a human resource planning process in your organization?
- If there is, what is your role in the planning cycle? What do you think it should be?
- Does your plan *anticipate* economic fluctuations, and do you influence your management to keep their *options open* to maintain the flexibility necessary to manage recessionary forces?

If that is your role, did you recommend and implement plans prior to and during the recent recession which *balanced* considerations of issues such as EO, excessive overtime or employee relocations? Did you, and do you, develop strategies to balance needs or surpluses with transfers, retraining and carefully planned, but limited hiring? If business necessity required cost reductions, what impact did you have in insuring the continued financial well-being of your organization, without allowing cost considerations to disproportionately affect employee relations? Did you plan programs to reduce business cost, conserve energy, and enhance benefit programs at minimal cost?

What was your response to worldwide inflation? I don't mean recommending simple modifications to your salary or wage programs; as inflation eroded your basic compensation objectives, had you anticipated, or were you caught by surprise? What did you do? In the United States, we all recall the experience we had earlier in this decade with the pay board and the effect it had on our compensation plans. As you think back to that era, how quickly were you prepared to seek approval of your compensation programs when controls eased? Did you come out of that period with your employees knowing, of course, that you followed the guidelines to the letter? Did they also believe that you did all your company could for them within the limits of the controls?

I think we, as professionals, have a role to play in the face of this trend toward more employee/management legislation. We must analyze proposed and pending legislation and advise management *in advance* of its passage, of its probable impact on the business. We should equip management to *speak out more* in Washington and in state chambers to bring *balance* to our legislation and regulations. That's a legitimate activity in a democracy, and we should be activists.

ASPA has been active and effective in Washington, as you know, on many issues including the selection and testing issue. This is to be commended.

- Were *you* heard in Washington before HMO, ERISA, and OSHA were enacted?
- Are you now involved in other issues looming on the horizon: privacy, mandatory retirement, full employment?
- If you are from Indiana or California, for example, are you involved in the pending privacy legislation? Not all legislation which has an impact on us comes from Washington.

Be active—monitor and understand legislative processes. Prepare your management. We must plan, *and anticipate* economic impacts, *and recommend correct actions to our management.*

This is hard to do. You've heard, I'm sure, the line from a news magazine article, that if you placed all the economists in the world end to end, they'd never reach a correct conclusion. But *we* must reach correct conclusions in order to help plan labor expenditures. That's the only way we can avoid drastic fluctuations in staffing and balance our companies' people resources effectively. That is our job.

Another trend which has pushed personnel into the limelight is the *worldwide thrust of legislation* into areas of our concern: employee privacy, health, safety, pensions, handicapped, affirmative action, training, full employment, selection and testing, and others. We have many laws and an extraordinarily complex set of regulations throughout the world which affect employee relations. And they demand *more* than routine competence in traditional personnel subjects if we are to be called professional people. To deal with this complex legal environment requires more than a good knowledge of the legislation and regulations. It requires planning, anticipating, and factoring in such things as legal considerations without abdicating the responsibility for decision making to the lawyers.

Actions prior to legislation are one thing. Actions to comply are another. We have to prepare first by getting our own house in order. Prepare managers to cope with and respond to audits. And advise management on what to expect and what they must do to comply. In fact, you may want to propose action *before* legislation, especially if the legislation is inevitable.

- Have you planned and announced an affirmative action program for the handicapped? Does it include measures of handicapped employment, advances, and accommodations? Have you complied with the 1976 reporting requirements?
- Have you briefed your management on the possible full employment legislation and its potential impact on your ability to manage resources? Full employment regulations would impact each of us.
- Have you offered the required HMO alternatives to your employees in those areas where one is available? You should plan for the certain rapid expansion of this program.
- Are you following the bill on the Senate agenda, S.1, which would hold corporate executives liable for "reckless default"—violation of federal regulations committed by subordinates? The possible criminal penalties were outlined in *Business Week* on May 10th.

- For those of you with corporate responsibility in an international firm, are you aware of Code 32 in Sweden? Co-determination in Germany? What steps are you taking to plan for pending implementation?
- What was your reaction to the French government's Sudreau Report?
- What are you going to do if mandatory retirement age is abolished?

On the whole, the legislation I've cited is good. The personnel role is to assure that we, as well as our management, contribute our best thoughts to the formation of legislation and regulations which affect our enterprises and our people.

Another major cause for the growing importance of our role is the *cost* of the human resource in any public or private enterprise. Labor costs are the most significant investment in many organizations, public and private alike. The answer to increasing labor costs is obviously improved productivity. What have you recommended to improve productivity in your organization?

The so-called noneconomic motivators seem to become increasingly important as compensation and job skills increase. If this is true, we need to concentrate, especially in an environment of rising costs, on the noneconomic motivators. For example, *the job itself.* After 20 years in personnel, I've concluded that the *greatest* motivator is the opportunity for interesting, challenging, personally rewarding work in an environment that offers training, advancement potential, and management that offers dignified treatment as an individual.

A lot can be said for job enrichment and job enlargement. But the territory that needs exploration is that which encourages people to *reach beyond,* to stretch themselves. We have to develop a *responsive environment.* The concept of making work more challenging and satisfying is perhaps the most worthwhile one that exists in personnel. This can become the most important personnel factor we deal with and, of course, an opportunity to affect in a positive way the health and productivity of our organization.

Because we deal with people, changing human values and attitudes toward business have had an impact on the personnel profession. In one respect, these changes are minor. For example, our internal research doesn't reveal any significant shift in what employees feel is important. And our newest hires show attitudes toward work remarkably similar to those who have been with us several years. This fact was also established in a U.S. Department of Labor monograph which found "no conclusive evidence of a widespread, dramatic decline in job satisfaction" in this country.

But what we think is significant, and very disturbing, is what I read about the general trend of increasing public distrust of business and other institutions reported in our society. A survey conducted last year showed that of 15 institutions, big businesses ranked next to the bottom in the public's trust and confidence. Only the stock market ranked lower, and that's not hard to understand, the market being where it was in mid-1975. Small business didn't do very much better than big business—ranking ninth.

Less than 18 percent of the public has a high degree of confidence in large corporations. Why? Lots of reasons. People believe they see misleading advertising; purchased products may fall apart; consumer complaints may be difficult to get heard. And, of course, we all have heard of instances of corporate bribery, kickbacks, and illegal political contributions. The media aren't in the business of reporting only good news. The fact that a company didn't bribe, and most don't, doesn't make the headlines. But enough have engaged in the illegal and the unethical to flood the public in a wave of reported corporate misconduct. No wonder the public is suspicious.

But what does that mean to us in personnel? We are, or ought to be, contributing to the conscience of the corporation. I believe it is our responsibility to develop codes of business conduct where they don't exist. We should educate all employees about the rules, and the penalties for not following them. We must advise management and help them assure that ethical conduct is a way of life.

Have *you* a set of guidelines outlining the principles which govern the conduct of your business? Are your managers and employees precisely aware of your business practices? Do they know the rules for:

- Dealing with competitors, suppliers
- Accepting and giving gifts
- Political activities
- Conflicts of interest

Is the guidance you give on these and other subjects specific and detailed? Is management trained?

I think the personnel professional, working with top management, can make a major contribution to restoring the faith of the American people in business. And there's no question in my mind that faith can be restored.

Personnel has been able to respond to the needs of business because we increasingly attract top-notch people. Management turns to us because of the problems they are having today. They do so with confidence because we have proven our worth.

But management has the tendency to ask, "What have you done for me lately?" Yesterday's performance won't win tomorrow's battle or solve tomorrow's problem. Our organizations and their environments are dynamic, and we must be also. We must concentrate on professionalizing personnel and being the very best staff in the organization to be ready for tomorrow's problems.

For the personnel professional, daily doses of new knowledge should be a requirement—like vitamins. I believe, for a personnel professional, the daily minimum requirement is reading one report from Washington or your state capital, or one article from the *Personnel Administrator*, or one chapter in a new personnel publication.

To improve personnel professionalism in IBM, we have implemented a number of personnel development activities. First, to provide the focus, attention, and coordination it requires, we have a director of personnel development, reporting directly to me, whose sole responsibility is the development of personnel people in IBM—worldwide. We conduct personnel seminars international in scope, where personnel professionals study a broad range of business and personnel topics.

We track the careers of identified high-potential personnel professionals to assure that they receive the variety of experience and training necessary, to assume greater responsibility as their careers progress. Nearly 200 individuals have had opportunities to participate in headquarters' rotational personnel assignments in the past four years. To broaden their perspective and skills, these assignments are typically two years in length, and upon completion professionals are returned to key locations or field positions. Additionally, seminars are conducted regularly on contemporary personnel topics for members of the corporate personnel staff. Recent topics have included HMO, ERISA, Affirmative Action for the Handicapped, and European personnel issues.

In addition, each year I produce a personnel overview videotape which is seen by all personnel people in my company, and is followed up throughout the year by both in-company functional training as well as some out-company training.

Professionalism in personnel requires another skill. In the growing body of literature, we must be able to separate the truly good ideas from those that are merely today's fads. That's what I call having a discerning eye. Every so often a "cure-all" sweeps over the country. Every so often we're sorely tempted to wrap our arms around an idea that turns out not to have very much true impact. Be careful of those temptations! There's no surer way to lose credibility and the confidence of management than advocation of an ill-conceived or inappropriate theory. There's no quicker way to lose impact and influence than by adopting something that is going to be commonplace—a "practice in industry"—only to find two years later that the practice can't be found anywhere but in your organization. That is *not* the path to a happy future!

While striving for and achieving professionalism, it's important to keep in mind the appropriate *role* of personnel. Classically defined, personnel is a staff function. That means we exist to provide advice and counsel in our area of expertise and decision-making management. We exist to add *value* to the operation—to add to management's knowledge, to improve their decision-making, to increase the individual dignity and efficiency of the human resources of the organization, to add the dimension that is the human factor.

Easy to say, hard to do—because we must stop short of practicing what we preach. We all know how easy it is to do the line manager's job—we've advised on it many times. Success in personnel depends on how well we *advise*, not do, the line manager's job. *Our* job is to *train, develop, educate,* and *influence* management, not usurp their line responsibilities.

Defining your place in the organization, and then implementing your role effectively, is critically important in establishing and maintaining an environment of personnel professionalism. The exact definition of the personnel role must take place in the context of the company's *policies, objectives,* and *principles.* Know those intimately. Our achievements must be measured against how well we contribute toward meeting corporate or institutional goals.

Over the years, I've developed a short list of the characteristics I've found to be major contributors to professional success in personnel. I'd like to share them with you.

1. *Knowledge*—Knowledge of the job, role, government activity, and knowledge of the enterprise's philosophies and objectives.
2. *Empathy*—We've all heard about the person wanting to get into personnel because he or she likes people. But simply liking people isn't enough. Empathy is the key—knowing people and having empathy for them and their desires and problems.
3. *Staff work*—A professional must be able to do completed staff work—analyze problems and recommend alternative actions so that the final decision is already self-evident.
4. *Healthy and well-rounded individuals*—True professionals must be conscious of their total welfare. The job isn't the only thing in life. We need a balanced background to make sensitive people decisions, and good health to function well in difficult, demanding jobs.
5. *Self-development*—This is critical. Professionals must keep up with the growing body of knowledge and theory in the profession, and contribute to the furthering of professional knowledge.

My list isn't complete. You may have other important characteristics. But the point is that we *can* determine within some common framework the elements needed for attaining professionalism in personnel and each of us can work toward their fulfillment.

Impact? Influence? What is it? It is the way you measure your day's work. Have you helped your organization move toward its own objectives? Do you contribute to the management decision process a personnel dimension?

If there is one measure of a professional, it is how much *influence* he or she has. Consider that, and if you are not satisfied—as a true professional is not—chart a course to improve your own skills to increase your impact—and improve your influence. This is the last quarter of the twentieth century: *People* management has reached its time. Be ready—the future is increasingly yours.

ORGANIZING AND STAFFING THE PERSONNEL FUNCTION

Fred K. Foulkes   Henry M. Morgan

We recently had the opportunity to study and evaluate the effectiveness of the personnel departments of several large organizations. During the study, line managers clearly indicated a desire to make the personnel function more effective. Typical of their many comments are the following:

- "We need better coordination into a corporate viewpoint on personnel practices—there are still too many instances of personnel practices and programs developed and pursued without recognition of the total corporate implication."
- "We need better methods of identifying and developing management talent. We also need help in finding ways to move out older managers with long service, short of terminating them and ending up with an age discrimination charge."
- "Reclassifications take months and they are tacky. There is confusion at the first level of personnel management. They are not about to get out of a reactive mode. They are just not able to say no to requests."
- "The image of personnel is zero, though some of the gripes are unjustified. Personnel is reluctant to get rid of its obvious nonperformers. The image of personnel in the community is poor."
- "Personnel should have more contact with line managers to exchange ideas before policies are frozen. They need a better knowledge of the profit impact of the suggested actions."
- "Personnel tends to be a tower unto itself. If personnel does not perceive a problem as important, it is not handled. It is too interested in new gimmicks, and ignores day-to-day needs."

Such comments raise questions, to say the least, about the performance of personnel departments in different companies. Why do other parts of the organization view personnel departments as so apparently ineffective? Why do line managers often view the personnel department with contempt?

In this article, we will focus on the critical issues of organizing and staffing the personnel department for greater usefulness. We warn at the outset that personnel programs of every sort, other than those involving routine service matters, often fail. Properly or improperly, personnel usually gets the blame for such failures, while line managers generally take

Reprinted by permission of the Harvard Business Review. *"Organizing and Staffing the Personnel Function" by Fred K. Foulkes and H. M. Morgan, May–June 1977. Copyright © 1977 by the President and Fellows of Harvard College; all rights reserved.*

credit for any successful personnel program. In reality, personnel programs succeed because line managers make them succeed.

The Jewel Companies, for example, have been very successful in attracting and retaining outstanding MBA students. It is significant that at Jewel either the president or the chairman interviews every MBA who is being seriously considered for a job. Jewel's innovative personnel program also features for each MBA a mentor or sponsor relationship with a senior executive.

We could argue that if an organization has both a top management that is involved in personnel matters and a reward system that gives weight to success in personnel activities by means of performance appraisals, merit raises, and bonus determination, then neither the organization nor the staffing of the personnel department really matters. Our experience, however, suggests that appropriate organization and staffing of the personnel department can enhance the effectiveness of the personnel function.

ORGANIZATIONAL ISSUES

The long-accepted approach to understanding the organizational role of the personnel department is through a discussion of line-staff relationships. On examining these relationships, however, we find little consideration of the complexity and geographical dispersion of large modern organizations. Is traditional line-staff language appropriate for discussing the multidivision, multilocation organization? Where do line and staff come into contact? Is the staff function performed only in central headquarters, or is there a line-staff relationship at each location? If so, are there differences in the roles and issues at headquarters and local offices?

We found that the tasks of the personnel department at corporate headquarters differ from those at operating offices. We also think that the old line-staff concepts are no longer completely adequate. An issue today is as much staff-staff relations (corporate staff versus division staff versus plant staff) as it is line-staff relations. Such geographically dispersed and functionally diversified corporations as Du Pont, General Motors, and Tenneco obviously require different personnel functions for different locations.

Consider a relatively modest-sized company such as Polaroid. With about 10,000 employees, 95% of whom work in laboratories, factories, and offices within 50 miles of its Cambridge, Massachusetts headquarters, it is less complex than Du Pont or General Motors but more so than a single-plant corporation.

In fact, most organizations that are large and complex enough to need a well-defined personnel department probably resemble Polaroid. Does Polaroid's personnel department need to provide the same service to its highly automated film division in Waltham that it does to the research laboratories in Cambridge—or to the camera assembly factory in Norwood, the patent department, or the international division? Is there one personnel manager's job? Or are there many similarities with some differences based on the client served? Does the location of the personnel department in any way determine the function?

From our studies we have developed a way of looking at the total personnel function and breaking out aspects that are best handled at different places by different people. Thus we can identify four distinct aspects of the personnel function:

1. Formulation of personnel policy—a top management responsibility.
2. Implementation of policies by the line managers—the service function.
3. Audit and control—the establishment of standards and procedures to see that organization policies are maintained.
4. Innovation—research and development of new practices, procedures, and programs.

We find that many personnel departments are not organized to get the whole job done. In fact, service and audit activities bog some of them down so that they can give only scant attention to policy formulation and innovation—the most important functions in the view of a number of line managers, including chief executive officers, whom we interviewed.

Most managers recognize the longer-range critical policy problems. Many of them, however, demand administrative or maintenance type of help at the expense of policy problem solving. The urgent always gets in the way of the important, and, consequently, the personnel function should be organized to get both jobs done.

Policy Formulation

Undoubtedly, a most critical issue for any organization is the formulation of personnel policy. In an evaluation of the personnel department of a large organization, we asked a high-level administrator how personnel policy was formulated. His answer was, "I don't know. I don't have a good picture of it." When the personnel director of the same organization was asked the same question, his answer was, "Each policy has a different process." When pressed, he said that policies were developed on an "as needed" basis in response to some new problem or crisis.

Confusion arises because people mean different things by "personnel policy." At the extremes, policies range from simple administrative procedures such as schedules for coffee breaks to crucial institutional issues relating to growth strategy, location of plants, and attitudes toward unions.

While much input from various people and in different ways is essential, we believe that top management should formulate the critical policy decisions relating to personnel. Such decisions should not be allowed to develop in response to crises, and they should be integrated with basic corporate strategies.

In general, the formulation of personnel policy is simply too important to be left to the personnel department alone. Personnel policies need to take into account the law, ethics, and the developmental needs of people and costs. Above all, they should reflect accurately the goals and values of the organization.

Edwin H. Land, chief executive officer of the Polaroid Corporation, describes the strategies of the company:

> We have two basic aims. One is to make products that are genuinely new and useful to the public, products of the highest quality and at reasonable cost. In this way we assure the financial success of the company and each of us has the satisfaction of helping to make a creative contribution to the society.
>
> The other is to give everyone working for the company a personal opportunity within the company for full exercise of his talents—to express his opinions, to share in the progress of the company as far as his capacities permit, and to earn enough money so that the need for earning more will not always be the first thing on his mind. The opportunity, in short, to make his work here a fully rewarding and important part of his life.

All personnel strategies at Polaroid flow from the second basic aim. The personnel policy committee consists of top corporate officers and is chaired by a senior vice president, with members of the personnel department serving as staff to the committee. In addition, all levels of the organization, through a "yellow draft" system, extensively review proposed policy changes before their formal adoption.

Needless to say, personnel policies have to be well administered, for the essence of policy is administration. In personnel, as in everything else, good policies poorly administered mean little.

There is no question about the role of personnel in the implementation of policy, but what should its role be in the formulation of policy? A good personnel department can provide feedback into policy from two directions. First, it knows the concerns of employees and traditionally has represented their views. Second, in response to a world of increasing complexity, it has an outward perspective on social changes and their resulting legislative and regulatory impact on policy.

Policy formulation has two aspects: the process and the content. In the personnel area, where effective implementation counts for so much, the process can be as important as the content of the policies themselves. Thus we would recommend that personnel join with others in top management as a partner in the balancing of values that is the heart of the process.

In one large company, a recent personnel policy change upset so many people that it had to be modified considerably. The company had long had a job-posting system, but the change called for selecting the most senior qualified applicant as opposed to the prior policy of selecting the "best qualified." This change raised so much havoc that the company went back to the old policy for all exempt jobs. The new policy continues, amidst much disagreement, for nonexempt employees.

Regardless of the equity of the approach, the issue would have fared differently, we feel, if it had been discussed by a method similar to that used by Polaroid's personnel policy committee of line managers.

In another case, Honeywell recently formed an executive employee relations committee composed of five operating group vice presidents and five staff vice presidents. This committee serves as a senior policy board in respect to employee relations. Commenting on this, Charles Brown, Honeywell's vice president for employee relations, said: "We go to the committee with one or more proposals for changing something at every meeting, and we have had practically 100% acceptance. Once an idea is endorsed by the committee, its implementation becomes relatively easy." The executive employee relations committee at Honeywell is also responsible for evaluating the top 200 management positions in the company.

At Honeywell, proposals approved during 1976 included a significantly upgraded employee communications program, improvements in the company's merit pay plan, and increased emphasis on recruiting talented minorities and women.

Does any set of personnel policies universally fit all situations? We think not. If they did, management could simply find and adopt them. The best personnel policies are like the best organizational strategies—they are contingent upon the particular situation and they depend on the strategy of the company.

Within a company, with respect to both setting and administering personnel policy, one must ask where and when uniformity is essential and when it is unnecessary. Given the different missions and diversity of some organizations, some local autonomy and flexibility is frequently desirable. While discretion can result in inconsistency, a certain amount of inconsistency can be lived with, at least in some organizations. And the price of a detailed set of uniform rules and regulations may be very much higher than the price of discretion.

We admit, however, that inconsistent policies at times bring difficulties in equitable administration and in compliance with government regulations. Good sense suggests that sometimes people are being treated fairly when they are not being handled in a uniform manner. Yet, unfortunately, the law sometimes makes it hard these days to justify such action.

The best personnel policies for Polaroid, Xerox, or IBM arise from different contexts from those for U.S. Steel, Kennecott Copper, and the Ford Motor Company. Good personnel policies must be judged by how well they serve the particular management and employees. Do they work? Are they easy to understand and implement? Do they contribute to the attainment of corporate goals?

Good personnel policies cannot stand apart from the basic strategies for the organization as a whole. The two aims of Polaroid, for example, each form an essential part of one inclusive corporate strategy, neither part separable from the other.

Policy Implementation

The "bread and butter" of the personnel job is service to line management. Personnel assists in the hiring, training, evaluating, rewarding, counseling, promoting, and firing of employees at all levels. Personnel administers the various benefits programs such as educational reimbursement, health and accident programs, retirement, vacation, and sick leave. The department also has a role with respect to grievances.

Personnel must, however, guard against becoming a servant to, as opposed to a service to, the line organization. As one personnel vice president put it, "if you get into that servant role, you're asked to arrange the Christmas party and the retirement parties and that's about it."

While most good managers recognize that dealing with personnel matters is an integral part of their own jobs and that they generally must retain the responsibility for final selection of job applicants and other crucial decisions, the personnel representative can provide valuable support such as the initial screening and all necessary signing-in processes after the final decision.

Although personnel departments have had to develop specialized expertise to maintain their usefulness and justify their existence, it is often this special expertise that brings about dissatisfaction with personnel departments. For example, dealing with people is a critical part of any manager's job, and most managers believe they are competent at the practical level. They may seek help when they are overextended, but they do not want the personnel department to do things for them that they feel competent to do.

Thus the personnel representative who provides service to line managers must understand their needs and provide the help asked for—help that may require little special expertise. The personnel representative at the decentralized level, working as part of the management team, must be more of a generalist. (We will discuss the role and place of the personnel specialist in a later section of this article.)

The personnel department must also be accessible. We observed that wherever there is a physical decentralization of operations, the personnel function should be similarly decentralized. Those performing the personnel function should be where the people and the problems are. There should be a strong sense of mutual "ownership" of the personnel department by both management and employees at the local level. Correspondingly, personnel needs to identify with the organization and feel a part of it.

Consider the recent experience of a large and highly decentralized company. One of its plants produces five major product lines. Within the past two years, product management teams have been established for each line consisting of two technical or operations people and one marketing person. Each team has the authority to draw on all resources available for the profitable production and sales of its set of products.

The company noted that because of the technical nature of the manufacturing and sales involved, these teams found a definite need for personnel planning within the organization. In fact, this need became so strong that, in three of the five teams, personnel people have been physically moved to the team location and are directly participating in the work of the team. The personnel people, moreover, have the same evaluation of their work as do the line managers under the company's management by objectives program.

In smaller organizations that are physically decentralized but without the resources to employ local personnel representatives, the personnel function can be performed on a part-time basis by someone other than a member of the personnel department. We believe it better to perform the service function locally, even if it is not assigned to a specialist in personnel, than to insist that a centralized personnel group try to serve where its people are not seen as members of that organization. One organization has made the administrative assistant to a department manager the official provider of personnel service to that department.

In a bank we studied, a line officer, who is responsible for a large clerical operation, said: "I wish Personnel would realize that this part of the bank is a factory with three shifts. What we need are blue-collar types rather than traditional bank types. If only the personnel people would visit us sometime, they might better understand what it is we do."

While this comment says something about the staffing of the personnel department, it is also relevant to our organizational point. It would probably be better to designate someone in the department as a personnel coordinator.

However, management can go too far with a decentralized approach. Decentralization in the personnel area has both costs and benefits. Ways need to be found to lower the costs. For example, at one large company, a former senior personnel administrator, who was promoted from personnel to a line job, said:

> I think our decentralized approach to personnel is one of our strengths and also one of our weaknesses. By aligning the personnel function with the line organization, it becomes much closer to the action, really learns to understand what pressures line people are under, and becomes actively involved in working with line managers to meet their goals.

> However, from a corporate standpoint, this results in a somewhat frag-
> mented personnel function. The separate groups tend to function independently
> and, as a result, much effort is spent in reinventing the wheel. It is very difficult to
> coordinate with this type of organization.

Therefore, as personnel service is provided locally and as implementation is decentralized, there is a corresponding need to strengthen, but not
necessarily enlarge, the centralized personnel function to help maintain organizational consistency and integrity. There should be strong and centralized auditing to ensure proper and consistent policy implementation by
the generalists at the local level.

Audit and Control

Of the four organizational issues we are dealing with here, a most critical one today is that of audit and control. The coherence and integrity of
the entire personnel service function depends on good personnel policies
that, in turn, require follow-up to ensure that they are indeed being properly practiced. This follow-up requires a strong and centralized audit of actual practice.

One organization we studied has recently implemented a job audit
program. Under this program, a central personnel member checks what
employees actually do on their jobs against the job descriptions to ascertain
whether there are any serious discrepancies. This company adopted its approach after some women employees filed an equal-pay suit.

Management, doing what it thought proper under its affirmative action plan, had consciously given these women additional responsibilities
for development purposes. The women, however, claimed they were doing
more than the men were and that they were not being paid accordingly. A
job audit revealed that this was indeed the case and thus the women were
given back pay. Afterward management adopted a job-audit program to
avoid future legal challenges.

The various requirements of state and federal regulations (for example, the Occupational Safety and Health Act, the Equal Employment Opportunity Commission, Wage and Hour Acts, Employee Retirement Income
Security Act) make increasing demands on both profit and nonprofit organizations. In 1940, the U.S. Department of Labor was responsible for en-
forcing 16 statutes and executive orders. By 1960, the number had grown to
40. Today it is more than 130.

While the reader could argue intelligently that the regulatory list is too
long to permit proper enforcement, in the meantime compliance is necessary. Responses and reports to these regulators can be made only from a
central group supplied with accurate information. In addition, this centralized group must be made up of specialists—well trained in legal require-

ments and in accounting and reporting techniques, and well reinforced by the full power and authority of top management.

Unfortunately, too many organizations suffer from inadequate and incompetent staff in their central audit and control group. This function should be in the hands of personnel specialists. Compliance with the laws relating to OSHA, EEOC, and ERISA demands expertise. Expertise is also needed in the content of, installation of, and administration of wage and salary plans; in the increasingly complex field of employee benefits; and in surveying what is happening in the outside world. Labor relations and grievance procedures also require the knowledge of an expert. And crucial to the entire audit and control function is the need for a superior employee information system.

Separation of the service function from the auditing function can relieve a large part of the anxiety and ambiguity of the service-control conflict. This will make the personnel function more effective and better accepted as part of the management team.

There should be more innovative ways to perform the audit and control function. Line managers need to develop further their personnel knowledge and skill. Two companies use impressive approaches to accomplish these objectives: one for labor relations and one for health and safety.

- One company has added a Step 3½ to its grievance procedure (Step 4 is arbitration). At this step, managers from nearby plants hear grievances. This procedure encourages a plant manager to get involved in day-to-day labor relations in order not to be embarrassed in front of his fellow plant managers.
- Another company requires that all of its plant managers devote two weeks a year to safety and health inspections at two plants other than their own. One week is spent at each plant. The inspection team, with the help of a company safety specialist, conducts a complete safety audit. This exercise not only educates the plant managers about safety and health and their importance but also motivates them to keep their own houses in order, since the manager knows that sometime during the year a team will be inspecting his plant and making a report to top management.

Innovation Role

The final important function of the personnel department is to provide up-to-date information on current trends and new methods of solving problems. We call this the innovation role. Personnel departments can escape their errand-boy guise and gain the respect of other members of management by providing credible information on trends concerning human resources and related policy proposals. Such a role will permit top management to plan its course of action rather than operating on an emergency basis. A personnel department able to provide timely advice to management on how to shape and use its human resources will have no trouble making its voice heard in executive councils.

Naturally, the innovative role must be in tune with the times and the set of issues confronting a particular company. In periods of rising inflation and escalating wage and salary demands, the emphasis may be on compensation issues. In times of retrenchment and falling profits, creative work sharing and lay-off plans may be needed.

Currently, there is a great deal of interest in improving the quality of work life to fight boredom and decreased productivity in both blue collar and white collar jobs. More and more promising executives in their 40s are deciding to get away from high-pressure, treadmill jobs and are abandoning careers they have pursued for years, thus leaving gaping holes in the ranks of the up-and-coming. Employees are demanding changes in the ways in which work is organized. There is an increasing concern and growing legislation about privacy. There are proposals to encourage employee stock ownership.

All these issues require the attention of personnel. And, since the issues change with the times, personnel must be responsible, adaptive, anticipatory, and, especially, innovative. Because of the changing nature of demands, the personnel function must be characterized as pragmatic rather than doctrinaire.

Let us look at some of the specific issues and consider how and where innovation can best take place according to our concepts of central versus dispersed operations.

Attitude Surveys: The purpose of this activity is to assess and evaluate employees' attitudes. Who needs this information? The central office of corporate headquarters? The plant or office manager? Or both?

It seems to us that attitude surveys trigger action at the local level. The local manager certainly needs to have the survey information as a measure of the local pulse. Does a central office need the same data? Is a local situation purely local, or is it often part of a large system trend? We believe that attitude surveys should be made locally and sent to central office for audit, since action and service belong at the local level with auditing and control at the central level.

Work Hours and Work Life: Can management allow flexible working hours at one location and not at another? Should local personnel managers be allowed, or encouraged, to engage in research and experimentation, or should this research be done only at a central point to maintain equity and uniformity?

Depending on the status of union contracts or the potential for union organization, local experimentation and research can be desirable or disastrous. Basic changes in working conditions and hours of work are critical issues of policy and should be carefully controlled corporation wide. This does not mean that variations cannot be allowed or encouraged in response to local conditions, but they should be administered in the light of overall policy.

Job Design: It can be argued that job design is an integral part of a compensation system and must be developed and audited centrally. But the knowledge about the jobs and persons holding jobs obviously resides at the local level. Compliance with corporation-wide standards can be too rigid, so that managers have little or no incentive to try something new in job design.

Perhaps central specialists should assemble the basic tools of job design, with the information gathered and the implementation carried out at the local level. When job redesign involves new classifications and hence changes in compensation systems, some central authorization and monitoring is necessary; but, without local initiative and participation, it is unlikely that much will ever change.

Pay and Benefits: Because of the critical factor of equity, pay and benefits must be established and controlled centrally. The requirements of various governmental regulatory bodies, on top of the continuing need to ensure conformity with corporate strategy, have forced greater uniformity and less arbitrariness in compensation.

Government regulations form part of a societal trend that is sounding the death knell for many types of merit pay plans. Too many of these plans have been administered in such a way that the recipients cannot comprehend them. As a result, most wage and salary plans have become minor variations of a straight seniority system.

This subject is too complex for detailed discussion in this article. For our purposes here, however, we should simply remark that compensation requires centralized standardization.

Our analysis and prescriptions for the placement of different activities could be called a contingency approach to organization. Basic to this approach is task, since we find that certain tasks are better performed in different places.

Another element of concern in the contingency approach is the environmental forces. Many of the pressures on the personnel department today arise externally, as we have discussed. It is exactly these external changes that an innovative personnel department must sense and track to anticipate the need for internal response ahead of situational crisis.

PERSONNEL AS 'CHANGE AGENT'

One danger requires a strong warning. That is the self-appointment by personnel to the role of "change agent." Any personnel director who appoints himself his company's change agent is presumptuous. Anybody in a business who sets out without invitation to reform his senior colleagues is headed for trouble. In addition, simply as a practical matter, the role of internal change agent is difficult, especially on a part-time basis, added to the administrative responsibilities of an entire department.

On the other hand, if the personnel director is indeed to be a part of the executive team, can he also be a satellite of the organization? Are these two functions, personnel manager and change agent, compatible? Many organizations, struggling for stability in a stormy sea of external change, will not look kindly on the change agent in their midst.

In our experience, most of the people who try to fill this role do not see themselves as trying to institute the change, but sincerely consider that they are helping the organization respond, adapt, and survive. But their colleagues in management see them as the proverbial messenger bringing bad news, creating change, and creating trouble. And, like the messenger, they often suffer a disastrous fate.

As a consequence, the personnel manager often works himself into the position of feeling excluded from major management decisions and then, donning the robe of missionary and reformer, the position of defender of the downtrodden with whom he identifies. This role will further alienate him from management, because he will be seen as working against things as they are, and against established policy. He will be seen as leading the charge against the ramparts of status quo. At this point, the only direction for the personnel manager to charge is out the door.

One personnel manager we knew felt it was his responsibility to educate his top management. He developed training programs to identify and deal with social change issues. Although the effort was well intended, it required that a cultural change take place within that company. The company's operative style was one of reaction to crisis, and these training programs required an anticipatory or proactive response. These programs required more than the support of top management; in fact, top management had to institute and lead them. The personnel manager as change agent, as a satellite, cannot even produce an adaptive mode, let alone produce change itself. As one company chairman put it:

> One weakness of personnel people is that they think they are God's favorite children. Too many simply want to rock the boat rather than solve the problem. They need to take responsibility. It is easy to come up with ideas. But there is a need to

think things through. Things can't be done that quickly, especially when they involve sales and production people. Personnel people don't seem to understand that things can't be implemented tomorrow.

With respect to change, the personnel manager plays a role similar to the one he plays with respect to personnel policy. He should be the agent to look at change rather than the change agent. Personnel can be the expert staff that identifies areas of concern, researches choices, and provides certain skills in training and implementation. But personnel alone does not decide what changes are needed, nor does it deliver the solutions. Change strategy, like policy information, must be "owned by" the appropriate leaders in the organization. There must be an institutionalized process for developing policy and for change.

In our view, it is important to recognize, however, that while it is difficult and frequently inappropriate for the personnel officer to assume a Janus role, the chief personnel officer should be sufficiently tuned to the needs of employees via his personnel network to make certain that the employees' viewpoint is given appropriate consideration on critical matters. Sometimes it is legitimate for a personnel director to play a change agent role. As one personnel vice president put it:

> The ideal situation is when the personnel guy is a consultant. But in the real world there are a number of people in responsible positions who have no interest at all in the growth and development of their people. Personnel may be the only one an employee can turn to in a nonunion company. Sometimes I have to be a bad guy with the manager. I have to be a change agent or a catalyst.

What makes this personnel vice president's behavior appropriate is the fact that he has the backing of his company's president and chairman. Personally recruited for his job by the president, this man has a value system congruent with the value system of the president and chairman of this family-controlled company.

In summary, self appointment to a change agent role can be suicidal for the individual and dysfunctional for the organization. For the change agent role to be effective, not only does the personnel officer need to be part of top management, but other members of top management need to be committed to the appropriateness of one of their members in a change agent role.

Earlier we referred to two aspects of policy formulation, process and content. In regard to change, we see the personnel manager as the custodian and protector of the process of change. In this role, he keeps channels of communication open—channels up and down and sideways, channels that flow in and out of the company.

Line management, particularly at and near the top, must be responsible for the content of change. In assuming process as a fundamental part of his job, the personnel manager gains strength and avoids the risk we have warned against.

STAFFING CONSIDERATIONS

While the personnel function must be organized properly to be effective, competent staffing is equally important. Though we have already said a little about staffing, we wish to deal more explicitly with this subject. How large should the staff be? What is a competent personnel department member? How has he or she been trained? How can competence be recognized and rewarded?

Too often, personnel members have been called incompetent. Too often, other departments have used personnel as a dumping ground for their failures. Some personnel departments are staffed by people recruited from outside. They do not know the business, and sometimes they show no interest in learning it. Some company personnel departments are staffed by people who have been somewhat less than successful in the line organization. Weak people who do not engender respect and who cannot hold their own at staff meetings do not add to a department's credibility. Too often, people seek personnel work because they "like working with people."

Effectiveness in much of personnel work has little to do with liking or disliking people; rather, it requires a willingness to take the time to understand the individual needs of employees in order to identify with their problems. This is true in a direct counseling session, in labor negotiations, or in dealing with another member of senior management or the chief executive officer.

While many companies have faced up to the need to get properly trained, talented, and motivated people into the personnel function, the old image is sometimes still there. Personnel people, to be effective, ought to have a working knowledge of what goes on in a plant or office.

Specialists and Generalists

We recognize the need for a wide variety of talents. We see the need for the specialist, particularly in the areas of audit and innovation. However, we also see a strong need for the generalist in the areas of service and policy.

As we have described it, the auditing function requires detailed knowledge of the legal and regulatory aspects of personnel. It requires the development and understanding of systems, and the collection, storage, and use of large quantities of information. Personnel must have the ability to understand the needs both of the line organization and of the various branches of state and federal government.

In many respects, all elements needed cannot be found in any one person. Rather, we suggest that a team be developed. This team would include specialists trained in personnel compensation and benefits, in the uses of computers and data systems, and in law, either in the department itself or on call.

However, because a team of personnel specialists will lack the ability to understand the needs of the line client, both manager and nonmanager, we suggest that people trained in other ways should supplement the auditing and control part of the department.

Line Managers and Supervisors

One source of talent will come from line managers and supervisors who have needed personnel information themselves to help them be good managers. In effect, these are the consumers of personnel services. They will bring to personnel the knowledge, language, and requirements of the line. Such managers will improve immeasurably the communication links within the company, and line managers will get help from someone who talks their language.

After a stay of perhaps two to five years, when the temporary member of personnel returns to the line, he or she will serve as a valuable ally of, and interface with, the personnel department. Half of IBM's corporate personnel staff consists of line managers who remain in that function for no more than two or three years.

The increasing demand for personnel to be better integrated with the rest of the organization appears in nearly every situation we have met. A woman personnel officer at a trade association talked about the changes she had noted in the caliber of people going into personnel work in an industry that increasingly draws union interest. Commenting on this, she said:

> Top management has finally realized that the people costs are as important as other costs. Lately, I've noted more forceful people in the personnel and labor relations field. They now have more of a voice in top management. You can't just talk it; you have to do it. The person entering the field today isn't the 'has been' who used to hang around in this field.

Current and Future Superstars

Management now pays greater attention to who heads the function. Where seniority and grandfather clauses used to prevail, many organizations today ask their current and future superstars to lead the personnel department. In one company, after a long conversation about personnel's role and other topics, the vice president of personnel casually stated, "When the president is away, I run the company." Attracting and holding a person of this caliber, one who can and does take over the reins when necessary, is becoming increasingly common.

One of the immediate effects of asking a superstar from the line organization to head the personnel function is to increase the salary of the position, for good people do not move for less money. Thus it is important not only to rotate managerial talent into and out of personnel but also to alter the reward system to show that the organization values such service.

In addition to having credibility with top management, the line executive who becomes the personnel vice president has to, in turn, rely on the staff people because they possess the specialized knowledge that he is lacking. Staff people thus have greater influence.

It is also more natural, perhaps, to put the personnel vice president with line experience on the executive committee and on the bonus committee, positions that indicate influence to other line managers. Such status and influence have been and will continue to be obtained by the well-prepared and trained personnel specialist who becomes a personnel generalist through his training and experience.

But does this mean that there is no great future for the well-trained specialist in the personnel department? No, but the well-trained specialist must learn the language of the rest of the organization and go beyond his own special language, jargon, and concepts. Some who have done so have become very effective personnel vice presidents.

Just as we have suggested that line managers and supervisors take a turn through personnel, so should the personnel specialist take a rotation through a line job in order to increase the ability to understand and deal with the organization as a whole.

It may be, however, that some personnel staff jobs have become so specialized that such people cannot handle a line job. If this is so (though we suspect these cases are rarer than is commonly thought), then such people should, in addition to teaching or taking courses in psychology, law, human relations, and personnel, take courses in marketing, finance, and general management. They also need to find ways to spend more time in offices and plants so that they become more familiar with what actually happens on a day-to-day basis.

Interested Employees

Many nonunion companies have still another source of personnel talent. These companies generally have highly developed communication networks for a two-way flow of information. Employees must know what management is thinking, and managers must also know what employees are thinking.

In such companies, interested and articulate members of the non-salaried, nonexempt ranks can become important resources for personnel. In fact, the best potential new members for personnel have often been the harshest critics. Far from bringing such employees into personnel to co-opt or silence them, the company should give them an opportunity to make improvements in the very things they found to criticize.

In one company, several key division personnel managers had been at one time hourly employees. The training in personnel, coupled with their previous hourly work experience, had made them effective with both management and workers.

While such a transition may be more difficult in unionized companies, those companies ought to have people in personnel who have seen a side of the company other than that learned through the route of college, an MBA, and several years of management experience. It is just as important for personnel people to understand the language, goals, and values of top management, we should add.

Thus we see many sources of talent for a well-rounded, effective personnel department: the college-trained specialist, the line manager taking a rotation through personnel, the line manager with a career commitment to the function after years in the line, and the hourly employee who is upwardly mobile. Above all, look for talent, not among those who "like working with people," but among those who want to be effective and who like to be part of the total organization.

Naturally, besides selecting people for personnel, management must think about their development. To provide the focus, attention, and coordination this activity requires, IBM has a director of personnel development who reports to the personnel vice president. His sole responsibility is the development of personnel people in IBM on a worldwide basis.

GUIDELINES FOR EVALUATION

We are left with one final question: How does management evaluate the effectiveness of the personnel department? This question obviously needs to be thought through in the context of the particular organization and its specific goals. What is effective for Texas Instruments may not be for Polaroid, or vice versa. But there are some common questions and guidelines.

While people like to think that their organization is unique, the personnel job in reality does not differ greatly, whether it takes place at Macy's, INA, Citibank, or IBM. Organizations do face common problems. In the area of personnel, the similarities may in fact be greater than the dissimilarities. Every organization has to handle people and define personnel's role, particularly how it relates to top management, and to develop the appropriate policies.

From our study of personnel departments and interviews with line managers, we can define three important measures for evaluating the effectiveness of the personnel functions.

1. Operating measures: Budget for the function as a percentage of company or division sales. Size of personnel staff to size of employee group serviced.
2. Quantity measures: Number of nurse visits and of industrial accidents per month. Cost per professional employee hired. Number of days to process insurance claims.
3. Quality measures: Analysis of grievances and of the issues personnel is involved in plus the nature and level of its involvement. Employee feedback on specific corporate issues. Effectiveness and professionalism of personnel staff (that is, group as well as individual performance).

Undoubtedly, other criteria could be added to this list. But the point, it seems to us, is that personnel, like all staff work, has to be evaluated with rigor, and not only as to its results but also as to how efficiently those results are achieved. To do so, the organization should develop measures and criteria in accord with its objectives. Any such evaluation should include periodic checks with line managers, the clients of the personnel department.

Part IV

Selected Topics of Continuing and Strategic Importance to Both Human Resources and Line Managers

If the authors of this book were polled to ascertain their views on those topics of continuing importance that they would like to see addressed, the list would be a very long one indeed. Even if the question were qualified by asking only about topics of strategic importance, the list would still be quite long. There are many topics that could be covered; I have included four: labor and employee relations; pay and executive compensation; the quality of working life; and human resources planning and management development.

LABOR RELATIONS

No aspect of human resources management has changed more dramatically during the past 25 years than the field of labor relations. Although union membership as a percentage of employees in nonagricultural establishments increased from 12 percent in 1930 to 35 percent in 1945, it declined from approximately one-third to less than 20 percent between 1955 and 1985. The changing economic, social, legal, and political environments have altered permanently the institution known as collective bargaining. In 1975, virtually no one would have predicted that in 1985 there would be nonunion automobile plants in the United States owned by Japanese companies (Nissan at Smyrna, Tennessee, and Honda in Marysville, Ohio). Nor would anyone have predicted that Toyota and General Motors would operate a joint venture in Fremont, California, a facility where the United Auto Workers and management have agreed to conduct business in radically different ways involving changes in work rules and lines of demarcation. General Motors' Saturn Unit, moreover, reached an innovative "memorandum of agreement" with the United Auto Workers in 1985. The agreement not only gives GM unprecedented flexibility in paying and assigning workers to jobs but also gives the UAW much greater involvement in business decisions. Among other features, the agreement also provides for employment security for one class of workers or "members," member pay tied more closely to profits, straight salaries rather than hourly pay, elimination of time clocks, and common parking and cafeterias for labor and management.

In "Straight Talk From a Union Leader," Douglas A. Fraser, retired president of the United Automotive Workers, talks about what is happening in the American labor movement and the new era of labor-management cooperation.

Bruce D. Henderson, founder and retired chairman of the Boston Consulting Group, writes in "Adversaries or Partners?" of the necessity of developing a whole new culture of cooperation and commitment, similar to the mutual commitment of Japanese labor and business. Calling for an end to labor wars, Henderson argues that in their own best interest, labor and corporations must work together toward their common purpose, prosperity.

A veteran of the labor-management scene is Arnold Weber, president of Northwestern University. He has been a student of collective bargaining and a contributor to a better understanding of it for many years. In "Lifeboat Labor Relations: Collective Bargaining in Heavy Seas," Weber presents an analytical framework that will help the reader better understand the "new and boldly changing strategic labor relations environment."

Finally, to conclude this section, I reprint "How Top Nonunion Companies Manage Employees," my *Harvard Business Review* article on the personnel policies and practices of over two dozen large companies. Many managements today have a strategic choice. If they elect to operate on a nonunion basis, then it is imperative that they have in place certain philosophies and personnel policies and practices. There is, however, much in the article that could improve labor relations in unionized companies as well.

PAY AND EXECUTIVE COMPENSATION

It is frequently said that if one wants to understand a corporation and what it really values, one should simply ascertain both how people are paid and who gets promoted. Companies express their values by the actions they take with respect to key compensation and promotion decisions. In this section, we examine compensation in general and executive compensation in particular. Later in Part IV we focus on career and management development and succession planning.

Executive compensation in recent years has become a matter of public concern. Management incentive compensation plans have been criticized because they force managers to become overly concerned with short-term results to the detriment of long-run performance. The size of executive bonuses, moreover, sometimes seems excessive, in light of company performance and return to shareholders. Some plans, too, seem poorly designed in light of the strategic posture of the business unit or corporation. If one is going to pay for performance, generally relative performance, then one has to define performance in measurable terms. And if it is really important to motivate key executives to achieve good long-run results, then it is extremely important that there be effective long-term incentive compensation plans in place.

Professor Edward E. Lawler, III, of the University of Southern California is this nation's leading academic expert on the subject of pay. In "Determining Total Compensation: Strategic Issues," he analyzes compensation from both the individual's and the organization's perspective. Lawler discusses the importance of developing a compensation "philosophy" and reviews nine strategic decisions to make in designing a compensation plan.

If Ed Lawler is the leading academic expert on the subject of pay, "Bud" Crystal and Fred Cook are clearly the leading consultants in the field of executive compensation. In "Maximizing ROI Through Effective Compensation," Crystal, a vice-president of the consulting firm of Towers, Perrin, Forster and Crosby, explodes some myths about compensation. He argues compellingly for developing executive compensation plans with the right incentives and for making sure that risk is part of incentive compensation plans.

Frederic W. Cook, the founder and chairman of the consulting firm that bears his name, is also a profound and imaginative thinker with respect to the executive compensation area. In "Long-Term Incentives of Management, Part 1: An Overview," he explains in understandable terms the complex subject of designing attractive rewards for good long-run performance. Cook helps companies design effective compensation plans that not only provide real assistance in achieving strategic business objectives but also provide an "integrated, balanced, total compensation program for their key employees." For one wanting to learn of some of the intricacies and complexities of long-term plans, Cook's overview is essential.

QUALITY OF WORKING LIFE

The three articles in this section explore the subject of job design and enrichment, a topic of increasing importance. Although many better-educated and less docile individuals are seeking jobs that offer greater responsibility and challenge, at the same time many companies are worrying about alienation, high turnover, absenteeism, poor quality, labor shortages, and a loss of motivation. Many organizations, consequently, are experimenting either with the restructuring of existing jobs or the design of new work systems that are more responsive to human needs. The objectives of such programs are both to improve productivity and to enhance the quality of working life. The article by Irving Bluestone, formerly of the United Auto Workers, entitled "Toward New Freedom at the Workplace," is a plea for greater worker participation in deciding the methods and means of production. Similarly, the article by Donald N. Scobel, "Doing Away with the Factory Blues," is a fascinating account of how one corporation revitalized its work climate by doing away with the dehumanizing policies that can be typical of factory life.

Different companies have attempted to resolve work-force management problems in a variety of ways. But as the article by Professors Walton and Schlesinger ("Do Supervisors Thrive in Participative Work Systems?") makes clear, if job redesign programs are to be successful, top management commitment, support, and involvement is a must. Similarly, if the company is organized, union cooperation is essential. Experience has shown that the creation of more meaningful jobs involves much more than the addition of or a rearrangement of responsibilities: because work redesign efforts involve much supervisory risk-taking and behavioral change, the selection, training, and evaluation of the supervisor is critical. No program can succeed unless it has the support of the majority of supervisors. The reward system, too, must be consistent with the intent of the new work design.

These articles, then, will suggest ways in which working life can be improved and conditions under which such improvements are most likely to succeed.

HR PLANNING
AND MANAGEMENT DEVELOPMENT

Increasingly, writers in the human resources field have observed that personnel policy must be integrally related to the objectives of the business. The way to make this happen is to relate personnel planning to strategic planning. It has also been increasingly recognized that the really scarce resource in most companies is outstanding managers. If this second problem is to be addressed, then it is essential that companies not only do an excellent job in the area of initial selection, but also offer effective management development programs and opportunities. This section of Part IV, consequently, concerns both personnel planning and management development, two crucial processes.

No book that included a section on personnel planning would be complete if it failed to contain some of the work of James W. Walker. Walker, a vice-president and director of Human Resources Consulting Services in Cresap, McCormick, and Paget, has probably done more for the field of human resources planning than any other single individual. In "Human Resource Planning: An Evolution," he presents a complete overview of the field's origins and evolution, the state of the art and approaches that work. As Walker states:

Planning for human resource needs is more than a set of techniques and a system that is part of the personnel function. Today it is widely viewed as the way management comes to grips with ill-defined and tough-to-solve human resource problems facing an organization.

Eric W. Vetter, personnel vice-president at Gould at the time of his speech ("The Role of Human Resource Planning in Corporate Management") and now senior vice-president of personnel at Crocker National Bank in San Francisco, emphasizes that the dominant concern of the human resource function in personnel planning should be profits: "We must think profits—talk profits—make profits." With profitability as the standard, companies are unlikely to make the mistake of adopting programs for their own sake without regard for their ultimate value to the company.

When most successful general managers are asked to cite the significant developmental experiences of their own careers, they often reply "good jobs" and "good bosses." In the past, getting the right assignment or the understanding boss has generally been a matter of good luck. But if management development is as important as major companies have come to believe it is, the development of future leaders cannot be left to luck or chance. Succession planning, management development programs, and career planning processes, too, need to be managed with great care, high standards, and well-defined objectives.

The article by James F. Bolt ("Management Resource Planning: Keys to Success") describes the key policy and administrative issues in designing a management resource planning system. Bolt, director of human resource planning and development at Xerox Corporation at the time he wrote this article (he is now president of Human Resource Associates, a consulting firm), reviews the way succession planning is actually done at several large corporations. He identifies the requirements for success as well as the typical problems encountered.

An interview with Robert N. Beck, executive vice-president of personnel for the Bank of America, was the first reading in this volume. In the next article ("Developing Managers to Bank On") Beck discusses the need for good people managers and the Bank of America's management development strategies, including the important roles of performance planning, coaching, and evaluation and integrated management training approaches.

Training, however, is not something reserved for classes and formal programs. The final article ("Why Training is the Boss's Job") in this section is by Andrew S. Grove, president of Intel Corporation, a leading manufacturer of microprocessors and computer memory devices. In this article, Grove reminds us that a significant part of every manager's job is training. Recognizing the consequences of insufficiently trained employees, Grove convincingly argues that "training is one of the highest-leverage activities a manager can perform." Managers are role models and teachers, and Grove shows how managers themselves benefit from doing a good training job.

STRAIGHT TALK
FROM A UNION LEADER

Douglas Fraser

In recent times, workers and bosses in some companies have come to see that by working together both can benefit. No one has been in a better position to observe and foster this shift from antagonism to cooperation than Douglas A. Fraser, who retired last year as president of the United Automobile Workers union.

Fraser spent his entire career in the UAW. In 1980 he became a member of Chrysler Corp.'s board of directors—the first union leader to be elected to such a post in a major corporation. He played a leading role in rescuing Chrysler by persuading his union members to make concessions to keep the company afloat.

As Fraser makes clear in this interview with Reader's Digest Roving Editor Irwin Ross, the key to this new era of labor-management cooperation is something he recognized when he emerged from a Chrysler shop at age 25 to head his local union: a worker's need for goals beyond money.

Q. What's happened to the American labor movement? Less than a quarter of the nation's nonfarm workers belonged to unions in 1980, down from a third in 1955.

A. We live in a different world today. In the 1930s, when I first got involved, there was no organization at all in the steel, rubber and auto industries. Before the union, the auto shops, for example, were authoritarian. You couldn't challenge or talk back. Wages were pretty good. What we wanted was dignity and security.

The major thrust in auto and steel was for seniority, which meant that when a company cut the work force, there was no favoritism about who stayed. Before, a worker was captive of the whim of the boss. When I worked at Chrysler, two things drove me nuts—the company soccer team and the Chrysler chorus. Those guys never got laid off. I used to joke, "We either have to organize a union or learn to sing or play soccer." Seniority represented a tremendous measure of security to the workers—a tremendous advance.

"Straight Talk from a Union Leader: An Interview with Douglas Fraser," reprinted with permission from the March 1984 Reader's Digest. *Copyright © 1984 by The Reader's Digest Assn., Inc.*

Q. But why are there almost no big organizing successes these days?

A. The old saying is true: the union doesn't organize workers, the bosses do. Employers have learned to treat workers with more dignity and even-handedness. Bosses are avoiding mistakes their predecessors made, so the union has a tougher time.

Most people join unions when some profound grievance motivates them. But one shouldn't join a union just to get better wages or working conditions. I would say: "Join a union to get democracy in the work place, because without a union, you get what the bosses choose to give you. You don't have it as a right."

Q. What characterizes employers who are most successful in resisting unions?

A. First, they make wages and fringe benefits comparable to the unionized shops in the industry. Second, they provide as much job security as they can. Third, they train personnel people, right down to the line foremen, to be leaders rather than bosses, and to be sensitive to the worker's dignity.

Q. Exactly what do you mean by dignity?

A. I used to be infuriated, as a shop steward, when I saw a foreman chew out a worker in front of his fellows. I remember one of the worst examples of indignity when I had a job in a factory where the toilet was in the middle of the factory floor. The upper half of it was enclosed in glass, so supervisors could see whether anybody was loafing there. Later, some General Motors plants took the doors off toilet stalls. The union got them put back. An employer who doesn't want a union doesn't do these things.

Q. How can the union movement grow in the face of increased sophistication by employers in handling labor relations?

A. With less unemployment, less fear and insecurity, it will be somewhat easier to organize in new fields. We have to explore new recruiting techniques. You can't organize workers by passing out leaflets at plant gates. You have to make personal contact. Many unions have begun to recruit people from the local community as temporary organizers. That overcomes the complaint that the union representative is an outsider. Community education is also important. The UAW and other unions have increasingly used TV advertising to create a more favorable impression.

I also think that, as a matter of law, a union should have the same right of access to a plant that the employer has. That is, if the boss campaigns *against* the union on company property, the union should have the same privilege. In my view, that would be fair. We almost got access in 1978, as part of labor-law-reform legislation. The bill passed the House and could have passed the Senate, but was stopped by a filibuster. We need a renewed push for it.

In addition, I believe unions will gain strength from the changing attitudes of women to jobs. When they thought of themselves as only temporary members of the work force, they were not much interested in unions. Now they are likely to be much more receptive to the union message.

Q.   Will unions show the same understanding of the problems of industry that they displayed during the recession?

A.   I think so, particularly people who are being called back to work. They know that companies have to prosper if employees are to prosper. But this realization depends on corporations' continuing to inform workers' representatives of what's going on. We had more of that in the recession than ever before.

I think the long-term trend is toward a less adversary, more cooperative relationship than we've had.

Q.   What will be some of the elements of this more cooperative relationship?

A.   Profit sharing, for one. We now have this at General Motors and Ford.

The concept is simple enough—let's divide the pie on the basis of results. Let's have profit sharing instead of a continual escalation of wages and fringe benefits. There has to be a floor—for example, you can't say, "You'll get health insurance if the profit level is high enough." But beyond the basic wages and benefits, the better the company does, the better the workers do. At GM for the year 1983, profit sharing is likely to mean $400 to $600 for each full-time worker.

Q.   Why have some unions resisted profit sharing?

A.   Part of the resistance is doctrinaire—a fear of being co-opted by the employer, of getting too close to him. This is a theoretical, juvenile objection. The fact is, the worker's future is tied to the future of the corporation. They're inseparable. Others argue that if workers share in profits, take-home pay for the same jobs in different companies will vary. But what's the alternative? To let GM, for example, keep that $600 instead of distributing it to employees?

Q. Do you foresee more programs to increase productivity—things like the quality-of-work-life movement in the auto industry, and quality circles in others?

A. I think so. Quality-of-work-life really means democratizing the plant floor. Management treats the workers as intelligent, innovative human beings who can come up with ingenious answers that hadn't been thought of before. And once people experience democracy, it's not easy to take it away. The worker gets a greater sense of achievement. And companies get better quality and increased productivity.

Q. In talking about the labor movement, we can't avoid the problem of corruption, including the practice of some convicted union officials' staying in office until they've exhausted all appeals.

A. I don't approve of that. I would remove them. Nor should acquittal by the courts automatically mean that they're absolved. Suppose a guy is indicted for taking a kickback from an employer, but the prosecution has insufficient evidence to secure a guilty verdict. The union should make an independent investigation after the trial and make its own judgment.

Q. What do you see for labor ten years down the road?

A. A stronger union movement; I think we can get back up to 25 percent of the labor force organized in unions—perhaps more. Unions will have to be more sure of themselves and sophisticated about the problems of the employer and the economy. I expect more profit sharing. And more shared decision-making, as we have at Chrysler. Workers *must* have a greater voice in shaping their own future. Labor-management relations and the whole economy will be better off when that happens.

ADVERSARIES OR PARTNERS?

Bruce D. Henderson

The labor wars must end. Hostile confrontation between members of the same organization is a barbaric legacy of a past that we should put behind us. It is a fundamental defect in Western productivity. A company divided against itself cannot compete.

The Japanese are teaching the West a humiliating object lesson. One by one the Japanese have entered industries in which the U.S. has led the world. Now Japan is becoming the new world leader in these industries. It is doing this without significant resources or advantages except the ability of its people to cooperate. The time is overdue for the West to reexamine its fundamental assumptions about business cooperation and competition. The starting point should be cooperation, coordination and teamwork within the firm.

Philosophy is not a substitute for action. The action must come after rethinking:

- The labor/management hostility
- The logic of labor monopolies, industrywide bargaining and the social sanctity of labor negotiation by threat, strike and interfamily war
- The lifetime role and mutual commitment of employers and employees in an increasingly specialized society
- The role of the face-to-face group and its function in our society

The debilitating "English disease" of labor strife is the bitter fruit of the Industrial Revolution. In the beginning the need for production equipment and machinery required factories. But factories broke down the intimate and personal communication of the farm families, the tradesmen and the artisan guilds. The factory substituted the faceless indifference and jostle of a crowded city. The small groups that formed within the factory banded together to control the hostile, prison-like environment within which they struggled. The factory itself became the enemy.

The upper Clyde River near Glasgow was once the greatest ship-building complex in the world. Eventually small groups of organized craft unions found that by respecting one another's picket lines each in turn could hold for ransom every ship under construction. Cooperation led to suicidal destruction.

Bruce D. Henderson, "Adversaries or Partners?" Perspectives # 250, *The Boston Consulting Group, Inc., 1983. Reprinted with permission.*

In Japan cooperation led to the opposite result. The production of the ship became the common cause, rather than the welfare of the small group at the expense of the common purpose. Each worker, to the limit of his ability, did whatever was needed most at a given time. Japan became the world's dominant shipbuilder.

During World War II, the British rose to the heights of courage, heroism and cooperation. Against impossible odds, they fought, survived and won against the enemy. But with the return of peace, the cooperation ended and the English disease slowly reduced the U.K. from the greatest of the industrial powers to the most stagnant.

Perhaps Japan was favored by skipping the Industrial Revolution and going almost directly from feudal baronies to a modern industrial society. For Japan the process from world isolation to world leader took less than a hundred years.

CONSTRAINTS ON PRODUCTIVITY

Deep in the heart of our self-inflicted constraint on productivity is the myth that we must decrease our individual productivity in order to create additional jobs so more people can share an unchanged total net output. Every society should take care of its own to the best of its abilities, regardless of the capabilities of its individual members. But anything in a culture that suppresses the productivity of any individual or limits achievement of any individual's potential is destructive of the common good.

Where industrywide labor bargaining monopolies are supported by law, competition between corporations based on productivity is suppressed. The whole industry suffers. Where competition is worldwide, as it is in steel and automobiles, the whole industry withers whenever labor acts as a monopolist. Competitively the result is that such an industry cannot supply value equivalent to that of foreigners.

Parasitic work practices that kill the host are not uncommon. Railroad work rules required a fireman for an engine with no fire. Railroad work rules limited the mileage of a train crew per day no matter how fast or steadily the train ran. These practices were major contributors to the decline and decay of the railroads. Strikes by such public services hold the entire economy for ransom regardless of the damage done to innocent third parties.

Corporations have prospered and grown to towering heights of achievement, then sunk into obscurity and been forgotten. All of them started with small groups with extensive face-to-face exchange and consensus on goals and values. All prospered as extended families with shared objectives and a common cause. All failed when they became pitted against themselves internally instead of coordinating and cooperating to achieve common purposes.

Whatever the services of organized labor have been in the past, its role as an adversary is self-defeating. Its future role must be that of communicator. Whatever the perceived role of management has been in the past, its future role must be as internal coordinator and external interface. All employees of a corporation, like the crew and passengers of a ship, have a common destination.

THE SOCIAL COMMITMENT

The payments and benefits of a company to its employees are typically many times greater than those to its shareholders. For that reason, employees are the true beneficiaries of a corporation's prosperity. But the changes in benefits to employees that are practical, or possible, are trivial unless matched by a change in productivity per employee when compared to the company's competition.

The ever greater specialization inherently required for increased productivity means that labor skills are not ordinarily transferable or fungible without very high cost. The labor market becomes increasingly thin and inefficient. The relationship eventually represents mutual dependency.

The long term services of any organization's employees represent a substantial investment by both the individual employee and the organization. The knowledge, skills, background, organizational fit and teamwork interactions are often not transferable to another organization. Even if they are transferable in some measure, they have far less value. These capabilities represent a major investment on the part of both the organization and the employee.

That investment is the true basis for the Japanese commitment to lifetime employment. That commitment must represent a social contract. The obligation of the employee to the firm can be no stronger than the obligation of the firm to the employee. For it to be effective, it must be part of the firm's culture, not public law.

The Japanese have set a standard of achievement and internal integrity others cannot match unless they rise above their past cultures and make common cause. Non-Japanese can outperform their competitors by learning from the Japanese just as the Japanese learned from Westerners. The Japanese did not copy Western practices. Instead they learned from us, adapted our practices to their own culture and then began to outperform us. We can do the same, perhaps even better.

A whole new culture must be built in Western business if it is to realize its potential. True cooperation is based on mutual commitment. True commitment is based on mutual purpose, mutual evaluation and mutual trust. For that to be possible, the corporate purposes and the implicit responsibilities of each member of the organization must constantly be reaffirmed.

For that to happen, management must be more than coordinator; it must be leadership. In the future this probably means that:

- Industrial organizations will move steadily toward smaller and smaller separate factories of 500 or fewer employees with work teams of 10 to 25 members.
- Labor unions will become primarily company unions in those companies that survive.
- Work rules will become a relic of the past. Instead, each member of the team will do whatever is most valuable.
- Permanent employment will come after an extended courtship that leads to long term mutual commitment and responsibility to the members in an extended family.
- Productivity will become a measure of corporate citizenship and status.
- Corporate stature will be measured by the corporation's ability to provide personal security to its employees, outperform its competitors and support the norms of its society and culture while repaying its moral obligation to those who make its existence possible.

These things can all be done. They are a matter of will, morality, energy and culture. Those who can and do will be the survivors. Failure to achieve them in real time is to invite mutually assured destruction.

LIFEBOAT LABOR RELATIONS: COLLECTIVE BARGAINING IN HEAVY SEAS

Arnold Weber

A sweeping change is taking place in labor relations strategies and tactics in the United States. This development has been occurring with such precipitous speed that no expert could have predicted it as recently as three years ago.

In fact, the leading issue in labor relations that titillated attorneys and arbitrators three years ago was the neutrality clause. For those who do not remember this debate, the neutrality clause was incorporated in collective bargaining agreements so that a company, in effect, waived its right under Section 8(c) of the National Labor Relations Act to express free speech in the context of a union organizing drive. Had that tendency persisted, this practice would have raised interesting legal questions. It certainly was viewed as further evidence of the "muscularity," or monopoly power, if you will, of unions such as the United Auto Workers, the rubber workers, the paper workers, and others which were making demands for such neutrality clauses.

Three years later, however, we are talking about a different set of adversities and legal issues that reflect a completely contrary labor-management environment. If I have any text to my sermonette, it is that the current interest in the use of the bankruptcy procedure to abrogate union contracts is best understood within the context of pervasive and profound changes in the labor relations environment. Beyond the important legal considerations, the issue itself is overshadowed by broader issues of structure and strategy within the labor relations area.

It is important first to specify the dominant characteristics of the American industrial relations system, in order to provide a framework for the changes that have been working themselves out during the past few years. Once we look at these ascriptions, we can then identify what, in fact, has happened and is likely to happen in the years ahead. With this perspective, we can perhaps better understand the implications of the bankruptcy issue.

Arnold Weber, "Lifeboat Labor Relations: Collective Bargaining in Heavy Seas," in Labor Relations in Transition: Bankruptcy Law vs. Labor Law, *proceedings of a conference, Kenneth W. Chilton and Ronald J. Penoyer, eds. (St. Louis: Center for the Study of American Business, 1984). Reprinted with permission.*

Let us look at the American labor relations system as it existed in the mid-1970s and toward the end of the decade. On the one hand, we can say there was a certain element of self-congratulation, if not smugness, in viewing the American industrial relations system. It had certain problems. Stereotypes such as the hyperaggressive shop steward, the union leader pursuing self-defeating wage policies, and the willful employer had some basis in fact. But by and large, the system had worked and it reflected the character of the American environment. Even the most distraught employer, if he wanted to mitigate his own feelings of oppression, could look at England where unions would literally shut down a plant at the drop of a teacup. Or he could compare his situation with his Italian counterpart, where if a company were to consider shutting down a plant, the head of the union would appear with the mayor, with a green sash across his ample abdominal area, to take over the plant in the name of the workers and engage in other sportive exercises in proletariat romanticism.

In the United States, however, regardless of deficiencies in labor relations practices, there still was a comforting quality of stability. It was a framework within which, at the end of all the posturing, you could "make a deal."

BASIC ELEMENTS OF U.S. INDUSTRIAL RELATIONS

Three basic characteristics of the labor-management system were taken as given at the end of the 1970s. First, union membership and strength had been maintained in the dominant sectors of the economy, and that strength was accepted as a given. Unions in the United States have had a unique and anomalous role: statistically, they have always been a minority. But in terms of their impact in the labor market, through their emulative impact on the non-union sector, unions have always had a majority effect. Union membership at its peak (and nobody knew it was peaking in 1958) was around 28 or 29 percent of the labor force. Nonetheless, unions clearly have been viewed as a constant in the heartland of the American economy.

Heartland Strength of Unions

Union strength traditionally has been in manufacturing, in the "blue collar alley" curving from Pittsburgh to Cleveland, up into Michigan, and across to Chicago. Construction, the extractive industries such as mining, and particularly the transportation and printing industries defined the deep genealogical roots of the trade union movement. The assumption had been that steel would always be 100 percent unionized, and certainly that the automobile industry would be unionized, even though a company such as

General Motors might be emboldened to move a few plants to the South to avoid unionization. But if anyone thought that the United Mine Workers would not be the dominant union in coal, that was *prima facie* justification for the revocation of his or her Ph.D. in whatever subject, be it economics or religious studies.

Adjusting Wages by Formula

The second basic principle governing the labor relations system at the end of the 1970s was the widespread acceptance of a formula approach to compensation. Wage increases were linked to macroeconomic factors rather than to firm- or industry-specific factors. When this development took place, it was proclaimed—and with some justification at that time—as the triumph of statesmanship and long-term perspectives over short-term avarice.

The basic element of this approach was something called the "annual improvement factor," or AIF. In its explicit and robust form, the Annual Improvement Factor was developed in the General Motors-United Auto Workers contract of 1948. Basically, labor and management said, "We are going to change the ouija board, which works on differential pressure, into a slide rule (we would say a computer now) in determining how we divide up the pie." The governing factor was what happened to national trend productivity, which was fixed at that time at 3 percent. We should remember that this approach was greeted with loud hosannahs—Walter Reuther, in fact, established his credentials as a bona fide labor statesman because of it. The AIF approach spread in one form or another to most other industries, even those which did not explicitly adopt the 3 percent standard. The primary consequence was to break the linkage between wages and the firm or industry measures and, instead, tie wages to some macroeconomic variable.

The next step in this formula approach to wage adjustments was to protect the real gain in earnings associated with the Annual Improvement Factor by adding on a cost-of-living adjustment clause, or COLA clause. The explicit theory behind COLA adjustments was that the appropriate approach to collective bargaining and wage determination is to establish a real increase based on the AIF or on productivity, and then protect the value against changes caused by inflation through a COLA clause.

COLA clauses became widespread and, in most cases, were uncapped, so that the median recovery rate amounted to around 70 percent of the inflation rate—although there was tremendous variance around that percentage. In autos and steel, agreements would start at 90 percent and then be reduced by the mathematical effect of the formula. Even if they did not have an AIF or a COLA clause, most union agreements reflected this concept in one form or another.

To present a specific example, in one of my earlier incarnations I worked with the paper industry. In that industry it was a sacrament that you should not give a COLA clause. And, of course, if you did not give a COLA clause, the terms of trade demanded agreements of less than three years because a COLA clause was one way that a firm accommodated the anticipatory anxieties of union leaders in entering into multi-year agreements. I did a calculation of the wage gains in the paper industry relative to what was given in the UAW over a ten-year period. The paper industry conceded just about the same amount, except that it never received the advantages of "time-weighting" associated with the operation of a COLA clause. That is, when an agreement has a COLA clause, the wage adjustment is not made until after the fact. If there is no COLA clause, then wage adjustments are given "up front" in the form of money increases, which are associated with some imputed or prospective impact of inflation.

The third element of the formula approach to wage increases was coincidental with the emergence of fringe benefits as a major element of compensation. This took place in the 1950s and 1960s. Every employee has since been exposed to the erosive economic impact of "benefit creep." This phenomenon arises from the fact that employers prefer to negotiate benefit levels rather than costs, because if they became involved with costs, the unions would push for the last nickel or dime. So, labor and management began, instead, to negotiate the benefit package—that is, whether lobotomies and hysterectomies and all sorts of medical expenditures would be covered by the fringe benefits. It turned out, however, that as the price of these services went up, firms did not negotiate the benefit down to, say, seven-eights of a lobotomy. Rather, it was the worst of all worlds. In real terms, the benefits might cost the employer 50 percent more over time, but management received no credit for it from an imperceptive work force.

So the second principle in what we perceived to be a highly stable and constructive system of labor relations—which developed over a forty-year period until the end of the 1970s—was the formula approach to wage and compensation determination. This formula approach linked together an implicit or explicit notion of national productivity trends, protection of real value through COLA clauses, and "benefit creep."

Consolidated Bargaining

The final element of the pre-existing system was the development and entrenchment of highly consolidated bargaining structures. These structures are of two basic types. The first is a straightforward, garden-variety, multi-employer bargaining arrangement. The most robust examples are found in the steel and railroad industries where all the employers sit down with the union on the other side of a table and all the firms explicitly enter into the same deal.

In its more subtle and extended form, bargaining structures were consolidated through "pattern-setting"—which developed in rubber, autos, retail food, and a whole range of other industries. This pattern following developed its own protocols which, in some ways, were predictable. For example, in the automobile industry everybody knew if a union wanted to win a principle, it went to Ford; if it wanted to get the money, it went to General Motors; and if it wanted to have fun, it went to Chrysler. The process of bargaining in the auto industry consequently had a highly stylistic but predictable form.

Although it was maintained that these highly consolidated structures were further evidence of union power, in most instances they were accepted or actively promoted by the employer. This type of bargaining was protection against whipsawing and against the other axiom of union behavior, "He who settles last, settles dearest." From the union's point of view, it was a way of taking wages out of competition.

In my judgment, these three elements—the predominance and acceptance of union organization in the heartland of the economy, the development of a formula approach to wages, and the establishment of consolidated, well-defined bargaining structures—were the pillars of the American labor relations system. They stood for a thirty-year period. Lost time from strikes in a bad year was on the order of .18 of 1 percent, which was probably less than the lost time associated with golf.

THE CHANGING
LABOR-RELATIONS ENVIRONMENT

The system worked, and we thought it was an expression of maturity. At the same time, it almost had a Toynbee-esque quality. But changes were taking place in the environment which would undermine existing practices and set the stage for the tactics and developments that we identify today— of which resort to bankruptcy is an element.

International Competition

One of these major changes is the emergence of unrelenting international competition. Many industries did not understand this development; they imputed the apparent success of companies and industries to their own managerial genius when, in fact, that success was attributable to their position in national economic development—the fact that many companies operated in protected markets. This was certainly the case in airlines, steel, rubber, autos, and a whole range of industries within which protective practices took root.

It is clear, for example, that there is no such thing as a domestic automobile industry anymore, and there never will be again. The automobile industry is now an international industry in which, ten years from now, there may be only six or seven producers worldwide. Similarly, the agricultural implements industry is now becoming less of a domestic industry (and with diminished American dominance in world markets) and is entering a highly competitive environment. That is why Caterpillar, almost in an act of anticipatory desperation, withstood a 150-day strike in an effort to change the union's approach to labor costs. Caterpillar was, in effect, getting ready for Komatsu—and it did so in a manner that was only a little more effective than the way in which Ford and General Motors got ready for Nissan and Toyota.

Deregulation

Secondly, and most dramatic, has been the impact of deregulation, particularly on transportation. Ten or fifteen years ago, Jimmy Hoffa of the Teamsters was a folk hero in labor relations. Hoffa was a larger-than-life figure who stood astride the Central States Master Freight Agreement like the Colossus at Rhodes. We can recall the legendary stories of Hoffa negotiating global contracts and also serving as the court of last resort in the resolution of grievances. And if Teamster business agents strayed from the existing contract, methods were found to try to bring them back in line.

But look at what is happening now in the deregulation of industries. The best Master Freight could do was agree to a wage freeze which has subsequently been widely eroded through the fragmentation of what appeared to be a monolithic bargaining structure.

Effects of the Recession

A third factor is the extended, deep recession which began in 1979. In this recession we have seen a discontinuity in the trend growth rate of the American economy. Many of the principles inherent in past labor-management relations arose during the era of what I call the "Great American Schmoo Machine"—the Schmoo being the mythic character in the Al Capp comic strip, every part of which was convertible to a delectable pork chop, that would split by binary fission as a gesture of love. That is the situation we thought we had for thirty years. Real GNP was increasing by roughly 4 percent a year, productivity was going up 3 percent, and everybody fell into the trap of linear extrapolation: the expansion was going to go on forever. We finally reached a discontinuity in the 1970s.

Looking back, the end of the Schmoo Machine started to emerge at the beginning of the decade, with a significant drop in productivity associated with OPEC oil prices as well as a range of other factors. But by the time we came out of the 1970s, productivity was not 3 percent, it was zero, and the real increase in GNP was not 4 percent, it was doing its best to valiantly keep up with trend rates of 2 percent. Of course, the recession also left a legacy of high levels of unemployment.

The Sun Belt Shift

The next factor of change was the failure of unions to follow geographical and industrial shifts in the labor force. What happened was that the trade union movement, like almost every other institution, acquired a certain "organizational arteriosclerosis." That is, it is much easier to have an office on Sixteenth Street in Washington, and go across the street to the White House, than it is to get out and hustle in small towns in Tennessee and pass out handbills at 5 o'clock in the morning or go around to peoples' houses and try to organize them. In other words, there was a loss of initiative within organized labor.

Data from the National Labor Relations Board show that the geographical incidence of union representation elections today is almost the same as it was 20 years ago. The highest incidence of representation elections is in the Northeast, the Middle Atlantic states, and the Midwest. The strength of union membership is not where the "action" is taking place now—in the Sunbelt, the South, and the West.

Professionalization of Personnel Administration

Another factor which altered the labor environment was the maturation of the personnel administration movement. I think this aspect plays a very important part in understanding the unions' difficulties, because workers now perceive that there are reasonable, non-tyrannical alternatives to joining a union. In the past, when you talked to people who were in personnel administration and you asked them why they entered this field, they always gave two reasons: 1) "I did it in the Army," and 2) "I like people." But those reasons should have disqualified them for the job.

In the past, management had no deep sense of professionalism, nor a capacity to offer other alternatives in what Clark Kerr calls a "pluralistic labor relations environment" in which a web of rules defines the relationship between the employer and the employee. Labor used to think that labor-management relations could be changed only by the government or in the context of a collective bargaining agreement. In short, labor could not trust the employer. That perception has clearly changed with the professionalism of personnel administration that has taken place during the past twenty years. Sophisticated personnel systems may offer a credible alternative to unionism in advancing and protecting employee interests.

Influence of the PATCO Strike

The last important element of change is the following: in order to crystalize any event, there has to be the "Sarajevo phenomenon." That is, World War I was not caused by the assassination of a hapless archduke; it was an incident which merely captured a whole set of historical events.

In American labor relations, in my judgment, the Sarajevo phenomenon was the Professional Air Traffic Controllers' strike. When the PATCO strike took place, many of us dismissed it as exotica. In a way, it *was* exotica. But the very fact that it happened was extraordinary. The fact that the President of the United States—the chief personnel administrator, if you will—took on this group and broke the strike gave it tremendous significance. This was the largest strike broken by any employer since the steel workers' strike in 1919. I do not think there was anything malicious in what Secretary of Transportation Drew Lewis did or in what the President did. After all, the strike was viewed, in the end, as a test of the authority of the government of the United States.

The PATCO strike lay bare a whole range of considerations. For one thing, the strikers had average salaries in the range of $40,000 a year, a salary that sounded pretty good to a fellow in Kearney, Nebraska, or someone working at a pecan shelling plant in Georgia. And yet the air traffic controllers were going to bring down the entire structure of the American transportation system simply because they wanted to make $48,000 a year or adjust their working hours, or what have you. That just did not wash with the American public.

Moreover, another ironic factor played a part. The PATCO strike did not really inconvenience most people—that is, people on the South Side of Chicago or the South End of Pittsburgh. The people it inconvenienced were the John Chancellors and the Dan Rathers of the world and the other "opinion makers" whose lives are defined by jumping on a shuttle and going someplace to engage in "itinerant punditry."

In the instance of the PATCO strike, these factors contributed to a subtle change in public opinion. In my judgment it redefined what was considered both feasible and acceptable in the labor relations game.

In a consequential way, the PATCO strike created the environment that permitted Continental to file for bankruptcy. What is more significant are the recent events [in late 1983] at Greyhound. Imagine calling the union representative in and saying, "You take a 9½ percent wage cut, and if you do not take it in a week we are going to replace you." Furthermore, Greyhound is a company that has been unionized for decades. Such a challenge to an established union would have been unthinkable a few years ago. The Continental bankruptcy issue, the Greyhound showdown, and a range of other episodes are efforts to redefine the current limits of acceptable behavior. This redefinition process is a legal, managerial, tactical and, if you will, moral issue.

IMPACTS ON U.S. LABOR RELATIONS

Shrinking Unionism

The question is, how have these changes affected the three basic elements of the labor relations system that I outlined earlier? Unions will not disappear or decline to insignificance, but they are clearly defending a shrinking perimeter. Their membership has fallen from a peak of 28 percent of the labor force to 20 percent as of two years ago, and membership to about 18 percent today. They have failed to keep pace with the growth of the labor force in areas such as health services and microelectronics. In addition, unions are now losing membership in sections of former strength through the development of what I characterize as the "neo-open shop movement."

Who would have thought that a major automobile producer could come into an industrial metropolis such as Smyrna, Tennessee, set up a major assembly operation, and then keep it non-union! If that is not enough proof of declining unionization, look at the Honda situation in Marysville, Ohio, an area that was a union stronghold for thirty years. Several key industries have moved from the presumption of unionization to an emphasis on maintaining a non-union edge—even in market sectors such as the construction of utilities and in coalmining. We have seen the last national emergency strike, under Taft-Hartley Act or otherwise, in the bituminous coal industry. The United Mine Workers' perimeter is circumscribed by Pennsylvania, Kentucky, and West Virginia, but most of the strip-mining is taking place in the West.

Breakdown of Formula Bargaining

Secondly, the formula approach to bargaining is clearly losing ground. There has been a sharp deflation in union wage gains beyond any reasonable expectations, a deflation which has been associated with moving away from the formula approach. Look at the data. In 1981, wage gains in all major bargaining agreements averaged 9.6 percent. Four years ago, a self-respecting union leader would not dare come forward and say the union had a three-year agreement for anything less than 30 percent. But in the first nine months of 1983, wage gains averaged 1.7 percent. If interest rates had dropped from their peak as much as first-year wage increases have declined, they would be down to about 4 percent.

In one way or another, the AIF has been eroded and COLA clauses are being modified. Co-payment has been introduced into a wide array of benefit plans in order to deal with the "benefit creep" problem. Thus, the automatic features of wage adjustments are being altered dramatically.

The next step in the evolution of labor bargaining is the one where the bankruptcy issue comes in. Labor and management have altered the rules of the game with respect to the rate of wage increases, but in many industries that is not perceived as an adequate adaptation. The next step, in management's view, is rationalizing the wage structure.

For example, it is one thing for a firm in the meat-packing industry to declare a zero percent wage increase. But if that wage freeze leaves the firm with employees earning $12 an hour while a competitor such as the old Iowa Beef Company (now MBX) or a non-union city packer is paying only $6 or $7 an hour to its workers, then it is the competitor's wage rate that defines the adjustment which management will seek.

The use of bankruptcy law has taken place in these types of circumstances. The major issue in these cases has not been reducing the rate of increase in wage, but rationalizing the wage structure and labor costs in light of a new economic environment. That is the context in which Continental Airlines and Wilson Foods have attempted to make use of the bankruptcy law.

Fragmentation of Bargaining Structures

The third major change is the fragmentation of large bargaining structures. Indeed, in my judgment, this is probably the most important development in shifting from macro considerations to micro factors in wage determination. For instance, can Uniroyal, when talking to the rubber workers, make its own case or must it always deal within the shadow of Goodyear and Firestone?

The true test of this process of decentralization, the "World Series" for bargaining structures, will come next September when the automobile unions step to the plate at Ford and General Motors. During the last bargaining round, for the first time in 40 years, a pattern did not emerge in the automobile industry. The existence of a "dog which did not bark" was at least as significant as the wage freeze and the fringe reductions that were implemented. In dealing with the economic problems that beset them, it is essential that the companies attain greater individual discretion in bargaining outcomes.

PROSPECTS FOR THE FUTURE

Are these trends likely to change? John Dunlop, who is a respected authority in this area and a man of great judgment, basically views all this as a perturbation. Historical parallels can be made with changes in the hosiery industry outside Philadelphia in 1934 and other past episodes; that is one way you can look at current trends. Dan Mitchell at UCLA also takes this view. I do not think what is happening now is a perturbation. I believe the changes are durable and are likely to continue over the next five or ten years.

Several things are changing the current environment. The first of these is government policy. We certainly do not see consequential labor policies coming from President Reagan. As a matter of fact, the curious thing is that the Reagan Administration is the first administration of any party in 50 years not to have an explicit labor policy. Its labor policies are derived from other economic policies. What is happening in the airline and trucking industries comes from the Carter-Reagan policy toward deregulation. What happened in construction and autos, in a real sense, was a consequence of tight money, which dried up demand and put excruciating pressure on the bargainers. Even the most myopic manager has to realize that "the times, they are a-changing."

Even if there is a change in political parties in the White House and Congress in 1984, I do not think we will see a major change. Any President is unlikely to be enthusiastic about increasing a broad array of tariffs, or placing more limitations on employer discretion in plant shutdowns, or altering the array of economic forces that are producing these changes in labor-management relations.

Secondly, are we likely to get any relief from the labor market? In my judgment, the answer is no. Given current unemployment rates and the breakdown of immigration controls—which maintain sort of a permanent elasticity in the labor supply—we will not see a change that would result in a labor shortage and thus tip the labor-management balance of power.

And third, will some Mosaic leader emerge from the unions, as we saw in the 1930s? Is there lurking in some textile mill a prospective John or June Lewis, ready to lead labor out of the wilderness? I see no evidence that this will happen.

What we are more likely to see is the power of the American labor movement diminished at the bargaining table. Unions will then switch toward increased political action in closer accord with the European model. And indeed, in my opinion that is the significance of the bold step taken by Lane Kirkland of the AFL-CIO in having formal labor representation in the high councils of the Democratic Party as well as the early endorsement of political candidates.

Setting aside collective bargaining agreements via bankruptcy poses an interesting and challenging policy issue that will, in one way or another, be worked out. But its true significance can be seen as a tactic within a new and boldly changing strategic labor relations environment. In a tactical sense, I do not know whether filing for bankruptcy is better or worse than threatening to hire replacements or shutting down plants peremptorily. But, in fact, these methods are part of a new array of tactics in a game in which the parties are divesting themselves of previous virtue and trying to redefine the character of new, more difficult, and probably less generous relationships.

How TOP NONUNION COMPANIES MANAGE EMPLOYEES

Fred K. Foulkes

What is the primary advantage large corporations gain from operating without unions? Many might answer that the biggest advantage is lower costs for pay and benefits.

I would strenuously dispute that answer, however, on the basis of a study I recently carried out of 26 large corporations that are either predominantly or entirely nonunion. My study suggests that such companies benefit most from the flexibility they have to improve productivity in both the short and the long run.

I should add right away that these 26 companies were not chosen randomly. Rather, they were picked because they are respected leaders in their fields and, in many cases, are recognized for their innovative personnel policies. The corporations studied include Black & Decker, Eli Lilly, Gillette, Grumman, IBM, and Polaroid. (For details on the study, see the box on page 209.)

The experiences of these companies are especially instructive for companies without unions, because these experiences suggest that companies willing to take creative approaches to employee relations can improve productivity. The experiences are also potentially useful for unionized companies, since innovative approaches to employee relations are possible for them too.

Executives of the 26 companies studied believe they achieve higher productivity than they would if they were organized. Their companies, they say, have achieved a high degree of employee loyalty, a low rate of turnover and absenteeism, and a low degree of worker resistance to technological change. One of the companies studied, for example, enjoys a turnover rate of .5 percent monthly, considerably below the average for its industry. The annual turnover rate of another of the companies studied is 3 percent. A third company employs fewer people per dollar of sales than any other company in its industry. And a fourth has achieved such a reputation as an attractive place to work that it has its pick of job applicants—it receives an average of 8000 to 10,000 applications annually for its 500 nonexempt job openings.

Reprinted by permission of the Harvard Business Review. *"How Top Nonunion Companies Manage Employees" by Fred K. Foulkes, September–October 1981. Copyright © 1981 by the President and Fellows of Harvard College; all rights reserved.*

In the view of many of those interviewed, such benefits accrue from their freedom to experiment with employee relations plans, their opportunity to deal directly with workers, and the absence of an adversary relationship between employees and management.

Not surprisingly, the accomplishments of many of these companies cannot easily be copied or duplicated. My study revealed that strong top management concern for employees becomes institutionalized through implementation of various policies. Also important are the intangibles of leadership, personal example, and use of symbols. These companies' rich legacies and traditions affect their managers and employees profoundly.

My study disclosed a set of nine common attributes, policies, and attitudes among large nonunion companies against which the managers of nonunion as well as unionized corporations can measure the effectiveness of their own personnel practices.

1. A SENSE OF CARING

First and perhaps foremost, many of the founders of the nonunion companies in my sample held fiercely egalitarian views about treatment of employees. Today, many of the customary symbols of corporate rank and status are absent. In many of the companies, everyone from vice president to sweeper has access to the same parking spaces, receives identical medical benefits, and eats in the same cafeteria. Frequently, executive offices are Spartan or even nonexistent. Employees at all levels call each other by their first names.

Moreover, the salaries of some of the top-level executives are modest by *Fortune* "500" standards. Many of these companies eschew such perquisites as company cars and club memberships that symbolize a visible ruling class of management.

Top management's commitment to employees is demonstrated not only symbolically but also through certain policies and practices. Hewlett-Packard, for example, is committed to job security, innovative training programs, promotion from within through job posting, cash profit sharing, an attractive stock purchase plan, widely granted stock options, and flexible working hours.

In most cases, the founders articulated and put in writing top management's commitment to effective personnel practices when the companies were quite small:

- At IBM, Thomas Watson stated almost half a century ago the personnel principles that still govern the company; respect for the individual was and is one of those principles.
- Edwin Land, founder of Polaroid, spoke early in the corporation's life of Polaroid's objectives: "We have two basic aims. One is to make products that are genuinely new and useful to the public, products of the highest quality and at reasonable

cost. . . . The other is to give everyone working for the company a personal opportunity . . . to make his work here a fully rewarding and important part of his life."

- At the Eli Lilly Co., J. K. Lilly wrote in 1916 a *Report on the Subject of Employment* that still guides the company. He noted in part, "The employment function is so important to good organizations as well as right relations that the 'Hiring Office' should be looked upon as one of the most important departments of the Company."

- Some of Hewlett-Packard's corporate objectives with respect to employees are as follows: "To help HP people share in the company's success, which they make possible; to provide job security based on their performance; to recognize their individual achievements; and to help people gain a sense of personal satisfaction and accomplishment from their work."

What is important, of course, is the way Hewlett-Packard or any other similarly committed company achieves its objectives. While philosophy is important, it is action that counts.

2. CAREFULLY CONSIDERED SURROUNDINGS

Several situational factors are also important both in fostering an effective personnel program and in encouraging a climate of trust and confidence. These factors include, among others, plant location and size and the handling of "sensitive work" and particular employee groups.

Determining Location and Size. The companies I studied consider carefully effects on employees and the chances of remaining nonunion when they select sites for new plants. Among the criteria used by one company are the quality of the public schools and the proximity to a university—as well as the area's attitude toward unions.

A personnel vice president at another company reported why a certain city would not be a good place to construct a blue-collar, production-type plant: "That city is sixth among the top 50 cities in the United States in downtime due to strikes, jurisdictional disputes, and other, related union conflicts. Moreover, there are more EEO charges in that city than in all but two other major cities. It is third in the number of fair employment practice cases and unfair labor practice charges. The city has several militant and aggressive unions."

Not only do many of the companies carefully choose rural or suburban plant sites, but they frequently limit the size of their facilities—between 200 and 1,200 employees—to promote personal and responsive employee relations. In the words of one personnel director, "We like to keep our plants small. We don't want them to grow larger than 200 employees. Beyond that size, both management and personnel lose personal contact with the employee."

Taking Care with Traditionally Union Work.   Many of the companies studied are also careful about how they handle sensitive work—work that unionized employees often do. Some companies subcontract sensitive or strategic jobs. One company, for example, subcontracts its printing work, while many of its unionized competitors do their own printing. Sometimes sensitive jobs are done in-house but by the unionized employees of a sub-contractor.

The idea is to make an organizing drive less likely. If a company's own nonunion employees do sensitive work, management usually pays close attention to their working conditions and wages, attempting to ensure that their treatment is equal to or better than that of comparable unionized personnel.

3. HIGH PROFITS, FAST GROWTH, AND FAMILY TIES

Certain financial and ownership characteristics seem to have an important bearing on personnel policies. Most of the companies studied are profitable—some, extremely so. Many are high technology growth businesses, have dominant market positions, and are leaders in their industries. Growth enables them to offer many promotion opportunities, provide full employment, and make profit sharing pay off.

Another important company characteristic is close ties between ownership and management. Two of the companies in my sample are privately owned, and members of the founding family are still active in management. In several of the public companies, a significant percentage of the stock is owned by one or more families, whose members remain active in top management. Thus, management is pushed to endorse the ideals of the founders and owners.

I should emphasize that no company studied displays all these attributes. Nor are these factors a sine qua non for achieving the desired organizational climate. They can even get in the way. For instance, while rapid growth provides many promotion opportunities, it also sometimes leads to such problems as communication difficulties and cramped quarters.

4. EMPLOYMENT SECURITY

Many of these companies attempt to minimize workers' usual nagging uncertainty regarding future employment. Several of the companies use various techniques to ensure full or nearly full employment.

During its early years, for example, Hewlett-Packard rejected large government contracts that would have created huge fluctuations in work

load, forcing the company often to lay off and then rehire people. Moreover, during the 1970 recession, Hewlett-Packard cut everyone's pay and
work time to 10 percent for a six-month period rather than lay anybody off.
The pay cut applied to everyone, from chairman of the board to assembly-
line worker, as did the practice of not working every other Friday.

Other methods of weathering peaks and troughs in the work load include hiring freezes and the use of temporary or retired workers. This latter
method, of course, simply transfers unemployment from the permanent labor force to part-time and temporary workers. Some companies prefer to
devote periods of overstaffing to building up their inventories. Others encourage employees to take voluntary leaves of absence—thus guaranteeing
continued employment.

Permitting employees to bank their vacation time can also ensure
some flexibility in lean times. Work sharing is another way in which some
companies avoid or minimize layoffs. Some companies that experience sea-
sonal work loads hire their own retired or former workers during the peaks.

To some extent, one company's full-employment practice becomes its
subcontractors' unemployment problem. At one company studied, part of
the full-employment strategy is to use subcontractors to help absorb necessary production cutbacks. During tight periods, such subcontracting is
curtailed or eliminated.[1]

Costs of Full Employment

Although companies that provide employment security boast of the
flexibility gained from their nonunion status, they of course lose their option to lay workers off in response to changed business conditions.

The Exhibit catalogs the costs and benefits of avoiding layoffs. As it
indicates, the costs can be significant. Yet the benefits of employment security cannot be overestimated. Eliminating workers' fears about layoffs can
be a cornerstone of effective employee relations.

If layoffs become necessary nonetheless, management must implement a system that is perceived as equitable. The companies in my sample
that do not practice full employment rely nearly exclusively on the principle
of seniority. They also attempt, through a variety of means, to delay layoffs
and cushion their impact. Curiously, none of these companies uses a supplemental unemployment plan.

A point to remember about full-employment practices: they always require effectively coordinating manpower planning and business planning.
If a company has a policy of no layoffs, personnel people and line managers
must cooperate when formulating strategies.

---

[1]See Warren M. Lowry, "Two-Way Contracting," HBR May–June 1967, p. 131.

5. PROMOTION FROM WITHIN

A policy of promoting from within—accompanied by training, education, career counseling, and (frequently) job posting—is most attractive when a company's growth rate opens up many advancement opportunities. When computerized operations were expanded at one company, it chose to train current employees to be programmers instead of hiring qualified applicants. The training opportunities were simply posted, and interested employees who bid and passed the aptitude tests were trained to be computer programmers on company time and at company expense.

Like employment security, such efforts go a long way in building employee loyalty. Indeed, two-thirds of the companies in my sample have institutionalized the principle of promotion from within by routinely posting job openings. Some companies even provide plant workers extensive training and education so they can move into white-collar positions.

Promotion of insiders to good jobs gets attention from company employees. Up-from-the-ranks supervisors who have benefited from such a policy have reason to be loyal and enthusiastic. Indeed, their attitude may contribute to the higher rates of productivity that many of these companies claim.

Promotion from within also helps a company maintain a consistent philosophy as the organization grows larger. Homegrown managers know and respect the company's values and traditions. Unlike newcomers, veteran managers know many employees personally and are familiar with sev-

---

How the study was designed

The 26 companies in the study were defined as nonunion based on the fact that all or nearly all of their production and maintenance employees located in the United States were not members of any union. Twenty of the companies in the sample appear on the *Fortune* "500" list of industrials; and five other either privately owned or service companies had sales figures that would have qualified. Half of the companies studied had sales of $1 billion or more at the time of the study.

The companies each employ between 2200 and 150,000 people in the United States; 60 percent employ more than 10,000 in this country.

All but three of the companies are engaged in manufacturing, in a range of industries. The three remaining companies are service organizations. No banks or insurance companies were included in the study. Many of the companies studied enjoy leadership positions in their respective fields. The names of most of them are household words. But the names of most are anonymous as a condition for their cooperation in the original study.

This field study used the case-study interview approach. More than 500 key line managers—including chairmen, presidents, operating executives, lower-level management people, and personnel executives—were interviewed.

eral different jobs and operations. They also serve as excellent role models for employees wishing to follow in their tracks. But remember: extensive reliance on promotion from within requires reliable initial hiring practices and good career development programs.

6. INFLUENTIAL PERSONNEL DEPARTMENTS

Not only are the personnel departments of the companies studied usually extremely centralized, they also have access to and in many cases are part of top management. More than half of the personnel vice presidents I interviewed report directly to the presidents of their companies. At a few of these companies, the head of personnel is a member of the board of directors.

The personnel departments of the companies studied are well staffed. Many have at least one professional person per 100 employees. Many also devote much attention to training and encouraging personnel people. At one predominantly nonunion company, trainees in employee relations get experience in a union plant, a nonunion plant, and finally in a corporate staff assignment. One company employs a staff person whose sole function is to help plan the career paths of the company's personnel people.

One reason for the influence of the personnel departments at the companies I studied is that line managers' competence is measured partly in terms of employee relations. When a department manager is accountable for the results of an employee attitude survey or the number of complaints filed by his or her subordinates, the expert advice of the personnel department suddenly takes on relevance.

7. COMPETITIVE PAY AND BENEFITS

As might be expected, the 26 companies in my sample work hard to ensure that employees perceive their pay and benefits policies as equitable. All of them, therefore, compensate their employees at least as well as their unionized competitors do. The companies studied thus pay well by both industry and community standards. The nonunion companies watch carefully the union settlements of competitors.

Also, the nonunion businesses make careful and thorough attempts to communicate with workers about their pay increases and benefit improvements. Few of the companies studied will likely ever be vulnerable to a union drive on the basis of either benefits or pay.

These companies also give particular attention to making their benefits visible. One company, for example, presents an annual slide show at each local office comparing its benefits with those of its organized competitors. Black & Decker personnel and benefits professionals present all major benefit changes in group meetings. They not only tell managers and supervisors about the changes beforehand, but personnel staffers also provide them with answers to possible questions from employees.

Some nonunion companies argue that what might appear to be very generous provisions are highly cost effective. For instance, the medical facilities for employees at some companies seem lavish. Polaroid, for one, has on call its own orthopedists, dermatologists, and other specialists in company facilities. Polaroid managers argue that this is much less expensive than medical insurance payments. Furthermore, employees spend less time away from work when medical professionals come to them.

Many nonunion companies also place heavy emphasis on merit increases, which either substitute for or supplement across-the-board pay increases. According to its proponents, such pay systems can serve as an incentive and will encourage greater work effort.

In the same spirit, many of the companies studied pay blue-collar workers salaries instead of hourly wages. About half of the companies have no hourly employees at all. The practice of bestowing the status of a salary on blue-collar workers represents another attempt to eliminate the "we-they" distinction between management and labor or between office and plant personnel.

The allowances for illness or personal business included in salaries impart respect and responsibility to the worker that are absent when labor is rewarded strictly by the time clock. Besides being consistent with the principle of equal treatment, salary plans differentiate the employee in status from his or her friends at other companies in the same industry or community.

Other common forms of supplementary compensation include profit sharing, company-matched savings and investment plans, and employee stock purchase plans. Profit sharing and stock ownership can also help employees to identify with the company, motivate them to work for its success, and further their understanding of the economics of the business.

Such programs often distinguish large nonunion companies from comparable organized corporations in the eyes of employees. For example, unionized employees at AT&T and General Motors were allowed to participate in their companies' savings and investment plans only two years ago, long after workers in many of the 26 companies I studied were offered that perquisite.

8. MANAGEMENTS THAT LISTEN

The companies studied use a variety of mechanisms to learn employees' views on various matters. Attitude surveys "take the temperature" of the organization and expose developing employee concerns. Some companies regularly conduct "sensing sessions," or random interviews to understand employees' sentiments.

A number of these companies exclude supervisors from the upward communication process, so employees feel freer to speak out. For example, one company keeps its local managers out of its annual benefits presentations, which include a suggestion, complaint, and discussion session.

These managers now conduct their own regular meetings with employees, in turn excluding the foremen and supervisors. In this way, management believes, it can forestall serious labor problems on the local level. Supervisors are also encouraged by this system to resolve employee problems quickly, because they may fear higher-level investigations or complaints to higher management that reflect negatively on them.

Speak-out programs, which allow employees' anonymously written inquiries to be answered by management, are another common communication device. According to executives of companies that use speak-out programs, 5 percent to 10 percent of their employees submit a question at least once a year.

Like other communication programs, speak-outs can backfire if handled gracelessly. At one company, a hardworking technician wrote to inquire why parking at the plant was not on a first-come, first-served basis. This man arrived early every morning, parked his car, and then walked one-quarter of a mile across an empty management parking lot. His letter was answered by a low-level official, who suggested that managers have a divine right to convenient parking. The president of the company later learned of this gaffe, so now a top officer at each location reviews and signs the answers.

The dominant grievance procedure in the companies studied is the open-door policy. However, two companies have (and pay for) formal arbitration programs for certain grievances that can't be otherwise resolved. Two other corporations have appeals boards to which employees can take their grievances. One of the boards includes hourly employees and makes recommendations to the president. The other, which consists of managers, is a decision-making body.

Discussions with representatives of several nonunion companies have convinced me that open-door policies whose reviews and investigations are formal and rigorous can be effective. The office of the chairman of one company usually receives several hundred open-door complaints a year. Investigators working out of the chairman's office follow up on these complaints under an exacting timetable. Because managers usually settle in advance those cases in which the employee is obviously right, the cases that reach the chairman's office tend to be those in which management is right; thus, about three-fourths of the decisions support managers and about one-fourth back employees.

Top management's reactions to complaints demonstrate to lower-level

EXHIBIT.   Costs and Benefits of a Full-Employment Policy

Costs	*Benefits*
Extra payroll and payroll-related expenses:	Flexibility to reassign workers
• Training costs • Extra overtime because of reluctance to hire • Possible temporary red circle rates • Extra costs of any special early retirement plans	Productivity advantages because of high employee morale Greater acceptance of changes in methods and technology Lower unemployment insurance costs
Extra employment costs associated with extreme selectivity in hiring	Savings of training costs due to layoffs
Productivity losses associated with people assigned to different jobs	Favorable image in the community and recruiting advantages
Moving expenses	
Extra financial charges because of larger-than-necessary inventories	
Possible slower delivery schedule	
Possible slower rate of change in methods or technology due to need to avoid displacing permanent employees	

management and employees alike whether the higher echelons care about the way employees are treated. When top management wants the decisions to be fair and is willing to investigate and review lower-level decisions, its credibility is enhanced.

The principal value of the formal complaint procedure seems to be the encouragement it gives to managers and supervisors to resolve employee problems before they become formal complaints. Management in a nonunion environment should not expect a formal grievance procedure to be used frequently; nor should such a procedure be relied on as a primary feedback device.

However, in my view, a nonunion company today should not be without some kind of formal complaint procedure. This is especially so in today's environment because employees who feel discriminated against because of race, sex, or age or who think their work area is unsafe can take complaints to an outside agency for investigation. Wise executives prefer to respond to complaints through their own mechanisms rather than deal with requirements set by a government agency.

9. CAREFUL GROOMING OF MANAGERS

Managers in these companies know that effective management of people is an important part of their jobs. Many of the companies studied avoid bonuses that reward short-term performance. Instead, they emphasize long-term results, including successful employee relations. They use stock options or other incentives associated with longer-term company success.

Thus, the selection of managers is a carefully considered procedure. Some nonunion companies use a series of panel interviews to evaluate potential managers instead of the traditional process whereby the boss picks his or her favorite for a promotion. Other companies send managerial candidates to "assessment centers" for a series of rigorous and imaginative tests that assess their ability to identify priorities and subdue crises in the managerial ranks.

At the lower levels of the organization, considerable resources are devoted to supervisory training. The supervisors, after all, deal with employees on a day-to-day basis, while top management has only occasional contact with them.

As a consequence of such training and reward systems, managers at all levels are keenly aware of the importance of good employee relations. Results of surveys are viewed as indicators of managerial competence. In many companies, managers believed that a stigma would be attached to their careers if their units had union-organizing drives or major personnel problems.

"People who demonstrate that they can manage well within the ethic of the organization are promoted," said a general manager of one company. At another company, performance is evaluated in terms of both "competence" and "relationships."

Because top management's personnel concerns often focus on the lowest-level employees, the supervisor may have the most difficult role of all in these nonunion companies. In some cases, the preoccupation of the founder with the welfare and security of the hourly workers appears to have depreciated the role of the supervisors, who may feel less secure than those they supervise. If supervisors come to feel insecure and experience too much anxiety, of course, the long-run health of the organization can suffer. Some of the nonunion companies have therefore begun tracking the feelings of supervisors through attitude surveys and other means.

PRIDE AND PROFITS

The 26 companies studied clearly try to create a climate of cooperation between employees and management. However, skeptics may still wonder if the rewards of positive employee relations are financially significant. I noted at the beginning of this article that the top managers of many large nonunion companies have expressed the belief that they can justify their personnel policies as providing great economic incentive. However, it may be impossible to determine precisely by what amounts the personnel practices previously outlined actually alter the bottom line. It certainly is costly to hire your own doctors, conduct attitude surveys, train your own employees for promotion, and offer profit sharing.

But in the view of many of those interviewed, the freedom to experiment with employee relations plans, the opportunity to deal directly with employees, and the absence of adversary relationships between employees and management result in a more profitable enterprise in the long run. Many of the managers take obvious pride in their personnel philosophies and accomplishments and are convinced that their efforts contribute directly and positively to productivity and profits.

Thus, I would argue that, for a large company to remain nonunion, top management needs to be personally involved in personnel management and to constantly demonstrate to nonexempt workers and managers alike its interest and concern for employees.

DETERMINING TOTAL COMPENSATION: STRATEGIC ISSUES

Edward E. Lawler III

The financial rewards that employees receive from their organization can, and typically do, come in a wide array of forms. Probably the most visible forms are cash compensation and such fringe benefits as vacation pay, health insurance, retirement pay, and life insurance. Some organizations, however, go far beyond such typical fringe benefits. For example, dental insurance is gaining in popularity, as are legal insurance, vision insurance, and supplementary unemployment insurance. When combined, the cash and fringe benefits that an individual receives from an organization constitute his or her total compensation.

The amount of an individual's total compensation is important for several reasons. From the organization's point of view, it is a major cost. Depending upon the type of organization, it may range from 10 percent of the organization's total operating costs to well over 50 percent. In addition to being a critical cost factor, the total compensation awarded an individual can have an important influence on his or her behavior. The total rewards an individual receives, when compared with what the individual feels he or she should receive, determine satisfaction. In turn, satisfaction strongly determines turnover and, to a lesser extent, absenteeism and tardiness. Thus the amount of an individual's total compensation can have an important impact on the individual's behavior with respect to organizational membership. It does not, however, directly affect the individual's motivation to perform. Motivation is a function of the degree to which pay is tied to performance and is only indirectly influenced by how much an individual receives in total compensation.

From an individual's point of view, total compensation is an important determinant of lifestyle and of the kind of activities that one can engage in off the job. In addition, it can be an important determinant of social status and esteem in our society. To many people, compensation is more than just a given amount of money and benefits that can buy a certain set of goods and services; it means social respectability, power, and influence.

Determining what is an "appropriate" compensation level for an in-

Edward E. Lawler III, "Determining Total Compensation: Strategic Issues," Pay and Organization, © 1981, Addison-Wesley, Reading, Massachusetts. Pgs. 28–42. Reprinted with permission.

dividual is an extremely important, difficult, and value-laden issue, as is determining the appropriate "mix' of benefits and cash compensation. Both of these issues involve sophisticated technologies and are fields of expertise in their own right. . . .

[The present paper, however, is not concerned with these technological issues. Rather, it focuses on strategic choices that the organization must make regarding its total compensation program. Nine such strategic issues are considered.]

DEVELOPMENT
OF A COMPENSATION PHILOSOPHY

Many, but certainly not all, organizations develop a compensation philosophy. Having a compensation philosophy is not an absolute prerequisite to having an effective pay system but, in many cases, it can be a significant aid. Thus, an important strategic decision is whether to develop a compensation philosophy and, if the decision is made to develop one, what to include in it. In general, the best decision seems to be to develop one.

Having a well-developed compensation philosophy certainly does not guarantee an effective compensation system. However, it can help to articulate the purpose of the compensation system and give the people involved in the day-to-day administration of the system an anchor to which they can tie their decisions and practices. The latter is particularly important since it is very easy to lose sight of the purposes of a pay system when thousands of pay decisions have to be made day-to-day. A well-developed philosophy can also provide an important stability to the compensation practices of an organization. In turn, this can give the system the integrity and credibility that are so necessary if it is to be effective. For example, it is particularly difficult to get employees to accept the fact that their pay is based on their performance when this is not a consistently articulated matter of basic compensation philosophy. Another example of the advantages of well-developed philosophy is provided by what often happens in times of high inflation. Salaries typically do not keep up with inflation because organizations usually tie the amount of pay increases to changes in the compensation market rather than to inflation. This approach is always difficult for organizations to explain and justify, but it is easier when they have had a consistent well-articulated policy of meeting the market rather than meeting inflation. No generally accepted list exists of what should be included in an organization's compensation philosophy statement; however, the following list represents 10 major issues that can, and in most cases should, be included:

1. Goals of a Compensation System.   Pay systems should have a purpose. They represent a major expense and, as such, should produce some benefits. Possible benefits range from motivating performance to reinforcing a particular type of organizational climate.

2. Communication Policy.   All organizations have communication policies concerning their pay systems. Careful thought needs to be given to them since they have a significant impact on the effectiveness of a compensation system.

3. Decision-Making Approach to the Compensation Issue.   Pay decisions can be made in a number of different ways in organizations. It makes a difference how they are made, and this area needs to be part of any compensation philosophy.

4. Desired Market Position.   The determination of whether an organization intends to be a high, low, or average payer needs to be made, and it needs to be made as part of an overall strategic business plan that looks at what the organization is trying to accomplish and how it intends to accomplish it. In some cases, it probably makes sense for organizations to be high payers; in others, it does not. In any case, what is needed is a clear-cut statement of what is supposed to be accomplished and the role of compensation levels in accomplishing it. A good example of what can be said in this area is provided by IBM. For years they have stated that they intend to employ the best available people by being the highest paying firm in their industry. In contrast, another computer firm states that it wants to attract and retain qualified people by paying wages that compete with those paid by all others in their industry, except IBM.

5. Centralization and Decentralization in Compensation Policy Formation and Administration.   Large multilocation, multibusiness organizations face some very interesting issues in the area of centralization and decentralization. As will be discussed later, there are a multitude of possible strategies, but whichever one is chosen, it helps if a clearly stated philosophy exists.

6. Desired Mix between Benefits and Cash.   Organizations vary widely in how they allocate their compensation costs between cash and benefits. There is no right answer, except that it often helps if an organization makes its strategy known.

7. Role of Performance-Based Pay.   In the government, performance-based pay traditionally has not existed, while in industry it is often claimed to exist. It is important that its existence be part of the compensation philosophy if it is to have its desired effect.

8. Performance Appraisal. Most organizations do performance appraisals, but it often is unclear why they do them and what they are supposed to consist of. This confusion can be lessened if it is dealt with effectively in a compensation philosophy.

9. Fit of Compensation System with Management Philosophy of an Organization. Compensation systems can help reinforce and operationalize the overall management philosophy of an organization. For example, by rewarding performance, compensation systems can help build a motivating work climate. They are particularly likely to reinforce and complement the desired management philosophy when their relationship is clearly stated.

10. Approach to Change in Compensation Policy and Practice. Good compensation systems are always changing. This change can be managed in a number of different ways. It may be done through a participative process or through a top-down approach. A clear statement of philosophy can help whichever one is used to be more effective.

PROCESS VERSUS MECHANICS

An early strategic issue that should be faced when compensation decisions are being considered is the relative weight to be put on the process issues and the mechanistic issues involved. All too often, the major weight seems to go into the development of the correct mechanics for administering pay. The assumption seems to be made that if the right technology can be developed, the right answers will be found. The problem with this assumption is there are no objectively right answers to what an individual should be paid. People's reactions to their pay and their perceptions of what is fair are subjective. As a result, there is no such thing as an objectively right pay that will be accepted by everyone. Unfortunately, what is perceived to be right by one individual often is not perceived to be right by others. Hence, pay determination involves differing perceptions, values, and conflict.

Precisely because there is no objectively right pay level for people, factors like communication policy and participation in the design and administration of pay systems can have an important impact on people's perceptions of their pay and their behavioral reactions to the pay system. Considerable attention should be given to deciding how these issues will be handled when pay systems are being designed, implemented, and administered. There are a number of interesting alternatives in this area that deserve consideration. However, before any of these innovative alternatives can be considered, the organization needs to come to the decision that they are important, and to the realization that the answer to developing an effective pay system cannot be found solely in the latest, most sophisticated approach to job evaluation, salary surveys, or any other salary administration technique. It needs to accept that the answer can only be found by dealing appropriately with the process issues involved in compensation in conjunction with having an appropriate set of procedures, methods, and practices.

PAYING THE JOB
VERSUS PAYING THE PERSON

Almost all job evaluation systems are keyed to determining the total compensation levels for jobs. They typically use a scoring system to assign points to all the jobs in an organization. Points are usually based on such things as working conditions and the amount of responsibility the job involves. These points are then converted into pay scales. Characteristics of the person are used to make small adjustments in what an individual is paid. In many cases, this is a reasonable approach, but not always. In fact, many times it can be dysfunctional for the organization in several respects. It can lead to further bureaucratization of the organization, and it can decrease people's motivation to acquire new skills and abilities. For example, evaluation systems that measure amount of responsibility rather than the skills an individual has, often encourage individuals to seek management jobs, even though they lack skills in this area. For them it is often the only way they can advance to higher paying, more prestigious positions. Similarly, these systems can encourage individuals to try to acquire more subordinates and more resources, even though they do not need these in order to do their job effectively. This comes about because job evaluation systems are often based on the size of people's budgets and the number of people who report to them. Job evaluation systems are also a frequent cause of individuals resisting reorganization efforts, since reorganizations often result in some jobs being evaluated at a lower level.

The obvious alternative to basing total compensation levels on the job a person does is to base them on the skills and abilities the person has. This can have two potentially positive effects. It can lead to increased rewards for highly skilled individuals and for individuals who acquire new skills, even though they are not promoted. It can also help tie compensation levels more closely to the value the person has to the organization, rather than to the value of the person's job.

No one has suggested that person-based job evaluation systems should totally replace job-content-based evaluation systems. On the contrary, there is reason to believe that person-based systems are limited to their applicability. Nevertheless, they are proving to be useful in certain situations, and the decision to encourage them and allow them where appropriate is a key strategic issue in the design of compensation systems.

One place in organizations where person-based evaluation systems are clearly appropriate is in those staff groups where technical expertise, rather than managerial responsibility, is critical. The so-called technical ladders of some organizations recognize this fact. Unfortunately, the technical ladders are often only offered to research and development employees and are not offered to other technical specialists in the organization (e.g., accountants, organization development specialists, and lawyers). In addition, they do not extend high enough in total compensation to allow for meaningful career advancement unless the technical specialist enters management. Clearly, if these systems are to work, the organization needs to make the decision that high total compensation is possible through technical expertise.

Until recently, the idea of paying for the person rather than the job has not been implemented with production-level employees. However, in an attempt to improve traditional job evaluation plans, some organizations have introduced skill-based evaluation pay plans at this level. In these plans, people are paid according to what they *can* do, rather than what they actually do. Most of these plans pay individuals according to the number of jobs in the organization they can perform, and do not take into account the job the individuals are actually performing at a given time. This has the effect of focusing on the individual rather than the job, and it encourages individuals to learn new skills. At present, the skill evaluation approach has enjoyed limited acceptance. Procter and Gamble, General Foods, and TRW are among the organizations that have tried it in their plants. . . .

MEANS-END RELATIONSHIP

Because compensation is such an important aspect of work organizations, the compensation system is an important part of their very fabric. It is so connected with other issues in the organization that it can become the dominant tool in the management and control of organizational behavior. There is nothing wrong with this since compensation should be an important part of the way an organization is managed. However, a means-end displacement can take place such that decisions in the organization get made in order to help the compensation system work effectively, rather than the reverse. Another way of saying this is that an effective compensation system becomes the end state that is sought by some, rather than organizational effectiveness.

There are a number of symptoms that appear in organizations when the compensation system has become an end rather than a means. Typical symptoms include: (1) someone not being moved to a job, even if it makes sense on a number of criteria, because the move cannot be fit within the compensation system (often because the individual's present salary is too high); (2) reorganizations that are abandoned because of the impact they would have on the compensation system; (3) paying salaries that are way above or way below market, simply because the job evaluation system indicates that this is appropriate; and (4) designing job structures and job descriptions such that they will fit into an appropriate category in the job evaluation system, rather than because they make sense from a motivational or some other perspective.

Other symptoms of displacement include such things as the total number of points the job evaluation system yields becoming a status symbol in the organization, and the inability of an organization to respond to its external environment because it requires a change in the pay system or pay policy (Galbraith and Nathanson 1978). The latter can occur when an organization moves into a new industry and finds that its compensation policies do not fit the industry. Rather than adopting new policies, some organizations stick to their traditional approaches, only to find themselves noncompetitive. This seems to be particularly likely to happen when conservative companies (e.g., utilities) try to enter growth-oriented areas (e.g., oil exploration). Rather than adopt aggressive performance-based pay plans, they use their same old system in order to maintain consistency.

There is no magic formula for preventing the pay system from becoming an end rather a means. There is a strategic approach that can help, however. It involves the flexibility of the compensation system and its permanency. A means-end displacement is particularly likely to occur when a compensation system has been in place for a long period of time, and individuals have a particularly strong interest in seeing it maintained as it is. This suggests that at a strategic level, fairly frequent changes, adaptations, and updatings of the compensation system are needed, and that it should always be treated as a system that is open to change. It also suggests that as a matter of basic corporate philosophy the pay system should be identified as a tool that is supposed to produce certain outcomes. It should go on to point out that the pay system will be evaluated regularly on the degree to which it produces these outcomes (Lawler 1971). It should emphasize that the outcomes are things such as attraction, retention, and effective performance, rather than such pay system goals as internal equity and well-developed policies and procedures. Finally, it should stress that it needs to fit the environment in which the organization operates.

INTERNAL VERSUS EXTERNAL EQUITY

In any compensation system, individuals can compare their pay to people both inside and outside the organization. Similarly, an organization can place primary emphasis on its internal or external pay relationships; which it chooses is a key issue in any organization's compensation strategy and one that needs to be considered very carefully because it can influence turnover and job satisfaction.

In most cases, it makes sense to focus on external pay comparisons as the major criteria for determining total compensation levels. Both internal and external inequity have serious consequences for the organization. However, the consequences of external equity (e.g., turnover and absenteeism) are the most severe for the organization and are the ones that deserve primary attention. In practice, internal inequity often gets more than its fair share of attention because of its immediacy in the organization. Nevertheless, requests for internal transfers to better paying jobs are less painful than external transfers (turnover), and complaining is more tolerable than either overpaying people with respect to the external market, or losing them to higher paying jobs elsewhere.

Striving for *both* internal and external equity can create another kind of problem in the organization. It can lead to individuals being vastly overpaid in terms of the external market, simply because their internal job evaluation demands that they be paid comparably with highly paid people inside the organization. In this case, extra costs are incurred in order to maintain the system internally. Strategically, unless there is some particular need for internal equity to be exceptionally high, it would seem to be advisable for organizations to emphasize external pay comparisons.

SURVEYING THE RIGHT MARKETS

Establishing external equity demands good market data. The problem is that organizations often do not spend enough time determining what constitutes the correct market data for the many different types of jobs they have. The key is to gather market data on those jobs that the individuals whose jobs are being evaluated might move to. This is no simple task because people tend to make very different comparisons and have very different mobility opportunities. Depending upon the individuals and their level in the organization, it might be one of a very small number of jobs in a local community, or it might be a large number of jobs located all over the country, or even the world. The former is particularly likely to be true for lower skilled jobs, while the latter is likely to be true for management and technical specialist jobs.

One thing is certain: in most organizations there is no single set of organizations that can be surveyed that will constitute an appropriate market for all the jobs in the organization. What is typically needed is a set of surveys covering the range of jobs which exist. This suggests that, as a strategy, organizations should use a wide range of surveys and should be open to individuals bringing in surveying data that are relevant to their particular technical specialty. It also suggests that they may want to make the survey data they collect public within the organization so that such data can be understood and challenged. In other words, the suggestion is that the salary survey process be "demystified" and made subject to participation, due process, and open communication. The negative consequences of surveying the wrong market are obvious. In some cases, it can lead to overcompensation and, in others, it can lead to undercompensation and a resultant loss of people who are needed. Open discussion of the surveying process can help prevent this from happening. It may also help to disabuse some individuals of the view that "all those other companies are paying a lot more."

CENTRALIZATION
VERSUS DECENTRALIZATION

The compensation system, like most aspects of large organizations, can be designed, implemented, and administered on either a centralized or decentralized basis. Neither a centralized nor a decentralized approach to compensation is always the right one. However, there is reason to believe that more often than is optimal, organizations opt for a highly centralized approach to compensation administration. Centralized systems typically have standardized pay rates, standardized job evaluation systems, and standardized policies and procedures that cover the entire organization. The presumed advantages of this are ease of transfer of people from one part of the organization to another, internal equity, effective cost control, and a tidy consistency across the organization.

A centralized approach to compensation administration is usually quite appropriate in small organizations, and in large ones that are in a single business and in a single centralized location. Its advantages, however, are considerably less obvious in large organizations which operate in multiple businesses and multiple locations. In fact, a number of examples exist where this approach is highly dysfunctional in large complex organizations. It is dysfunctional because it effectively takes away the local autonomy that is needed to fit the compensation to the local market and to the kind of business that the organizations find themselves in.

An example of the kind of dysfunction that can appear is provided by a large regulated gas company that decided to go into the coal business. Rather than develop new compensation practices, it simply put into place the same pay rates, fringe benefit package, and pay policies that it had used in the regulated industry. This turned out to be a grievous mistake because of the totally different pay practices in the coal industry. The organization ended up considerably overpaying its coal employees. Another organization decided to go into the oil exploration business and found itself unable to compete for engineers because it lacked any incentive pay provisions in its pay policy. They were not common in its previous industry, but they are quite common in petroleum exploration. Finally, the organization ended up changing its corporate pay policy to allow for this since it found that it simply could not operate in the oil business without this change in philosophy.

A centralized pay philosophy also has severe implications for the amount of employee participation that is possible at different locations in an organization. As will be discussed in the next chapter, it can mean that people will not have as much information about the pay system and will not feel as committed to making it operate because they have not had a hand in developing it.

Another way of describing the choice between a centralized and a decentralized approach is to say that it is a choice between a differentiated approach to compensation systems which allows parts of an organization to design a system that fits the business they are in, and an internally consistent one that treats everybody in the organization the same way. The choice between these two approaches is an important one for organizations, and one that is not to be taken lightly. Each one has its unique advantages and disadvantages. The effectiveness of the different approaches is determined by the environment in which the organization operates and by the business strategy of the organization. For example, the decentralized, differentiated approach seems to be advisable in large organizations that are in multiple businesses and that operate in multiple locations.

ROLE OF PERFORMANCE IN DETERMINING TOTAL COMPENSATION

Performance does not have to play a role in determining an individual's total compensation. In many organizations it in fact plays a very minor role. This comes about either because performance is not used to determine pay changes or because the only thing that is determined by performance is an individual's raise and the variance between the best and the worst performer is so small as to be insignificant. The result is that performance has a minimum impact on total compensation. Much more important is seniority.

In some cases, not relating pay to performance is best, but it eliminates pay as a motivator and can lead to a number of severe problems. Most important of these is the underpayment of outstanding performers and the overpayment of poor performers. This comes about because poor performers and good performers are paid about the same. This puts poor performers in a relatively favorable situation because if they were paid according to performance they would receive a much lower pay; and, indeed, they are probably paid more than they could receive in the outside market. In the case of good performers, just the opposite is true. They are paid less than

what is perceived to be fair by them since they feel that their high performance warrants high pay. In addition, they are also likely to be paid less than
the outside market is willing to pay. The result is predictable: turnover of
the good performers. The poor performer, of course, is hardly motivated to
leave and is likely to be locked into the organization permanently because
of his or her relatively high level of compensation.

Not paying for performance can also have an impact on who is attracted to the organization. There is some reason to believe that individuals
who are highly motivated toward achievement and accomplishment tend
to stay away from those organizations that do not reward performance. For
them, it is a comparative disadvantage to be in a system that does not reward achievement and accomplishment. Overall, then, it appears that
whether performance has a key impact on total compensation is a very important strategic issue in organizations.

COMPENSATION MIX

Organizations vary widely in the percentage of their total compensation
costs that are allocated to cash and fringe benefits. Some organizations operate strictly on a cash basis, while others have more than 40 percent of their
total compensation costs in benefits. Unfortunately, no matter what is done
with respect to benefits, it is often less than optimal for a number of people.
There are large individual differences in people's preferences for benefits
and cash. Some people prefer cash while others prefer benefits. Among
those who prefer benefits, important differences also tend to exist as to
what benefits are preferred. One approach to solving this problem is cafeteria compensation. It gives individuals a choice in how they receive their
compensation. In the absence of the ability to give people choices, organizations that have high benefit costs often end up spending money that is
not appreciated by the recipients. Thus, they end up spending more than
organizations with low benefit costs, but they may not end up getting a
good return on their additional expenditures.

It is also difficult to vary benefits according to performance. As a result, money which might be used to motivate good performance is lost as
far as this purpose is concerned. All this suggests that, in most situations,
it is better to put money into cash than into benefits. Still, a situational analysis is required before the decision to emphasize cash should be made. Such
things as the nature of the work force, tax laws, and the existence of a unionized work force can tip the scales in favor of an emphasis on benefits.
For example, in a situation where the white-collar work force is relatively
homogeneous, and where the production workers have a union contract
that is heavy with benefits, it often makes sense to provide a strong benefit
package in those areas where the tax laws encourage it. In this situation, the

benefits are likely to be appreciated by most and may have more value than their taxable cash equivalents.

SUMMARY AND CONCLUSIONS

The compensation system of any organization is composed of many strategic decisions. We have reviewed nine of them and have examined some of the options that are available with respect to each of them. In the discussion of each, it was pointed out that in no case is there a simple approach that will work for all organizations. Each organization needs to design its own compensation system to fit its own situation.

Maximizing ROI Through Effective Executive Compensation

Graef S. Crystal

As we all know, in the last few years the country has gone through the wringer. We have lost a great deal of our international competitiveness; we have lost thousands of jobs; we have seen profits drop tremendously; we have witnessed and continue to witness companies going bankrupt. We are told that the economy is recovering, but I'm not sure we can call it a recovery yet. We still have an unemployment rate hovering around nine percent and a $100-billion-a-year trade deficit.

You can't lay all the problems we have experienced at the door of executive compensation, but there's no question in my mind that had we done things differently over the last decade, we would not have as many problems as we do. I'd like to give you my thoughts on how things might be done in the world of executive compensation and, as the speech title suggests, discuss maximizing the return on investment through effective executive compensation. The subtitle of this speech is, of course, "Give Greed a Chance to Work." Greed, by the way, is an ancient motive. People my age know it even outlasts lust.

First, let's look at how we measure pay competitiveness. We rush out to the CEO with presentations containing nice graphs that show sales volume on a horizontal axis, pay on a vertical axis and trendlines with little dots clustered around them that indicate where jobholders in particular companies are located. If an executive's dot lies two inches north of the trendline, everybody automatically assumes that person is overpaid. But we trip over that word; so, we don't say overpaid, but highly paid—nevertheless, the implication is there. Anybody who is above the trendline is overpaid; anybody below the trendline, underpaid.

Thus, we invite perpetuation of a bureaucratic mentality for which the prime objective is not to improve profits but to increase sales volume as well as the number and level of employees under your supervision. We measure these things all the time through various regression analyses to test pay competitiveness. If given the choice, however, shareholders might pick other measures. Why, for example, can't we look at company performance

Graef S. Crystal, "Maximizing RIO through Effective Executive Compensation," *American Compensation Association*, 1983 Conference Proceedings. *Reprinted with permission.*

in measuring pay competitiveness, at least for compensation elements other than base salary?

Second, I think we need to reexamine the concept of industry pay differentials. Shortly after World War II, pay differentials among industries began to narrow because of the belief, fostered by executive recruiters, that a good manager could manage anything. The recruiters acted like bees pollinating flowers. They brought the news to executives who then used their own bodies, if you will, to arbitrage away industry pay differentials.

There were a few notable exceptions. The entertainment industry, for example, always marches to the beat of a different drummer and the banking industry, until recently, had its own slow cadence. Then in 1981 and 1982 we were faced with what is called the recession. But the impact was uneven. For many industries it was an outright depression, one that they still face. For others, it was business as usual.

I was reminded of this forcefully a year or so ago when I was doing some work for Alcoa in Pittsburgh. I don't think they will mind my telling the story; the facts have appeared in all the newspapers. I was sitting in Alcoa's offices and I looked out the window at the U.S. Steel building across the street. I noted that another client, the H.J. Heinz Company, was located on the sixtieth floor of the U.S. Steel building. I began to think about Alcoa and Heinz.

Heinz that year had approved a merit increase budget of about nine percent. Alcoa, on the other hand, was initiating a second pay freeze. Heinz had paid record bonuses; its profits were up 16 percent over the preceding year, and that constituted its fifteenth consecutive advance of that magnitude. Alcoa's profits had declined rapidly and showed no signs of turning around for a long time. There were no bonuses and little hope of any for many years.

Prior to the recession, the companies had similar philosophies, practices and pay packages. Now one wonders how many years it will take Alcoa to return to full pay competitiveness. Will there ever be a year good enough to allow companies like Alcoa or U.S. Steel to raise their executive pay 50 or 75 percent in order to bring it up to that of other sectors of the economy?

Yet there are many who still claim that equity demands that executives be paid the same for the same amount of responsibilities regardless of industry. But won't a low performing company damage the business further by paying too much? And, if a high performing company pays only the equivalent of a national average, won't it lose talent over a period of time?

In effect, can a motion picture company afford to pay someone only $300 thousand if it can make $100 million on a single picture? In the motion picture industry, people think nothing of asking for ten percent of the profits; that would be $10 million on a $100-million film. But Eastern Airlines or

U.S. Steel, both of which are hemorrhaging money so badly that they may have to ask the courts for relief, can hardly afford to pay $300 thousand to an executive.

So, with the return of industry differentials the free market again is at work, and we have to live with it. Those companies that tried to insure themselves against economic ups and downs by acquiring different types of companies and different types of businesses, in particular, will have to learn how to operate in a world of differentials.

There are two diametrically opposing approaches companies have taken. One client, for example, has taken the position that pay levels should be set by each market. Management couldn't care less if an executive in one division is paid $1 million a year while someone in another division receives $150,000. Its basic concern is being competitive in the appropriate market, not in internal equity.

Another client has taken a different approach. It, too, is engaged in multiple markets, but it sort of averages its pay across markets. This worked well when one industry did not differ much from another. Now the company finds that one market pays, for example, 85 to 100 percent more than another. It will be difficult for the company to continue its average approach without losing talent in its high-paying industry or without putting heavier cost pressures on those industries that are in trouble.

Ironically, both companies face internal equity problems. In the first company, it's as if all the wagons are in a circle and the divisions are, in effect, firing out at their competitors. In the second company, the wagons are still there but the people are firing in at each other because they do not want to lose their share of the corporate pie. I believe the cherished notion of internal equity probably has to give way to economic reality in most companies for years to come. If a company is in vastly different businesses in vastly different pay markets, the averaging approach will not work.

Another point: Obviously we've got to get the merit back into merit increases. I was reminded of that recently while looking at a client's grid— a very sophisticated grid where merit increases were a function of both position in the range, which increased eight percent a year, and performance level. Just for the fun of it, I said, "Suppose we slotted someone who was considered outstanding at the minimum of the range. How many years will it take for that person to reach the maximum of the range?" The answer was 17 years. That seems like an awfully long time for an outstanding performer to get to the top of the range.

That kind of system probably didn't do any harm when the economy was expanding at such a rapid clip that the real payoff in a corporation was promotion. And, if you missed one promotion, another opportunity came along quickly. But, we don't have that anymore. Companies are stagnating. And if you miss a promotion, you may have to wait a long time for another opportunity.

Many companies are again focusing on pay for performance. For an outstanding performer, the only way to get ahead, given, say, a five-year wait for promotion, is to advance rapidly through the range. But companies will have to put their money where their mouths are. It seems to me that it's not unreasonable for an outstanding performer to reach the maximum of the range within two years. And if that takes 30-percent-a-year increases, so be it.

There's another area about which I have some emotional feelings now and again. I was reading a book the other day called *The Third Deadly Sin*. It's about a retired Chief Inspector of the New York City Police Department, whose name was Edward X. Delaney. In this particular part of the book, Delaney and his wife, Monica, were entertaining a friend named Rebecca. " 'Tell me, Chief,' Rebecca said in her ingenuous way, 'what do you really think of the women's movement?' Delaney kept his eyes resolutely averted from Monica and addressed his remarks directly to Rebecca. 'What do I really think?' he repeated. 'Well, I have no quarrel with most of the aims.' 'I know,' she said, sighing resignedly, 'equal pay for equal work.' 'No, no,' he said quickly, 'Monica has taught me better than that; equal pay for comparable worth.' "

Well, if you begin to read about comparable worth in a popular novel, then perhaps the idea's time has really come. Sure, I can write snotty articles about the comparable worth of Beethoven and Aristotle, but it is time for me to recant, at least partly. If you want to get "intellectual," how can you really compare Beethoven and Aristotle and how can you really compare a nurse and a machinist? But those are *reductio ad absurdum*-type arguments. The real issue is not comparing nurses and machinists; it's comparing occupations that really aren't too difficult to compare. This is a piece of unfinished business that people in compensation have to work on in a more positive way.

In the area of short-term incentives, a lot of unfinished business remains to be accomplished. Let's assume that back in the '50s you had $1 million to invest. You could have invested it in Treasury bills, with an annual return of three percent. So, you would have had a $30,000 pretax return, in a noninflationary environment. Alternatively, you could put the $1 million into a business. But, you would have reasoned that unless that business could earn more than a three percent aftertax return on its equity, there would be no point in going into the business.

That sort of reasoning led a lot of companies to introduce so-called thresholds in their bonus plans. They said to executives, "Unless we have a substantial return on equity, we are not going to pay any bonuses." In the '50s, the typical threshold was six percent; return on equity had to reach six percent after taxes before any money was diverted to executive short-term incentive awards. That was three full points above the so-called riskless return rate—the Treasury rate. Indeed, it was about two-thirds of the nine percent return on equity that the typical company was achieving in those days. So, it was a fairly gutsy threshold.

If you reason the same way today, you'd be dealing with about a nine percent riskless return rate. If you want a three-point cushion, then you need at least a 12 percent aftertax return on equity before diverting any money to executives. But, interestingly, if you analyze current bonus plans, you find the thresholds are still six percent. Companies have basically kept their plans the same since the '50s. Today, with inflation (and we still have inflation), if a company consistently achieves only a six percent aftertax return on equity, it heads right into bankruptcy.

Moreover, in the '50s, a company that had a six percent threshold might have said that it would, say, divert ten percent of the profits above the threshold to a bonus fund. But remember, inflation swells the profit figures. And even without inflation, the number of eligible executives does not grow at the same rate as profits do. In fact, if the number of executives grew correspondingly, the profits couldn't grow by that percentage because of increased overhead. So, because the number of eligibles grows more slowly than profits, in theory you don't need a full ten percent of the excess to fund the bonus.

Yet I know of only one company that ever cut back on its formula. That was General Motors. On two different occasions GM asked its shareholders to approve decreases in the bonus funding formula. Ironically, both times six percent of the shareholders voted against the resolution. I guess that six percent would vote against anything that management proposed, even cutting the bonus plan.

But GM was the exception. Many more companies have ended up with slushy funding formulas. The formulas generate too much money early in the profit stream; they carve out too much of the profit incrementally, and they create bloated funds. Then, interestingly, because the fund becomes so large, the money isn't all spent in a year and the excess is carried forward.

Let's say a company generates $60 million of bonus money and spends only $30 million of it. The following year profits drop. Someone says, "Gee, we're not going to pay bonuses." And someone else retorts, "We can pay $40 million worth of bonuses this year, because, although the fund has dropped, we spent only half of it last year." The theory was, if you recall, that as profits increased, the leverage nature of these incentive funds would cause executives' bonuses to increase at an even faster rate. So, if the profits went up ten percent, the bonuses would go up 20 percent. The same applied in reverse—if the profits dropped ten percent, the bonuses would drop 20 percent. But, in fact, that hasn't happened.

Now we find that with a ten percent increase in profits, the bonus fund goes up three percent. With a ten percent decrease in the profits, bonuses may drop three percent or they may not drop at all. They may go up two percent and someone will defend that by saying it is less of an increase than inflation and therefore the bonuses really went down. But they don't apply the same logic to the profits themselves, which are also affected by inflation.

Many companies are enamored of the concept of paying bonuses whether or not they make their budgets. That in itself is an interesting incentive game. If you budget a disaster and make it come true, you are showered with money. But, if you budget a triumph and fall a little short, then you take a savage beating. You don't make that mistake too many times. Other companies seem to be consciously trying not to use money to motivate. They have caps on their bonus plans; in fact, there are so many caps around that sometimes I think I am working as an orthodontist rather than as a compensation consultant.

Caps are insidious; they can cause all sorts of problems. In one major company, for example, the presence of caps caused a year's delay in the annual meeting because no one could trust the books. Management had told its divisions, "If you make budget, we'll give you 100 percent of our normal award. If you make 90 percent of budget, you will get only 80 percent of that award, and if you make 80 percent of budget, we won't give you any award at all. If you go above 100 percent of budget, to, say, 105 percent, we'll give you 120 percent of the normal award, but, once you get to 100 percent, we'll cap it. You get 120 percent and no more."

Toward the end of the year, several division managers asked the controller what sort of year they were having. They were told that the company would close the year at 150 percent of budget. And the division managers said, "My God, we can't do that. If we do, three terrible things will happen. First, those guys at puzzle palace will think we've been sand-bagging on the budget all these years because the only way you make 150 percent of budget is if the budget was wrong. Second, we won't get any money above the 110 percent of budget and, third, we will probably get an even higher budget next year, which will be hard to make."

So they decided to have their advertising agencies bill them now for the next five years' worth of advertising. And they asked anybody else they could find to bill them now. The aim was to drive down the profits to just below 100 percent. Actually, incentive compensation did work in this case; behavior was modified by the incentive.

Of course, the audit committee of the board was not amused. It had to delay the annual meeting for a year because nobody knew what the company's profits were. This all shows that caps usually have one of two effects—if they are too low, they cause people to behave in crazy ways to the detriment of the enterprise and the shareholders. If they are too high, they don't mean a thing; they are just cosmetic.

Another issue involves what I term divisionalization. Many incentive plans pay on the basis of corporate performance, even though the company is highly decentralized and highly divisionalized. I submit that if you want to make greed work for you, you need to offer division-level incentives that are funded in advance and are independent of the corporation. Then people who work in a division will have the opportunity to make a good deal of money if they produce a good deal of performance.

Of course, you have to struggle with the issue of whether a division is truly a discrete profit center. It seems to me that a candidate for a divisionalized incentive plan is a unit that could be spun off tomorrow and still retain its heart and its kidneys. It might be missing a few fingernails, which regrow easily. But, it would have its vital organs, its ability to live as an independent economic entity. It would not have significant transfer pricing problems; it would have little or no exchange of people or of R&D. If a division has those attributes, management should seriously consider setting up separate incentive plans to get people to maximize the return on investment in the division itself and, hence, in the corporation.

True, in many companies there are no real divisions, they're only on paper. Some years ago, the Chrysler people told me a great story that illustrates this. Chrysler had a consulting firm do an organization study because the company, even then, was experiencing profit problems. The consultants looked at Chrysler's functional form of organization. There was a Vice President of Manufacturing with some 270,000 workers under him and a Vice President of Marketing with some 30,000 salesmen. The consultants recommended divisionalization but, try as they might, they couldn't come up with any real divisions. So they renamed the functions. The Manufacturing Department became the Manufacturing Division and the Marketing Department became the Marketing Division.

They instituted a transfer pricing process, whereby the Manufacturing Division "sold" cars at an agreed-on price to the Marketing Division. That price then became the Manufacturing Division's revenues and the Marketing Division's cost. The Marketing Division, in turn, sold the cars to the dealers. After a couple of years, Chrysler executives discovered that the Manufacturing Division was earning hundreds of millions of dollars in profits and the Marketing Division was losing its shirt.

They called a crisis meeting. One of the vice presidents announced, "Gentlemen, I've been looking over these numbers and you can see at a glance that we have a magnificent, indeed, uncanny ability to manufacture our cars. But we do seem to have some trouble selling them. What it tells me is that we should make the cars and not sell them. We have huge parking lots around each plant, so why don't we just make the cars and leave them in parking lots. At a stroke, we will cut all our losses."

Naturally, there was dead silence in the room. But this typifies the kind of games that are played with transfer pricing. And, of course, you would not want to divisionalize in those cases. By the way, that vice president is no longer with the company.

But surely where there are true divisions, there ought to be true incentives. I remember one division manager saying to me quite pointedly, "We are not dumb around here. We look at the risks and we look at the rewards. Suppose I make this tough decision to do something and it's a great success. What do I get for it? Maybe a 10 percent merit increase instead of the usual seven percent. Maybe I get a bonus that's 35 percent of salary instead of 30 percent. Maybe I'll even get promoted, but that's probably the least likely of all. There's an UP-side, but not much of one.

Now what is the DOWN-side? They could fire me. They could stifle my career. Obviously, the UP-side rewards are never equal to the DOWN-side penalties. So, we don't take risks around here."

The reward in many companies becomes very bureaucratic. Some years ago, Clark Kerr, who was then President of the University of California, was sacked by then Governor Reagan. In his farewell speech Kerr said to the assembled crowd, "You know when I became President of the University of California seven years ago, I was fired with enthusiasm. Today, seven years later, ironically, I find myself in the same position."

What then are we to do with these short-term incentive plans? I think we have to tighten the funding formulas and let bonuses swing with performance a great deal more than they do now. We have to divisionalize where it makes sense to divisionalize and reward people in a division that does well even if the corporation loses $50 million. Maybe the rewards won't be as great as they might have been if the corporation had also done well, but at least part of the social contract, if you will, is guaranteed. Above all, I think we should get rid of the caps and let money work.

Does it really matter if a group of executives make $100 million if the shareholders make $1 billion? What shareholder will object to that proposition? Yet compensation committees in many companies do not accept that reasoning. They scurry behind the safety of the average and become very uncomfortable anytime you talk about paying somebody above that trendline.

In a case about 20 years ago, the United States government brought a company to court in an effort to disallow some above-average executive compensation payments under defense contracts. The judge wrote an interesting opinion. He said, in effect, "I'm not a mathematician, but it seems to me, dimly, from my days of college math or even high school math, that if you have an average, then somebody must be paid more than the average for the numbers to work out right. If everybody is paid at or below the average, the average would not be the average. Therefore, how can you, the government, say that anybody who pays above the average is unreasonable? It is an absolutely illogical proposition."

The judge established the idea that you might even be the highest paying and still be paying reasonably. As I said, that is a proposition that compensation committees have trouble accepting. But if somebody has to be at the 100th percentile—and if your company is the highest performing company—then why not you?

Let me move on to the area of long-term incentives, an area that is constantly discussed in newspapers and magazines. A recent *Business Week* article, for example, reporting on Tandy Corporation said, "One problem with Tandy's bonus system is that the company employees often pay too much attention to short-term savings. At some Radio Shack Computer Centers . . . the response to soft sales this summer was to reduce sales staff."

The article goes on to decry that move, implying that if you sell sophisticated computer systems, you need staff to explain them to buyers. If you cut staff to cut costs, you hype current profits, and sow the seeds of long-term disaster.

What's it all about? Long-term incentives have changed over the years. For a long time, companies backed away from the price earnings multiple; they did a Pontius Pilate act over it: "It has nothing to do with us." Instead, they set internal performance targets, such as earnings per share growth. If the company didn't make the targets, then management set new, lower targets. Then they set still lower targets, if necessary. Finally when they couldn't clear a four-inch hurdle, they just gave up the targets altogether and started giving the money away.

In effect, we had companies giving huge grants of, say, restricted stock to executives who had only to breathe in and out 17 times a minute for five years while on the company's payroll. In other cases, companies were swayed by relative performance. You're in the steel industry, for example, and it's in terrible shape, but you performed no worse than the typical steel company. So that entitles you to a reward.

Of course, not all companies have lost their bearings and forgotten that money is supposed to reward, and that if we have poor performance, we have lower rewards. Unfortunately, some people get hurt in the process.

What should we do? I believe we have to continue to emphasize market price in long-term incentive plans because ultimately market price is a good arbiter of performance. The fact is that the stock market was right all those years. The reason price earnings multiples dropped was that real earnings were terrible, but the fact was masked by funny accounting. We need to adopt meaningful, not snap targets. We need to be willing not to pay anything for poor performance. We need to be willing to pay the moon for tremendous performance.

We need to divisionalize again. If you take the time, you can set up an artificial stock market price in a division. Or you can use other appropriate measures. You can even do the unthinkable—sell part of the division to executives. I throw out the thought. It may not work in a lot of companies but, then again, it may. Why not sell somewhat less than 20 percent of the stock to a group of executives in a division? Arrange it so when they leave the company or when they retire, they sell the shares back. Value the share at a book value if you can't find anything else. Give the executives an interest-free loan to pay for it, so they don't have any cash flow problems. It's an interesting thought because, if the division triumphs, the executive will make a lot of money; he might even become a millionaire. And if the division goes down the tubes, he'll lose lots of money, which is what entrepreneurs have done through the centuries.

Some years ago, a huge company came to me with a problem. They owned 60 percent of the stock of a computer software house. Twenty percent was publicly owned, and the other 20 percent was owned by five officers of the software company. So there was a public market for the stock. The company acted on the assumption that if owning 60 percent of something was wonderful, it would be much more wonderful to own 100 percent.

For starters, they were willing to offer the software executives an incentive to sell their shares. They asked me to design a plan that would give these executives the same sort of aftertax benefits, under roughly the same circumstances, that they would have received had they continued to own the shares.

That wasn't too hard to do. I designed a sort of phantom plan. When the chairman of the parent company saw it, he said, "Hey, these guys can make $3 million each off this plan." I said, "Yes, they could; that's what they're making now." Well, he didn't like that at all. He retorted, "That's more than what I earn." I felt like saying that, although he had made an interesting observation, it had nothing to do with the situation.

The point was that these people were earning a huge amount of money through the stock market mechanism, but it didn't show up on the company's books. So the chairman had not had to face the issue until now. The company decided to go ahead with the acquisition. They bought up all the shares but did not offer this replacement plan to the top people. Rather, they offered them a band-aid.

Within one year, the five executives had gone off and formed a separate software firm. The parent company had to write off its entire $50 million investment. Was it, in this case, worth owning everything? Was this not a case where you can do better by giving people a chance to make huge amounts of money by establishing a symbiotic relationship and letting them act like the entrepreneurs they are supposed to be? Most executives' idea of heaven, a compensation equivalent of heaven, is to have an unlimited opportunity.

So I repeat that there are good reasons for divisionalizing incentive plans in many companies. You may ask, what happens if you have a poor performing division and want to transfer someone into it? How do you get people to move if they are not going to get annual bonuses? Probably by using the same entrepreneurial principle that other companies do—give them a large opportunity. It's fraught with risks, but you are saying, in effect, "If the ship comes in, you become a multimillionaire. We can't give you much in the way of salary; we may not grant any bonuses for two or three years. But if you turn this place around, you can really 'make it.' "

As the lights were going out at Chrysler several years ago, I was asked what I thought the company executives might do. I replied, "They obviously can't do much in salaries; they will probably have to cut salaries. They can't do anything in bonuses; there are no more bonuses. The only thing I can suggest is that they plaster the walls with stock options." And that's what they did. I reasoned that if Chrysler turned around, people would get back the opportunity to make enough money to overcome the bad years. And if Chrysler went belly-up, it wouldn't make any difference.

Chrysler did turn around. Today, there are a lot of very satisfied people there. I doubt that many Chrysler executives would say they were underpaid in total over the last four or five years. They obviously had a somewhat uneven incidence of income, but they got theirs back. It worked! I wish I had bought some stock but I didn't have enough faith, and so one pays the penalty.

In addition, I think we need to pay more attention to the cost-effectiveness of incentives than we have in the past. Let's look carefully at the gimmicks that come out of the woodwork every few years promising to be the alchemist's compensation dream. The latest is junior stock.

Here's how it works: Assume the company stock is selling for $50 a share. You set up a plan to sell someone a different class of stock—junior stock. You get your investment banker to agree that the junior stock is worth only $5 a share. This is somewhat hard for an investment banker to do because, through the years, he has been educated to tout the company's shares and tell the chief executive that the shares are worth far more than they actually are.

Now investment bankers have to recycle themselves. But they are a hardy breed; they adapt quickly to change. You hedge the offer with all sorts of restrictions—certain profit goals, for example—and provide that, if these goals are met, then the person can convert the junior stock into an equal number of common shares.

Let's say an executive buys 1000 shares for $5 and gives the company a check for $5000. Over time, the goals are achieved and the shares become convertible. By now, the stock has moved up from $50 a share to $100. Here's your executive with a $95,000 profit, because he paid $5000 for shares that are now worth $100,000. That's a long-term capital gain, which you hope the IRS will sustain. If the IRS does, then the $95,000 gain is taxed at 20 percent, or $19,000, giving the executive $76,000 in income. The cost to the company was $95,000 because it sold property worth $100,000 for only

$5000. And the company received no tax deduction because it was a capital transaction.

The company could have avoided all that fiddling around and all those fees to the investment banker by granting an executive a non-qualified stock option. Let's say the company granted 1600 shares under a discounted option at $5 a share. That's 60 percent more shares than the junior stock plan offers. Assuming that the stock went to $100, the executive has the same $95 gain at exercise as he or she had on junior stock. The $95 gain times 1,600 shares comes to $152,000 in pretax income. At a 50 percent tax rate instead of a 20 percent tax rate, the end result is $76,000 in income.

That's the same amount that the individual would have received through the junior stock plan. The aftertax cost to the company, however, is about 14 percent lower because the company can take a 46 percent tax deduction. The company pays out more, but the government pays a hefty piece of the cost. When a company loses its 46-point tax advantage (or its tax deduction), who gets the 46 points? The executive gets only 30 of the 46 points. That's the difference between the 20 percent long-term capital gains rate and the 50 percent ordinary rate. Who gets the other 16 points? If you analyze the transaction, you find the 16 points go to the IRS.

It seems to me that the IRS, rather than hassling companies on junior stock, ought to buy spots on prime-time TV to advertise it. It's a great money-raiser for the United States Treasury. But we all reason in funny ways. If it's someone else's cost, and your benefit, then it is that much more appealing to you. You don't worry about the company side. All you look at is the fact that you save 30 points of tax.

We also have to pay less attention to accounting costs. I'm not going to get into the details of how accounting works, but there are too many senior executives around this country who will look you right in the eye and say, "If there is no charge to the earnings, there is no cost." So, they see a stock option plan as a cost-free device.

There is always a cost. Any time a company gives someone an economic benefit of $100,000, there is a cost of $100,000 minus the tax deduction. If the accountants don't want you to put it in the income statement, they say you don't have to charge it. But it has to show up somewhere at some time. You are going to see a reduction in shareholder equity or a drain in cash or an increase in the number of shares outstanding or something. Yet the accountants play all these games, alleging that the tax or accounting consequences of some types of compensation are different from those of others. They, thereby, send out signals to people to conform their thinking to accounting consequences.

To my mind, that's the wrong way to go about things. You should design plans that make motivational sense—and to hell with the accountants. Even now, the Financial Accounting Standards Board is being confronted with demands for change. In fact, a Board-appointed Task Force has recommended changing current accounting practices for stock options and requiring everyone to take a charge to earnings, just as if there were a stock appreciation right attached to every stock option. If that happens, we will at least get back to a point where we have to recognize that there is a cost. Then we can decide whether the cost makes sense.

Finally, it should go without saying, perquisites ought to be downplayed if you want to maximize return on investment. Fortunately, we don't have the tremendous number of perquisites that they do in Britain and some other countries. Probably U.S. companies could offer even fewer perks than they do now with no ill effects. If you are really going for return on investment, for maximizing profits over the long term, many of these fancy perquisites just don't make sense. And they tend to turn people off.

In summary, we need to bring executive compensation back to its original goal. The original goal—as I see it—was to set up plans that replicate ownership through incentives for professional managers; to give these hired guns a chance to participate in the profits as if they were owners. Thus their interests and those of the shareholders would be inexorably tied together, and the executives would do those things that, over the long run, made the shareholders and themselves very wealthy. That means we have to inject more risk into incentive compensation plans than we have in the past. We have to accept the fact that pay should go down sometimes. At the same time, we need to offer limitless reward and the chance to become multimillionaires.

As I said at the beginning, the subtitle of this speech is, "Give Greed a Chance to Work." That's the ending, too. I implore you, I beg you, give greed a chance to work.

LONG-TERM INCENTIVES FOR MANAGEMENT, PART 1: AN OVERVIEW

Frederic W. Cook

For years, the predominant form of long-term incentive award for corporate executives was stock options. This was because certain now-defunct tax benefits and high tax rates on current income made tax-qualified stock options the only viable alternative. Whether "restricted" as before 1964 or "qualified" as after, tax laws virtually governed plan design.

Just when compensation planners were secure in the knowledge that stock options were a stable element in managerial compensation programs, Congress slowly but surely erased the special tax advantages of qualified options and reduced high marginal tax rates on ordinary income, creating a situation in which tax considerations no longer dictated plan design.

To complicate matters, outside forces started to erode the incentive value of stock options. Inflation, high interest rates, and depressed price/earnings (P/E) ratios suddenly revealed the weaknesses of stock options that, though they had existed all along, had been masked by tax considerations. The result: a burst of creative energy in compensation planning that has led to a wide variety of alternative longer-term incentive vehicles available and in use. And the design challenges are not yet over.

The basic *raison d'être* for this new crop of plans, as for the time-honored stock options, is to motivate and reward management for the corporation's long-term growth and prosperity and to balance the short-term earnings orientation of annual incentives or bonuses. As such, long-term incentives are one of the five major elements of pay in a soundly designed total compensation plan for management-level personnel. (See Figure 1).

THE ALTERNATIVES AVAILABLE

This article is the first in a series that will explore long-term plan alternatives in detail. Stock options, which have by no means been put to rest, and several other new devices will be examined—namely, stock option/stock ap-

Frederic W. Cook, "Long-Term Incentives for Management, Part 1: An Overview," reprinted, by permission of the publisher, from Compensation Review, *Second Quarter, 1980, © 1980 by AMACOM, a division of American Management Associations, New York. All rights reserved.*

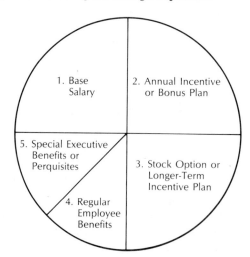

FIGURE 1.   A Balanced Management Compensation Package

preciation rights (SAR) plans, stock purchase plans, restricted stock plans, formula-value plans, performance share/unit plans, and combination market/performance plans. In this article, we will help set the stage for those that follow by covering:

- The longer-term incentive alternatives available
- The alternatives top industrials are adopting and trends in the offing
- The significance of currently available alternatives in terms of an executive's total compensation
- The challenges and opportunities presented by these alternatives

A rose may be a rose but a long-term incentive may be many things. Just how many forms it will eventually take is anybody's guess—but a look at the major plan alternatives that have emerged so far shows the level of diversity involved. Definitions of six key long-term incentive alternatives are given in the box on page 248. Figure 2 shows how these plan alternatives relate to one another on the basis of what an executive can hope to gain from their application.

DEVELOPMENTS DURING 1979

A look at long-term incentive developments among the *Fortune* "Top 200" industrials is probably a good way to sight precursors of trends in this area. Among the Top 200 (as ranked by *Fortune*, May 7, 1979, with certain agri-

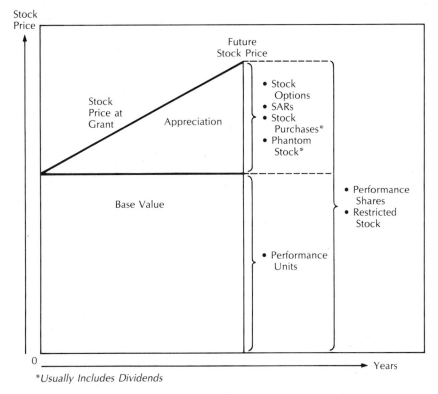

*Usually Includes Dividends

FIGURE 2.   The Gain to Executives under Different Long-Term Incentive Vehicles

cultural cooperatives and other companies excluded), 184 have some form of stock option or long-term incentive plan for their executives. Figure 3, which examines the major changes in plan categories in the Top 200 during 1979, shows that:

- 19 companies adopted SARs, bringing the total to 121 (60 percent)
- Nine companies added performance share or unit plans, increasing the total to 63 (32 percent)
- Five began restricted stock grant plans, leading to a total of 23 (12 percent)

A review of these firms' proxy statements revealed that 35 of the Top 200 companies made changes in their long-term incentive plans for executives during 1979; six dropped plans or plan alternatives, and 29 added plans or plan alternatives.

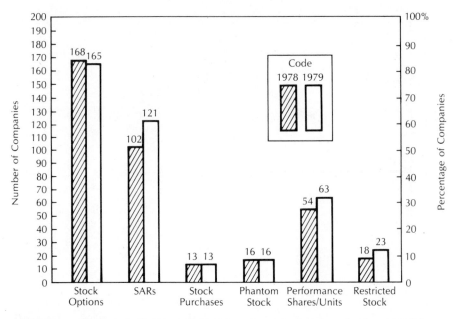

FIGURE 3.   Changes in the Use of Long-Term Incentives among the Top 200 U.S. Industrial Companies: 1979 vs. 1978

TRENDS IN PLAN DESIGN

Research has shown that large companies are moving away from stock options as their sole long-term incentive/stock ownership vehicle for executives. And in response to a number of factors, including economics, legislative action, and changes in management philosophy, other long-term incentives are beginning to share the stage with the stock option. In particular, there have been trends toward these types of plans:

- Plans that do not require executive investment
- Plans that relate all or part of the executive's reward to actual multiple-year company financial performance as opposed to stock price movements
- Multiple plans or combinations of plans that offer a more sophisticated and flexible incentive vehicle

Let's look at each trend more closely.

High interest rates, a desire by companies to limit executive risk, and the SEC's recognition of SARs in 1976 all helped put the first trend into motion. In 1979 alone, 27 of the Top 200 added plan alternatives whereby executives could realize a payment or reward without making an investment. The previously mentioned increase in SARs, performance share/unit plans, and restricted stock plans emphasize this trend toward noninvestment. The second trend—toward financial performance-based plans—was also strengthened in 1979 when nine of the Top 200 added performance share/ unit plans. As a result of the adoption of these plans, almost one out of every three of the largest U.S. industrials have performance-related long-term incentive plans. This is particularly interesting since these firms had no such plans in 1970.

Why has this trend emerged? Obvious answers are the volatile stock market and the depressed P/E ratios experienced in recent years. Both have made executives rethink the values of incentives, such as stock options, that are based on the premise that the market price for their company's shares will reflect earnings growth. A further reason is the desire by companies to provide direct incentives for executives to achieve strategic business objectives. This is an outgrowth of the management by objectives philosophy that gained many adherents in the '70s.

The third trend—toward multiple alternatives or combinations of alternatives—is supported by the fact that 54 of the Top 200 companies (27 percent) have available three or more categories of award alternatives. (Care should be exercised in interpreting this trend, however, since all the alternatives available to companies may not, in fact, be used—and different alternatives may be used for different levels of executives.) Companies have been moving in this direction for a number of reasons. Some want to be able to provide funds from one alternative—say, performance units—to help executives finance another alternative, such as stock options. Others want to give the company flexibility to shift incentive vehicles in response to changing company directions or economic conditions. Yet a third group wants to target particular mechanisms to meet specialized needs instead of applying them across the board (SARs, for example, would be used for officers subject to special SEC rules in buying and selling company stock, or restricted stock would be offered especially to attract and hold experienced executives and middle management).

These trends are not new; they have been evolving for a number of years. Most certainly, the adoption of certain plans by the top industrials in 1979 gave continued impetus to these trends, but they are not irreversible. Certain critical factors dictate their continuation—so changes in the directions of long-term incentives *could* occur, for example, in the event of:

- A return to low interest rates and stable or increasing P/E ratios for company stock
- Significant decreases in capital gains taxes or increases in the marginal tax rates on ordinary income
- A reenactment of favorable tax legislation for stock options

PROJECTIONS OF VALUE

Not only are companies confronted with an increasing array of long-term incentives from which to choose, they are also faced with a major problem if they decide to move to the newer forms of longer-term incentives for their executive compensation package. Stated simply: How do you determine the appropriate size for an award—appropriate in terms of maintaining competitive grant values to executives? This problem is increasingly critical because many of the emerging alternatives involve real payments from the company and accrual of compensation expense on the income statement, as opposed to traditional stock options, which have positive cash flows to the company. This situation is made more sensitive by the fact that annual accruals of contingent long-term incentive payments for higher-paid executives must now be reported in company proxy statements.

While it is true that many stock options have been worthless, it is also true that many others have produced millions for the executives who held them. Surveying *realized* value is a tricky process that produces tremendously volatile results from year to year and doesn't contribute to calculating guidelines for making competitive grants. It's analogous to driving a car by looking into the rear-view mirror.

Although compensation specialists do disagree on the value of stock options, most would agree that stock options and other forms of long-term incentives provide *opportunity* for future gain. If a company granted its key employees the same gain opportunity under a long-term incentive plan that other companies did under a different plan, then the company's granting practice would be "competitive" under similar future performance assumptions. If that grant produced above-average gains because of above-average performance, this would be quite appropriate and defensible to shareholders since they would have received above-average returns. Thus the concept of "opportunity value" provides a basis for comparing dissimilar forms of long-term incentives and assessing competitiveness.

Even though opportunity value solves some problems of comparison, however, others still remain:

- Some plans make annual grants while others employ less frequent or irregular granting practices.
- Some plans relate rewards to growth in earnings or other financial performance while others use growth in stock price.
- Some plans provide that gains may be realized over long periods in the future (up to ten years, for example, under stock options) while others pay off three to five years after grant.

If, however, we are willing to make certain explicit assumptions similar to those made by the financial community in valuing stock options, then these problems can be solved and comparability established. (See Black and

Scholes, "The Pricing of Options and Corporate Liabilities," *Journal of Political Economics,* May–June 1973.) Say, for example, that we were to agree that:

- Grants during a multiple-year historical period could be averaged and annualized.
- Stock price and earnings would grow at a common rate (12 percent a year, for example).
- Stock options would be exercised five years after grant.
- 100 percent pay-out would be achieved under performance-based plans.
- All future gains would be converted to their present-value equivalent at an appropriate discount rate (for example, 7 percent a year) to wash out differences in realization timing.

Given these conditions, historical research would show us that the average annualized present value of long-term incentive grants as a percentage of annual direct compensation (salary and annual incentive awards) would be approximately as follows:

	Annual Present Value of Long-Term Grants as a Percentage of Direct Pay
Chief Executive	50 percent
No 2. Executive	45 percent
No. 3 Executive	40 percent
Average for the Top Five Executives	42 percent

Of course, different percentages result if different assumptions are used. And our experience shows that results obtained tend to be higher in certain industries, such as energy, than in others, such as consumer foods.

By converting the above present-value gain amounts to the more typical "investment multiple" for stock option plans (that is, shares granted times option price divided by annual direct pay), we derive the following investment multiples:

	Stock Option Investment as a Multiple of Direct Pay	
	Annual	Five-Yr.
Chief Executive	.90	4.50
No. 2 Executive	.82	4.10
No. 3 Executive	.74	3.70
Average for the Top Five Executives	.77	3.85

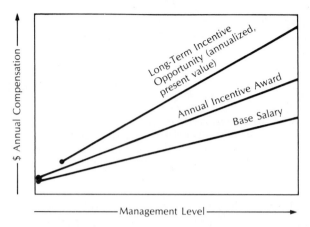

FIGURE 4.   Comparative Value of Long-Term Incentive Opportunities as Managerial Level Increases

What this all adds up to is that stock options and other forms of long-term incentives can significantly increase the value of the total compensation package, not just for top executives but for lower management levels as well. Figure 4 shows the escalating value of long-term incentive opportunities at increasingly higher management levels.

Definitions of Long-Term Incentive Alternatives

The following definitions apply to six key long-term incentive alternatives.

Stock options: rights granted to executives to purchase shares of their company's stock at a fixed price (usually market value when the option is granted) for a fixed period of time, typically ten years.

Stock appreciation rights (SARs): rights attached to stock options that enable executives to receive a direct payment for the related stock option gain during the option term without exercising the option.

Stock purchases: opportunities for executives to purchase shares of their company's stock valued at market or by formula value at full or a discount price, often with the company providing financing assistance.

Phantom stock: rights that, though not related to stock options granted to executives, entitle them to receive payment for stock price *appreciation,* measured by market or formula value, often with dividend equivalents, over a period of years.

Restricted stock: grants to executives of stock or stock units that are earned out through continued employment.

Performance shares/units: grants of stock, stock units, or contingent cash amounts—the *full payment* of which is contingent upon the company's achieving certain long-term performance goals.

EMERGING PROBLEMS AND OPPORTUNITIES

Most of the long-term incentive arrangements that have emerged in recent years have been developed in response to problems with previous plans. Thus SARs were developed because of high interest rates, the risk inherent in a volatile stock market, and the special problems officers face with stock options. And performance share/unit plans arose because the stock market did not reflect actual improvements in company performance. Born of problem parents, the newer plans in time create their own problems and present new opportunities for further development. Recent company experiences suggest the following as emerging problems and opportunities.

Several companies with *nonqualified stock option plans* have seen the market price for their shares increase dramatically. While this is a "high grade" problem, it nonetheless presents difficulties for managers in financing the option exercise and resulting taxes in times of high interest rates. If shares are sold or SARs used, significant ownership and leverage for further appreciation is lost. And once the stock price levels off or the P/E ratio declines, a new generation of managers may find stock options inequitably less attractive and motivational than did predecessors.

Companies that adopted *performance share/unit plans* early and enjoyed the prosperity of the mid-to-late 1970s found these plans highly effective incentives for management. Yet most of the plans are based on growth in earnings from a base period just preceding grant. Coming off a high period and facing uncertain recessionary times, companies are concerned about the motivational effectiveness of these plans for the 1980s if executives believe the goals set are unrealistic.

Currently, *restricted stock* is a much talked-about device. But the advantages are all up front; the problems emerge in future years when the restrictions are lifted and taxes are due. Furthermore, the restrictions can lapse in years of low or no bonuses. Unrestricted shares may need to be sold to raise tax funds, but this may be contrary to the plan's purpose.

Companies with *performance share/unit plans* typically use only corporate performance as the measurement of value for participants. This is logical because the plans replaced stock options that also embodied one measure of performance—stock price. This single focus on corporate performance has the additional benefit of stressing teamwork, thereby freeing annual incentives to focus on unit and individual performance. But while there is only one market price for a company's stock, there are numerous measures of internal financial performance. With the increasing emphasis on strategic business planning and development, it is likely to be only a matter of time before performance share/unit plans fragment, with different goals established at the division/subsidiary and even individual level.

Last, many of the newer plans and combinations are unfortunately more complex than the traditional "plain vanilla" stock options. This complexity arises not because of inept plan design, but as a side effect of creating more direct incentives, additional flexibility, and other advantages for executives (such as voluntary deferrals), or meeting other specific plan objectives. But a plan cannot motivate if it is not understood. Thus increased complexity creates a parallel need and opportunity for more and clearer plan communication to participants.

IN CONCLUSION

Stock options and other forms of long-term incentives for executives are an important, potentially powerful component of a complete management compensation package. Numerous plan alternatives are available—some still evolving, others being refined. Although such variety leads to design and communication complexities, it also offers companies the flexibility and opportunity to design plans that support and reinforce achievement of strategic business objectives and provide an integrated, balanced, total compensation program for their key employees.

TOWARD NEW FREEDOM
AT THE WORKPLACE

Irving Bluestone

Improving the quality of worklife is rooted in the democratic values unique to a free society. Our democratic heritage promises that each individual will have the opportunity to achieve a sense of personal dignity and worth through the exercise of free will—the freedom to choose, to make decisions. The opportunity to assert meaningful control over the forces that affect one's life is indispensable to freedom.

The application of these fundamental values of a democratic society to the workplace is essential in improving the quality of worklife. The worker as citizen enjoys the opportunity to participate in the decision-making process within his family, the community, the nation. The citizen as worker lives almost half his waking life in a workplace dominated by managerial authoritarianism.

Improving the quality of worklife means bringing to the workplace the maximum in democratic lifestyle, balanced between the needs of production and the needs of the worker for self-fulfillment.

The world of work in industrialized society will be undergoing gradual but inexorable change in the decade or two ahead. The change will be dominated by the persistent demand for dignity on the job, by resistance to the authoritarianism of the boss-worker relationship, by the thrust for workers to participate meaningfully in the decision-making process at the workplace.

Needless to say, union contracts have made enormous strides in enhancing the dignity of the worker at the workplace and gaining him rights without which he would be subject to the whim and caprice of management. Nevertheless, labor contracts, even with their hundreds of provisions, substantially leave to management the "sole responsibility" to determine the products to be manufactured, the location of plants, the schedule of production, the methods, means, and processes of manufacturing, and the general managerial decisions governing financing, marketing, accounting, pricing, purchasing, and the like.

Slowly, however—even hesitantly—a fresh evaluation of the world of work is stirring forces aimed at new directions for worklife. Two distinct yet

Irving Bluestone, "Toward New Freedom at the Workplace," Employee Relations Law Journal, *Winter 1977. Reprinted with permission.*

overlapping approaches are indicated. One relates to "managing the worker's job"; the other relates to "managing the enterprise."

Decisions involving seniority layoff and recall, transfers between jobs, promotions, shift preference, and literally hundreds of other "working conditions" are customarily—perhaps traditionally is the better term—covered by the terms of labor contracts. In more recent years, decisions involving subcontracting of work or product, both inside and outside the plant, moving all or part of a plant to another location, the introduction of new equipment, health and safety matters, and other issues affecting the worker's security and welfare have become front-and-center bargaining issues as they affect workers' job security, personal welfare, and income. Decisions such as those involving the type of product to be manufactured, marketing it, purchase of materials, setting aside reserves, pricing policies, accounting procedures, distribution of dividends, and other similar determinations are more remote from the workers' immediate interests. They have not yet entered the usual and customary collective bargaining arena.

Issues related to managing the job receive most immediate and persistent attention since, aside from wages and benefits, they concern the working conditions most immediately and noticeably affecting the workers' welfare.

Increasing attention is currently being devoted to this problem of managing the job. Rising rates of absenteeism and labor turnover, deterioration in the quality of the product or service, the revolt against supervisory authority—these are some of the factors motivating employers to reevaluate current practices and customs governing management-worker relationships. Concurrently, the worker rebels against the authoritarian atmosphere of the workplace, against the subordination of his personal dignity, desires, and aspirations to the drive for more production at lower cost; he finds little challenge, satisfaction, or interest in his work. While his rate of pay may predominate his relationship to his job, he is also responsive to the opportunity to play an innovative, creative, and imaginative role in the production process.

In Europe, significant changes in the workplace are already commanding attention. In January 1973, Willy Brandt, then chancellor of West Germany, stated:

Co-determination [*Mitbestimmung*] is of the essense of democratizing . . . society. It is part of the historical development of those reforms which in their totality constitute a free society.

. . . The new *Mitbestimmung* law in Germany will now provide the opportunity for a comprehensive test of the concept, since the law is applicable in all plants of 2,000 or more workers. Thus, the auto plants owned by Ford and General Motors Corporation in West Germany will now fall within the orb of the law establishing co-determination. No doubt these stalwart pillars of the free enterprise system, accustomed to exercising their "sole prerogatives," will nevertheless adjust to this new scenario, just as over the years they have been learning to adjust to the union's presence in their plants and at the collective bargaining table.

But what about the concept of co-determination in the United States?

Unions in the United States traditionally have moved in the direction of improving wages, benefits, and working conditions. Generally, they have left managing the enterprise to management, reacting to managerial acts objectionable to the workers. They have not embraced a political philosophy to motivate their overall politics and programs. This is not to say that U.S. unions have no socio-politico-economic concepts. Quite the contrary; but they are not married to an "ism" governing and directing their behavior.

Rather, U.S. unions move to meet practical problems with practical solutions. It is highly improbable that they would approach the problem of worker participation in decision making by way of fierce ideological struggle founded in socioeconomic theory. They are not prone to beat their wings in ideological frustration.

Where workers feel victimized they combine their forces to correct the situation—case by case, problem by problem. Gradual, persistent change, not revolutionary upheaval, has marked the progress of the American worker. When explosions occur—as they did in the 1930s—they are responses to specific problems that arise in the search for specific solutions. We can therefore anticipate that worker participation will manifest itself in a step-by-step effort to meet specific problems affecting the welfare of the worker.

Decisions regarding purchasing, advertising, selling, accounting, financing are far more remote from the immediate problems facing the worker than are decisions concerning his job. In the vast range of managerial decisions that are made, the immediacy of impact on the worker varies enormously. Thus, the average worker in a gigantic enterprise usually displays less interest in the selection of the chairman of the board than in the amount of overtime he receives.

What direction, then, will the drive toward worker participation in decision making take? To begin with, it seems safe to say that any further encroachment on so-called management prerogatives will spell "revolution" to management, while to the worker it will simply represent a nonideological effort to resolve a problem that bothers him.

Certain areas of possible confrontation come to mind. Management, by way of example, controls the decision to shut down a plant or move all or part of it to another location, often hundreds of miles away. The union bargains for severance pay, early retirement, the right of the worker to transfer with the job and to receive moving allowance, etc.

The worker is the victim of such a management decision. He may be thrown out of work, or, given the right to transfer with the job, he must pull up stakes, cut off the roots he has in his community, leave family ties and friends, and begin a new life in a strange place, with no assurance of permanence. Management wields the decision-making authority; the workers (and the community) dangle at the end of that decision.

Similarly, management generally controls the final decision to subcontract work out or to move work about among its many facilities in a multiplant corporation. It is the worker who faces the ultimate insecurity.

Management holds the authority to discipline. All places of work (like society at large) require rules and regulations for people to live by. But discipline can be a fearful weapon in the hands of a ruthless employer, even when subject to a collectively bargained grievance procedure.

Production scheduling can be a serious source of friction. In an auto assembly plant, for instance, changes in line speed to meet changes in production schedules, or changes in model mix, require rebalancing of jobs and operations. This in turn gives rise to disputes over production standards and manpower. Frequent changes in line speed or model mix disturb agreed-upon production-standard settlements and manpower agreements, often resulting in crisis bargaining and, on occasion, strike action.

The never-ending yet necessary introduction of technological innovation results in alteration of jobs, cutbacks in manpower need, and effects on skill requirements. All of these factors generate new problems, emphasizing the concern workers naturally have for their job security.

The call for excessive overtime is a source of unhappiness and discontent.

These are but a handful of the kinds of confrontation issues directly affecting workers and increasingly subject to worker participation bargaining.

Other types of issues also command attention, for democratizing the workplace carries considerations beyond the worker's immediate job.

The double standard that exists between the managers and the workers comes into question. Symbols of elitism, traditionally taken for granted in industrial society, are challenged: salary payment and its recognized advantages as compared with hourly payment; time clocks; paneled dining rooms versus spartan cafeterias; privileged parking facilities nearest the plant entrances; etc.

Democratizing the workplace may entail organizing the work schedule to enable the worker to manage his personal chores: visiting the dentist or doctor; getting his car repaired; visiting the school to discuss his children's problems with the teacher; etc. . . .

. . . [A]s the worker increasingly recognizes the direct connection between the top-level managerial decision and his immediate welfare he will clamor for the right to influence that decision-making process. This may or may not take the form of co-determination as it evolved in West Germany, but it will certainly involve the workers—through their elected representatives—in decision making currently foreclosed to them.

Managing the enterprise is quite a different concept from "managing the job," although admittedly the areas of overlap are considerable.

The American Assembly noted at its Arden House Conference in November 1973:

> Unions have since their inception been seeking to 'humanize' work. The current ideas of improving the quality of working life are basically an extension of this long-range goal. Unions have primarily sought and have achieved significant economic gains and have substantially increased job security. This should not obscure their long-term struggle for improvement in the quality of working life.

Innovations in employer-employee relations are spawning a new nomenclature: "job enrichment"; "job enlargement"; "job rotation"; "humanizing the workplace"; "democratizing worklife"; and, in another context, "co-determination." I prefer the term "improving the quality of worklife," for this encompasses an unlimited scope of possibilities for worker participation in the decision-making process. These innovations relate essentially to the issue of managing the job. They do not as a rule impinge on administrative decision-making relative to pricing, marketing, purchasing, accounting, etc. . . .

Let us explore various aspects of worklife in which the workers can play a significant decision-making role. Projects could then be improvised to improve the quality of worklife in these subject areas. The following emphasize primarily areas of concern having to do with managing the job rather than managing the enterprise. They are in this sense worker shop-floor subjects for decision, as contrasted with concerns of walnut-row executives relative to marketing, pricing, investing, or accounting practices.

● **Plant Layout.** In developing the layout for a new plant, or in remodeling an old facility, it is customary that the architects and engineers make the decisions. Workers do not share in blueprinting the facility even though they possess intimate and direct knowledge of product flow, need for equipment location, and facilities to expedite the production process.

● **Methods and Means of Operation.** Many managements recognize the creativity latent in workers with experience on the job to develop improved ways and means of manufacture. Suggestion plans are designed to appeal to the individual worker's desire for financial gain; but they are no substitutes for direct participation by workers as a group in deciding on different, more effective methods and means of operation. Rarely are affirmative programs developed actively to afford the workers the time, space, and opportunity to participate in these types of decision-making activities.

● **Tools.**   Almost invariably it is management that decides upon the tools to be used in the performance of specific jobs. The worker's role is relegated to learning how to use the tool. Yet, it is the worker who is closest to the job and whose knowledge and experience can be tapped to improvise new and more efficient tools. As a matter of fact, as any old-time foreman knows, workers do indeed devise their own tools to make the job more efficient or easier to perform, but this unique capability remains largely unused and unorganized.

● **Preventive Maintenance.**   The habit usually is to provide maintenance to repair a breakdown in production. Some preventive maintenance is undertaken, planned by maintenance supervision, but the first-line trained maintenance worker is rarely consulted and plays hardly a role in determining the course of preventive maintenance programs. Yet, these highly skilled workers have much to offer toward developing and fulfilling preventive maintenance programs that will keep the production process running more smoothly and with fewer interruptions.

● **Scrap and Repair Reduction.**   Few workers—and this includes foremen and engineers—are given special training in problem-solving techniques. Experience indicates, however, that when workers are trained in the rudiments of problem solving and meet regularly in groups of common work function to find answers to the problems of scrap and product repair, the results can be quite remarkable. The usual practice is to exhort the workers to "produce quality" and to discipline when scrap or excessive repairs occur. Finding the proper solution to scrap and repair is a far more satisfactory procedure.

   Without going into detail, let me cite a few additional subjects of in-plant life which could be relegated to the group worker decision-making process:

- Counseling with chronic absentees
- Developing a reasonable system of working hours, including "flextime"
- Equalizing overtime hours within work groups
- Vacation scheduling
- Transfer requests
- Product flow and routing

These by no means exhaust the list of possibilities

   We are already familiar with joint union-management cooperative efforts in maintaining health and safety procedures; developing new-hire orientation programs; alcoholism, drug, and other troubled-employee rehabilitation programs; United Fund drives; etc. There is no end to the worker-participation programs that management and labor, working together, can devise. Suffice it to say that the workplace can be democratized.

Work can be made more satisfying and rewarding. People can and must win greater control over their working lives and the production process, for people at work can indeed manage themselves to a far greater degree than the present authoritarian workplace permits.

We must stop treating workers as nonadults at the workplace, telling them what to do, when to do it, with what tools, in how much time and space, in what sequence—and threatening them with discipline for violating orders. Enhancing human dignity at work means bringing into the workplace the same opportunities to exercise freedom of choice and decision-making power that lie at the heart of our democratic values outside the work arena.

DOING AWAY WITH
THE FACTORY BLUES

Donald N. Scobel

During the past few decades, the financial lot of the U.S. factory employee has been enhanced immeasurably by beneficial laws, organized and persuasive representation, economic clout, and, until recently, a generally increasing economy. The factory employee now also has more avenues than ever before to lodge specific protests and to achieve some social equity through grievance procedures, courts, labor boards, equality commissions, safety councils, and arbitration hearings.

Despite these social and economic advances for the factory employee, however, the factory itself has retained much of its classism and discrimination. Even with the dissections of academia, decades of behavioral science, theories of job enrichment and of human relations, new styles of management, and concepts of organizational development, the factory remains the kind of place *non*factorymen hope their children never have to work in as well as the kind of place factorymen hope their children can get out of. Why?

Why must the U.S. factory cause unhappiness for so many of its inhabitants? Why is it that an average of a few hundred people spending more than a third of their lives under a common roof cannot seem to find there a sustaining measure of equity, understanding, or even friendship? How can this mini-society called the workplace, where members are truly dependent on each other for economic security, remain so socially and emotionally sterile?

Part of the problem is that most people concerned with improving the lot of "people at work" fail to see the workplace holistically. Behavioral scientists, managements, unions, consultants, and legislators often concern themselves with separate segments of the industrial complex. Those who are concerned with styles of management do not worry about how the job is separate from the environment. Those concerned about worker alienation generally leave problems of the white collar force to others. Still other groups work to improve laws for the nonexempt. Yet these individual ef-

Reprinted by permission of the Harvard Business Review. *"Doing Away with the Factory Blues" by Donald N. Scobel, November–December 1975. Copyright © 1975 by the President and Fellows of Harvard College; all rights reserved.*

forts rarely succeed in establishing a work culture where internal social values and business objectives are congruent.

In the past six years, however, considerable work has been done at several U.S. Eaton Corporation locations to provide the foundation for a workplace culture quite different from the more common industrial environment. At the outset, management did not form work teams, thrust a system of enriched jobs on the workplace, or even presume that the participation of people in decisions directly affecting them is a necessary ingredient of a healthy work culture. The thrust at the Eaton plants was simply for a climate of responsible industrial freedom, where the respect, dignity, and trust due a "man at work" is not culturally different from those due a man at church, a man bowling, or a man in tune with his own family. Management's effort was to achieve a happy, responsive work culture that would respond constructively to job enrichment, decision participation and involvement, or whatever grassroots needs, as they emerged.

The "Eaton story" may at times seem as if it were a fairy tale. Indeed, the approach used at Eaton has been spawned and nurtured more by innocence than by behavioral analysis, and that may have been part of its magic. Regardless, since 1968 about 13 Eaton manufacturing plants, involving over 5000 people, have tried and succeeded in establishing a responsive workplace. Each plant's approach is tailored to the needs of its employees, which include foundry workers, truck transmission and axle makers, lift truck and auto parts makers, and forestry equipment and hardware builders.

It all began seven years ago when the manager of Eaton's Battle Creek, Michigan engine valve plant decided to build a new facility in Kearney, Nebraska. He asked his managerial staff and the Cleveland headquarters employee relations people how he might avoid the deterioration in employee/management relationships in Nebraska that had occurred over the decades in the Michigan plant.

In response to his challenge, a few managerial people representing the full spectrum of functional disciplines at Eaton isolated themselves to discuss and evaluate traditional policies and practices that affect employee relations. They summarized their composite critique in a report to the Battle Creek manager that took the form of a letter written as if by a factory employee who is explaining why he brings so little of himself to his workplace.

THE EMPLOYEE'S LETTER

Beginning in the Nebraska cornfields and spreading to other new facilities and, more recently, to some older plants, Eaton's revolt against the factory blues began with this "letter."

Dear Sir:

What you are asking me, as I see it, is why am I not giving you my best in exchange for the reasonable wages and benefits you provide me and my family.

First, I'm not trying to blame anybody for why you don't see the "whole" me. Some of the problem is company policy, some is union thinking, some is just me. Let me tell you why, and I'll leave it to bigger minds than mine to figure out blames and remedies.

I'll begin with my first day on the job eleven years ago—my first factory job, by the way. I was just 19 then. Incidentally, my cousin started work in your office as a clerk typist on the same day. We used to drive to work together. She still works for you, too.

The first thing I was told that day by the personnel manager and my foreman was that I was on 90 days' probation. They were going to measure my ability and attendance and attitude and then make up their minds about me. Gee, that surprised me. I thought I'd been hired already—but I really wasn't. Although the foreman tried to make me feel at home, it was still sort of a shock to realize I was starting out kind of on the sidelines until I proved my worth. In fact, the only person who told me I "belonged," without any strings attached, was my union steward.

You know, that first day my foreman told me all about the shop rules of discipline as if I were going to start out stealing or coming to work drunk or getting into fights or horseplay. What made it even worse was when I later found out that no one told my cousin she was on probation. I asked her if she had seen the rules, and here it is eleven years later and she still doesn't know there are about 35 rules for those of us working in the factory.

What it boils down to is that your policies—yes, and the provisions of our union contract—simply presume the factoryman untrustworthy, while my cousin in the office is held in much higher regard. It's almost like we work for different companies.

After I had been here about eight months, a car hit my car broadside on the way to work. My cousin and I were both taken to the hospital right away and released several hours later. As soon as I was released by the hospital, I called the plant to tell them what happened. I couldn't get through to my foreman, so I told my tale to a recording machine. Whey my cousin didn't show up by nine o'clock, her boss got worried and called the house and then the hospital. When he found out my cousin had a broken arm and some cuts, but was basically okay, he sent for a taxi to take her home.

Both my cousin and I ended up missing four days' work. On each of the next three days, I called and told the tape recorder I would not be in. I never heard from anybody in the company and when I got back to work later that week, my supervisor said, "Sure glad to see you're okay . . . it's a shame you spoiled your perfect attendance record. . . ."

Sir, I don't come to work to be worried about by someone. But I have some difficulty understanding why, when I'm absent, nobody really cares. It seems as if the company's just waiting for me to do something wrong. When I got back to work from that car accident, you started getting another little chunk less from me. Does that sound crazy? Or does it seem selfish?

Sir, why must I punch a time clock? Do you think I'd lie about my starting and quitting times? Why must I have buzzers to tell me when I take a break, relieve myself, eat lunch, start working, go home? Do you really think I can't tell time or would otherwise rob you of valuable minutes? Why doesn't the rest room I must use provide any privacy? Why do I have to drive my car over chuck holes while you enjoy reserved, paved parking? Why must I work the day before and after a holiday to get holiday pay? Are you convinced I will extend the holiday into the weekend—while, by the way, my cousin is thought to have more sense than that?

I guess I'm saying that when you design your policies for the very few who need them, how do you think the rest of us feel?

Sir, do you really think I don't care or don't know what you think of me? If you are convinced of that, then you will never understand why I bring less than all of myself to my workbench.

You know, sir, in my eleven years, I've run all kinds of machinery for you, but your company has never even let me look at what the maintenance man does when he has to repair one of my machines. No one has ever really asked me how quality might be better or how my equipment or methods might be improved. In fact, your policies drum it into me good and proper that you really want me to stay in my place. And now, *you* want to know why *I* don't pour it on? Wow! Don't you realize that I may want to contribute more than you let me? I know the union may be responsible for some of this—but again, I'm trying to explain why, not whose fault it is.

You know, sir, I would like a more challenging job, but that isn't the heart of the matter, not for me at least. If there were a sense of dignity around here, I would not hold back the effort and ideas within me, even if my particular job was less than thrilling. Many of my buddies do not want a greater job challenge, but they do want their modest contributions respected.

You know, my neighbor is a real quiet, sweet old man who just retired from here last month. When I ask him how he sums up his life's work, he says—and I can almost quote him exactly—"A pretty good place to work—only thing that really bothered me was that warning I got 26 years ago for lining up at the clock two and one-half minutes early."

Well, sir, I suspect that 26 years ago, you may have corrected this quiet, nice guy for lining up early at your clock. But the price you paid was making him a "clock watcher" for 26 years. I wonder—was that warning all that necessary? Why couldn't you have just told him why lining up early isn't a good idea and then relied on him to discipline himself? I wonder.

It has been said, sir, that factory people look upon *profit* as a dirty world. I don't feel that way, but you know, it's almost as if *love* is the dirty word here.

Why don't I give my best? Well, I guess I have a kind of thermostat inside me that responds to your warmth. Do you have a thermostat inside you?

Very truly yours,

THE COMPANY'S ANSWER

The above letter all but spells out its own solutions. The epilogue of the report to the Michigan manager said: "To avoid industrial decay, build a plant around the presumed correctness of the letter writer." And this is what the manager of the new plant in Nebraska, and all managers of new Eaton plants built since then, set out to do. Critical to solving inequities and problems cited in the letter is that management's commitment to the new approach be made explicit from the very beginning and that supervisors reexamine factory relationships.

The First Steps

At the new Eaton plants, management puts out a written handbook in which it commits itself to a counseling rather than a rules-penalties process; to weekly departmental meetings where employee inputs are sought; to manager roundtables and an "open floor" concept; to a uniform office-factory benefit system; and to a foundation of concern, trust, and participation. The handbook states that ". . . an important concept here is that people are individuals . . . and a company must relate to uniqueness if there is to be a full measure of personal growth and contribution to organizational objectives. The emphasis is upon employee involvement in matters that affect him and sharing the responsibility for an effective operation. It's a mutual fulfillment."

What Eaton does in the formal training of supervisors under the new model is remarkably minimal. In a two-day seminar, the group of supervisors spends the first day just talking abut why people work and what they want out of life. The consensus usually is that "we are all into this for pretty much the same reasons." The group invariably believes there are personal differences in motivational priorities, but does not believe these differences can be categorized for any class or group of employees, or that different categories of motivational factors are inherently more important. Although behavioral scientists have dissected this premise almost to death, it is true that most people desire a sense of community at work. Recognizing this fact helps supervisors and managers see that treating employees under the same roof with different value systems does not make much "human" sense.

During the second day of the seminar the supervisors review the basic components of the new approach and consider how that approach helps build a common value system of respect and participation. The reason training can be minimal is that the supervisor steps from the seminar into a workplace where the new commitments and ground rules are in effect immediately. Another plus is that it is not necessary to have "behavioral science superstars" to understand or apply the new approach. Supervisors of varying competencies are usually at ease with this approach after only brief exposure. Very few clamor for the old regimentation, or see it as essential to their ability to supervise. One supervisor simply said, "Nothing fancy about this. It's just being human with biblical roots." Eaton is trying to resurrect fairness through identifiable policy changes that are fundamentally fair.

Policy Changes

Space prohibits listing all aspects of this new approach. In essence, personnel policies and presumptions that are based on mistrust and lack of care are discarded and replaced, where necessary, with ones that reflect concern and mutual respect. The following are a few examples of how this attitude is applied to actual policies and processes.

- At the new Eaton plants, the hiring process is a meaningful, two-way exchange, which replaces the structured interview and the more common "get-me-twelve-warm-bodies-by-Tuesday" factory-hiring syndrome. Applicants and their spouses are invited in small groups to an after-dinner "coffee" where the plant's products, processes, and philosophy are discussed. Both factory and office employees take the group on a plant and office tour and encourage the applicant to spend additional time in departments that seem most attractive to him. Personnel people ask the newcomer to express his job preferences within his general skill level for initial placement or for later transfer if there is no opening in the department he selects. The people conducting the tour introduce the applicant to people he may be working for and with. With this open review of the job, the job seeker ends up knowing more about the company and its people than they do about him. This process extends to a drill press operator or a file clerk the concern and dignity that industry usually extends only to its applicants for managerial posts.
- There is no probationary period. Supervisors evaluate individually any problem that might arise with a new person. Although it can happen that supervisors may have to let someone go, the policy presumes that people are eager to work and to be dependable employees, rather than the opposite.
- The plants do not use time clocks, buzzers, or similar controls. Although the company needs records of time allocations for many legal as well as good business reasons, it assumes that individuals can accurately record their own times.
- The dual value system mentioned by the "letter writer" no longer exists. Many companies, including Eaton, have traditionally maintained reasonable, responsible relationships with their office and supervisory staffs and have solved prob-

lems with these employees by carefully appraising the facts of each case, counseling employees according to individual circumstances, and assuming that the employees are able to direct themselves rather than relying on a rigid penalty schedule for correcting behavior. This approach is now being used for all factory employees who once were subjected to a formal disciplinary system that had numerous posted rules and a sliding scale of penalties that went with them.

- All factory and office people also share the same benefit package. Levels of certain benefits vary with salary, but the system is uniform. Payment for casual absence is often a dynamic distinguisher between office and factory status. At the newer Eaton facilities, all people are paid for both casual and long-term absences and are under the same pay system for long-term absences.
- Office and factory supervisors hold departmental meetings at least once every two weeks to discuss issues that the employees themselves raise. Often the supervisor will have an employee lead the discussion.
- The plant manager chairs a periodic roundtable with representatives from all office and factory departments who are selected in whatever way the department decides. The participants prepare the agenda of concerns and the minutes, as well as post follow-up action notices on central and departmental bulletin boards.
- An "open floor" concept replaces the old "open door" policy. The "open door" implied to a factoryman, "If you want to do business with a staff person, you must come up to his front office." The new approach makes the factoryman's workplace as important an "office" as anyplace else in the facility. So that territorial barriers are specifically torn down, the personnel department and other staff people make a point of conducting business at the employee's workplace as well as at their own.
- In a variety of ways, factory, supervisory, and lower-level office people participate in managerial meetings and functions. For example, the manager invites some factory and office people to his weekly staff meetings. Similarly, there is regular factory representation at production planning meetings, as well as factory participation on methods, products, and process engineering committees.
- At some locations, factory and lower-level office people are editors of the plant's newssheets. Often the recreational, social, and community affairs activities are independently managed, including direction of the fiscal aspects, by joint committees of factory and office people. Special committees (little ad hocracies) are formed from time to time to handle contingencies.
- It is common for factory people to volunteer to be plant tour guides, to be involved with food service, plant safety, and fire protection matters, even to the extent of codirection of these activities.

I hope the above list gives the reader some idea of what Eaton is trying to do. In addition to these items, there are two important kinds of experiences that flow from this approach. For employees who want them, there are opportunities to be involved in developing the scope of their jobs or in increasing their participation in decision making.

Job Involvement.   From the beginning of the workplace renaissance, Eaton has not tried to implement new work structures or process designs. Each of the newer plants began with updated versions of the same basic technologies and procedures used at its older counterparts. Management wanted first to restructure the work climate and then to be responsive to spontaneous employee drives for greater job involvement as these drives emerged. What followed clearly, and almost quantifiably, resulted from the new work culture.

In the new plants, almost all employees seek better and more rapid performance inspection and feedback. In some cases, some of the inspection duties have been taken over by the employees themselves and blended into their own manufacturing responsibilities and operations. Interestingly, until people achieve job proficiency, they want guidance on how to improve their performance.

About one third of the people seek some involvement in their equipment repair. A significant number do not seek this enrichment, but for those who do, it is meaningful, and most maintenance people are willing trainers. Although maintenance time does sometimes rise briefly, it soon goes down, and preventive maintenance practices become more routine.

On the average, three quarters of the factory employees want to learn more about the whole production process, and those familiar with the process sequence soon develop an "early alert" system that warns them of trouble elsewhere on the line. Often these employees ask for temporary reassignment to help resolve the production holdups. It is startling how quickly employees become familiar with the total manufacturing process and how many of them aid the supervisor in product flow planning and problem solving.

Almost a third of the work force diagnoses its own job methods and scopes. At one plant, a janitor persuaded his boss that he, rather than the purchasing department, could order local cleaning supplies because he would give it higher priority than they would. He was allowed to do so, while other janitors wanted no part of the telephoning and paper work. At another plant the lathe operators insisted they be allowed to join a meeting of equipment engineers to learn why their lathes were malfunctioning. Many times people come forth with combinations of jobs or changes in sequences that can improve output. Some improvements require that the job and pay structure be changed, but many can be accommodated by the existing system.

These experiences in job involvement result from a specific policy of laissez-faire. Management responds positively to involvement but does not attempt to structure it.

Participation in Decision Making. It is integral to many aspects of the new approach that employees should participate in decisions. This extends to specific decisions that affect work and the work life. For example, if a plant is on a two-shift, five-day operation, and business expands, the different departments will discuss different work-schedule options, such as weekend work, extended daily hours, or a third shift that could be used to handle the increase. Often management will express its thoughts and invite reactions; more often, the options are put to a vote. In either case, employee inputs are specifically invited before any decision is made.

At one plant several employees suggested the company try a four-day week. The suggestion was put to a vote—and passed; in another plant, it failed. Elsewhere, management asked the employees in one departmental unit to restructure their own job contents and assignments when the current system was obviously inequitable. At a few locations, employees have nominated and selected candidates for supervisory positions, and in one situation, the employees said another supervisor was not necessary!

Even in layoff circumstances, decision participation is invited. Although people do not like to vote on only negative alternatives, such as a reduction of the work force versus a reduction in working hours, if the company submits its preferred course to employee consideration, it will often find the attitudinal "pulse" and more often than not receive ideas for policy redirection. During one temporary layoff, plantwide discussion brought forth more layoff volunteers than were needed! In almost all cases, when the employees participate in decisions, they cooperate to the full with the final decision. As one manager put it, "I can no longer conceive of making a decision of major impact on any segment of that work force without first inviting meaningful dialogue."

THE RESPONSE

Although some problems have arisen under the new approaches (I will discuss these below), nothing so far indicates that the basic concepts are off the mark. In fact, there are some interesting comparisons that can be drawn between the new model facilities and the older plants, indicating that the new approach increases both productivity and worker satisfaction.

Measures of Success

At the new plants, absenteeism (casual as well as sick leaves) ranges from 0.5 percent to 3 percent, compared with 6 percent to 12 percent at traditional locations. Turnover is similarly reduced. With the new approach, voluntary separations average under 4 percent annually, compared with up to 60 percent at traditional plants.

In the new plants the hourly product output (for identical blueprints of products run on similar equipment) will range from parity to 35 percent more than at the traditional plants. Of more importance to Eaton, however, is the longer range performance where trends are comparable. Management in the new locations actually hopes that productivity will fall off at times. A dip in productivity indicates that improvements are being made in the manufacturing process, which will lead to greater gains in the long run. It is interesting that some new locations report up to 15 percent less scrap and rework costs. Nevertheless, those plants that have the highest output gains report the least savings (if any) in the quality area. Most report reduced maintenance costs per unit of output once start-up problems are resolved.

On the other hand, new facilities often have a worse plant safety record than the older plants. Management speculates that this decline in safety is caused partly by the new work force's unfamiliarity with industrial hazards and by the fact that carelessness creeps in when people strive so hard to increase production. In any event, the safety problem has led employees to involve themselves more in plant and departmental safety activities.

Actions Speak Louder than Words. These measurements are interesting, but are subject to all the problems involved in accurately comparing even seemingly like facilities. Although many of the plants compared are "paired" in terms of product and basic machinery, there are crucial differences, such as age of equipment; length of production runs; availability and quality of raw materials, parts and supplies; climate; and reliance on a parent plant for services. These differences make it difficult to isolate and measure the involvement and effectiveness of people. One can tell what is happening at the new plants and what the work force's effect is on productivity more by examining actual events than by measuring output.

- At one plant an employee literally broke in to go to work. The first day his shift went to ten hours, requiring a 5:00 A.M. starting time, he arrived at 3:30 A.M., as was his usual habit of showing up an hour and a half early. Finding the whole place dark, unoccupied, and locked, and even though he lived nearby and could have returned home until the plant officially opened, he climbed a fence, pried open a window, turned on the lights, cleaned his area, and started up the heating equipment to warm his "plating" bath.
- At another facility, a significant number of day-shift people, while taking the family out for an evening "Dairy Queen," stop by the plant just to make sure everything is going all right on the night shift.
- A plant manager at one of the older plants visited a new model facility and wrote in his report to a vice-president, ". . . I'd sum it up by reporting that when the first shift ended you couldn't tell it was quitting time! No clocks to line up at! No rushing to cars! No tires screeching! Some people finished the last piece in their machine. Many casually took showers. Some went out to the picnic area and gossiped over a bottle of pop. Several stayed to play baseball or horseshoes in the back field. Some went to a variety of committee meetings. The point is that the exodus was so gradual it was unnoticed. Unbelievable!"
- A group of employees, on their own time, used company materials to build a special scooter to enable an employee who had become permanently handicapped in an automobile accident to return early to his job.

- At a facility where overtime work is assigned on a voluntary basis, for three months 97 percent of the people worked seven days a week with less than 2 percent absenteeism *during* the week, even though casual weekday absence would have been paid for.
- There have been no employee-initiated EEO or OSHA complaints at any facility where this approach to employee relationships is practiced.
- At a southern plant where 30 percent of the work force is black, the factory people selected five supervisors; three of them were black.
- Although there are not many transfers between office and factory positions, it is just as common to have office people apply for transfer to the factory as the other way around. At one plant, five office people volunteered to run factory machinery so five avid deer hunters could catch the first day of the season!
- At one location, a high-ranking visitor reported, among other things, ". . . the most remarkably constructive graffiti I have ever read . . . the few cartoons, poems and song parodies are genuinely witty and poignant and prideful. What a difference from the traditional back walls of industry!"
- One New Year's Day, almost all the employees at one plant responded to a TV news bulletin that the plant was within an unexpected flood area. Most labored around the clock so the plant could be fully operational the next day.
- At one plant, if at the beginning of his shift an employee registers his choice of lunch food, he will have a tray waiting for him at lunchtime. A cafeteria employee who thinks that "people's lunch break should be spent eating and gabbing and not waiting in line or kicking a vending machine" introduced the idea and carried it out.

These examples show how the new approach affects employees at work, and were perhaps best summarized by one manager when he said, "On those especially frustrating days I still know in my bones that nothing intentionally destructive is going on around here."

Problems of Implementation

Although the humanistic approach to employee relationships has not failed at any location, there have, nevertheless, been growing pains. With varying degrees of severity, most of the following problems have occurred at one or more plants.

Initially, Eaton concentrated its effort on employee relations in the factory. Although very few office people were averse to bringing dignity and fairness to the factory employees, when the factories were filled with camaraderie, the office people became envious of the "feeling." The office people did not have the sense of involvement with their workplace that management had assumed they did, and once the issue was raised it was clear why. Some plant managers did not include the office people in their roundtable discussions, and when they did conduct departmental meetings, which was infrequently, the meetings seemed pallid in comparison to factory meetings.

Management in the new plants solved these problems by stressing participation in the offices and ensuring more meaningful interaction between the office and factory employees so that all could share the same work climate. What Eaton had seen originally as a factory revitalization now involves the entire workplace.

Another related problem is what Eaton now calls the "up-the-ladder" disease. The first symptom appeared at a retreat that the manager of the new Nebraska plant held so that the supervisors could talk in a relaxed atmosphere about how things were going. This quasi-recreational gathering turned out to be a pressure cooker for the plant manager. The supervisors said most discreetly that their relationships with the factory employees were more spirited and participative than their rapport with higher management. They felt they were "short circuited" up the hierarchy. The plant manager realized he would have to be more awake and responsive to his supervisors and their ideas. Invariably, the cure for this disease is exposing higher management levels to the plant culture itself.

At one very small location, the plant manager ignored the espoused policies. The hiring orientation process fell short of the commitment, and departmental meetings did not occur. In reacting angrily to an employee soliciting money for his "cause," a department manager ignored individualized consideration and posted a mass denouncement on the bulletin board. As was immediately evident from the horrendous absentee and turnover experience, the managers were not treating the employees with respect and dignity. Luckily, the plant manager recognized what was happening and called the work force together to admit the hypocrisy and to pledge a speedy "new beginning," which has taken place.

There are different problems that arise when things go almost too smoothly. At a few places, for instance, the sense of goodwill was so pervasive that the company did not react to a few individuals who were exploiting the trust placed in them. The other employees became restless and brought pressure on these people directly as well as on management to deal with these individuals. In most cases, the peer pressure and counseling procedure has been effective, and the individuals responded positively.

Despite the implementation problems I have cited, the approach has been accepted in most new locations. Although not without its skeptics, the concept is now a familiar idea throughout the company, and many managers of traditional plants, which have varied histories of problems with factory and office employees, are searching out ways to apply the new approach at their own plants, where practices, policies, and attitudes are already firmly established.

The Backward Glance

Eaton's efforts at some older plants are still in early stages, and it is too soon to report significant successes or failures. It is already apparent, however, that remodeling is slower and more complex than building anew.

It is equally evident, nevertheless, that meaningful changes can be made at traditional locations without great risk or investment. As at new locations, the company must express its commitment; the absence of commitment makes the ideas seem vague and philosophical rather than action oriented.

Understandably, it is much more difficult to convince supervisors, employees, and their unions in the older plants that change is not threatening and can take place with fairness and dignity. This task has become easier at Eaton since the word has now spread that the new plants are such fulfilling places to work in. It is still, however, a great challenge to managers in the traditional plants to bring everyone together without fanfare into a common constructive process, to get them to believe that management means what it is saying. If management tries to impose the new approach, it runs the risk of appearing as if it were just another management attempt to impose its will upon the employees. Because of these problems, managers in some older plants are using different approaches to attain the same ends.

At one old plant, there is a joint company-union initiated effort to transform the workplace climate through a variety of participative endeavors. These include such experiences as employees themselves rearranging an entire stockroom area more efficiently or management entrusting employees in a certain department with the responsibility of resolving their own absentee problems. At another location, the company has approached the union to recast the provisions of the labor agreement in language that assumes trust and respect between parties. The point is to see whether constructive relationships can emerge from changes in legalistic language and principles previously inscribed in stone.

More commonly, however, Eaton is trying to adapt its new plant experiences to traditional places. There is no theoretical reason that the new hiring procedure, the "open floor" policy, departmental meetings, the manager's roundtable, and the counseling approach to discipline cannot be initiated by managers in the plants. In fact, some of these changes are in process at older places and seem to attract voluntary union involvement and cooperation.

The union, of course, must be integrally involved in the entire change process. As management takes on a new role, so must the union and the employees. All three must involve themselves in some new processes that have them working together toward some common objectives. Working together seems to bring about change far sooner than do eons of dialogue.

From our early efforts to reduce alienation at traditional workplaces, it seems that decision participation must come into play early in the process. This comes slowly at first for people not accustomed to participating, but the encouragement to participate begins to narrow the credibility gap and most people join in after a few invitations.

Lastly, management must discard traditional policies and practices that presume or embody mistrust. Where these policies are rooted in provisions of a labor agreement such as the probationary concept or a host of other rigid systems, the company and union must work these out together. And this teamwork is not likely to occur unless the union and employees are playing a part in the entire change process.

P.S.

What Eaton is doing is not complex. When one observer suggested we were only getting the "Hawthorne effect," we glowed and said that was exactly right. All we are trying to do is "bottle" the Hawthorne effect, and share respect and concern with employees.

It is significant that about a quarter of the companies that research the Eaton approach and visit a facility adapt some form of the process for one or more of their own locations. Of equal significance, however, are some of the reasons cited by those who do not make changes in their own organizations. In some cases, the inquirer is personally enthusiastic but sees no chance to influence traditional higher management in his company. This happens mostly with people from small companies where the chief executive officer is seen as having a negative attitude that dominates the entire organization. In larger, multiple plant facilities, such as Eaton, the change is often introduced at an interested branch, and then spreads throughout the organization.

Conversely, in some cases the chief executive officer, impressed by the concept, expresses doubt that other key people in his organization could implement these new processes.

Some people say they are hesitant to propose such an approach in their own companies because there are so many seemingly complex theories of behavior now on the shelf that the company fears embarking on any particular course when it may soon be outdated. Some inquirers are actually startled to find that Eaton people are not steeped in any particular behavioral school.

Those companies that have tried the Eaton approach have confirmed our experiences. They report:

1. This approach is fundamentally fair and makes sense even if it doesn't prove to be a panacea.
2. It is based on some very specific and simple actions that can be implemented by existing personnel.
3. The company can rely on its own innovators, and not, as one inquirer put it, on "a behavioral guru."
4. The approach does not require a large financial investment, and even a 1 percent increase in plant utilization or a 2 percent drop in absenteeism brings a substantial return on investment.

At Eaton we are convinced that concern, respect, and trust in people produce a cohesive and effective workplace. Complex evaluation procedures, behavioral science theories and analyses, job design, and individual consultations are not primary and often not necessary. In fact, the process is more akin to an attitude than to a detailed intellectual plan. Most supervisors and managers boast of the esprit de corps and excitement that builds as the approach takes hold. One manager, when asked by a visitor just beginning his tour, "What will I see different out there?" responded, "A feeling."

Perhaps behavioral science's gallop is leaping over some very simple and moving truths. When bird hunters spontaneously prepare a duck casserole luncheon for the entire work force; when a fifty-seven-year-old-man boasts how his wife of thirty-seven years has finally got him bowling and dancing " 'cause I come home so rarin' "; when a plant's annual aspirin consumption is down to a small bottle; when hospitalized employees are visited by about 20 percent of the work force; when the plant community spontaneously plants trees and shrubs to create its own wooded picnic area; and when a guitar-playing employee sits in that picnic area and sings his own folk song about a "workplace havin' soul," then something constructive and productive is truly happening somehow.

DO SUPERVISORS THRIVE
IN PARTICIPATIVE WORK SYSTEMS?

Richard E. Walton   Leonard A. Schlesinger

In order to generate improvements in employee productivity and the quality of work life, social scientists and managers have embarked on a number of efforts to fundamentally restructure the manner in which work is performed. Such work restructuring efforts have addressed the way tasks are organized into jobs, the way workers relate to each other and to management, the way performance is measured and rewards are distributed, the way positions of authority and status symbols are structured, and the way career paths are conceived. They invariably have provided for increased levels of employee participation in the management of organizations, often utilizing team structures.

In a recent paper (1976), we reviewed a number of work restructuring projects in an attempt to portray the risks and opportunities that face the parties involved in such efforts. Our analysis at that time indicated that a particularly troublesome aspect of these projects was the appropriate reformulation of the first-line supervisory role.

That the traditional supervisory role needs to be modified is generally acknowledged by those initiating work restructuring. Also, they usually agree upon the general direction of change in behavior. A more consultative pattern of supervision is seen as a way to avoid the common reaction of subordinates to get turned off when someone is "breathing down their neck." Wider participation is viewed as a way to enhance the quality of information available for decisions and increase the commitment to those decisions. Assigning a group of subordinates joint or collective responsibility for performing certain functions is intended to encourage a variety of emergent patterns of cooperation and a team-level identification, with potential benefits for the task and for social satisfaction.

This article presents, in a preliminary fashion, our findings regarding the nature of the difficulties surrounding the supervisory role in participative work systems, a conceptualization of the supervisor/work group interface, and some action implications for the management of organizations. These findings are based on the experiences of 12 manufacturing plants in

Richard E. Walton and Leonard A. Schlesinger, "Do Supervisors Thrive in Participative Work Systems?" reprinted, by permission of the publisher, from Organizational Dynamics, Winter 1979, © 1979 by AMACOM, a division of American Management Associations, New York. All rights reserved.

which we have served as consultants or researchers. In nine of the plants, the work restructuring efforts were plantwide and had been introduced during the plant start-up. These plants ranged in age from one to nine years, the median age being about three years; they ranged in size from 70 to 1,500 employees, the median size being 350 employees.

The work restructuring projects introduced in the three older, established plants were confined to one or two departments per plant, these departments ranging in size from 25 to 150 employees. The sample included a mix of technologies—continuous flow, batch, and assembly process—in paper, food, automotive, and farm equipment industries. Subsequent reports will present the findings of a more systematic and intensive study of supervisors in six of the plants.

Supervisory role difficulties have been manifested in many ways: Those who occupied the role often expressed dissatisfaction and evidenced high levels of ambiguity about their responsibilities and authority. One supervisor said of this situation: "I'm like one of those lizards that are always changing colors, except that I don't have any control over what color I am. When the workers want me I've always got to be there. When they don't, I have to tread lightly."

A large number of supervisors complained that they lack the skills and organizational support to do their jobs well. In one large manufacturing plant, for example, daily team meetings of workers and supervisors were instituted without any training for the supervisors assigned to lead them. Many of these individuals had not held meetings in over 20 years! Their response to these meetings was predictably negative.

Others voiced disappointment because whatever recognition they got for the accomplishments of their units was not commensurate with the effort they had invested in their work. One said, "With the system we've got here, all the attention is focused on the hourly workers. They get most of the training opportunities and rewards from management. When things are going well, no one recognizes how I've busted my butt to get the team working together. But when things are going poorly, they let me know right away."

Typically, supervisors have assumed that they could not get their own concerns attended to as readily as most other groups in the organization. Such assumptions tend to reinforce personal feelings of marginality and uselessness in the supervisory role.

Although some of the grievances are not unlike those voiced by supervisors in more conventional organizations we believe they have tended to be more pronounced in many of the participative work systems studied, an observation supported by the self-reports of a number of supervisors who have had experience in both kinds of plant organization.

Our sample of 12 plants contained a range of supervisory satisfaction from high to low. Even within a single plant, the range of individual supervisors' experiences was substantial. Finally, the degree of satisfaction for a supervisor tended to change considerably with developments in the organization, especially during the first few years of newly established plants. Nevertheless, in most cases, there was relatively less satisfaction or more dissatisfaction at the first-line supervisory level than in positions above or below them in the same plant organization hierarchy. Where dissatisfaction was voiced by the supervisors themselves, it was matched by similarly negative comments about the supervisory level voiced both by their organizational superiors and by subordinates.

As we shall see, these striking levels of frustration in the sample of plants result from a variety of unrealistic expectations and a number of shortcomings in implementing more realistically formulated roles.

A PROPOSED CONCEPTUALIZATION

By providing workers with an opportunity to assume additional responsibility and autonomy, one blurs the distinction between what has been traditionally conceived as managerial work and hourly employee work. Consider, for example, Dunnette's (1974) critical dimensions of effective leadership performance of traditional supervisory roles:

1. *Know-how.* The supervisor keeps thoroughly informed of organizational needs and keeps up to date technically.
2. *Responsibility.* The supervisor is ready and able to accept personal responsibility for actions.
3. *Integrity.* The supervisor maintains high standards of business, professional, and social ethics.
4. *Wisdom.* The supervisor exhibits informed commitment and loyalty to organizational goals, policies, and practices.
5. *Empathy.* The supervisor shows personal concern and understanding for other persons.
6. *Communication.* The supervisor communicates effectively, thoroughly, and accurately.
7. *Representation.* The supervisor presents a positive organizational image to the public.
8. *Motivation.* The supervisor motivates subordinates and others through example and challenge.
9. *Training.* The supervisor determines subordinates' training needs and institutes programs to meet them.
10. *Coaching.* The supervisor provides direct performance feedback to subordinates and shows them how to improve performance.
11. *Coordination.* The supervisor negotiates with and cooperates with other organizational units for optimal use of all resources in meeting organizational goals.
12. *Innovation.* The supervisor develops and applies innovative procedures to accomplish organizational goals.
13. *Planning and allocation.* The supervisor forms goals and allocates resources to meet them.

14. *Delegation.* The supervisor assigns tasks to others and monitors performance.
15. *Accomplishment.* The supervisor persists with consistent high effort in all facets of performance.
16. *Crisis action.* The supervisor recognizes critical problems and acts promptly and decisively to alleviate them.
17. *Follow-up and documentation.* The supervisor documents actions and keeps accurate records of results.

These 17 statements of what the supervisor ought to do presumably are valid and integral elements of his ideal role definition in a more conventionally organized work system.

In participative work systems, the burden of a cluster of additional *oughts* is placed on the supervisor. These 17 elements of leadership ought to be relatively widely diffused throughout the work unit for which the supervisor is responsible. The supervisors should supervise in a way that enables them to assume responsibility for most or all of the required coordination internal to the unit and some external to it, to train each other, to take on many of the planning functions of the unit, to solve problems in crisis situations, to develop innovative procedures to improve upon normal operations, and to coach each other and impose sanctions on counterproductive behavior of fellow workers. In other words, one might say that the supervisor is expected to delegate as much as possible of his functions. He ought to work himself out of a job completely or to some significant extent. Thus, while delegation is an issue in any managerial position, both conceptually and practically it is the cornerstone dimension of the supervisory role in participative work systems.

Figure 1 outlines a conceptualization of the supervisory/work group interface that depicts the delegation of previously managerial functions to workers and work groups as their skills develop over time. Figure 2 itemizes some of the additional self-management capabilities that are contemplated in work restructuring projects of the kind we studied.

As Figure 1 indicates, at the outset new workers and newly formed work groups are assumed to possess limited technical know-how and limited skills in organizing themselves to coordinate their efforts to make decisions and solve problems. Therefore, in order to fulfill the technical, administrative, and social requirements of the task addressed, supervisors (or some other resource) must supply much of the expertise and play a largely directive high-profile role. With time and the provision of appropriate training and development for workers, the load of day-to-day responsibilities should shift. As workers and work groups develop the capacity to direct their own activities and increase their technical capabilities (Space A), the supervisor's active role relative to the group and the task should tend to shrink in a directly corresponding pattern (Space B), freeing up a capacity for supervisors to assume other functions (Space C).

A number of additional *oughts* for the management organization can

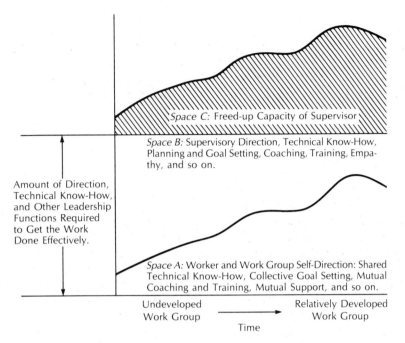

FIGURE 1.   Supervisory-Work Group Interface for Delegation

be readily derived from the foregoing conceptualization. For example, the organization must provide for investment in training to develop the technical and organizational skills required in order to make delegation a viable option. The organization must ensure that the supervisor has some net positive incentive to delegate functions to the work group. And the organization must consider how to employ productively the freed-up capacity of supervisors when they do succeed in working themselves out of some of their supervisory tasks.

ANALYSIS OF ROLE DIFFICULTIES

Contributing to the difficulties that we observed as the management/workforce interface have been a number of common fallacies that underlie the design and implementation of work restructuring.

Neglect of Start-up versus Steady-State Distinctions.   In several instances, there was an implicit assumption that the work teams would start at an advanced state of development. Neglected was the important distinction between conceiving of the design of the steady-state organization and

FIGURE 2. Illustrative Self-Direction Capability by Work Teams

Area	Some Capability	Moderate Capability	High Capability
Team's social capability in terms of knowledge, skills, and team culture or climate	—Cooperative norms and effective sharing of work by members. —Team able to allocate tasks to team members —Self-discipline by team members —Peer pressure precludes blatant counterproductive practices	—Team able to assimilate new members rapidly; handle moderate levels of turnover of membership without deteriorating self-direction capacity —Team members able to counsel and to give and receive feedback —Team able to allocate learning opportunities, with future implications for pay —Peer pressure can deal with certain moderately controversial issues, such as absenteeism	—Able to identify, diagnose own social problems. —Able to preserve cohesion and team loyalty and yet also handle high level of diversity —Able to make allocations of pay (with its practical-economic-family implications)
Technical and economic capability	—Knowledge of basic operating requirements of several jobs —Knowledge of basic maintenance requirements —Knowledge of basic quality specifications —Understand a few performance objectives	—Knowing how one's current tasks are affected by previous operations and what to communicate to whom —Understanding more complex maintenance requirements —Understanding multiple objectives and the current priorities to place on quality, quantity, waste control, labor efficiency, machine utilization, and so on	—Team able to diagnose complex problems in each of a number of performance areas —Possess the basic economic information to make trade-off decisions affecting two or more performance objectives —Team able to evaluate own proposals for improvements recurring investments, including stream of savings or earnings by computing return on investment

designing the initial organization. Thus the role responsibilities described for newly hired workers and interface managers reflected those idealized in the steady-state organizations. In fact, initially work team members lacked the technical and human skills and their teams lacked the problem-solving capacity to be self-managing and perform effectively. When it became clear that it was necessary to raise the profile and involvement of the first-line managers whose teams were floundering, the unrealistic expectations of team members had to be revised downward, thereby risking the cynicism of teams and complicating supervisors' efforts to gain legitimacy in the exercise of directive supervision.

Interestingly, in at least two plants where the need for more supervisory direction was neglected during plant start-up, the teams that were most advanced in self-management after 15 months were among those whose supervisors had held a tight rein initially. At first, these more structural supervisors had been the cause of concern for both subordinates and superiors—concern that they were not supporting the participative work system. Of course, not all supervisors who provided relatively high structure initially were effective in encouraging subsequent development toward self-management; in some cases the teams became more firmly dependent on supervisory direction.

The extent of the difference between start-up and steady-state conditions and therefore the length of time it will take to develop capacities of the workforce to handle large doses of delegation significantly depends on the technical complexity of the production technology. An insufficient understanding of production technology has led to problems in a number of the sites studied. One plant, for example, started up manufacturing a new product with substantial amounts of new technology, yet chose a design that called for no direct supervision and limited technical training of hourly employees. The results were predictably unsatisfactory. Another plant, with a stable, simple, labor-intensive technology started up with a design incorporating a three and one-half year learning curve for tasks that employees could master in five months. As a result, supervisors have experienced great difficulty in coordinating a development process that is proceeding much more rapidly than planned for. This has added to significant interface problems.

The avoidance of major start-up problems requires a detailed understanding of the production technology and its implications for task complexity, necessary operating skills, and the amount of time and talent required to learn them.

Unrealistic Assumptions Regarding Work Group Developmental Trends. Managers often operate as if there is an identifiable trend line toward the self-direction that never plateaus or reverses itself, even where it is recognized that work groups take time to develop. Consequently, organizations and supervisors are not prepared for the possibility of supervisors having to resume a higher-profile role as a result of a drop in a group's self-direction capacity. Our conceptualization of Figure 1, which depicts a possible development path of workers' and work groups' self-direction capacity, shows a few temporary setbacks in the maturation process; it also can plateau at a level below its peak. Many conditions can lower the level of development: Interpersonal conflicts or rival cliques can emerge that decrease the ability of a group to reach consensus; an additional shift or unit can be started up, creating turnover that will lower the level of technical skill in the initial work group; technological developments can render workers and work groups temporarily or permanently more dependent on external direction and support.

The fact that work teams within the same plant do develop at different rates and may plateau at different levels of self-management capability requires management tolerance of diversity. Some managements have not explicitly accepted such diversity, and therefore have not managed it well, especially when the interteam differences in autonomy are discussed in terms of equity.

Managers would be well advised not to think in terms of completely eliminating the role of first-line supervision and to plan for contingencies that require an *increase* as well as a decrease in the amount of supervision over time. They should also recognize and legitimatize diversity among teams in terms of the amount of responsibility and autonomy delegated to them at any point in time.

Insufficient System Stability.   Managers often pay inadequate attention to the need for stability in implementing innovative supervisory roles. For example, after adopting a self-managing team concept for employees who worked single shifts in a three-shift operation, supervisors in one plant continued to rotate shifts every six months. Six-month tours with a group did not permit the development of effective personal relations and shared understanding regarding role responsibilities. This, in turn, retarded the achievement of effective self-management capabilities.

Care must be taken to minimize further disruption of an already dynamic system. However important it is to have a clear philosophical understanding of team development and progressive delegation by supervisors, these processes remain basically transactions among specific individuals who must know, respect, and trust each other.

Underestimating in Recruitment and Selection.   In most instances, the recruitment and selection of employees for this dynamic supervisory role has received inadequate attention. In some instances, individuals with no technical or managerial experience were hired to start up a plant that used complex technology and had inexperienced employees. These supervisors had little to offer their work groups in this early developmental phase and were rapidly relegated to a "go-for" role. In other instances, plants hired highly experienced supervisors who could manage this early phase but did not have either the requisite attitudes or skills to let go of their functions and assist work groups in their development. In yet another situation, college-educated supervisors were brought into an organization for an initial assignment designed to last one to two years and were moved out at the point when they had developed sufficient skills to make a contribution to their work group's development.

Supervisor selection is a matter which must be addressed in concert with the management organization's analysis of four characteristics:

1. The requirements of the technology.
2. The experience level of the workforce.
3. The availability of career paths beyond the supervisory level (lateral or upward).
4. The skills and capabilities of management above the supervisory level.

Failing to Provide Adequate Supervisory Skill Development. Many projects we observed, including some with a heavy training effort directed at workers and work groups, failed to recognize fully the need for new supervisory skills. As a result, inadequate training generally has been provided for supervisors who must deal with highly participative work groups. Further, these organizations offer few role models for supervisors whose role it is to develop subordinate groups to the point where the supervisors themselves are no longer needed. At higher levels of management, generally little attention has been paid to the importance of exploiting the informal coaching opportunities that are available in manager/supervisor interactions. Such developmental activities can provide a model to guide the supervisor's behavior vis-à-vis work teams.

Of major importance is the development of a list of skills necessary for supervisory success in individual plants and the allocation of adequate training resources, both formal and informal, to assist supervisors in obtaining these skills.

Failing to Tie Supervisory Evaluation and Reward Systems to Team Development. Few of the workplace innovations we have studied have tried to tie evaluation, measurement, and reward systems directly into the supervisor's mandate to reduce his presence considerably or work himself out of a job. Most managers and supervisors we have studied have not outlined in operational terms the extent to which they wish workers to participate in the management of their organizations. Consequently, developmental benchmarks around technical, administrative, and social skills are not built into the systems. In two organizations, an attitude developed among managers which tended to overemphasize the uniqueness of their particular organization and rejected the application of traditional managerial tools, such as evaluation against goals.

In the absence of more systematic timetables and incentives, we observed different forces working toward the same end. In one case, the plant manager acted on a theory of agitation. When he sensed that a team was capable of taking on another significant chunk of responsibility, he would agitate the team members to put pressure on the supervisors to help them take another developmental step. A second case involved first-line supervisors who were college graduates in their initial management assignments. Their promotion from the supervisory position (which would get them off rotating shift work) was dependent in part on whether their team was sufficiently developed that the transition would not adversely affect team performance.

It is appropriate for managers to work with a supervisor to establish time-tables for his or her responsibilities as a developer of a work group, and it is also appropriate to establish benchmarks for determining to what level a group's capabilities have been developed. This strategic aspect of the supervisory role is clearly amenable to some form of goal setting, systematic assessment, and reward. It tends not to be treated this way. It should be.

Absence of Supervisory Support Systems.　Surprisingly, many projects have been developed in a way that belies an early assumption that no provisions had to be made for supervisors' needs to share their feelings with each other about this tension-laden role and to develop their own voice in the organization. In most projects the recognition comes after the need is felt most acutely. The efforts to build a team of supervisors have usually been well received. The underlying fallacy may be some idea that only the quality of work life of *workers* counts. The worst thing that can happen, and it has happened, is that supervisors, too, accept that underlying fallacy.

The remedy for this difficulty is relatively straightforward, once the need is recognized; namely, anticipate the need to build relationships among superiors and take steps to legitimize concern about their productivity and the quality of their work life.

Lack of Plans to Utilize Freed-up Capacity.　We found that supervisors were in most cases charged with working themselves progressively out of a job without any systematic planning for utilizing the managerial capacity that would become surplus. A number of utilization options have been explored at the sites studied. In some cases these options have been implemented effectively; in others they have merely generated new problems.

The first considered solution to freed-up capacity is to deploy it within the team. Thus, in two plants, management addressed the issue of freed-up capacity by adding a number of new functions to the role. For example, supervisors were expected to hold regular one-to-one meetings with each of their employees and document each meeting as well as develop and implement plans to reduce equipment down time. They were also expected to participate in a number of meetings on issues that prior to this time had never been considered. This merely delays the problem. Moreover, if the added functions are important, it can be argued that they should not wait until time permits—maybe they are even more important during earlier developmental stages.

Some managements have progressively enlarged the supervisors' span of control, perhaps with an eventual goal of eliminating supervision. In some cases, supervisors have been able to take on a second adjacent team on the same shift or assume responsibility for the second- and third-shift crews. Sometimes this has created concern, especially among other supervisors who, if displaced, would not be promotable.

There is a cost to building new supervisory skills that will soon become obsolete. Some plants have invested significant amounts of supervisory training time in individuals who quite possibly will perform the role for a limited time. In organizations with widespread availability of supervisory or other alternatively acceptable positions, this is not a major problem, but for most organizations the problem is considerable.

Some participative work systems have assumed that this freed-up capacity of first-line supervision would be utilized by pulling down functions from higher levels of management. In one positive case, as the plant marked its first anniversary supervisors were quite upset over the amount of "dead time" they were beginning to find themselves having. The plant manager encouraged them to meet as a team and determine the functions currently performed by higher management that they would like to assume. The follow-through was less than the promise. As in other cases, such transfers have tended not to happen in practice, in part because people hired into first-line supervisory positions have tended not to have the basic analytical and technical capabilities to perform the higher management functions in question. Perhaps, too, it is in part because having supervisors perform middle management functions is potentially as threatening to some middle managers as having workers perform supervisory roles is to some supervisors. If higher-level managers delegate some of *their* functions to the freed-up middle managers, the implications and potential for resistance move up yet another level. When plant management is unable or unwilling to provide new and attractive tasks and responsibilities to various levels of the existing hierarchy, difficulties can be anticipated.

Basically, the same argument holds for situations in which staff specialist functions have been transferred to supervisors. Staff specialists have resisted yielding parts of their domains of expertise. In addition, staff functions that serve in a monitoring role have resisted the notion of having supervisors monitor themselves by performing their own quality control checks and so on.

Managers are in a position of having to provide gap-filling opportunities to supervisors while at the same time keeping similar gaps from opening up at other levels of the organization. Although there are no clear solutions to this problem, we have found that developing an explicit awareness of the problem and promoting open discussions among the affected parties have been of significant value.

SUCCESSFUL STRATEGIES FOR ADDRESSING THE SUPERVISOR ISSUE

While these pages have focused attention on the problems and root causes of the role difficulties experienced by supervisors in work restructuring projects, a number of the organizations studied have experienced significant success in addressing these issues. One company—let's call it XYZ, Inc.—has had a number of years of experience in the implementation of work restructuring programs in both new and existing operations and has made great strides in providing supervisors with relatively satisfying roles despite all the potential problems. What follows are the highlights of a number of its efforts.

Recruitment and Selection.   XYZ deliberately strives to achieve a mix of skills, backgrounds, age, and educational experience in its supervisory force. While a sizable number of supervisors are recent college graduates who assume the supervisory role on a short-term (one- to three-year) basis, they are complemented by a contingent of up-from-the-floor promotions to supervisor as well as a number of individuals brought in from the outside who have extensive manufacturing or military backgrounds. The intent of this recruitment strategy is threefold: (1) It ensures continuing technical and managerial skills at the base of the managerial hierarchy. (2) It provides potential high-level managerial personnel with an in-depth understanding of and appreciation for participative work systems through an initial supervisory assignment. (3) By fostering formal and informal interaction among the supervisors, it promotes the interchange of individual skills and competence—for example, assigning a supervisor with extensive manufacturing experience to help a new college-educated supervisor in learning the technology and assigning the new supervisor to help the experienced supervisor in writing reports or organizing meetings.

This strategy has generally been quite successful and, where the organization has been able to foster close working relationships among the supervisors, has developed into an extremely powerful socialization and training vehicle.

Training.   All supervisors are provided with extensive formal and on-the-job training in human relations skills—performance appraisal, problem solving, team meetings, communication, and so on—as well as in the manufacturing process. New supervisors are provided with an 8- to 12-week training period that allows them to gain an in-depth knowledge of the work system and the personnel at all levels of the organization without the pressure of meeting daily production demands.

In addition, a great deal of training is directed at assisting the supervisor in gaining an appreciation of group dynamics and group development in the context of his or her role as the person who will assist a work group in developing the capacity for increased self-direction.

Evaluation and Reward Systems.   At XYZ, Inc. the evaluation and reward systems are closely tied to the supervisor's achievements in team development. Supervisors are expected to regularly provide their superiors with training plans for individual workers that cover a 6- to 12-month time frame, and many further prepare team development game plans that establish measurable benchmarks for the team in a number of key areas. All these plans grow out of extensive consultation with the shop floor workforce.

Performance appraisals for supervisors are conducted within a group's format, with appraisal feedback supplied by workers and supervisory peers as well as by their managers. The results of these appraisals feed into both the salary system and the career planning system.

Supervisory Support Systems.   At regular intervals supervisors are provided with the opportunity to have offsite meetings that allow them to address a number of issues of personal and general concern. On a number of occasions these meetings have been facilitated through the use of organization development consultants. These meetings provide for the sharing of experiences, tensions, and frustrations among peers, which is so difficult to accomplish during the normal workday.

Also, through the establishment of a supervisory team of sorts, they have been quite successful in increasing the importance of their voice in the organization.

Utilization of Freed-up Capacity.   XYZ, Inc. has experimented with a number of strategies for utilizing freed-up supervisory capacity and has settled on a deliberate mix of strategies to be tailored to the individual needs and desires of supervisors as well as to the needs of the business. The high level of activity engaged in by supervisors around individual and team training and development limits the amount of their free time to a greater extent than at the other sites studied. Yet we found supervisors involved in higher-level budgeting and project work, plantwide training and development programs, and individual development activities. In one area, shift supervision has been completely eliminated, the supervisors having been transferred to satisfactory assignments in other areas of the organization.

The strategies used by XYZ have not eliminated the problems that have concerned us here, but have alleviated them significantly. The supervisory workforce at XYZ is recognized as an important and effective group throughout the organization, and the levels of satisfaction reported by supervisors at XYZ ranked at the top of the sites examined.

SUMMARY

In sum, supervisory roles within innovative work systems can be analyzed and improved by emphasizing task accomplishment through increased employee participation and self-direction. Many of the problems that currently surround the supervisory role are an outgrowth of inadequate conceptualization of the dynamic nature of the role relative to the work group and consequently to the larger organization.

A number of common problems have an impact on the supervisory role, as we have seen, and one company's efforts to address the issue reflect considerable progress. Additional research is underway to generate further insights into the subject.

As workplace innovations that promote employee participation and self-direction become more widespread, models of collaborative leadership are needed that can provide the operating manager with tools for the design and management of organizations capable of enhancing both employer productivity and the quality of working life.

SELECTED BIBLIOGRAPHY

First, of course, are the two articles we mention in text: Leonard A. Schlesinger and Richard E. Walton's "Work Restructuring in Unionized Organizations: Risks, Opportunities and Impacts on Collective Bargaining" (Proceedings of the Industrial Relations Research Association, September 1976) and Marvin Dunnette's "The Hawthorne Effect: Its Societal Meaning" in Cass and Zimmer's Man and Work in Society (Van Nostrand-Reinhold, 1974).

Other works that are important in this area are George Strauss's "Managerial Practices" in J. Richard Hackman and Lloyd Suttle's Improving Life at Work (Goodyear Publishing, 1977), which presents an overview of many of the issues that confront supervisors in quality of work life projects; J. R. Hackman's "Is Job Enrichment Just a Fad?" (Harvard Business Review, September-October 1975), which reviews on a more general basis the problems that have contributed to less satisfactory outcomes from work restructuring; Robert Tannenbaum and Warran H. Schmidt's "How to Choose a Leadership Pattern" (*Harvard Business Review*, May–June 1973), which introduces the notion of a leadership continuum that is situationally based and clearly appropriate to the ideas we develop in this article; and Robert A. Luke's "A Structural Approach to Organizational Change" (*Journal of Applied Behavioral Science*, September-October 1973).

HUMAN RESOURCE PLANNING: AN EVOLUTION

James W. Walker

A decade ago, human resource planning was cited as an emerging function of management responding to demands for new talent and improved development and use of existing talent. Has the function emerged since then? In what ways has it changed? What exactly has become of this promising new dimension of human resource management?

How human resource planning has evolved and how it is taking shape to meet the changing needs of the years ahead will be described here. Techniques have become more sophisticated through years of application and research, but the crux of human resource planning's development has been its capacity to help managers satisfy needs for talent to achieve organizational objectives.

Effectiveness of human resource planning practices depends largely on how relevant they are to practical managerial concerns and prevailing demands on an organization. Planning for human resource needs is more than a set of techniques and a system that is part of the personnel function. Today it is widely viewed as the way management comes to grips with ill-defined and tough-to-solve human resource problems facing an organization.

ORIGINS AND EVOLUTION

Since the origins of the modern industrial organization, management has been concerned with human resource planning. Economist Alfred Marshall observed in 1890 that "the head of a business must assure himself that his managers, clerks, and foremen are the right men for their work and are doing their work well." Division of labor, specialization, organization, work simplification and application of standards for selecting employees and measuring their performance: all were principles applied early in industrial management. They were also applied in large nonindustrial organizations, including religious, governmental and military groups.

James W. Walker, "Human Resources Planning: An Evolution," Pittsburgh Business Review 47, No. 1, March 1979. Reprinted with permission.

Planning for the staffing of work to be done is not a recent concept. The relatively sophisticated techniques available in management today are the outcome of a long period of evolution in practices, beginning decades ago with simple, pragmatic, short-term planning. The methods used by management have tended to fit the contemporary conditions and events. During the first half of the century, for example, the focus of manpower planning was on the hourly production worker. The aim of improved efficiency through work engineering and early industrial psychology applications was consistent with the need to improve productivity and introduce greater objectivity to personnel practices.

During World War II and the postwar years, the focus intensified on employee productivity. Concern also was great about the availability of competent managerial personnel due to a talent shortage coupled with a significant demand for goods and services. New technologies and interest in behavioral aspects of work also added complexities to the manpower planning task.

Expanded demand for high-talent personnel in the 1960s resulted from the high-technology programs involved in the space race and rapid corporate expansion and diversification. In response, manpower planning practices were focused on balancing supply with demand, particularly for managerial, professional and technical personnel. The demographic shortage of men from the age of 30 to 40 in general and shortages of specific engineering and scientific skills in particular were noteworthy during this period. The textbooks written during the latter part of the decade document these conditions and concerns well, with manpower planning viewed as a system linking the organization with the environment.

STATE OF THE ART

In the decade ahead, there may be less legislation, but administration and enforcement of laws will likely be strengthened and diverse regulations affecting company human resource practices will be consolidated. At the same time, employee desires for participation in decisions that affect their work and careers will become stronger, as will management desires for improved control over costs and profitability. As a result, companies will adopt work and career management practices of the type reflected in innovations under affirmative action programs.

By the year 2001 and beyond, today's radical practices will likely be considered commonplace. It is projected, for example, that workers will have reduced working hours and significant reshaping of work and work customs (such as not going to an office). Government may have more direct involvement in matching individuals with jobs both across and within organizations under equal opportunity objectives. Futurists anticipate continued work force expansion, limited availability of work, and strong desires for individual autonomy within large complex organizations.

Techniques and practices have therefore been developed and applied to satisfy needs resulting from managerial concerns and, indirectly, from economic, social and technological changes in the environment. The state-of-the-art practices applied in a few leading organizations indicate emerging needs and priorities that may ultimately affect other organizations.

For example, Sears, Bank of America, AT&T, and General Motors have led the way in developing advanced career management techniques, in part because of their EEO/Affirmative Action commitments. Many other retailers, banks, utilities, and large manufacturers have not felt the same degree of pressure to move that boldly into broad new programs.

A MODERN APPROACH

Effective human resource planning is a process of analyzing an organization's human resource needs under changing conditions and developing the activities necessary to satisfy these needs. It is essentially a two-step process. The emphasis is on techniques or systems to be applied. The *forecasting of needs* allows determining of priorities and allocating of resources to where they can do the most good.

Analysis of needs leads to *program planning*. While the activities and programs may run through the gamut of human resource management, the emphasis of new programs tends to be on the areas relating directly to current issues. During the 70s and 80s, four basic areas appear to be of primary concern to management. These concerns reflect issues identified in the above discussion of changing conditions and events:

- Needs forecasting: improved planning and control over staffing and organizational requirements, based on analysis of conditions.
- Performance management: improving the performance of individuals and of the organization as a whole.
- Career management: improving the performance of individuals and of the organization as a whole.
- Management development: activities to assess and develop the managerial talent needed to satisfy future succession needs.

In focusing on these four areas, the contemporary approach to human resource planning establishes a link between the broad range of external and organizational factors on the one hand, and specific personnel programs on the other. The planning approach defines human resource needs within the context of the organization's overall needs and defines a strategy to satisfy them. In this way, individual development, recruitment, compensation and other activities become integral parts of a dynamic process.

Training programs, for example, are warranted only if they are shown to be pertinent to prevailing skill or knowledge needs.

Decisions in different parts of an organization or in different functional areas are thereby brought into the same planning framework. Termination of employees for poor performance cannot logically follow sizable bonus awards or salary increases for these individuals. Laying off employees in one quarter while recruiting comparable employees in another would also be avoided. All programs are measured against affirmative action plans and against the other tests of necessity.

The contemporary approach also features a strong link between individual goals and plans and those of the organization. Historically, programs have been designed to meet organizational needs. But in the years ahead, it will be increasingly important to balance organizational needs with needs of employees and society in general. Employee career interests, relocation preferences, and development plans will be weighed in needs forecasting. Societal pressures for disclosure of company policies and practices for hiring of minorities, job sharing, more flexible work schedules and other new programs also will be evaluated. In the future, contrary to the adage, what is good for individuals may be what is considered good for the company, as well.

NEEDS FORECASTING

Few executives today are not concerned about controlling personnel costs. In an era of continuing inflation, rapidly rising costs, and increased competitive pressures on profits, personnel costs are a big concern. In many businesses, personnel costs rank near the top among all costs. In banks, they rank second only to cost of capital. In many manufacturing firms, labor costs have risen more rapidly than any cost except energy. There is therefore considerable interest extending into all ranks in improved forecasting and control of staffing, particularly professional and managerial.

The common approach to the problem of staffing is the planning and budgeting process, involving participation by successive levels of management. Properly conducted planning and budgeting yields estimates of future demand, supply, and net human resource needs accepted as valid by managers. In the past forecasting has been enhanced by:

- Including human resource forecasting in the budgeting cycle, requiring submission of plans along with financial budgets.
- Requiring estimates of needs from each organizational unit (bottom up), so that unit managers are committed to them.
- Analyzing supply through computerized models (forecasting flows of employees in, up, over, and out of the organization).
- Reviewing facts and forecast assumptions by senior executives, in authorizing future staffing levels.

To improve the objectivity of staffing plans, companies are also including human resource planning at an earlier stage in the planning cycle. It is not enough, many executives argue, for staffing plans to be budgeted. Human resource needs must be considered in the context of longer range, strategic planning. A number of firms have found themselves short of talent when they were all set to implement broad capital expansion programs. Others have found themselves heavily overstaffed with employees whose talents no longer fitted the company's changing needs, and thus in the uncomfortable position of having to terminate many individuals or force them to retire early. In the years ahead, increased lead time will be provided to allow advance planning for staffing, related career development and organizational changes.

More emphasis is being placed on the qualitative aspects of human resource needs. In many cases improved control of staffing is being achieved through closer attention to the actual nature of the work. Analysis and planning of work activities, organizational changes, and specific job requirements are an increasingly important part of needs forecasting. In an effort to manage the work as well as the people, companies are giving studies of work activities high priority in planning. Numbers alone simply don't tell the whole story.

Computers are also being used more extensively as reliable personnel data are maintained. Introduced in the early 70s into many companies, personnel data systems are only now starting to be used for analysis and planning purposes. Companies are now providing computer-generated analyses of personnel complement, attrition, movement and projected requirements. The use of mathematical models—largely experimental in this decade—will become more common in the years ahead. An incentive for the use of models has been the need for projecting career opportunities in affirmative action planning. To date, most models have focused on forecasting the talent supply. In the future, models will be used extensively for forecasting staffing needs in relation to both changing demand and changing supply. To achieve this, data on changing work activities, workload demands and organizational patterns will be necessary elements in the data systems. In large complex organizations (such as the military services), large-scale modeling is relied on to assure optimal staffing and organization to meet planned objectives.

PERFORMANCE MANAGEMENT

Many executives are convinced that company productivity can be increased through better management of employee performance. Although individual employee motivation is seen as a key factor, other factors such as the structure of jobs, individual competencies, and appropriateness of performance goals and standards of measurement are also considered important. The results of efforts to directly motivate employees to improve performance have, by and large, been disappointing. Companies are therefore trying alternative approaches to obtaining closer control of performance.

For many years, managers have relied on job descriptions and performance appraisals as basic tools in managing performance. Job descriptions are commonly outdated, however, not descriptive of the actual duties. Appraisals are often too general, too unrelated to the work being done (quality of work, initiative, cooperation, etc.).

To strengthen managerial skills in this area, companies are modifying their performance planning and performance appraisal systems. They are making them simpler and easier to use, tailoring them to overcome difficulties experienced in the past. Training and coaching for appraisers have been stepped up in many companies to help managers carry out their part of the process. In some large companies, for example, workshops help appraisers conduct the most difficult part of appraisal: actually discussing performance and future plans with the individual employee.

Employees are being brought more actively into the process: they are being asked to prepare their plans and past performance reviews before discussions with their managers. Management policies and statements of philosophy are being liberalized to encourage open and constructive discussions of performance plans and results. Too often, goal-setting systems were forced into organizational settings that simply weren't prepared to make them work.

An understanding of the work to be performed is a critical element of good performance. Many companies are supplementing their job descriptions with additional tools for analysis of the actual work requirements. Time sheets, activity reporting, special studies, and supplemental job analysis questionnaires are being used to build a broader picture of the activities actually performed and those desired on a job. Such activity/work analysis is becoming more common in part as a response to requirements for improved job-relatedness of employee selection, promotion, pay, termination, and other personnel decisions under EEO regulations.

Finally, companies are making noteworthy changes in working conditions. Experiments to improve the "quality of working life" have pointed the way toward flexible job design, flexible working hours, flexible benefits and compensation, more open communications, open posting/bidding for job assignments, and other innovations. Many companies are working to build rewards into the design of jobs and to make compensation incentives more meaningful to employees.

Overall, practices in managing performance are changing significantly as companies feel pressures to improve their productivity through improved management of people. Traditional practices such as performance appraisal and job description are being reexamined and given vitality through new approaches. As an important management concern, human resource planning focuses on improving performance.

Career Management

Companies are giving more attention to employee careers. With high turnover, a limited supply of competent talent and changing requirements, career development has become an important aspect of human resource planning. Retention and improved utilization of talent are receiving emphasis rather than external recruitment. This means greater attention to selection, appraisal, individual counseling, career planning and innovative training and development programs. Another factor prompting heightened interest in career management has been increased governmental intervention through EEO and Affirmative Action programs. To achieve EEO/AA objectives, companies have developed new job-matching/career progression systems, explicit career paths and job requirements, more objective ways to identify and evaluate prospective candidates for promotions and transfers, and expanded employee development programs. To achieve specific targets for utilization of protected classes, procedures are being adopted in recruitment, selection, placement and development.

Recruiting and selection practices are focused on job criteria. What are the skills, knowledge and experience really needed on a job? Can these requirements be demonstrated to be job related? Executives are increasingly concerned with the quality, not only the quantity, of talent employed. The concern goes beyond the initial candidate selection, progressing through each assignment.

For many employees, the focus of human resource planning is upon career development. The challenge is to develop individual talents fully and to match them with opportunities that best fit the organization's needs. While responsibility for career development rests largely with the employees, the organization can help by providing developmental resources and job-matching vehicles. Some companies, for example, have provided their employees with tools for individual career planning—workbooks, workshops, counseling and career information. The focus of career planning is on self-analysis and development planning. It normally includes examination of personal goals, interests and values; capabilities and limitations (assets); career options and how they relate to personal goals, values and assets; current job performance, so that development may begin immediately and not wait for a different job; and specific development action plans.

Training programs are being redesigned and expanded to meet identified needs. Tuition aid programs are being used more extensively to meet both company and individual needs. More job rotation and special assignments are allowing mutual assessment of individuals as candidates for different kinds of jobs. Data systems are being used to provide practical inventories of available job candidates, often as supplements to open job-posting or bidding systems. And appraisal programs are being expanded (or sometimes split into dual programs) to give improved consideration of individual development progress and plans.

Career development programs have been expanded. For example, special programs have focused on needs of women and minorities to acquire career planning skills and development assistance necessary for equal footing. But the trend is toward broadly based programs open to all employees. Even "fast-track" management development programs, popular in the 1960s to move young managers into executive ranks, have waned as the supply has become greater and the lead time for development planning has extended.

But companies are turning attention to the needs of one "new minority" group—the older workers. Careers of employees approaching retirement were never considered an issue until the Age Discrimination in Employment Act started having an effect. Performance appraisals are now essential in terminating employees over 40 if there is any chance of age discrimination charges. Also companies are providing special counseling and more flexible work/retirement options to employees facing retirement or career changes. Career planning is a natural way of life in many companies, and is likely to become commonplace in the future.

Overall, companies are adopting more formal and more objective systems for appraising individual capabilities and potential, identifying candidates for position vacancies, and guiding individual career development. While managing careers still is primarily on the shoulders of employees themselves, the trend is toward providing resources to aid their planning.

MANAGEMENT DEVELOPMENT

Developing future managers has long been a concern of executives. In the past, the key question dealt with the identification and development of backups for a few key management positions. The primary concern today, however, is to develop broadly experienced and seasoned managers in a way that is simple, practical, meaningful and fair. Companies are focusing on a talent pool, rather than on individual backups for key positions. This allows greater flexibility in planning developmental assignments across organizational/functional lines.

Planning for management development begins today with clarification of job requirements—exactly what do the management positions require? And requirements are changing as the business changes. Rarely do executives feel that their successors will closely fit their own image. Rather, new skills, knowledge and types of experience will be necessary. A number of companies developed Position Profiles, a sort of behavioral job description, for each key position based on inputs from the incumbents and senior management.

Assessment information on candidates is also changing. The trend is toward more specific job-related appraisals rather than global assessment of managerial qualities. The search continues for the basic qualities sought in every effective manager, and assessment programs and appraisals are focused on the qualities currently felt to be important. But the emphasis today is upon the skills, knowledge and experience that candidates may obtain through career development. Less weight is given to ratings of "potential" or "personal promotability" than to specific development needs and plans.

There is also greater consideration of individual goals, interests and preferences in management development. Many companies have acknowledged that they have little "hold" on high-talent individuals. To keep them in the organization and keep them motivated, executives are listening to individual desires regarding career paths, location and other factors. Young managers particularly vocal about their personal career goals and plans are being heard.

SETTING GOALS AND PRIORITIES

So where does a company begin? Varied needs for human resource planning come from internal organizational sources and external pressures. A first necessary step, therefore, is to weigh the various needs and determine their relative priority for management attention. Few organizations even try to respond to all of the concerns felt important to human resource planning. Of course, many external forces are compelling, such as affirmative action agreements and lawsuits. Labor shortages, economic pressures to reduce staff, technological changes, and even social attitudes are not felt evenly across companies, however. An organization may experience more difficulty than others in recruiting high-talent employees; another may have difficulty recruiting but not consider it a noteworthy problem. Those companies "in the crunch" respond with action, while others direct attention to other concerns.

The pressure of competitive employment practices is also unevenly felt. Certain companies and industries are more sensitive to competition than others. For example, the shortage of petroleum engineers, particularly female ones, is a concern of only the few companies aggressively trying to attract them. Retention and motivation of clerical workers tends to be a problem in urban areas and locations with a concentration of businesses.

Some companies have levels of profitability that allow them to implement human resource programs, whether essential or not. Utilities, oil companies and other capital-intensive businesses allocate staff and money to human resource programs under the philosophy that continued growth requires extraordinary attention to the development of required talent. In the first instance, human resource needs and costs are not felt to be particularly significant in the realm of business operations. In the latter instance, human resources are considered potentially key factors affecting future growth and profitability.

In many companies, the concerns, attitudes, values and personal managerial styles of key senior executives tend to set the priorities among human resource needs. In these cases, changing internal organizational conditions affect planning far more than changing external ones. Preserving the status quo is often a number one priority in the minds of conservative executives. Only when external factors or changing internal conditions result in mounting pressures do human resource policies and programs begin to change.

Naturally, executives have primary responsibility for identifying, sorting and initiating action for human resource needs. It is important that their judgment be based on objective analysis of conditions, not on their personal biases or assumptions. In many cases, priorities for human resource planning are selected on the basis of:

- Minimum costs and lowest risk of upsetting existing practices
- Previous personal experiences
- Practices and concerns of other companies
- Consultant advice
- Package approaches readily available on the market

These factors are commonly considered in human resource planning but should never obscure current needs. Goals and priorities should be determined by business plans, obstacles and changing external demands on the organization. The key to effective human resource planning is the analysis of the factors representing change—change that potentially affects the survival, growth, profitability or efficiency of the business.

THE ROLE OF HUMAN RESOURCE PLANNING

IN CORPORATE MANAGEMENT

Eric W. Vetter

. . . The basic thesis in my talk is that human resource management has a major contribution to make in organizations; but only when we learn how to relate our efforts to the primary needs of corporate management.

I shall not, therefore, praise our cause or tout its future. Rather, I am concerned that we may miss our opportunities unless we change some of our ways. I am especially concerned about the organizations whose economic performance suffers because of some of their human resource practices.

For example, we know that the shelves and closets of many organizations are filled with managerial performers. We tolerate "pop gun" managers in positions that require the fire power of a howitzer. We add analysts to do studies that others ignore. We spend money on expensive management development programs that yield little if any payoff and we invest in managers who should be headed for the exit.

To prevent these situations, we must demand that human resource management meet rigorous performance tests. I found that MBA students learned more when the standards were high. I've found Gould managers perform better when the standards are high. Is it possible that the growing philosophy of developing "real understanding" of people and their behavior can subtly cause us to tolerate mediocracy, let alone incompetence?

As human resource types we must be wary of the idea that we are "professionals" rather than "managers." Professionals study, analyze, understand and recommend. Successful managers "make things happen." They practice the Peter Drucker thought of "First things first; Second things not at all."

Therefore, if we are to gain influence with corporate management, we must think and act like those who hold the power in the corporation. When we are perceived as the thinkers, as the nice guys, as the chaplains, it is

Eric W. Vetter, "The Role of Human Resource Planning in Corporate Management," reprinted by permission of the publisher from Human Resource Planning, *Spring 1978. Copyright 1978 by the Human Resource Planning Society.*

because we behave that way. Too often we have accepted these roles. Why? Probably because we want to be liked. Because we prefer to think, to study, to solve problems. Because we are good at conceptualization and planning and at taking a systems view.

And along the way we (i.e., the collective Human Resource manager) become identified with a tolerance of mediocrity, of softness, of a lack of impact. One observer remarked that human resource planners are often among the first to go in a cutback in force. If that is so, then it probably is deserved.

I protest against any department, and especially any in the Human Resource field, that is staffed with second team players, that is weak in will, that is out of touch with operating management.

HUMAN RESOURCE ROLES

How do we alter this role trap of the human resource function? We begin by making corporate profits our dominant concern. The measure of corporate performance is the profit produced. The decision makers in the company worry about ROA, EPS, margins and cost reduction. To influence the power holders we must be bolder. We must do less thinking, less analyzing and less talking. We must be action and results-oriented. We must design programs our operating managers need and want; ones that don't get cut. We must staff our unit in a lean and mean fashion. We need a sense of urgency; too much to do and too little time. We must worry about today's impact and not just tomorrow's. We must want to be winners. We can still be understanding and compassionate—but selectively and with an eye on the vital welfare of the company. We can conceptualize—but not over design solutions. We can be nice guys—but we can also be tough minded. We can do studies—but not make them ends in themselves.

A profit mentality will cause us to make more decisions that are business management oriented and fewer of those that primarily serve our professional interests. Let me illustrate.

At Gould we use outside managerial psychologists to consult with our senior executives and division general managers on organization and people problems. They are useful to organizations' diagnosis and help solve individual people problems. Last year we engaged them to do depth interviews with 15 of our recent top young managerial hires. They were to provide us an evaluation on how well these young managers were meeting our criteria for future general managers, how our recruitment process was working, and what we might do to improve on career management.

The project was a success. One result was a well received special training program on interviewing at Graduate Business Schools for our hand-picked campus interviewers—all drawn from our operations. Included were our senior operating executives, top division general managers, and some of our most promising young managers.

My human resource planner recommended we continue the depth interviewing this year and indeed expand upon it. I asked what will we do with the additional data? How will we use the depth interview conclusions in career planning? What new information can we expect from further studies, and why? I didn't get good answers, but, $25,000 was included in the 1978 budget proposal for the program because it was a highly visible, successful effort. The staff had scored points with corporate management with the first effort and wanted to keep scoring with a repeat performance.

I used the budget discussion to suggest that the $25,000 was not our money. It was stockholder money. If we didn't spend it, the funds went directly to the bottom line. I asked, "If this were your wholly-owned company—100 percent yours—would you put the twenty-five thousand in your pocket or in the study?"

Profits must be our business—it is what corporate management is all about. We must Think Profits—Talk Profits—Make Profits.

KEYS TO PROFITABILITY

In human resource planning, I suggest that we adopt the surrogate: Products + Productivity = Profits.

It is products (and services) which generate revenue. This means that if we are profit conscious, we must look to the product function as an area to direct major effort. More specifically, the product development area—where new products and where modifications to existing products are developed—is a key to our very business survival.

Every quality human resource planning effort must, therefore, direct major attention to the product development function. We must have our finest systems and procedures in this area. Our career development programs must be very operational. Our recruitment and selection must be well planned and executed. Our longer term needs must be anticipated. We must have star performers in place to set the tone for the entire product development function.

When we talk about productivity, we also immediately are talking the language of corporate management. Sadly, however, many of the modern personnel ideas are either non-productivity related or even anti-productivity.

As a professor, I was keenly interested in the changing values of our society; especially, as they relate to work. The decline of the work ethic, the shallowness of the workaholic, the pursuit of leisure, the whole man concept. These are some of the "in" behavioral subjects of the '70s that result in calls for changes in managerial practices.

Human resource planners have unfortunately added their voice to those who suggest we must lower our expectations of job behavior and job performance (read productivity) because of the changing values. Suggested is that we can't expect to see the old work ethic. If we are not careful, however, we will forget that most great achievements of mankind are produced by workaholics and, we will fail to acknowledge that the "whole man" is a solid performer on the job.

The productivity of the managerial workforce is adversely affected by some of the reforms we have encouraged. We tolerate managers who set poor examples. We have lax discipline because we are confused about our performance standards. We fail to communicate an expectation of quality work. Our compassion causes us to assume the blame and feel guilt for marginal workers.

To the extent we foster a gentle approach toward performance problems, we encourage over-staffing, poor organizational tone, weak decision making and the loss of able managers. The bottom line is obviously lower productivity. We must be concerned about employee morale in a demanding environment but high morale of a group of weak performers is not worth much.

Our challenge, then, is to support change, but in a manner that makes good business sense; that increases productivity; that adds to profits. We must avoid being foolish. Fortunately, some excellent productivity work is being realized in factory situations. But more can be accomplished. One approach is to use nonprofessionals in human resource projects. At Gould, we now have an experienced plant manager whose task is to go into plants to help raise labor productivity. He can identify low productivity areas in a plant ten times faster than I can. He does it without a PhD, or consulting experience, or all the reading I've undertaken. He likes factories that hum—and he isn't shy about taking on hard nosed production guys because he is one. He believes in people and their capabilities. He is a practitioner of clear and frequent two-way communications. He sets and communicates high standards. He won't tolerate poor work habits. He is a human resource manager in the best sense.

In one plant on the day of a very severe blizzard about 170 workers showed up even though the police said not to travel. Most Chicago plants didn't open that day. Joe unlocked all the coffee vending machines at 6:30 A.M. and put a note on them saying: "Free Coffee—thanks for your dedication—Joe Gorn." Joe is a non-professional.

ASSESSING THE PROCESS

Two other elements of successful human resource planning should be addressed. One is the process we use in our programs. We should ask three questions about every program (assuming we know who needs the program, why they need it, and that they at least dimly feel they need it). The questions are:

- Is the process understandable?
- Is the process results-oriented?
- Is the process reasonably self-maintaining?

The classic bit of process error from my consulting experience involved a new performance appraisal program. The human resource planner proposed to add a career planning page to the appraisal for exempt employees (later he proposed to add the non-exempts). The process was to involve an open-honest discussion (who can be against that?) between the supervisor and the employee. Self-development goals, counselling on potential and strengths and weaknesses, and a written pact between the two would result. A copy of the form would go to corporate for review and advice, and for analysis to help govern the design of training programs.

We knew the company had over 6000 exempt employees. We asked some questions. The answers were as follows:

"Yes, foremen and salesmen are included; all exempts are included."
"No, we haven't had requests for the program—but our career planning is poor."
"No, most supervisors can't really discuss the jobs above them or outside their department."
"Yes, we will have to add a few specialists at corporate to review the submitted forms."
"No, we probably can't alter the current selection procedures for promotion."
"No, we don't have a program to train supervisors to do the career counselling."

The effort was killed because the process was going to guarantee a disaster. The problem was that the planner loved career planning. He used his needs and his style of management as the model for operating managers.

SENSE OF PURPOSE

A third key element in successful human resource planning is that a strong sense of purpose must exist. We must want to be among the best performing departments in the corporation. We must staff with dedicated, results-oriented, tough-minded, smart people. We must demand the best they have to offer so they will stretch and grow. We must excuse those who can't make the grade; not find a shelf for them. Excellence in our endeavors is therefore part of our sense of purpose.

Another purpose is a strong personal desire for recognition and responsibility. We must want to achieve and excel as individuals. If we don't, we cannot give our function the energy it needs, or the leadership, or the ability to withstand the criticisms that will come our way when we goof.

Finally, at Gould we have a thought that guides our human resource planning. It perhaps is one you use. It is simply: "Raise the Average." We ask division general managers how the average quality of their direct reports are going to be improved over the planning period in terms of performance and potential. We ask each department head that question and importantly, we ask R&D lab directors that question. This simple, but basic idea, can help give purpose to human resource planning.

In summary, a mentality that focuses on profits, products and productivity should be reasonably easy to develop. Then, combine this mentality with sound process and strong purpose. The result, it seems to me, should be a human resource planning effort that is part of the mainstream of events in an organization and one which is able to meet the many potential opportunities of the future.

MANAGEMENT RESOURCE PLANNING: KEYS TO SUCCESS

James F. Bolt

What do IBM, GE, Du Pont, Exxon and Xerox all have in common? Despite their obvious diversity, they have in common a deep concern for the development of their management resources (MR). There is nothing new about that. No self-respecting CEO or other senior executive would argue against the fact that the long-term growth and success of their enterprise requires a certain number and quality of seasoned managers to run the organization. In recent surveys, CEO's and personnel executives ranked this subject as the most critical issue facing their organization. However, the expressed concerns regarding this subject seem to be taking on a sense of urgency. The reason is straightforward enough—competition! Whether it's from the Japanese, the Germans or newer U.S. competitors, the competition is significantly better than we've ever faced before. One reason is the narrowing of the technology gap. Even though these large corporations generally have superior resources to apply to R&D, much of the new computer technology cannot easily be protected by patents. Also, some previous technological advantages have been lost through legal action, e.g. in 1975 Xerox was required by the FTC to license virtually anyone who wished to use its copier technology.

In addition to the narrowing technology gap, many of these competitors are very well managed. The management gap may also be narrowing. In fact, many of the successful new companies in the computer industry have been started by young entrepreneurs who came from larger organizations where it was difficult to express their entrepreneurial spirit and skills. It's only recently that American businessmen have come to realize that a major reason for the Japanese success is excellent management practices.

Lastly, the average level of education has improved so that the MBA is almost common now. Combining these elements, it can be argued that technological superiority is declining and that among the companies competing, the quality of management is more even than in the past. Therefore, a significant competitive edge that these large companies must have is su-

James F. Bolt, "Management Resources Planning: Keys to Success," reprinted by permission of the publisher from Human Resource Planning, Vol. 5, No. 4, 1982. Copyright 1982 by the Human Resource Planning Society.

perior management talent in their key management positions and superior bench strength to fill those positions when vacated.

Management quality and depth may be more the source of competitive advantage than it has been in the past. Thus, the intense interest in this subject, in terms of being required for survival versus the general statements one often hears. Rather than expounding on the importance of the subject, this article deals with the common and critical elements in management resource planning (MRP) processes currently in place in major corporations and will then explore some of the persistent problems in this field. The following case is used to illustrate a typical Management Resource Planning system of a major corporation.

THE CASE

J. B. Carlisle, CEO, was about to go into the monthly meeting of the corporate management review committee (CMRC). Carlisle chaired this committee which was made up of the top six senior executives of the company. This group also formed the central policy committee which met weekly on matters of key policy and operational significance. Management development is an important subject at this company as evidenced by the fact that this committee exists and that they recently decided to expand the amount of time dedicated to management resource planning (MRP) considerably. The purpose of the CMRC was to review the key management positions and people in the company in terms of their performance and developmental needs, and to plan the replacements for these key people/jobs.

Top management felt that MRP was an important part of their responsibility. Carlisle felt especially strong about this. In fact, he was personally responsible for setting up the extensive process used throughout the company nearly eight years ago. XYZ, a four billion dollar company, had nearly 70,000 employees and was organized on a divisional basis. Every effort was made to provide the divisions with maximum autonomy. The MRP process was a bottoms-up approach, not complicated but time consuming. It was corporate policy that all divisions use the same process for middle-level management positions and above. Therefore, once each year the process was reviewed and updated for all middle manager positions and above. The division had an option to do the same for lower levels of management. There were two fairly simple forms. One was completed by the employees and contained a summary of their work experience and their career goals. The second form was filled out by their managers and summarized current performance levels, long-term potential, specified the most likely next jobs for each person, identified specific developmental needs as well as appropriate developmental actions such as special assignments or training. It also specified the names of two to three people who could re-place the incumbent.

The division presidents were responsible for management succession within their organization and were required to use the corporate system. Most of the division presidents had formed their own version of the CMRC with their division senior executives, performing similar functions as the corporate committee but within their division. Beyond that, in several of the divisions, such committees were common at lower levels, e.g. the manu-facturing plant manager headed a committee which oversaw all manage-ment succession activities for management positions in that plant. No assignment could be made without their review and approval. This was done in order to assure that management developmental needs (not just the immediate needs of the business) were a primary factor in assignments. The plant manager felt that this was important because there was a natural tend-ency for managers to fill critical jobs with the most qualified candidate due to the pressure in meeting near-term business objectives. Naturally, these were the assignments which were also best for testing younger managers who showed exceptional potential.

The divisions have considerable autonomy in their management re-source activities. However, in addition to the requirement to use the cor-porate process and forms, there were other corporate "demands." Once each year, the division presidents had to visit corporate headquarters spe-cifically to review their management resources with the CMRC. It was re-quired that they review each of the senior positions reporting to the division president. Those reviews covered the incumbent's management resource information as well as the two most likely replacements for each of those positions. It was common for these meetings to be lively since many of these people were known by the members of the CMRC, and these meetings had to end in agreement on the next moves, replacements and development for each person and position reviewed.

It was also required at these meetings, that the division presidents dis-cuss lower level "high potential" managers who would be put through spe-cial developmental experiences to test, challenge and prepare them for senior division positions within the next 10 years. Lastly, each division pres-ident was required to review people who had been identified as having the potential to fill the most senior corporate positions within the next 10 to 15 years. The CMRC took great interest in this group because they were po-tentially their replacements. Once they were approved by the committee, these people became "corporate resources" and all developmental plans, job assignments and compensation actions had to be approved by the CMRC.

Carlisle felt that this was necessary in order to assure the identification and long-term development and preparation of the future senior executives. It was natural for the division presidents to want to keep their best people within the division. In fact, many of them felt that they could provide these people with adequate development opportunities within their division without any corporate involvement. Carlisle strongly disagreed. He believed that future senior executives needed assignments in several businesses and functions, in at least two different divisions and preferably an international assignment, to have the thorough understanding and knowledge of all key aspects of the business and to have a broad perspective. Therefore, these corporate high potentials became part of a separate process. This process was administered by the Manager, Management Resources on the Corporate Personnel staff. He was responsible for coordinating all the management resource actions for the corporate high potentials, which involved about 200 people. More detailed, long-term developmental plans were created for each of these people. These long-term plans were created by the division but required the approval of both the Manager, Management Resources and the CMRC.

In reflecting on the meeting he was about to start, Carlisle was proud of the company's program and of his own foresight in setting it up despite cries of corporate bureaucracy from the divisions, and the fact that it was established when the company was much smaller and the need less clear. Of course there were some problems, but for the most part he felt it had worked quite well as evidenced by the fact that in the last three years they only had to go outside the company twice to fill key executive positions.

However, he knew this meeting would be a difficult one. The president of the largest division was in for his annual MRP review. Carlisle knew he had some specific gripes which would be aired in the meeting. First of all, he and his senior people were upset because a new senior corporate position had recently been created to manage a new acquisition and the job had been filled from outside the company because "we didn't feel anyone inside had the appropriate understanding of the technology needed in the newly acquired company." Secondly, the division did not meet its sales and profit targets for 1980 and the division president felt it was partly because two of his most talented people in critical assignments had been moved for developmental purposes to other divisions. The performance of their organization had declined during the transition to their replacements.

Carlisle was not satisfied with the number of minority and female names on the division's management resource review last year and was looking for significant improvements. Also, during the past year, Carlisle had received an open-door letter from a middle manager in that division who "sensed there were very few opportunities for development in that division and wanted to know what top management could do about it." A similar letter was received from a manager who had been there for 20 years and who felt that the division management resource process was discriminatory because none of the division high potentials were over 40 years of age.

CRITICAL ELEMENTS OF A MAJOR MANAGEMENT RESOURCE PLANNING EFFORT

This case is not representative of a specific company, but is a composite made up from a study of the processes used in several major corporations. As such, it provides a useful way to illustrate elements which seem to be common and which apparently are critical to successful programs. Although these represent large companies' practices, I'm sure it will be clear that the principles would apply to many small and medium-sized companies as well, although perhaps in a scaled-down version. What then, are these keys to success or critical, common elements?

Extensive Involvement of Senior Management

The CEO sets the example by his or her personal involvement in the process. Often the CEO is the head of the system and the most prominent proponent of the Management Resource Process. Senior line managers see themselves as being responsible for management resources with the staff (usually the Personnel function), playing a supportive role and being responsible for administration of the process. In other words, the development of management resources is clearly seen as the responsibility of line managers versus the staff role of advising and managing the *process* or system. In many cases, the CEO personally approves the replacement plans for the key positions and the long-term development plans and assignments of high potential employees. Typically the CEO and his equivalent of the CPC spends 40 to 50 hours per year in formal management resource reviews with the operating divisions.

An Institutionalized Process

A single, consistent process, institutionalized over time, is used throughout the company. Divisions have the responsibility for the development of management resources within their divisions, but they have little choice in the process or system used, which is mandated by corporate headquarters. There are written development plans for all people included in the program. The MR process has become a way of life in the company, almost ritualistic and a part of the corporate culture. There are dedicated support staffs. No one debates the value or need for management resources, it's just done as part of the ongoing management process.

An Overall MR Strategy

The long-term development of management resources in these companies is usually only a part of a broader management resource strategy, although it is infrequently articulated or even conceived as such. There is an overall strategy based on the basic philosophy that it is better to grow your own management talent than to hire from outside. Recognizing that there are some risks to this approach, e.g. possibly less creativity than might result from infusing the organization with outside talent, they are willing to accept these risks in exchange for what they feel are off-setting benefits. Namely, the motivational aspects of reserving promotional opportunities for their own employees and the ability to "grow their own," steeped in their corporate culture, values, management philosophy and practices. Their overall strategy, not necessarily articulated as a coherent, comprehensive strategy, is to grow their own talent. This normally includes a promotion-from-within policy backed up by a practice of assuring that external hires are generally recent college graduates who can advance as their talent and experience allows. Many even have dedicated college relations staffs to assure that they get their share of the best college graduates. These graduates can then be groomed over a long period of time for managerial responsibilities.

Formal, mandatory internal management orientation and training programs are used to teach management philosophy, skills and practices. This is seen and used as a way of imbuing new managers with the corporate philosophy, values and key management practices. Subsequently, advanced internal management training programs purposely review and reinforce these values and philosophies throughout the manager's career.

These companies tend to pay their employees very well compared to other companies in their industry and have executive compensation practices which are designed to retain their management talent. At the same time, there is strong emphasis on a merit pay system in order to reward performance.

Lastly, the importance of developing management resources is reinforced through the reward and incentive systems in general. Typically, the performance appraisal for all managers must appraise the managers on how well they have done in this area, and specifically in coaching, counselling and developing their own employees.

MR Committees Throughout the Organization

It is common in these major corporations that MR committees have expanded below the level of top management. Frequently there are a series of committees performing much like the CMRC illustrated in the case. Table I illustrates a typical system. In this example the Division President serves

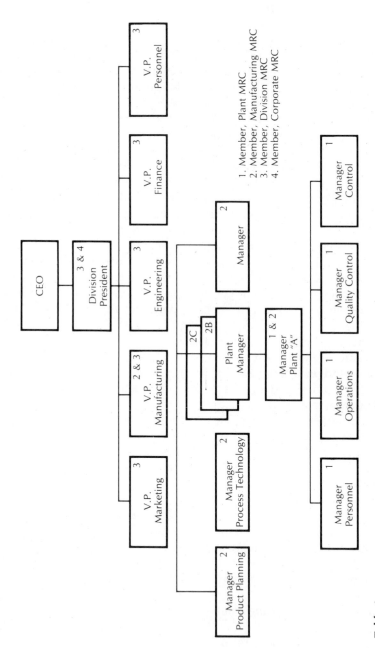

CEO

Division President — 3 & 4

V.P. Marketing — 3

V.P. Manufacturing — 2 & 3

V.P. Engineering — 3

V.P. Finance — 3

V.P. Personnel — 3

Manager Product Planning — 2

Manager Process Technology — 2

Manager — 2

Plant Manager — 2C / 2B

Manager Plant "A" — 1 & 2

Manager Personnel — 1

Manager Operations — 1

Manager Quality Control — 1

Manager Control — 1

1. Member, Plant MRC
2. Member, Manufacturing MRC
3. Member, Division MRC
4. Member, Corporate MRC

Table 1.

as a member of the CMRC. He is also the Chairman of the Division MR Committee which oversees the MRP for the division and approves all key developmental plans and assignments for managers who are in the MRP. In this example, the V.P., Manufacturing is a member of the Division MRC but is also Chairman of the Manufacturing MRC. The Plant Manager is a member of the Manufacturing MRC as well as Chairman of the Plant MRC, etc. There is a "layer" of line committees which meet regularly to plan and manage the development of their management resources.

Special Process for High Potentials

Both in the divisions and at corporate headquarters, there is a special effort made beyond the normal replacement planning process. This effort is aimed at identifying managers early in their careers who have the potential to fill key senior leadership positions in the future and to plan developmental experiences over a relatively long period of time (approximately 10 to 20 years). These experiences are designed to test and help prepare these high potential managers. In the divisions, people are identified who can eventually fill the senior division jobs. At corporate headquarters, a pool of "corporate resources" are identified who have the potential to fill the key corporate jobs including president and CEO. Generally, these corporate plans assure developmental assignments across functions, within different divisions and internationally, to assure sufficient breadth, perspective and understanding of the entire enterprise.

Internal Management Training

Although these companies believe that development occurs primarily on the job, all of them have extensive internal management training programs to support and supplement on-the-job development. These programs are generally designed and run internally simply because the company feels it can do it better than any outside organization could. There is usually a series of programs offered (attendance is mandatory) at key career points. This includes programs for newly appointed managers, programs for middle-level managers who must manage other managers and then programs for more senior managers and executives as they move into positions requiring responsibility for policy and/or understanding of the management of multiple functions or businesses. The programs are aimed primarily at reviewing and reinforcing key corporate values, management philosophy and practices, and at providing training on the management knowledge and skills required at that management level. The lower level programs, offered early in the management career, tend to be highly oriented toward skill building, whereas the senior level programs are less so and more focused on building a broad perspective of the company and the outside world, e.g. world economic factors, government relations, environmental factors affecting the business, etc. In other words, these programs are designed as a series of learning experiences to supplement on-the-job development. They are aimed at imbuing the values, philosophy and management practices which are felt to be needed throughout the company and at imparting the key knowledge and skills required on the job. They also help broaden the perspective of those moving into more senior positions. It is not unusual for the most senior level programs to be run by outside faculty from major business schools.

Executive Education

All of these companies use external executive education programs such as Harvard's AMP and PMD, MIT's Program for Senior Executives, and the Stanford Executive Program, to supplement job assignments and their internal management training. These are used as a planned part of the management resource process versus having people attend on an ad hoc basis. These companies seem to feel that they are most valuable for the development of a general management perspective. That includes developing a broad knowledge and understanding of all major functions of the business, reviewing major world economic, political and social issues, and exposing executives to their counterparts from other organizations from which much of the learning comes. These programs are invaluable for senior managers or those about to become senior managers whose work experience has been totally or primarily in one functional area. Surprisingly, this is the case in many major corporations. These programs are expensive and time consuming. The programs run from 8 to 14 weeks.

Some Persistent Problems

If these are the common and critical elements in a major MRP effort, what are the persistent problems which seem to negatively impact the effectiveness of such programs?

The Basic Conflict: Short-Term versus Long-Term

As illustrated in the case, there always has been and perhaps always will be a troublesome conflict between a bottom line, near-term, results oriented management focus and the necessary long-term developmental process of management resources planning. Operating managers are driven to meet this year's (often this quarter's) product, sales or profit targets, and in order to do so, require the best available management talent in their key positions. Because they are key positions, they are usually the best developmental assignments for high potential managers in terms of testing their mettle and providing a significant learning experience.

However, frequently the developmental assignee has little or no previous experience in that function. Therefore, he or she is unlikely to perform at the level of performance the division would get if it put in the person most qualified, if they were solely concerned about meeting their performance targets. That's the heart of the issue. Human nature causes an obvious tendency to take the actions which result in the most positive, near-term consequences. The natural pull is for filling critical assignments with the best qualified candidate for that position now versus the developmental candidate. Despite long-time efforts to make management resources more important to the line managers, such as making it part of the performance appraisal and bonus plan, seldom are these efforts strong enough to overcome the pressure and importance of meeting this year's bottom-line results. Stories of managers being promoted because they did an exceptional job at management resource development, even though they missed their bottom-line sales or profit targets, are few and far between.

This difficulty is evidenced by the fact that even when these key assignments get reviewed by a group like the CMRC, a near-term, business "crisis" sometimes gets the nod over previously agreed to, long-term developmental assignments. Is there a way to satisfactorily resolve or eliminate this issue so that these needs are not in conflict? Probably not. The only answer seems to be brute force. The CMRC must assure that the long-term developmental needs are met by insisting on following long-term developmental plans for the division and corporate high potentials. They must review and approve all assignments for these key people and for all key positions. This will often not be satisfactory to the divisions since the short-term results may suffer, but it will assure that the long-term corporate management resource needs take precedence over short-term division requirements. Also, it sets an important example for managers in the division. This kind of action on the part of CMRC is more important to the organization than anything they say about management resources. In other words, it demonstrates their interest and belief in the importance of this subject.

Identification of Potential

Obviously, a critical factor in these MR processes is the accurate and early identification of people with exceptional potential for advancement. Despite the obvious importance of this, relatively little progress has been made. In most cases, there are virtually no criteria for including people in the MR process other than being at a certain job level and/or being "seen as a potential replacement" for a key job. Nor are there hard criteria for selecting people to be included in the high potential process. Some work has been done in the area of written tests. Generally, however, these companies do not use such devices. The assessment center approach, where potential is assessed by having people work in simulated management situations which are related to satisfactory performance in the future job, has tremendous face validity and when done correctly seems to actually work much better than more traditional methods of screening out or selecting people. Nevertheless, other than AT&T, few major corporations seem to use this process widely. In fact, even where these methods are used, the trend has been away from using them to select people and more toward their use for developmental purposes, i.e. to identify developmental needs and plan developmental activities.

A major reason for not using assessment centers more often seems to be that they are costly and time consuming. Yet they are surely less so than the disruptiveness and costs of management failures caused by poor selection processes. Is there an answer to this persistent problem? Probably. There is certainly little excuse for the relative lack of the use of assessment techniques. These processes must be based on actual studies of the key positions in question to identify the key success factors in the job. The technologies are available to build assessment programs or processes to test candidates through job simulation. Part of the problem is that many managers don't like it. They got ahead under the old system and they pride themselves on being able to spot talent. The facts suggest that the use of assessment technology is more accurate. There are significant front-end and ongoing costs involved. But, it only takes a handful of avoided management failures to defray these costs. The avoidance of the morale problems of management failures is also significant.

Other related techniques such as panel interviews, where several managers interview potential candidates based on a study of job factors which are critical, have also proven to be statistically more effective than traditional methods. Those methods which are based on a study of the actual job are more likely to be legally defensible since they reduce bias and increase objectivity in the selection process.

It is still commonly believed that the best test is the challenge of a new and difficult assignment. Being tested under a variety of managers reduces personal bias and provides the opportunity to work under different types of managers. It also provides the opportunity to be tested under different, challenging types of assignments, different functional areas, line as well as staff, etc. Not only is this a good test of abilities, but it is excellent in developmental aspects. What should be, and in some cases is, being done is more frequent rotational assignments, especially across functional lines and starting much earlier in a manager's career, often right after the first management assignment. Even when this approach is used now, it is often started late in the managers' careers after they have proven themselves for many years in a specific function and become overspecialized.

Planning for Long-Term Needs
versus Replacement Planning

Most of these elaborate MR systems are designed to identify and develop the replacements for current organizational positions and do it quite well. Generally, however, they do a poor job of planning future organizational requirements. In this case, Carlisle went outside to fill a key job because they did not anticipate the acquisition far enough in advance to identify and develop a manager internally. Unfortunately, this problem is not caused by or even aggravated by a weakness in their MR process. It is fundamentally a weakness in the business planning process. Even these major corporations are not as good as they'd like to be in business and strategic planning and, therefore, are generally unable to accurately predict significant organizational shifts which would require different types of technical skills or managers far enough in advance (10 years) to adequately prepare people internally.

Unless long-term business/strategic planning improves significantly, this problem is one we must live with. What can be done to alleviate it? First of all, it's essential that the MRP and business planning processes are clearly and actively linked so that the MRP can at least be as good as the business planning processes. In fact, it is wise to specifically require that division and corporate long-term plans include a section forecasting management resources requirements even if it has to be a little blue-sky.

If the other long-term developmental actions are taken as noted elsewhere in this article, there should be very few jobs that a manager who's proven himself/herself in assignments in several functions, divisions, in line and staff as well as international assignment, couldn't handle. Therefore, the replacement planning process coupled with long-term developmental plans would handle most cases. This would assure that external hiring would be only as a last resort to meet specific technical requirements which could not be forecasted or, perhaps, to occasionally bring in a fresh or innovative perspective.

It's best to not oversell your promotion-from-within policy or practices. People should understand that under certain, critical circumstances you will go outside so that when it does happen, it isn't read as hypocritical or a betrayal of a corporate promise.

CONCLUSION

Management resources is a serious business at these major companies and clearly should be. Extensive, comprehensive Management Resource Planning systems have been developed and are in place and work pretty well. The larger and more diverse the company, the more MRP is seen as essential to the long-term growth and survival of the enterprise. There's much to be learned from what's being done in these companies.

In general, their MRP processes include all management positions at a certain level and above, and require planning of assignments and the development of the encumbents of each job as well as their replacements. Senior level positions and high potentials are reviewed annually and approved by the CMRC. This includes the identification of people with high potential to fill the senior corporate positions. Developmental plans, compensation and all assignments are then approved by the CMRC for these people. The role of the CEO and other chief executives is prominent.

There are some persistent problems. Short-term business needs versus long-term developmental needs and the identification of potential seem to be manageable with special effort, time and financial resources. The difficulties caused by insufficient, long-term business and strategic planning can be alleviated with careful management attention. The emerging issues of the '80s and '90s need to be carefully studied and plans put in place to deal with them. This type of forecasting of emerging issues and contingency planning should be an integral part of the planning system rather than waiting until the issues are upon us when only a reactive position can be taken.

In summary, applying to your own organization a careful planning and development process for your management resources is clearly an opportunity to make management talent a true competitive advantage.

DEVELOPING MANAGERS TO BANK ON

Robert N. Beck

A tidal wave of change has given managers in the once-staid financial services industry a good dunking. As they dry off and look around them, managers are finding that the world in which they're operating is quite different from the one to which they'd been accustomed. And it's no secret that the continuing change and deregulation that lie ahead are going to both open up new competitive opportunities for banks and stretch the capabilities of all of us. New services, new competitors, new technology, and new methods of operation will have a dramatic impact on how we as managers do our jobs and how we relate to our customers and our staffs.

Some people instinctively accept change and flow with it; others, just as naturally, resist it. But as a management team we must recognize that many of our old procedures no longer apply to the new environment. In the past, the bank operated in a secure world neatly structured by regulations. Bankers didn't always like these constraints, born of the disasters of the Great Depression, but during the last half-century they became accustomed to operating within their tight perimeters. As they did, they felt compelled to check and recheck each step of each operation to be certain they were complying with these myriad regulations.

But, now, in moving from an era of controls into one of deregulation, the bank must respond creatively, effectively, and quickly to this change. In such a fast-moving environment—in which technological, political, or economic influences can change overnight—Bank of America's management team . . . will have to make decisions before corporate policies and procedures can be studied and codified. Often, these decisions may have to be based strictly on the facts at hand. . . . Today's Bank of America needs managers who can look at the long term, as well as focus on the short term. Most of all, it needs flexible, able managers who can cope with new processes, products, and structures.

When a large organization, accustomed to running itself with a "steady as she goes" approach, collides with massive, dynamic change, a "clash of values" can occur. Individuals may wonder, "Just who are we serving around here?" Or, "Are we changing our goals? Are we forgetting our traditional customers?" As managers, one of our most important re-

Robert N. Beck, "Developing Managers to Bank On," Management Quarterly, *Summer 1983,*
Vol. 1, No. 1 (copyright by BankAmerica Corporation, 1983). Reprinted with permission.

sponsibilities will be to communicate the bank's values to our employees and help them understand and work with these values.

The strategy we're developing to respond to change includes a close look at the bank's values. The examination isn't finished, but we know it will place an emphasis on performance, on communication, and on developing a unique managerial style. In part, it will be based on understanding that the future is necessarily ambiguous. The rigid bureaucracy built up by the world of regulation and compliance has developed in many managers a fear of ambiguity. We must rid ourselves of the security blanket of bureaucracy and liberate managers to manage, based on the fundamental values and goals of the bank.

President Sam Armacost has described the current situation: "Bank of America needs a strategy that's flexible and a management team that thinks through all possible outcomes and is ready, no matter what. The bank needs to build flexibility into its organizations, to develop creativity, innovation, and entrepreneurship throughout the system. And it must reward and reinforce these qualities in its team. The bank needs to change its habit of worrying more about penalties for failure than rewards for success. It must cultivate the judgment of knowing when to stick to a plan and when to deviate from it. It even must induce and seek out contrary opinions. We need to be sure that people can disagree without personal risk. To meet the future, the bank must adjust its management style and corporate culture to work with its new strategy."

THE PEOPLE MANAGER: MANAGING INDIVIDUAL AND ORGANIZATIONAL PERFORMANCE

In this changed world, managers are going to be more entrepreneurial in running their units, managing them as if they were small businesses. They will make decisions based on the goal of achieving the success of their unit—that is, on meeting the needs of their customers, whether those customers are the public or other bank units. Competitive success in the marketplace will depend upon people training and management style. Branch managers, for example, will be more people managers than asset or credit managers. In the past, the bank managed people as it managed credit—with endless signoffs. Now, the bank is going to give managers more responsibility and autonomy to manage their people.

As part of our response to today's business environment, people management is the key process for managers throughout the bank to achieve their unit and corporate goals. It is a skill managers can use to help their staffs cope with the rapid organizational changes that may be necessary to stay competitive. It is a skill managers will use to develop and to motivate their employees. Each people manager must help his or her employees understand the mission of the organization and what their contributions are toward the realization of the mission. Just as managers must focus their units' efforts toward the success of the corporation, so they must inspire their staffs to focus on personal goals that contribute toward the success of the unit. In this atmosphere of commitment instead of compliance, we will aim to "Improve the system," not just "Follow the system." We will be moving from risk avoidance to "smart" risk taking, from a philosophy based on catching something wrong to one of discovering something right. And, most of all, we will be moving from management based on procedures to management based on people.

THE MANAGEMENT DEVELOPMENT STRATEGY

Our goal is to develop in our managers the skills to cope with the period of change ahead—to produce leaders who manage people, products, and services effectively to attain profitable results. At a time when many organizations are reducing their management development expense, Bank of America is increasing its investment in this area.

The three major entities in a manager's system are: the customers, the business, and the employees. The role of the manager is to balance these forces so that the needs of all three are met. In the past, we had piecemeal training of managers. They learned here about one aspect of the job and there about another aspect. The result was unfocused. Now, we're trying to reach instinctive management in the bank. We are integrating the personnel training effort, with Jenifer Renzel, Senior Vice President of Management and Employee Development, guiding it.

This new training program is being developed in-house, *with* Bank of America people *for* Bank of America people. Classes are being tailor-made to fit this bank's needs, rather than being bought from a vendor who markets training programs to many different organizations. By tailoring our training programs ourselves to our own needs—and at a fifth of the cost of buying them from vendors—we will have one concept of management throughout the bank. The programs will be owned by the bank. Because we are developing and conducting these programs ourselves, we will be better able to monitor quality control and evaluation. Also, through constant revision, we can keep all content timely and relevant.

This management development strategy is structured to be "top-down" training, in order to provide a support system for the middle and first-line managers. All levels of managers are taking the classes, so any manager can assume that his or her manager will support the methods and concepts taught in them. . . .

The guideline for the management development strategy is the "change of role." When people become managers for the first time, they've changed roles. They can benefit from a class on how to manage people. When first-line managers who've been managing non-managers move up to second-line, or middle-management jobs, they now are managing managers. That's a change of role. Finally, senior managers all the way up to top executives, such as executive vice presidents, vice chairmen, chairmen, and presidents, can profit from additional people-management training appropriate to their level. This training emphasizes achievements and results. Managers will have to do a better job in establishing performance objectives, in coaching individuals, and in fairly evaluating performance. This will include a new managerial style, based on example. Each people manager in the bank will be expected to be a role model for his or her staff. We are aiming for what Tom Peters and Bob Waterman call the "Loose-Tight" organization style in their book, *In Search of Excellence*. This style is based on accountability, responsibility, and trust. We must eliminate the old "transparent manager" attitude, in which each level of manager points to the next in line, saying that the program is his or hers, and the responsibility is his or hers, but never "mine."

We will frequently examine the training accomplishments, the evaluations of the class participants and teachers, and the feedback from management. This feedback process on all levels will be an important part of the ongoing management development strategy. Management development is an investment in the bank's future, and we expect to get interest on the investment. We are convinced that this program is the leading edge of management training in the country.

PERFORMANCE PLANNING, COACHING, AND EVALUATION

In the future, a significant part of the manager's own performance review and salary will be based on how well he or she manages people. This reward system not only will support good people management, but also productivity, because all real productivity is based on good management of people.

The Japanese have developed a managerial system that emphasizes trust between employees and managers. Waterman and Peters discuss this system in their book. If performance evaluations are on a one-to-one basis, with input from both manager and employee, and are based on well-defined criteria, the employee will have less reason to worry about trusting the manager. And an employee who trusts his or her manager will not be afraid of innovation or risk taking on the job. At least, the employee will dare to make suggestions without fear of being shot down. In addition, because the manager will be running his or her unit as if it were an independent small business, with a genuine concern for the welfare of the employees, a new sense of trust will grow between manager and employee. Without an adversarial relationship tainting the manager-employee alliance, they will be able to work together to achieve the common goal of productivity and quality of service. This approach to managing will enable managers to reward high performers and to counsel and work with poor performers in a more effective way, including managing them up or out appropriately and with sensitivity.

Supporting this improved relationship between manager and employee is the new performance evaluation system. A redesigned Performance Planning, Coaching, and Evaluation (PPC&E) form—what I call our new "People Maximizer"—has been developed to help the individual employee recognize his or her place in accomplishing the mission of the branch or unit. The new form emphasizes a spirit of communication between employee and manager by focusing on goal setting and accomplishment. The employee and the manager together define the employee's role in achieving the unit goals; this definition becomes the basis for the objectives against which the employee's performance will be evaluated. The emphasis will be on positive planning, coaching, and career building.

With these tools, managers will be better able to maintain a supply of experienced staff to meet work needs, and, at the same time, the current work staff will be more likely to grow and develop in ways that meet the bank's needs. Instead of managing people in a crisis environment, we will be managing people in an environment that anticipates change. Finally, we will be able to build careers and plan for succession throughout the organization.

INTEGRATED MANAGEMENT TRAINING

Traditionally, the bank has trained managers using a module system of classes. Each of the subjects covered—communications, leadership, compensation, performance evaluation, career planning, interviewing and selection of employees, creation of a positive work environment—was approached separately. Typically, the manager was responsible for integrating all of these lessons into a cohesive whole. The new system is an integrated approach, based on business needs.

Our management development program is divided into three tiers, all based on the "change of role" concept I discussed earlier. First-line managers (those who manage nonmanagers) take a course called the Effective Leadership Program (ELP). Middle managers (who manage other managers) are in the Advanced Leadership Program (ALP). Members of senior management participate in Executive Seminars. After the first year, which ends in March 1984, the week-long Effective Leadership Program and Advanced Leadership Program classes will be required only for managers who have changed roles, including newly hired managers. Forty hours, including a three-day Core Curriculum, will continue to be required for all managers each year. ELP gives first-line managers basic training in managing people; communications; performance planning, coaching, and evaluation; and policy implementation. For middle managers ALP focuses on managing managers, making decisions, pre-formulating policy, interpreting policy, and supporting top management. The senior managers in the Executive Seminars will discuss strategic planning, formulating policy, managing change, leadership, studying external and international environments, and corporate citizenship. The annual Core Curriculum for all three tiers will evolve from the business plan each year, but it will include such subjects as managing change, bank strategies, equal opportunity, performance planning, giving opinion survey feedback, and compensation.

At all three levels, courses are held in a location removed from the workplace, where attendants live for the duration of the class. A quota system set by Management Development, a unit of Corporate Personnel, determines the number of participants divisions may send to the classes at any time. Participants are nominated by the heads of their departments, who have the responsibility for deciding—according to individual unit needs—which managers should take the classes first. The nominated students then are scheduled into classes through the training coordinators of division personnel departments. An effort is made to mix students from all divisions in the United States, and from some overseas units, to encourage cross-pollination of ideas and experiences.

Between March 1983 and March 1984, some 9000 managers will participate in either ELP, ALP, or Core Curriculum classes. Approximately 200 top managers are taking the Executive Seminars. Currently, the classes are being held in hotels located in the north and south of California, but the bank plans to develop one residential facility for all classes. This facility will be in the San Francisco Bay Area to enable top senior management from the world headquarters to participate as instructors or discussion leaders.

Just as managers attending these classes are expected to act as role models for their employees when they return to their units, the instructors are selected to serve as role models for the managers in the training program. Because of their experience on the firing line, the manager-instructors can highlight and illustrate the concepts presented in the program with on-the-job examples; speaking from experience, rather than theory, enhances their credibility. Nominated by unit and division heads, these instructors all have been recognized as outstanding people managers. Approved by senior management, they come from Retail Information and Processing Services, from World Banking Division, from Retail Banking Division, and from administration. They are on loan from their units for approximately one year, after which they return to the field, to the same level jobs they left or higher, to continue to act as super-role models.

Obviously, a one-week course can't make a manager an "expert" in all facets of his or her job. That's not the objective of this program. The management development courses are intended to give managers a conceptual overview of the major elements and activities of their roles. The program also is designed to explore how the application of these concepts and skills is at the heart of independent managerial decision making. One of the advantages of this type of education is that it relieves managers of the need to memorize endless details and rules or to continually search through rule books for precise answers. This program makes it possible for managers to trust themselves and to trust their people.

The curriculum is graduated to the requirements of each respective management level, while still encompassing the overall philosophy of the program. For example, senior managers need to be more concerned with longer-range strategies and with the implications of changes in the marketplace than do lower-level managers. However, all courses include discussions of the bank's values, a review of leadership styles, and an examination of the role of communication and performance planning in effective management.

While many of the elements that make up the curriculum have been around for some time, this is the first time courses have been assembled to demonstrate how certain basic subjects and concepts affect all aspects of the manager's job. For example, communications is an important, and complex, process in managing. If done well, it can enhance and improve the interactions among the people in the manager's group. Communication in management can be taught as a separate subject, but examining its importance in relation to each of a manager's activities offers managers an integrated view of their job that can provide new insights and help them to greater excellence of achievement.

ELP and ALP classes will help managers perfect or brush up on their skills. But good management doesn't depend on checklists or recipes. Situations that appear to be the same nevertheless aren't and can't be the same. The people involved in each situation are unique individuals who are at different levels of personal and job maturity. A manager who handles job situations by rote and without evaluation is doing his or her position, the people involved, and the organization a great disservice. Management is a dynamic process, not a static condition. These courses are designed to give the manager the skills to deal with each unique situation as it deserves to be dealt with. At Bank of America, we manage people, not "positions," which is why the classes include role playing and video sessions based on actual problems that the participants encounter in their people-managing careers.

A PLACE IN THE BANK'S ARCHITECTURE

It's a little early to judge the overall success of the program, but the first graduates have been enthusiastic, commenting particularly on the intensity and stimulation of the week-long session. The sharing of experiences between students and teachers and the mutual growth of everyone involved creates an exciting sense of camaraderie among the students in each class. The emotional impact comes, I think, from the fact that many of them are learning to *care* again—about the skills and about their own contributions to the bank. They feel again their own place in the whole architecture of the bank.

One assistant branch administration officer who took the ELP class said that he discovered where his short-comings lay as a people manager. The leadership survey that five of his employees filled out (anonymously) as part of his pre-course preparation, coupled with the lessons he learned during the week, showed him precisely where he needed to improve, he said, and he was grateful. "I know I have a long way to go to be as good at people managing as I want to be," he said, "but at least I'm aiming in the right direction, now, and I feel good about that. And I think my staff is feeling better about me, now, too."

Other people managers who have gone through the class report how helpful they find the Action Plan feature of the program, which helps them to implement on the job the skills acquired in class. "I learned to focus on real problems," said one woman who manages 20 tellers, "instead of side issues. And I've turned our teller meetings from a lecture format, where I told them what was wrong and what they ought to do about it, to a brainstorming format, in which they're encouraged to share ideas to solve problems. The tellers have responded wonderfully. They're more excited about their jobs than they've ever been. And they're coming up with solutions!"

Another graduate of the ELP class was enthusiastic about the support he received from his manager when he returned to the job. "We're going to have a 'State of the Branch' meeting," he reported, "to discuss the goals of the branch and how each of our units works toward meeting those goals." He added that the classes left him intellectually beat, but on fire— really charged up about working for Bank of America. And a lot of that enthusiasm grew out of what he learned about the bank and about himself during those five days. Reports such as this convince us that these classes are going to be a great help to people managers at all levels in the bank and will point every branch and unit toward a successful, entrepreneurial approach to its mission.

We hope graduates of these classes will have reaffirmed their own mission to effectively manage and lead people, to enhance within their units the culture and values the bank is striving for during the 1980s, and to reflect in their own actions their genuine care and concern for the individuals in their units. At the same time, they will understand more clearly than ever how to plan, organize, and direct the operations in their units within an environment of change. Above all, they will be more skilled at communication on the job—upward communication, downward communication, and lateral communication. Much of this can be summarized in stating that they will be people oriented—motivating and inspiring their staffs to work for the success of the organization as a whole.

WHY TRAINING IS THE BOSS'S JOB

Andrew S. Grove

Recently my wife and I decided to go out to dinner. The woman who took reservations over the phone seemed flustered and then volunteered that she was new and didn't know all the ropes. No matter, we were booked. When we showed up for dinner, we quickly learned that the restaurant had lost its liquor license and that its patrons were expected to bring their own wine if they wanted any. As the maitre d' rubbed his hands, he asked, "Weren't you told this on the phone when you made your reservations?" As we went through our dinner without wine, I listened to him go through the same routine with every party he seated. I don't know for sure, but it's probably fair to assume that nobody instructed the woman taking calls to tell potential guests what the situation was. Instead, the maitre d' had to go through an inept apology time and time again, and nobody had wine—all because one employee was not properly trained.

The consequences of an employee being insufficiently trained can be much more serious. In an instance at Intel, for example, one of our sophisticated pieces of production machinery in a silicon fabrication plant—a machine called an ion implanter—drifted slightly out of tune. The machine operator, like the woman at the restaurant, was relatively new. While she was trained in the basic skills needed to operate the machine, she hadn't been taught to recognize the signs of an out-of-tune condition. So she continued to operate the machine, subjecting nearly a day's worth of almost completely processed silicon wafers to the wrong machine conditions. By the time the situation was discovered, material worth more than $1 million had passed through the machine—and had to be scrapped. Because it takes over two weeks to make up such a loss with fresh material, deliveries to our customers slipped, compounding the problem.

Situations like these occur all too frequently in business life. Insufficiently trained employees, in spite of their best intentions, produce inefficiencies, excess costs, unhappy customers, and sometimes even dangerous situations. The importance of training rapidly becomes obvious to the manager who runs into these problems.

For the already overscheduled manager, the trickier issue may be who should do the training. Most managers seem to feel that training employees

Andrew S. Grove, "Why Training Is the Boss's Job," Fortune, January 23, 1984. Reprinted with permission.

is a job that should be left to others, perhaps to training specialists. I, on the other hand, strongly believe that the manager should do it himself.

Let me explain why, beginning with what I believe is the most basic definition of what managers are supposed to produce. In my view a manager's output is the output of his organization—no more, no less. A manager's own productivity thus depends on eliciting more output from his team.

A manager generally has two ways to raise the level of individual performance of his subordinates: by increasing motivation, the desire of each person to do his job well, and by increasing individual capability, which is where training comes in. It is generally accepted that motivating employees is a key task of all managers, one that can't be delegated to someone else. Why shouldn't the same be true for the other principal means at a manager's disposal for increasing output?

Training is, quite simply, one of the highest-leverage activities a manager can perform. Consider for a moment the possibility of your putting on a series of four lectures for members of your department. Let's count on three hours of preparation for each hour of course time—12 hours of work in total. Say that you have ten students in your class. Next year they will work a total of about 20,000 hours for your organization. If your training efforts result in a 1 percent improvement in your subordinates' performance, your company will gain the equivalent of 200 hours of work as the result of the expenditure of your 12 hours.

This assumes, of course, that the training will accurately address what students need to know to do their jobs better. This isn't always so—particularly with respect to "canned courses" taught by someone from outside. For training to be effective, it has to be closely tied to how things are actually done in your organization.

Recently some outside consultants taught a course on career development at Intel. Their approach was highly structured and academic—and very different from anything practiced at the company. While they advocated career plans that looked ahead several years, together with carefully coordinated job rotations based on them, our tradition has been more like a free market: our employees are informed of job opportunities within the company and are expected to apply for desirable openings on their own initiative. Troubled by the disparity between what was taught in the course and what was practiced, the participants got a bit demoralized.

For training to be effective, it also has to maintain a reliable, consistent presence. Employees should be able to count on something systematic and scheduled, not a rescue effort summoned to solve the problem of the moment. In other words, training should be a process, not an event.

If you accept that training, along with motivation, is the way to improve the performance of your subordinates, and that what you teach must be closely tied to what you practice, and that training needs to be a continuing process rather than a one-time event, it is clear that the *who* of the training is *you*, the manager. You yourself should instruct your direct subordinates and perhaps the next few ranks below them. Your subordinates should do the same thing, and the supervisors at every level below them as well.

There is another reason that you and only you can fill the role of the teacher to your subordinates. Training must be done by a person who represents a suitable role model. Proxies, no matter how well versed they might be in the subject matter, cannot assume that role. The person standing in front of the class should be seen as a believable, practicing authority on the subject taught.

We at Intel believe that conducting training is a worthwhile activity for everyone from the first-line supervisor to the chief executive officer. Some 2 percent to 4 percent of our employees' time is spent in classroom learning, and almost all the instruction is given by our own managerial staff.

We have a "university catalogue" that lists over 50 different classes. The courses range from proper telephone manners to quite complicated production courses—like one on how to operate the ion implanter, which requires nearly 200 hours of on-the-job training to learn to use correctly, almost five times the hours of training needed to get a private pilot's license. We train our managers in disciplines such as strategic planning as well as in the art of constructive confrontation, a problem-solving approach we favor at Intel.

My own training repertoire includes a course on preparing and delivering performance reviews, on conducting productive meetings, and a three-hour-long introduction to Intel, in which I describe our history, objectives, organization, and management practices. Over the years I have given the latter to almost all of our 5000 professional employees. I have also been recruited to pinch-hit in other management courses. (To my regret, I have become far too obsolete to teach technical material.)

At Intel we distinguish between two different training tasks. The first task is teaching new members of our organization the skills needed to perform their jobs. The second task is teaching new ideas, principles, or skills to the present members of our organization.

The distinction between new-employee and new-skill training is important because the magnitudes of the tasks are very different. The size of the job of delivering a new-employee course is set by the number of new people joining the organization. For instance, a department that has 10 percent annual turnover and grows 10 percent per year has to teach 20 percent of its staff the basics of their work each year. Training even 20 percent of your employees can be a huge undertaking.

Teaching new principles or skills to an entire department is an even bigger job. If we want to train all of our staff within a year, the task will be five times as large as the annual task of training the 20 percent who represent new members. Recently I looked at the cost of delivering a new one-day course to our middle-management staff. The cost of the students' time alone was over $1 million. Obviously such a task should not be entered into lightly.

So what should you do if you embrace the gospel of training? For starters, make a list of the things you feel your subordinates or the members of your department should be trained in. Don't limit the scope of your list. Items should range from what seems simple (training the person who takes calls at the restaurant) to loftier and more general things like the objectives and value systems of your department, your plant, and your company. Ask the people working for you what they feel they need. They are likely to surprise you by telling you of needs you never knew existed.

Having done this, take an inventory of the manager-teachers and instructional materials available to help deliver training on items on your list. Then assign priorities among these items.

Especially if you haven't done this sort of thing before, start very unambitiously—like developing one short course (three to four lectures) on the most urgent subject. You will find that skills that you have had for years—things that you could do in your sleep, as it were—are much harder to explain than to practice. You may find that in your attempt to explain things, you'll be tempted to go into more and more background until this begins to obscure the original objective of your course.

To avoid letting yourself bog down in the difficult task of course preparation, set a schedule for your course, with deadlines, and commit yourself to it. Create an outline for the whole course, develop just the first lecture, and *go.*

Develop the second lecture after you have given the first. Regard the first time you teach the course as a throwaway—it won't be great, because no matter how hard you try, you'll have to go through one version that won't be. Rather than agonize over it, accept the inevitability of the first time being unsatisfactory and consider it the path to a more satisfactory second round. To make sure that your first attempt causes no damage, teach this course to the more knowledgeable of your subordinates who won't be confused by it, but who will help you perfect the course through interaction and critique.

With your second attempt in the offing, ask yourself one final question: will you be able to teach all members of your organization yourself? Will you be able to cover everybody in one or two courses, or will it require 10 or 20? If your organization is large enough to require many repetitions of your course before different audiences, then set yourself up to train a few instructors with your first set of lectures.

After you've given the course, ask for anonymous critiques from the employees in your class. Prompt them with a form that asks for numerical ratings but that also poses some open-ended questions. Study and consider the responses, but understand that you will never be able to please all members of your class: typical feedback will be that the course was too detailed, too superficial, and just right, in about equal balance. Your ultimate aim should be to satisfy yourself that you are accomplishing what you set out to do.

If this is your first time teaching, you'll discover a few interesting things:

Training is hard work. Preparing lectures and getting yourself ready to handle all the questions thrown at you is difficult. Even if you have been doing your job for a long time and even if you have done your subordinates' jobs in great detail before, you'll be amazed at how much you don't know. Don't be discouraged—this is typical. Much deeper knowledge of a task is required to teach that task than simply to do it. If you don't believe me, try explaining to someone over the phone how to drive a stick-shift car.

Guess who will have learned most from the course? You. The crispness that developing it gave to your understanding of your own work is likely in itself to have made the effort extremely worthwhile.

You will find that when the training process goes well, it is nothing short of exhilarating. And even this exhilaration is dwarfed by the warm feeling you'll get when you see a subordinate practice something you have taught him. Relish the exhilaration and warmth—it'll help you to arm yourself for tackling the second course.

Part V

New Directions

In the concluding section, some of the country's leading personnel executives, senior line managers, and other experts offer their own prescriptions for successful human resources management in the '80s. In light of the forces that are shaping the direction of human resource management today—changing demographics, the shift to a service economy, and the altering expectations of the work force—these professionals recommend a number of policies and practices to improve the effectiveness of personnel management, which in turn will help organizations better meet their business objectives.

Douglas Reid, a graduate of the Cornell School of Industrial and Labor Relations and a personnel professional for over 20 years, was promoted to a vice-presidency at Xerox at an early age. In "Managing Human Resources in the '80s," an address prepared for members of the American Compensation Association, Reid reviews the major forces of change affecting human resource management. Drawing on his extensive experience, he defines what makes Japanese personnel management successful and suggests what Japanese practices ought to be imported to the United States. In order to implement the practices he recommends, Reid suggests developing a strategic personnel plan that holds the human resources manager accountable for its success.

Randall Schuler and Ian MacMillan, both of New York University's Graduate School of Business, examine the ways in which a number of highly successful companies have gained a significant competitive edge through superior management of human resources. The authors of "Gaining Competitive Advantage through Human Resource Management Practices" describe how these companies first identify their particular personnel requirements and then deliberately design policies to meet them. Sometimes highly original, these policies are often hammered out as part of long-range company strategy, and in the examples cited, the initiative has obviously paid off.

Homer Klock spent more than 25 years in a variety of personnel and industrial relations assignments both at the Burroughs Corporation and at the Celanese Corporation before joining the investment banking firm of Morgan Stanley & Company. In "Decentralization—The Key to the Growth of the Human Resource Function," Klock argues that the decentralization of support functions "is the most effective way for the human resource professional to become part of the team, to better understand corporate goals, and to be a confidante of management." While recognizing that decentralization generally increases headcount and is, therefore, more expensive, he nevertheless finds that "the added value of on-the-spot expertise results in management productivity improvement and a decreased risk in people management decisions."

In the remaining selections in Part V, senior line managers define the traits, experience, and knowledge that the ideal human resources manager will bring to the job in the '80s. Almost all these company leaders expect the top human resources officer to assume power and status equal to line management, in exchange for thorough understanding of and tangible contribution to the business goals of the corporation.

In "The Role of the Personnel Manager—As I See It," Paul Gordon, vice president of ITT and chairman and president of Federal Electric Corporation, discusses a concept of magnetic management in which the personnel manager is at the center of a hub of many activities. He or she is thoroughly aware of the company's financial record and goals, and goes to his or her boss with personnel policies that will improve the record and help meet the goals. Gordon identifies seven important activities that will mark the "business-oriented" personnel manager, and distinguish him or her from the mere "keeper of the personnel files, the arranger of employee activities, the processor of wage increases, and the handler of insurance claims." The business-oriented personnel manager, on the other hand, will become, and will remain, an important, respected, and influential contributor to his or her company's success, an executive who will be consulted on every major management issue.

Robert Berra, now senior vice-president of administration at Monsanto but vice-president for personnel at the time of the interview, is a recognized leader within the personnel profession. Focussing on the changes in the personnel profession, this seasoned practitioner discusses the type of personality, education, and training that best prepare a human resources manager. Berra also looks at the changing role of personnel and today's special challenges.

Herbert Hubben went from a key personnel job at Corning Glass to one at Eaton, where he is now vice-president of the international division. He is, therefore, uniquely qualified to look at human resource management from the perspective of line management. In "What Line Management Expects of Human Resource Managers," he offers a set of guidelines for personnel managers to follow to achieve the respect and become members of the top management team.

Finally, in "Selection and Performance Criteria for a Chief Human Resources Executive . . . A Presidential Perspective," four chief executive officers discuss what they expect from and look for in a chief human resources executive. Their comments reinforce the theme of this book—developing a personnel plan in cooperation with top management that is related to the needs of the business.

Managing Human Resources
in the '80s

Douglas M. Reid

. . . This afternoon I would like to make some comments about the dynamics of "Managing Human Resources in the 80's." The major points included in my remarks are outlined below:

I. Forces driving change
    Legislation
    Competition
II. Legislation
    Affirmative action
    Other
III. Competition
    De-regulation
    Japan
IV. Japan
    Reason for success
    Employee involvement
    Differences and similarities
    Applications for U.S.
V. Cost effectiveness in manpower management
VI. How to seize opportunities
    Strategic personnel plan
    Line manager
    Accountability
VII. Summary

Focus on Change

. . . We live in a world which is jolted almost daily by change, whether it be economic, political, military or social. These macro forces impact the organizations we serve. How many companies here are going to have their third quarter earnings depressed by the devaluation of the Mexican peso and the continuous fluctuation of other international currencies?

Douglas M. Reid, "Managing Human Resources in the '80s," 1982 Conference Proceedings, American Compensation Association. Reprinted with permission.

EXTERNAL FORCES
IMPACTING HUMAN RESOURCES

As I reflect on the major external forces that have resulted in significant change within the human resource function in the last decade or so, I conclude that legislation and competition have had the greatest impact. Impact, resulting in changes not only in our business practices, but as we human resource professionals wrestle with these changes, we have been presented with outstanding opportunities to significantly expand our influence over the management of our respective organizations.

LEGISLATION

The government has been prolific. Consider the impact of:

- Civil Rights Act   1964
- Age Discrimination Employment Act (amended 1978)   1967
- Occupational Safety and Health Act   1970
- Employee Retirement Income Security Act (ERISA)   1974
- Revenue Act of '78   1978
- Economic Recovery Tax Act (ERTA)   1981
- Proposed 401 (K) REGS   1981
- Tax Equity and Fiscal Responsibility Act   1982

AFFIRMATIVE ACTION

However, in my opinion, the most important piece of legislation, in terms of its impact and the opportunity it has provided human resource professionals, is Affirmative Action. Although it took a long time for the Civil Rights Act of 1964 to gain momentum in terms of changing practices in the workplace, this legislation certainly had significant impact in the '70s.

What the various Affirmative Action regulations have done is forced those organizations who were otherwise reluctant to do so, to look at virtually all their personnel policies and practices in the area of selection, compensation, performance appraisals, training, promotion and most other areas.

With very few exceptions, this intensified mandatory revisiting gave top management an opportunity to review the adequacy of their many policies in these areas, not only for members of the protected classes, but for all employees. Affirmative Action regulations have provided us with the opportunity to take advantage of a much greater segment of the labor force and to insure that all our personnel practices make sense for all people.

Some personnel departments were vaulted into key roles and elevated status within their respective hierarchies the hard way with multi-million dollar suits against their companies based on past discriminatory practices. Other managements had enough foresight to see what could happen if they did not pay attention to this area and took aggressive action. And, of course, some managements were responsive to the requirements of the law from the beginning.

The key lesson to be learned from Affirmative Action is that issues that initially appear as concerns affecting only protected classes are usually issues that are of concern to all employees. And resolving these issues benefits all employees.

FUTURE LEGISLATION

The impact of government is continuing to be felt. Legislation to regulate plant closings has been introduced in the past and will probably be a continuing governmental attempt to force employers to assist affected employees.

The employment "at will" concept, which is receiving increased attention in California and other parts of the country, is forcing management to implement sensible performance improvement practices when they realize they can no longer fire people "at will."

Not all the legislation has been popular. Increasing the retirement age to 70 has introduced an additional time delay in many companies' manpower planning and succession strategies. And, as you know, Congressman Pepper is currently advocating elimination of any retirement age.

ACTION REQUIRED
BY HUMAN RESOURCE PROFESSIONALS

What this all means is that companies must be much more pro-active in influencing legislation by letting their point of view be known to the appropriate congressional committees, actively supporting professional organizations which can also have considerable influence in Washington. Too many of us say, "we can't make any difference," "we don't have the time," and so on. This attitude must change or we will risk having legislation that may be contrary to the best interests of business or unnecessarily complex.

COMPETITION

I mentioned earlier that one of the most significant external forces impacting human resource professionals is competition.

Competition comes in many forms. De-regulation has played havoc with the airline and trucking industries, and is in the process of doing so with the banking industry.

When principal competitors were American-based the cost of contracts between U.S. labor unions and companies tended to be much the same. Thus, no single company could gain a significant competitive edge as a result of contract settlements. But, in today's world of rising international competition, a costly wage settlement in the United States can provide a major advantage to non-U.S. firms.

Wage differences among countries—especially between the United States and Japan—are a major handicap to U.S. companies. In 1981, the average U.S. production worker was paid 76 percent more than a Japanese counterpart—$10.97 per hour for the American versus $6.24 for the Japanese (these numbers include the cost of benefits).

IMPACT OF JAPAN

But it is really many major U.S. manufacturing industries that are reeling under the onslaught of the Japanese—steel, TV, consumer electronics with auto being the best known example.

American auto companies report a current wage and benefit total of $20 per hour versus about $11 for Japanese competition—significantly higher than average U.S. rates.

In addition, it's been estimated that the typical Japanese production worker is on the job at least two weeks a year more than the average worker in U.S. heavy industry. The difference, which doesn't include overtime, is due to more paid time off for the Americans.

In 1960, Japan did not export one automobile! In 1982, they are capturing close to one out of three auto sales in this country!

The obvious question is how do they do it? There are lots of reasons, including lower wages, which I will comment on later.

Xerox's major business—office copying and duplicating—is under attack from the Japanese, so we have spent a lot of time trying to understand the reasons for their success. I have made several trips to Japan, visiting many different industries, as well as visiting our own operations in Japan.

In my opinion, the key reason for the Japanese success is human resource management.

Many Japanese companies have as their primary mission statements such as, "to do well by our people" and back up this mission statement with statements such as, "in order to do well by our people we must build quality products at a low cost" and so on.

"When western firms fail, workers lose their jobs, but management stays. When Japanese firms fail, managers lose their jobs but the work force stays," the Chairman of Sony Corporation, Akio Morita, recently quoted earlier this year while making a speech in London.

Mr. Morita's remarks captured what western analysts say is the most exportable feature of Japanese management: "A greater sense of managerial responsibility to the company work force."

So, ironically, the key to competing with Japan is to emulate some of the people management practices that are being so effectively utilized in Japan.

There are many examples that demonstrate that Japan's human resource practices are exportable. At Sony's ultra modern plant in Brigend, Wales, British workers have raised their output to 1000 television sets a day from 250 seven years ago. At the same plant, absenteeism has dropped from 12 percent to 4 percent. Production is consistently over the company quota, and there has never been a strike.

Closer to home, Sanyo acquired an Arkansas TV manufacturing plant in December, '76 that had a record of poor quality, highlighted by a reject rate of 10 percent.

Under Japanese management, this rate was brought down to less than two percent.

KEY JAPANESE
HUMAN RESOURCE PRACTICES

In my opinion, if we, as human resource professionals, want to maximize our effectiveness, we must understand why Japan is so successful in the market places they have chosen to compete in, and we must understand which Japanese human resource practices we can successfully emulate.

Japan has taken several steps to enhance the quality of their human relations. For example:

- The intense labor management strife in the mid-1950s had to be stopped. Three major understandings, age/seniority pay, lifetime employment and labor management consultation, eliminated this strife by forging a cooperative national productivity effort. I will come back to the age/seniority pay and lifetime employment issue.
- Ironically, studies of the American management theorists were taken seriously. Group effort and teamwork were seen as a major key to organization development.
- Inflationary pay practices were controlled through national level negotiations.
- The workplace has been established as a socially attractive place. The Japanese live to work, rather than work to live. The relationship of the male worker to his family and to women in society is culturally different from the United States.
- The typical work week is 5½ days. The work day is normally 9 to 5 with breaks of 10 minutes in the morning and afternoon and a 45 minute lunch. However, people stay at their post until their supervisor leaves. Thus, the worker level usually works from 9 in the morning to 7 at night, if not longer. People do not use all of their vacation, are rarely late or absent.

Overall absenteeism rates in plants are reported at 1 percent and 2 percent (U.S. average = 6 percent).
- Communication is enhanced by open office designs. Therefore, memo writing and telephoning is replaced by continuous contact. Each department sits in the same area. Sections see each other and the functional head is located in an office located directly in the area. Thus, people know more about each other's daily work and assignments. Information sharing, two-way communications are continually practiced in all aspects of Japanese work life.
- Selection into the enterprise is a key decision for both the company and employee under the lifetime employment system. The interviewing process often lasts days with the personal involvement of senior managers. Both parties become honor bound to support each other.
- On the employee's part, loyalty, hard work, quality and excellent performance become an obligation.
- The employer strives to maintain employment. The boundary defining business is much thinner providing diversification. Examples: distilleries moving into publishing and pharmaceuticals; shipyards into computer peripherals and building, consumer electronics into insurance and fast foods.

The rotational transfer system generates broad working networks among professionals and managers. Appreciation for total business needs is, therefore, at higher levels.

The Japanese lifetime employment system has received much favorable publicity. But it is important to understand that in many industries, over 50 percent of the workforce are so-called temporary or contract workers. Beyond the obvious implication of not being guaranteed lifetime employment, these employees are paid about 50 percent of the "permanent" workers' wage rates and have very marginal benefits. When the economy starts to slow down, these are the first employees to be "laid-off." But it is through these manpower buffers that Japanese management can offer lifetime employment to a significant portion of their workforce.

STATUS, ROLE, AND POWER OF JAPANESE PERSONNEL DEPARTMENT

William Ouchi, author of *Theory Z*, tells the story of how he asked Japanese executives, "Which, of all the managing directors, is the most influential?"

The response was always a variation of one theme: "We manage as a group, we are all equals."

After further probing, the final reply in every case surprised him: "Well, ordinarily, the most senior and the most respected managing director is in charge of Personnel."

There are many reasons for the power and significance of the Japanese personnel department. One example of this power is that the personnel department head can order talented people transferred from one division to another even over the objection of the division manager, who understandably wants to keep the best talent.

Most U.S. personnel departments, in the final analysis, do not have this kind of influence. There are some notable exceptions, such as, Du Pont and General Electric. Appointments to senior management positions are approved by senior management selection committees with personnel having key input.

At Xerox, we have spent considerable time studying how the Japanese personnel department works. Our key findings are as follows:

1. Of all the functions, personnel is perhaps the most powerful and prestigious.
2. The personnel function has the final say in almost all promotions and transfer decisions.
3. The personnel function is highly centralized.
4. Personnel is a full business partner in long range strategic planning.
5. Personnel serves as a center for organizational learning by exchanging information between managers on corporate goals, performance toward achieving those goals and corporate-wide manpower requirements. In this way, the Japanese personnel department integrates the efforts of decentralized units.
6. Personnel manages traditional administrative programs and long range strategic manpower planning with equal vigor.
7. Japanese personnel departments are structured similarly to American personnel departments.
8. Japanese personnel departments appear to provide many of the same services that American personnel departments provide.
9. The Japanese personnel function is much leaner than its American counterpart (approximately 1:100 in Japan versus 1:80 in America). However, Japanese line management's people practices are supportive of all personnel policies and practices.

Not all is perfect in Japan. There are fundamental differences—historical, cultural and sociological—between Japan, a closed, homogeneous, disciplined society, and the United States, open, heterogeneous and nonconformist. In many ways these differences make the Japanese model difficult to import in its entirety.

BASIC CHARACTERISTICS OF JAPANESE

The basic characteristics of Japanese society that account for its relative success are a high level of universal and uniform education, sense of duty, conformity and acceptance of authority and a survival mentality. These are characteristics deeply rooted in the Japanese psyche and not easily exported.

These simply are prices Americans will not pay to achieve Japanese style economic and social success.

Another benchmark of strength for the Japanese is education. Japanese economists and analysts attribute high Japanese productivity in large part to the high level of education of the Japanese worker. The level of mathematical and scientific instruction is reputed to be the highest in the world.

The Japanese reinforce their heavy academic training with continuous training on and off the job.

In contrast, the American educational level is universally acknowledged to be declining steadily (to the point where educators view the problem with some alarm).

Competition to do well in the Japanese school system is intense and begins at a very early age because academic performance, in large part, dictates the role you will play in life. The higher your marks, the better the university you get into, the better the university, the better the job.

A negative by-product of this intense pursuit of academic excellence is that Japan has one of the highest suicide rates in the world among its teenagers.

EMPLOYEE INVOLVEMENT

One of the key reasons for Japan's industrial success is their ability to systematically utilize all the talents of all their people in improving in their individual group efforts. This process comes under many names, Quality Control Circle, Employee Involvement, etc., but it is a subject that we should understand and that we should emulate and build upon.

Effectiveness through involvement is a systematic process to improve the effectiveness of our business by tapping a key resource—the minds of its employees.

Employee involvement is based on sound assumptions:

- All people, no matter what they do or where they work, have ideas about how to do their work more productively.
- This represents a source of knowledge and creativity which has gone relatively untapped. This is clearly unproductive.
- The great majority of employees are willing, even eager, to share their thoughts with management. They are knowledgeable, they have a personal stake in performance, and they want to contribute.
- People whose contributions are recognized will take more pride in their jobs. People who are involved in decisions will be more committed to carrying them out. Being more involved results in greater motivation and, therefore, in better performance.
- Management does not have all the answers. It needs ideas from the people closest to the problems and opportunities.

TYPES OF INVOLVEMENT

There are as many ways to involve employees in improving effectiveness as there are jobs to be done. But generally speaking, there are three general phases in the problem solving and decision-making processes where employee participation can be valuable:

- **Analysis:** Determining the cause of a problem or the nature of an opportunity which has been identified.
- **Design:** Looking for innovative solutions to problems, or for strategies to exploit opportunities.
- **Implementation:** Making the actual changes called for. The basic problem solving process can take place at any level of an organization. What is important is to include the thoughts and recommendations of all those employees who are doing the work and who desire to be involved.

Three common methods of implementing employee involvement are:

- **Day-to-day involvement** in which individuals are asked to identify opportunities or problems and find solutions, in their own work.
- **Representative groups** that focus on a unit's ongoing problems or involve employees throughout the organization on a single issue.
- Projects or **task forces** that consider problems shared by several units or organizations.

Employee involvement programs provide an outstanding opportunity to marshall all a company's resources to systematically increase production. Most of the publicity surrounding quality circles has been about hourly workers, but it can also be successfully applied to salaried employees.

Although the current prolonged recession has quieted many of our employees, their expectations will quickly surface again when the economy has turned around.

Employee involvement can go a long way to satisfy their desire for job autonomy and greater participation in decisions affecting them in the workplace.

Indeed, we should learn from the European experience, where such participation has been legislated—Germany, Holland, Sweden.

EMPLOYMENT SECURITY

It is difficult to expect employees to willingly offer suggestions for productivity improvement if one of the consequences of their actions is involuntary manpower reductions. On the other hand, manpower costs are often one of the most significant costs of business.

One way to accomplish both objectives is through re-training of employees whose skills become redundant. This is a difficult task. In addition to the obvious short term costs—although, in some cases, these can be offset by the policy required severance payments—our experience at Xerox has been that employees are extremely reluctant to . . . give up the perceived market value of their years of experience.

Nevertheless, it is clear that job security is becoming an increasingly important objective of many employees.

Japanese human resource practices have received so much attention over the last two or three years that the media have tended to ignore several major U.S. companies which have been living by sound people practices for years—Eastman Kodak, Procter & Gamble and IBM are just three examples; the list is much longer.

What the various analyses of successful companies in Japan and the United States have shown is that sound people management practices transcend national boundaries and different cultures. These sound people practices do contribute to bottom line results.

Since Japan will continue to have a significant wage advantage for the foreseeable future, and quickly match and often lead the technological development of their chosen industries, the U.S. industries impacted by the Japanese must significantly slow down, stop, and in some cases, reverse their historical wage progression practices. The beleaguered U.S. auto industry has obtained some relief through "take away" bargaining.

Japanese wage comparisons have focused on hourly workers. U.S. salaried employees also earn significantly more than their Japanese counterparts. The fact that it is not as easy to export the salaried work to Japan as it is to fabricate and assemble products in Japan, should not mask the salary premium impact on U.S. overhead costs and resultant higher price levels in the marketplace.

COST EFFECTIVENESS IN MANPOWER MANAGEMENT

The significant cost advantage enjoyed by the Japanese, other international competitions, increased competition with the United States, mandate that we approach our manpower and organization responsibilities much more aggressively and tough-mindedly.

Compensation professionals are in an excellent position to lead this attack. You are all aware that compensation expenses can account for up to 70 percent of an organization's total expense base—the opportunity for significant cost savings is obviously significant.

There are many opportunities to be cost effective in manpower management.

COMPETITIVE BENCHMARKING

I think we have to re-look our competitive benchmarks for salary reviews. Too often we have adopted the "me too" approach to compensation. Company X is giving X percent so we have to give X percent or worse, the "ratchet" theory comes into play and we have to give X plus one percent. Far too often these actions result in increases that bear little resemblance to the productivity gains and profit needs of the firm.

Further compensation cost increases without offsetting productivity gains will be inflationary and will seriously hamper U.S. firms' ability to compete in world markets, thus causing additional erosion in America's shrinking portion of world trade.

Competitive benchmarking means that we select our most formidable competitors, or potential competitors, and insure that our compensation levels are, in fact, competitive with these benchmarks. Competitive benchmarking should be taking place in all aspects of the business—purchasing, quality standards, direct to indirect ratios, etc.

Benchmarking must include benefits. Depending on how you do your accounting, benefit costs range from 20 percent to over 50 percent of covered pay. Clearly expenses of this magnitude must be managed. The decade of the '60s and '70s saw a major expansion in employee benefits such that many industries have now covered most catastrophic and non-catastrophic needs. American industry can no longer afford the "add-on" enhancement tactic it has used in the past.

CAFETERIA BENEFITS

One of the most significant features of so-called, "cafeteria benefits" or "flexible compensation" is that it educates employees to the real costs of benefits and provides them with the means of making effective cost trade-offs based on their particular individual needs. We will see more "flexible compensation" in the future.

I think the heads of compensation and benefits should report to a common senior executive. Their combined total cost impact is so significant that trade-offs should be made between the two with employee preferences being fully considered before such decisions are made.

JOB ANALYSIS

Through one of the basic tools of your trade, job analysis, you are in an excellent position to identify job responsibility overlaps, outright duplication, and to challenge the incremental value of each position. You can identify opportunities to reduce levels of management and expand spans of control. You can use the results of job analysis to establish measurable standards of performance, and provide helpful information for meaningful career-planning.

MARKET PRICING

Cost effective manpower management requires that regardless of what job evaluation plan you use to determine job value, you must relate the dollars you pay to the person in that job to the marketplace which pays engineers more than accountants.

AREA DIFFERENTIALS

It is surprising to me the number of companies with operations across the United States that still pay the same for non-exempt positions regardless of location. In the continental United States alone, non-exempt wages vary by at least 40 percent. Millions of dollars can be saved here while still paying competitively in the local labor market.

INDUSTRY DIFFERENCES

Organizations which are in different businesses must have compensation levels that are cost effective within their industry. You can hardly hold the general manpower accountable for growth and profit targets within his industry if you direct him to pay salaries at a higher level than his industry. For those companies that operate in many different industries, complete cost effectiveness requires that inter-divisional salary equity be tempered by the realities of the division's marketplace salary practices.

SALARY ADMINISTRATION PRACTICES

Salary administration practices provide a gold mine of opportunities for cost effectiveness. I smile when some of my colleagues suggest that they could never adopt the Japanese age seniority pay system. They seem to forget that many technical people are paid on maturity curves. In the administrative area, instead of calling them maturity curves, we call them "job families" or "generic progression," associate accountant, accountant, senior accountant, and so on. The facts are that there is a correlation between age and pay.

In many ways, the Japanese seniority pay system is more forthright than our so-called pay for performance systems.

Personally, I would like to consider paying people up to the mid-point—which I would call their job rate—on a go, no-go basis; the time level varying with the complexity of the job. For example, for the janitor, his starting rate would be his job rate; for the Chief Executive Officer, it might take him five years to reach his job rate. Compensation above the job rate, formerly the mid-point, would be provided in the form of annual payments paid from a pool based on the company's overall performance and distributed on accomplishment against individual targets. If the company had a very bad year, there would be no bonuses. This pool could be based on overall company performance or on individual division performance, or some combination of both.

My thoughts here are precipitated in part by the Japanese semi-annual bonus system.

ALTERNATIVE TO PAY INCREASE

As competitive realities force constraints on historical salary progression practices, more attention should be spent on non-economic forms of recognition. For example: memos of commendation, plaques, task force participation, acknowledgement of unique contributions in group meetings and so on. Employees cannot live forever on these "soft" forms of recognition, but they do go a long way in the interim.

PERSONNEL RATIOS

In addition to competitive benchmarking salaries, personnel professionals must be concerned with the comparative costs of running their departments. The same way marketeers are concerned with selling costs, so should we be concerned with personnel costs.

A pragmatic way to get at this issue is to determine the number of personnel people you have as compared to your product market competitors. This technique is commonly referred to as the personnel ratio—the number of people dedicated to personnel per 100 employees. A recent survey by Xerox revealed that major companies in the U.S. have an average of 1:79 with an overall industry average of 1:100. The average for all Japanese companies is 1:200, although for major Japanese companies, it is considerably less.

In addition to staffing levels, you must also examine expense levels.

LINE MANAGER
VERSUS PERSONNEL MANAGER

As legitimate pressure is applied by senior management to reduce the total cost of providing personnel services, we must take steps to insure that all managers—line and staff—recognize that they are really the personnel managers for their own people. This means that they must view their human resource responsibilities the same way they view their revenue, production, expense responsibilities.

In order to make this desired change a reality, we must provide "management of people" training to all managers and measure them against these responsibilities.

OFFICE AUTOMATION

Clearly, one of the ways to increase productivity is to increase the utilization of office automation machines such as the Personal Computer and the professional Work Station. The challenge here is to insure that the capital investment required is offset by manpower reductions and/or significant reduction in administrative costs. Hands-on training is required to insure that the productivity inherent in the machine is fully realized.

STRATEGIC PERSONNEL PLANNING

Now, how does one go about systematically managing the major variables I have described this afternoon? One way is to develop a strategic personnel plan. The starting point is the corporation's articulation of its major strategic mission or missions, and the major objectives it needs to accomplish if its strategy is to be successful.

Then the human resource people need to understand what is happening in the external environment and how those activities might facilitate or obstruct achievement of the strategy.

Clearly, one of the variables in the environment that has and will impact our businesses is the employee relations implications of proposed legislation. What will happen to the turnover rate of high potential middle-level managers if Congressman Pepper's drive to eliminate any retirement age is successful?

One of the most significant variables in the external business environment is, of course, your competition. Xerox's most significant competition is Japan, Inc., and their comparable cost advantage. I identified, earlier in my remarks, some of the manpower and compensation actions we could take to increase our cost effectiveness.

Another increasingly important area for examination in human resource planning is demographics. For example:

- The population growth, in developed countries: there will be a relatively small net addition to the population over the decade; some nations may even experience a decline in total population (West Germany and United Kingdom) unless there is a net increase of immigration into these countries.
- Population growth in developing countries: in contrast will increase (especially Mexico, Brazil, India).
- In the United States: the end of the "baby boom" bulge in workforce entrants will produce secretaries, clerks, typists, and low skilled workers. This may give further impetus to efforts to increase office and factory productivity through capital investment or increase the number of immigrants into the United States.
- Labor force skills in the United States: Assuming normal economic growth, will experience shortfalls in production of certain skills (electronics engineers, programmers, computer scientists) may hinder the ability of U.S. industry to introduce new products and improved manufacturing processes.
- The number of women in the labor force is increasing at a rapid rate. There are twice as many dual earning families than single earning families. Forty percent of all preschool mothers are in the labor force. Implications, of above are significant, as witnessed by the demand for day care centers, flex hours, etc.

When you consider the future impact of economics, technology, demographics, a major shift of manufacturing to Far East Countries—Japan, Korea, Singapore, and eventually India, with their plentiful supply of inexpensive labor—suggests a permanent and major restructuring of many industries. I think we will see more multinational alliances such as American Motors in the U.S. and Renault in France, General Motors in the U.S. and Toyota in Japan. The implications of these trends for manpower planning are monumental; the short term impact of permanent unemployment for hundreds of thousands, perhaps millions, is critical. Sponsorship of retraining and support of job security legislation can also be expected.

REQUIREMENTS FOR SUCCESSFUL PERSONNEL STRATEGIC PLAN

My experience has been that developing a credible, workable human resource strategic plan requires:

- A well articulated corporate strategic plan.
- Intimate involvement of your key human resource people in your day-to-day operations and development of the strategic plan. You cannot develop the plan in a vacuum.

- Trade-offs—it is not possible to tackle all the issues. You have to decide which ones have the highest pay-off.
- Clear linkage of the personnel objectives to the business strategic plan.
- Objectives must be human resource objectives—not functional objectives like compensation, training, etc. Develop a human resource planning and development process to stabilize employment and meet future manpower requirements. Functional objective:
—Manpower forecasting
—Re-training
—Sourcing
—Management development
—Affirmative Action

- Patience (trial and error)
- Personal endorsement of highest level management.

But once you have a personnel strategic plan, it provides you a pragmatic guide to keep you focused on the high payoff items where eventual success increases your visibility and credibility with senior management. In return, for results against your strategic plan, you are rewarded with opportunities to be of even greater influence on the organization.

ACCOUNTABILITY THROUGH MEASUREMENT OF RESULTS

Now all the planning, all the analysis, and all the discussion in the world is wasted if you do not achieve results. In order to achieve results, my experience has been that you must hold managers accountable. If you are going to hold them accountable, then you must measure them against pre-determined standards.

At Xerox, up to 30 percent of a manager's merit increase is a function of his human resource management evaluation. For example, our field managers are measured on each of the following items:

- Affirmative action
- Career guidance
- Corrective action administration
- Employment
- Management development
- Succession planning
- Attitude surveys
- Employee involvement
- Performance appraisal/salary administration
- Communications

Some examples of the evaluation focus.

ATTITUDE SURVEYS

- Were problem areas surfaced by attitude surveys, and other means, effectively addressed? If necessary, did a substantial lasting change occur since the last surveys?

COMMUNICATIONS STRATEGIES

- Did the organization identify and communicate Xerox business issues?

COMPENSATION AND RECOGNITION

- Were special recognition awards and programs effectively utilized? Did protected classes participate equally in these programs? Were awards utilized in all job categories and levels?

DEVELOPMENT

- Were developmental plans established for managers and employees? Was there a tracking system in place to monitor developmental action plan status?

In summary, I would like to highlight my main points:

- Be proactive and participate in the early stages of development of proposed legislation and regulations.
- Understand your competition's strengths and weaknesses. Benchmark your product and industry competition's manpower costs.
- Learn all you can about the reasons for Japan's market share success and key human resource practices. Adopt those that make sense:
  —Employment involvement and
  —Employment security.
- Maximize the return on your substantial investment in manpower. Utilize all the tools available to you.
  —Job analysis
  —Area differentials
  —Critically examine our tradition-salary increase practices for higher pay-off opportunities
  —Expand utilization of non-economic recognition
- Develop a personnel strategic plan that directly supports the major business objectives and be persistent and unrelenting in your support of these objectives. Communicate your plan to key line managers and all your personnel people.
- And finally, measure your managers performance against their human resource responsibilities and hold them accountable for results.

I think the '80s will prove to be the most exciting time for human resource professionals with manpower and effective management of all its related costs being a significant factor in these highly competitive and cost conscious times. Compensation professionals have an outstanding opportunity to help their business and in so doing, advance themselves professionally. . . .

GAINING COMPETITIVE ADVANTAGE THROUGH HUMAN RESOURCE MANAGEMENT PRACTICES

Randall S. Schuler   **Ian C. MacMillan**

In an earlier article, MacMillan presented the concept of strategic initiative and defined it as the ability of a company or a strategic business unit to capture control of strategic behavior in the industries in which it competes (1983, p. 43). To the extent a company can gain the initiative, competitors are obliged to respond and thus play a reactive rather than a proactive role. Consequently, if it can gain a strategic advantage, a company can control its own destiny, and, to the extent it can gain an advantage difficult for competitors to remove, stay in control longer. Thus the financial benefits of gaining competitive advantage are enormous!

MacMillan (1983) suggests that gaining a competitive advantage requires an understanding and anticipation of response barriers, intelligence systems, preemption potentials, infrastructure requirements, calculated sacrifices, general management challenges, and punch and counterpunch planning. The purpose of this article is to expand upon his discussion of the *infrastructure requirements*. In doing so, we will show how companies can strategically utilize these infrastructure requirements to gain competitive advantage, particularly through their human resources and human resource management practices.

INFRASTRUCTURE REQUIREMENTS

Defined here, infrastructure requirements consist of those functions and activities necessary for the effective management of a company's human resources. The major purposes of these activities traditionally have been to attract, retain, and motivate employees. We refer to them as human resource management (HRM) practices (Schuler, 1984), and the key HRM practices include:

- Human resource planning
- Staffing, including recruitment, selection, and socialization

Randall S. Schuler and Ian C. MacMillan, "Gaining Competitive Advantage through Human Resource Management Practices," Human Resource Management, *Fall 1984, Vol. 23, No. 3. Copyright © 1984 John Wiley & Sons, Inc. Reprinted by permission of John Wiley & Sons, Inc.*

- Appraising
- Compensation
- Training and development
- Union-management relationships

The result of effectively managing human resources is an enhanced ability to attract and retain qualified employees who are motivated to perform, and the results of having the right employees motivated to perform are numerous. They include greater profitability, low employee turnover, high product quality, lower production costs, and more rapid acceptance and implementation of corporate strategy. These results, particularly if coupled with competitors who do *not* have the right people motivated to perform, can create a number of competitive advantages through human resource management practices. For example, according to Glenn Bailey, Chairman of Bairnco Corporation, compensation tied to performance is a powerful spur to management hustle. Under a system where officers with a salary of $100,000 a year can make that much again in bonuses linked to performance, the Kaydon bearing division of Bairnco has increased sales from $270 million in 1981 to $442 million in 1983.

Lincoln Electric is a leader in small motors and arc welders. Lincoln has a compensation system tied to the company's profits. This system has resulted in the average Lincoln worker making up to $44,000 a year. In addition to the high motivation to produce, Lincoln workers rarely quit. Their turnover rate is less than one percent.

Key to the success of the consulting group at the American Productivity Center is its HRM practice of selection. By hiring generalists, members of its consulting staff can "sell" any of the other specialty areas and also be effective in the delivery of those specific services.

As Peters and Waterman (1982) point out, all the excellent organizations surveyed made effective use of their human resources, and they did this through their personnel and human resource management.

A further bonus for a company's ability to attract and retain key people is its capacity to implement other critical corporate efforts and even ensure its survival and profitability. The essence of this is captured quite nicely by Walter Wriston's (outgoing Chairman and CEO of Citicorp) comment:

> I believe the only game in town is the personnel game . . . My theory is if you have the right person in the right place, you don't have to do anything else. If you have the wrong person in the job, there's no management system known to man that can save you.

Edson de Castro, president and founder of Data General, following up on Wriston's advice, hired a team of professional managers to direct the company, and thereby replace the previous leadership that excelled in technical and entrepreneurial skills. De Castro's strategic change of human resources appears to be thus far aiding the growth and profitability quite nicely. Commodore International illustrates the impact of not having the right people at the right time. In early 1984, Commodore's future was put in jeopardy upon the departure of several high-ranking, high-skilled managers. According to industry analysts these departures left Commodore without a clear product strategy for the future and cast doubt on the future of the company.

GAINING A COMPETITIVE ADVANTAGE THROUGH HRM PRACTICES

An initial understanding of where companies can gain competitive advantages through their HRM practices is facilitated by a discussion of

- Strategic targets
- Strategic thrusts

We shall briefly describe these via examples of companies that have gained a competitive advantage through the various targets and thrusts. Exhibit 1 identifies major thrusts and targets. After the description of thrusts and targets, we show how specific HRM practices can be used to gain a competitive advantage.

Targets

There are four targets of HRM practices that can be used for competitive advantage. These four targets represent upstream and downstream activities as well as the company itself. Accordingly, the four include: *self* (the focal company); *customers; distributors/servicers;* and *suppliers.* Our earlier examples illustrated uses of HRM practices only within a company. Companies can reach backward or reach forward to help shape the HRM practices of other companies. For instance, we find companies like Pepsico training store managers (Pepsico's *distributors*) in merchandising techniques to help

EXHIBIT 1. Matrix of Thrusts and Targets

	Target			
Thrust	*Self*	*Customers*	*Distributors and Servicers*	*Suppliers*
Cost/efficiency	Lincoln Electric	Unifi	McDonald's	Honda
Product differentiation	General Electric	IBM	Pepsico	Baltimore Orioles, Bell Labs

increase store sales as well as sales of Pepsico. Unifi helps *customers* with their performance appraisal systems, making their customers more competitive and thus better able to buy Unifi products. Mercedes has trained mechanics in service garages (their *servicers*) throughout the United States in order that Mercedes can offer 24-hour servicing anywhere in the United States. Nissan Motors and Honda Motors offer extensive training programs to their parts *suppliers* in order to enhance the quality of their products (both them as well as the suppliers). McDonald's offers extensive training to their franchise owners (i.e., their distributors/servicers).

Thrusts

There are two strategic thrusts, or ways to beat the competition, through human resource management practices. One is a *cost/efficiency thrust*. The case of Lincoln Electric is an example of the use of HRM practices to increase the efficiency of production and thereby lower the cost of the electric motors and arc welders. PEOPLExpress Airlines is a similar example of a cost/efficient thrust. Unifi, McDonald's, and Honda assist in the HRM practices of their customers, distributors, and suppliers, respectively, in order to help them keep costs down as well as to ensure a competitive, and thus enduring, set of customers, distributors, and suppliers.

The second thrust option is a *differentiation* thrust. The cost/efficient thrust represents HRM practices that are used to improve the efficiency of product production and thus to lower the cost of the product. The differentiation thrust uses HRM practices in ways to differentiate the product or the company from its competitors. Although this may not make them more efficient, their farm system and promotion policies help differentiate the Baltimore Orioles from competitors in the eyes of its *supply* sources—young talented baseball players. In a similar vein, for decades Bell Labs attracted the cream of the crop of engineering Ph.D.'s with a similar strategy. IBM was able to differentiate itself from competitors by providing programming training for *customers'* employees. As we have already mentioned, Pepsico was able to differentiate itself from competitors by providing merchandising training and store management training to a fast growing *distributor* group—the medium-sized urban supermarket. General Electric Power Systems division recognized that its sale of large equipment contracts worldwide depended on a challenging combination of traditional technical skills and radically new financing skills, so they systematically staffed up to secure these skills and now have differentiated themselves as producers of power systems, with affordable financing options, in third world countries.

The target-thrust matrix we showed in Exhibit 1 provides the firm seeking a competitive advantage with eight broad options from which to launch a strategic advantage. The next question is to ask what particular human resource practices the firm is exceptionally good at, and to see where these skills can be applied in the target thrust matrix. This we have done in Exhibit 2.

Planning

Increasingly, companies are being forced to link human resource planning with strategic business planning. Companies are taking note of recent census data—those data indicate that the number of young workers in the labor force peaked at 37 million in 1980 and will drop to 24 million by 1990. Meanwhile, each year 2.3 million 17-year-olds are added to the ranks of the functionally illiterate. Among Hispanic 17-year-olds, 56 percent are functionally illiterate while 47 percent of the Black 17-year-olds are functionally illiterate. In anticipation of a desperate need for literate young workers at all levels, companies such as Texas Instruments and New York Telephone are getting into secondary and primary education to help increase the literacy rate in the reduced supply of labor force entrants in the 1980s. Without such action, the very ability of some companies to survive is in jeopardy. According to Robert Feagles (senior vice president of Travelers Insurance Company), "The issue of functional illiteracy has coiled at the center of our unemployment problems and it threatens this country's ultimate ability to succeed in the world market" (*Business Week,* May 9, 1984, p. 81).

Another aspect of planning that companies are addressing is rather opposite to the one already described. It is that of the baby boom bulge (people aged 25–54) that is moving through the work force. This is creating a rapid expansion of potential managers with a narrowing base of managerial jobs. Added to this situation is the desire by many of those in this age category to be promoted and be successful. Meanwhile these changes are occurring in an environment that is becoming more turbulent and more demanding of change by the organization.

The intersection of these events is producing a company need for flexibility and current, up-to-date skills. Companies such as AT&T, Bank America Corporation, Sun Company, and Eastman Kodak Company are trying to gain this flexibility and skill currency by offering attractive early retirement packages for carefully selected groups of employees. Since it seems as if all the current demographic, economic, and technological trends will continue, it is reasonable to assume that the companies that most systematically plan with their human resources in mind will be most likely to gain a competitive advantage by having "the right people at the right place at the right time" to produce quality products efficiently.

Staffing

The American Productivity Center in Houston utilizes its staffing practices to gain a competitive advantage. Furthermore it supports its staffing

EXHIBIT 2. Matching HRM Practices with Targets and Thrusts

HRM practice	Company example	Target	Thrust
Planning	Texas Instruments	Suppliers	Cost/efficiency
	New York Telephone	Suppliers	Cost/efficiency
	AT&T	Self	Differentiation
Staffing	Sun Company	Self	Differentiation
	American Productivity Center	Self	Differentiation
	Data General	Self	Cost/efficiency
	Baltimore Orioles	Suppliers	Differentiation
Appraising	Unifi	Customers	Differentiation
	GTE	Self	Cost/efficiency
	Emery Air Freight	Self	Cost/efficiency
Compensating	Lincoln	Self	Cost/efficiency
	PEOPLExpress	Self	Cost/efficiency
	TRW	Self	Differentiation
Training and development	Hewlett-Packard	Self	Differentiation
	Delco Remy	Self	Differentiation
	Dayton Hudson/Pepsico	Self	Differentiation
	McDonald's Corp.	Distributors	Cost/efficiency
	Mercedes	Servicers	Differentiation
Union–managerial relationships	Ford Motors	Self	Cost/efficiency
	American Airlines	Suppliers	Cost/efficiency

practices with consistent training practices. According to Stu Winby at the Center:

> In hiring consultants we specifically look for the generalist; an individual who has high propensity to learn other areas in the productivity domain; an individual whose appreciation system and skills span both the qualitative and quantitative aspects of productivity and organizational effectiveness. A value of the organization is placed on organizational integration. We promote cross-training and a multi-disciplinary approach to consulting engagements. The competitive advantage is that most members of the consulting staff can "sell" any of the other specialty areas but can also be reasonably effective in the delivery of those specific services.
>
> Against consulting firms that are more specialized and do not seem to have this broad perspective emphasis on hiring generalists and promoting internal integration among consultants has provided competitive advantage.

The Baltimore Orioles also attain differentiation through their staffing practices, this time with their suppliers. Its farm clubs combine a selection policy emphasizing internal promotion and support this with an extensive training system (the farm clubs). Of these two HRM practices, it appears as if the internal promotion is more critical to their overall success. The result of both these practices, however, is a product that is clearly differentiated from other teams in the industry: a consistency at winning, yet retaining key employees at compensation levels far below many competitors despite the lucrative bidding that goes on for top players.

In order for Data General to successfully implement its new structure requiring professional managers rather than entrepreneurs, it has slowly replaced many of its homegrown managers with more experienced ones from outside. The results of this practice were mentioned earlier in this article. To ensure the success of this staffing practice, Edson de Castro and Hervert J. Richman, executive vice president, spent a vast amount of personal time on hiring only those managers whose styles and interests fit with Data General. The styles and interests that best seem to fit with Data General now are those reflecting a desire for organization, long-range strategic planning, and more stable and methodical growth patterns. This practice of careful selection to ensure a better fit between company and employee is also a critical HRM practice at Goldman Sachs. There, every partner interviews every MBA job applicant to ensure that the new employees "fit" the company.

Care in selecting to bring the right people on board leads naturally to another important staffing practice: *socialization*. Socialization represents the process used by companies to expose new employees to their culture and ways of doing things. When done successfully, it results in intensely loyal employees who are dedicated to the company. Companies that have perfected the socialization process include IBM, Procter & Gamble, and Morgan Guaranty Trust. Often the socialization process begins before the employee is hired. At Procter & Gamble for example, an elite cadre of line managers trained in interviewing skills probes applicants for entry level positions in brand management for such qualities as the "ability to turn out high volumes of excellent work." Only after successfully completing at least two interviews and a test of general knowledge is the applicant flown to P&G headquarters in Cincinnati where (s)he confronts a day-long series of interviews. If an applicant passes this extensive screening process, (s)he is confronted with a series of rigorous job experiences calculated to induce humility and openness to new ways of doing things. Typically this phase of socialization involves long hours of work at a pressure cooker pace. Throughout this phase and others of the socialization process, the new employee is constantly made aware of transcendent company values and organizational folklore. Such values and folklore include the emphasis on product quality and the dedication and commitment of employees long since past.

Appraising

GTE performance appraisals are viewed as one of the most important tools in the management arsenal. According to GTE Chairman Theodore F. Brophy, the GTE appraisal system complements the emergent strategic planning emphasis in all areas of the corporation. The appraisal reviews assist executives in clarifying and articulating objectives and expectations for themselves and their employees. They give GTE a realistic assessment of its strengths, weaknesses, and future requirements. As such, the company is now able to better utilize its human resources than at any time in the past.

Another critical aspect of appraising is correcting poor performance. At Emery Air Freight, the company was losing $1 million annually because employees on the airport loading docks were shipping small packages separately rather than placing those with the same destination in one container that would be carried at lower rates by air carriers. Management also found that the containers were being used 45 percent of the time when they should have been used 90 percent of the time. By establishing a program of positive consequences and feedback, the nearly $1 million annual loss was eliminated. Stories of similar changes in poor performance to good performance and labor dollar savings resulting from absenteeism reduction programs and employee assistance programs have been reported by many companies. The result is a tremendous gain in cost reduction and improved efficiency.

Compensation

In addition to PEOPLExpress Airline and Lincoln Electric, who use compensation practices to gain a cost/efficiency competitive advantage, TRW and the Hewlett-Packard Company use compensation to drive their search for innovative products and services.

At Hewlett-Packard, entrepreneurial behavior is stimulated in project leaders by tying more rewards to their success. Successful project leaders are being given banquets, stock options, and personal computers. At TRW, units or teams are given credit for sales generated in another department in return for helping that department. Consistent with the prescription by Rosabeth Moss Kanter in *The Change Masters,* TRW fosters innovation by stimulating interdependence through its compensation practices. And these companies do get what they pay for—a steady stream of product and service improvements and enhancements that help them stand alone among their competitors.

Another company that has used compensation to gain a competitive advantage is Nucor Corporation. It has simultaneously utilized four different group level incentive plans to increase its sales more than 6000 percent and profits 1500 percent in the past decade. At the equally successful Chaparral Steel, all employees are covered by profit sharing.

Training and Development

When Delco-Remy trained its employees in participative management, it succeeded in differentiating itself from all competitors in the eyes of Honda and others. The success of this training and resultant competitive advantage are described by Delco's Keith W. Wander:

> Honda of America was seeking an American battery manufacturer as a supplier to its auto plant in Marysville, Ohio. Honda wanted a plant which had a participative system of management and a reputation for producing a quality product at a competitive price. After a contact from the Delco-Remy Sales Department, two American representatives from Honda visited the Delco-Remy plant in Fitzgerald, Georgia. This visit was followed by a second one with Mr. Hoshita, President of Honda, in the group.
>
> During the second visit, plant tours were conducted by Operating Team (hourly employees) members. The tours were followed by Operating Team members explaining to Mr. Hoshita how people were involved in the Fitzgerald business, how Fitzgerald and Honda could be mutual resources to each other because of their participative systems, and why a Delco battery was the best-built battery in the world.
>
> Mr. Hoshita returned several months later to ask more questions of the Support Team (salaried employees) and Operating Teams. Shortly afterward, Honda of America announced Delco-Remy, Fitzgerald, as its sole supplier of batteries, based upon its (1) culture; (2) quality; and (3) price, in that order.
>
> To date, Honda has had zero returns of batteries and zero complaints on quality or delivery.

Dayton Hudson Corporation is using training and development skills to create future customers. B. Dalton Bookseller Division has earmarked $3 million over four years for a literacy training program. Their goals are to recruit volunteer tutors and to tell people without basic skills about the free teaching programs available in their communities. As a part of this, Dalton gives grants to local school districts to hire speakers who will persuade teachers to put more emphasis on teaching reading skills.

Texas Instruments is engaged in a similar program. While the result of both the B. Dalton and TI programs is of immediate benefit to the individuals gaining literacy, the companies broaden their base of potential customers over the longer run.

IBM has followed a similar strategy for many years in teaching programming skills to customers' employees—capturing unending loyalty of the firms and the employees to IBM products.

McDonald's uses training to ensure its distributors of a competitive advantage through cost/efficiency. McDonald's uses its intensive training program at Hamburger University to ensure that its franchisees or distributors run as efficiently as possible. Although training is also done in order to attain consistent quality, its competitive advantage from training is attained from a cost/efficiency thrust.

Union–Management Relationships

Critical to the success of many companies *vis-a-vis* competitors are their labor costs. In many industries today, companies face possible bankruptcy due to high labor costs. Helping to lower costs are wage reductions reached between unions and management. Recently American Airlines, Greyhound, McDonnell Douglas, Boeing, and Ingersoll-Rand have negotiated two-tiered wage systems to help reduce total costs by reducing labor costs. Without these jointly negotiated systems, these companies would not have survived. Thus, a company's relationship with its union can be critical to its survival, and the better its relationships are, the more likely it is to ever gain a competitive advantage.

Crown Zellerbach Corporation and the International Woodworkers of America demonstrated, however, that a competitive advantage can be gained without reducing total wages. In fact, based upon a recent incentive pay plan agreed to by the union and management, workers earn about $3 more per hour than before on straight wages. Because this incentive system makes the workers more productive, the company in exchange had to give the union greater worker involvement in work related decisions. Thus, the workers gain in involvement and salary and the company gains in cost reductions and greater competitiveness.

Ford Motor Company has engaged in a program of more worker involvement and more cooperative labor relations with the UAW. The results of this program are higher product quality than its competitors and a marketing campaign centered around "quality of Job 1." As with the two-tiered wage systems, this program of more worker involvement gains competitive advantage through cost reductions and improved efficiencies. Similar results of high product quality and efficiency have been obtained at Westinghouse Electric Corporation, Warner Gear Division of Borg-Warner Corporation, and the Mass Transportation Authority of Flint, Michigan. In these companies, gains in quality and efficiency have resulted from employee commitment associated with quality circle programs. In addition to increased quality and efficiency, these companies have experienced costs, higher engineering productivity, and fewer costly changes in design cycles.

Although the above examples suggest the importance of human resource practices for securing an advantage, they have not yet highlighted the benefits from delayed competitors' response. In the next section we highlight the difficulty competitors will have in countering such a competitive advantage when they so desire. These difficulties are due to a number of Inertia Barriers (MacMillan, 1983). Only by first overcoming these barriers can a competitor really counter HRM advantages.

BARRIERS TO COMPETITIVE RESPONSE

The first of four inertia barriers is the *needs-matching challenge*. To get the right person in the right place, as Walter Wriston suggests, requires a company to engage in extensive analyses. Jobs have to be analyzed, the needs and products of the company, present and future, have to be analyzed, and key individuals have to be analyzed. Then, once all of this analysis is complete, all the diverse needs have to be matched. These analyses are anything but straightforward—multiple approaches exist for analyzing jobs, yet none seems to be convincingly superior to the others—all have unique strengths and weaknesses. And since many companies are only just beginning to think strategically, many are unable to even begin articulating their future products and markets sufficiently to know what employees will be needed, i.e., what skills, knowledges, and abilities (SKAs) will be needed. Furthermore, even after years of selection research, identifying the SKAs job applicants for managerial positions may and should possess can still be regarded as an art more than a science (Skinner, 1981). All these uncertainties in analysis, let alone implementation, result in a serious challenge in trying to match the information across phases. Hence, there is a great reluctance to do it at all, and competitors will delay responding, as we have seen in industry after industry which has succumbed to foreign competitors.

Associated with the first inertia barrier is the second one—*attaining consistency*. For example, with the recent need to cut costs companies have been rationalizing their structures—a consequence of this has been the need to reduce the workforce. One popular way of attaining this is by offering early retirement benefits. However, companies such as Polaroid have found this practice to be completely inconsistent with their "retirement rehearsal" and "tapering off" programs. While the intent of these two programs was to ease the retirement process for its employees, the "golden handshake" retirement benefits have caused many employees to suddenly accelerate taking retirement. Not only does this result in inconsistency between their retirement practices, but often companies lose their best and brightest: these employees know they can take the retirement incentive payment and easily get another job elsewhere, perhaps even with a competitor. So, aware of the difficulties in attaining consistency across all their human resource practices, and the seriousness of the consequences for failure to do so if they do try, competitors shy away from changing the ways they manage their human resources and postpone meeting the competitive advantage we have created.

The third inertia barrier is *lack of commitment*. To change human resource practices consumes vast amounts of time and energy: As we have seen, merely attaining consistency requires a great deal of analysis, even under the best of circumstances, and even more is required to meet the needs-matching challenge. If this is combined with any past failures to change human resource practices, it makes it difficult to get organizational commitment to any more changes, starting at the top of the firm and working down. Yet it is at the top that commitment must begin. It begins there with the top level manager demonstrating concern, confidence, and excitement for the product and for the people. In turn, the rest of management and the employees begin to show the same concern and excitement in their jobs and products and confidence in themselves. Lee Iacocca has done exactly this at Chrysler Corporation. The results there have been astounding. Workers at the Smyrna, Tennessee, plant of Nissan Motor Manufacturing Corporation USA are producing trucks of measurably higher quality than their Japanese counterparts due in large part to Marvin T. Runyon, president of the firm. Runyon walks the floor of the plant to demonstrate his concern and confidence in the workers. He also lets the workers make decisions. According to Runyon, "decisions should be made at the lowest possible level."

Because the *time horizon* is so critical it is regarded here as a fourth inertia barrier. Skinner (1981) estimates that it may take as much as seven years for managers to: install, adjust to, and reap the benefits of major changes in human resource management practices; weed out unproductive employees; and create the new generation of employees. It may take the employees equally as long to accept the changes. This is because "effective relationships between individuals and companies rest on employees' trust that the goals [of the individuals and companies] are connected. But developing trust often requires overcoming years of bad experience and many employees' belief that companies exploit people" (Skinner, 1981, p. 114). Since many managers are rewarded for short-term performance, the time horizon in changing human resource practices becomes perhaps the most significant inertia barrier.

SUMMARY AND CONCLUSIONS

Although there are many ways by which companies can gain a competitive advantage, as MacMillan (1983) has suggested, one way often overlooked is through their human resource management practices. HRM practices enable companies to gain a competitive advantage in two major ways: One is by helping themselves and the other is by helping others. So there appears to be a significant benefit from having HRM considerations represented in the strategy formulation stage rather than only in the implementation stage.

Once the strategy is formulated and the appropriate HRM thrust identified, specific HRM practices need to be developed. These practices, such as staffing and compensation, are the ones that actually create the competitive advantage for the company. In addition, selection of the most appropriate practices should be appropriate to the strategy and lead to behaviors that are supportive of the strategy; for example, if cooperative behaviors are needed among employees, then group or organizational level compensation incentives should be provided rather than an individual-level incentive system. If product quality is critical, quality circles and union-management cooperation should be developed.

Once the strategy is formulated, the determination of the needed behaviors comes from job analysis. The HRM practices that stimulate those behaviors must be identified. They must be implemented so as to ensure consistency across HRM practices. It is this hard-won consistency which will help ensure that a competitive advantage through HRM practices is gained and sustained because of the barriers we have just discussed.

In addition to using their HRM practices on themselves, companies can also gain a competitive advantage through using their HRM practices on others. Specifically, companies can gain a competitive advantage by helping their suppliers, customers, or servicers/distributors with their practices. Recall, for example, how American Airlines and Honda assist their suppliers to ensure lower wages and better quality and how Mercedes trains servicers to enable Mercedes to sell its products with the guarantee of 24-hour service.

In this way they can secure a differential position in the eyes of their stakeholders—and this is often all that is needed to get priority of attention and support in times when this is critical. The fact of the matter is that the firm is stronger and healthier if its particular suppliers, distributors, and customers are robust and competitive.

While companies are better off when they gain a competitive advantage, few do it and even fewer do it through their human resource practices. There are, however, some notable exceptions and we have attempted to reference some of them here. For example, Lincoln Electric is extremely competitive in arc welders and electric motors because of its competitive practices; Delco-Remy produces high-quality battery products largely because of its participative management practices; and Morgan Guaranty, IBM, and Procter & Gamble are able to attract and retain highly skilled individuals due to recruitment, selection, and socialization practices. While there is no denying that all these companies have competitors, it is problematic that any are so successful as the companies mentioned thanks largely to their human resource management practices.

REFERENCES

MacMillan, I. C. Seizing Competitive Initiative. *The Journal of Business Strategy,* 1983. pp. 43–57.

Peters, T. J., and Waterman, R. H. Jr. *In Search of Excellence.* New York: Warner Books, 1982.

Schuler, R. S. *Personnel and Human Resource Management* (2nd ed.). St. Paul, MN: West Publishing, 1984.

Skinner, W. Big Hat, No Cattle: Managing Human Resources. *Harvard Business Review,* September–October 1981, pp. 107–118.

DECENTRALIZATION:
THE KEY TO THE GROWTH
OF THE HUMAN RESOURCE FUNCTION

Homer S. Klock II

Belt tightening and an increased push for profits in these hard economic times have put a great amount of pressure on human resource professionals to help wring the last ounce of performance out of a workforce that may be static or declining in number. As an important element in corporate planning, the human resources function should be able to accomplish this difficult task successfully and, in so doing, set an example of organizational efficiency. A primary step in achieving such strategic goals is the decentralization of the human resource function. Decentralization usually leads to greater success than a centralized structure, and is likely to be the way to go in the 1980s.

This trend is directly attributable to the changing emphasis in U.S. corporations today. Within most organizations the increasing drive for productivity and profits in each business unit has led to expanded responsibility and authority at lower levels of management. Focusing on product line control has thus resulted in a trend toward profit center structure. Along with this has come the enhancement of incentive and reward systems, leading to an increased competitive spirit and a sense of business unit identity.

Decentralizing support functions into smaller profit center staffs from the traditional large corporate central staff is the most effective way for the human resource professional to become part of the team, to better understand corporate goals, and to be a confidante of management.

This closer association allows the human resource organization to introduce improved management techniques at the user level and to better assist management in planning and control.

During the "growing pain" years of organizational transition—the 1960s and 1970s—many companies went full-circle from decentralization to centralized structure and back again. It was found that the matrix structure of decentralized management—solid reporting lines to the business unit and a dotted or functional reporting line to central human resource man-

Homer S. Klock II, "Decentralization—The Key to the Growth of the Human Resource Function," reprinted from the Spring 1983 issue of IAPW Journal. Copyright by and used with the permission of The International Association for Personnel Women.

agement—has its difficulties. But such a structure is very workable if human resource managers are selected for compatibility with the team as well as for technical expertise. The size of the organization also affects the optimal degree of decentralization. There are some companies, experience has shown, where due to their manageable size, relative ease of communication, and uniformity of corporate purpose, a centralized structure seems to be appropriate. The company, in effect, functions as a single business unit. But when, as is increasingly the case, a company is multi-product line oriented, has multiple subordinate headquarters units and profit centers, and several thousand employees, decentralization becomes the most appropriate human resource structure.

Decentralized management can be employed in a way which overcomes some of its previously mentioned difficulties. In one of my former positions, I had functional responsibility for three major business units (approximately 10,000 employees), each of which had its own human resource department. The manager of these areas participated in the consolidation of the groups' program results. My staff of five people was primarily responsible for management development and organizational planning, the key responsibilities of a group executive in assuring appropriate resources and succession of management for the whole organization. Another vital group function, which belonged to a peer of mine, was strategic planning. This process aimed to create an environment amenable to the good integration and coordination of our responsibilities. Participating in strategic planning is an important offshoot of the decentralized approach, since close proximity to decision makers tends to breed greater participation in the process. If we are to anticipate the needs of tomorrow, the human resource function must have a part in the strategic planning effort of any organization. Decentralization tends to foster inclusion of the human resource area in the planning process, and recognition of the equal importance of human and capital resources.

It is important to note that decentralization increases head count and therefore is more expensive. But the added value of on-the-spot expertise results in management productivity improvement and a decreased risk in people management decisions.

It must be stated that several human resource responsibilities should remain centralized, such as benefits administration, compensation planning, policy development and labor relations/contract negotiation. The reasons for this are clear: Consistency of philosophy, ease of interpretation of data on a total company basis, contractual relations with health care insurance carriers, and greater impact on labor-management relationships are pertinent goals in these areas. Decentralized staffs should nevertheless play a major role in reviewing central staff proposals and providing planning input. And of course, they play the sole role in implementing approved programs.

THE ADMINISTRATION
OF A DECENTRALIZED FUNCTION

To effectively function in a decentralized human resource environment, a manager must overcome fears that one may: (1) lose the loyalty of the decentralized staff; (2) be less informed on day-to-day matters; (3) need to share authority and responsibility with subordinates; and (4) be less influential at the profit center management level.

There is a good basis for these fears. The sophisticated professional, however, can readily see that the credibility of the function demonstrably increases with the psychological fact that the decentralized staff person is one of the business team and not a "foreigner in their midst." Therefore, decentralized staff participate in the business decision process, and the overall effectiveness of the function grows. This effectiveness reflects positively on the functional manager, whose role should become more conceptual and strategic, as advisor to corporate management and functional overseer.

The psychological impact of the human resource professional being a team member in the business unit cannot be overemphasized. Experience has proved that it is human nature for the business unit manager to take his or her own staff into confidence, rather than to seek out a corporate staff member. Politics being what they are, however, functional ties can be strained if the players are shortsighted in how the dual relationship is handled. It does put a lot of pressure on the decentralized staff to maintain communication with two bosses.

As a business team member, the decentralized professional has the opportunity to readily foresee the need for innovative programs and policies and to more knowledgeably convince management of their advantages. Then as always, the subsequent request from the line results in a more effective program. Meanwhile, the astute decentralized staff will call upon centralized technical functions for expertise, increasing the team effort between the functional areas and further strengthening the overall credibility and effectiveness of human resources as a key force in the business.

HOW DOES DECENTRALIZATION
AFFECT CAREER GROWTH?

Decentralization affects the professional qualifications and career opportunities of human resource people. Competition has required sharper skills in all business areas, including human resources. In fact, the external forces referred to earlier have driven complexity into various programs such as EEO, ERISA, and other policy areas to the point that the knowledge base required for human resource professionals is far beyond that of years ago.

A high degree of technical proficiency is now required to understand, let alone implement or administer, tax-effective compensation programs, pension and profit sharing plans, health care programs, and affirmative action policies. Cost savings aside, these areas of expertise are most effectively managed on a central basis rather than dispersed among the business units.

Decentralized staffs frequently include generalists who have had some experience in central staff. The generalist is best equipped with counseling skills, innovative and pragmatic in problem solving, and has an overriding business sense sufficient to understand the environment in which he or she is operating. Business sense first and personnel education second is the correct priority in selection of candidates for decentralized staff members. Of course, these same characteristics are necessary in those responsible for specialized areas, but they are even more important on the front line.

Decentralization offers opportunity for the human resource professional to gain experience in many product areas as well as in functional specializations, resulting in a person better equipped to rise to the top as a manager. These opportunities also make the professional more valuable to management as an advisor and counselor.

IN CONCLUSION . . .

Are there downsides to decentralization? Great efforts must be made to assure consistency of application of policy for EEO purposes and to encourage profitability between business units. One must be attuned to the potential breakdown of the solid and dotted-line relationships that can cause counterproductive effort, misunderstandings, and "bad blood," all of which add up to ineffectiveness and reduction of credibility.

But despite its admitted imperfections, decentralization is the logical choice for the sophisticated manager seeking to make the most of a complex organization's human resource potential.

THE ROLE
OF THE PERSONNEL MANAGER—
AS I SEE IT

Paul C. Gordon

If I were to ask each of you right now, I'm sure that you could rattle off, virtually from memory, the following personnel information about your company:

- The number of exempt, nonexempt, and union employees in your company. The absentee rate in each of those categories.
- Average sales per employee. The contributed value of the factory labor force to the finished product. The sales output per square foot of factory space. Your compensation-to-sales ratio and its trend for the last three years.
- The average rates of pay in your company and how they compare to the area.
- Your employee turnover rate, possibly even citing the job classifications causing the biggest problems.
- Your average cost-per-hire for electronic engineers, software programmers, and other critical classifications.
- The cost of operating your personnel department. The trend of those costs over the last three years—up or down—and why. The ratio of personnel employees to total employment (1 to 50? 1 to 100? 1 to 200?).
- The number of personnel requisitions that have been open for 90 days or longer.
- Your number and frequency of lost-time manhours due to on-the-job accidents.
- The number of pending workers' compensation claims and the amounts of money reserved for each. The amount of money your company paid last year to settle workers' compensation cases.
- The number of pending grievance and arbitration cases, the relative merits of the issues, *and* the company's potential financial exposure or possible operating restrictions.
- The average merit increase granted last year to exempt and nonexempt nonunion employees, and the average performance rating that supported those increases.

Undoubtedly, you could also tell us how your company's figures compare with the local area in which you work and with those at your company's two or three leading competitors, regardless of geographical location.

All of this information represents the basic databank of the personnel function. Each of you should have, and I'm sure does have, that information on the top of his or her tongue.

Paul C. Gordon, "The Role of the Personnel Manager—As I See It," speech given on December 10, 1982, in Paramus, New Jersey. Reprinted with permission.

So . . . I won't ask you about those routine personnel matters. You know all about them.

SOME DIFFERENT, MORE MEANINGFUL QUESTIONS

Instead, let me pose a different series of straightforward, perhaps even more meaningful questions to you. To do an effective personnel job, in my opinion, each of you *must* know the answers to these questions just as readily and as thoroughly as you do the personnel information I just mentioned. Moreover, you must *understand* the impact of the answers to these questions and how to *implement* that understanding in positive actions that will benefit your company.

- Let's start with an easy one. What were your company's sales and net income last year, this year, and what are the budgets for the coming year? What does the trend of these numbers mean to you as the personnel manager?
- If your company has more than one product line, or more than one factory or operating location, is any of them in a temporary or sustained loss position—and why—and is there something that you, the personnel manager, should be doing about it?
- What are your company's percentages of return on sales, return on assets, and return on total capital? What has been the trend of these vital ratios for the last three years—up or down—and why? What significance does this trend have for you as personnel manager?
- What is your company's standard cost of sales or standard cost of manufacture as a percent of sales? 50 percent? 67 percent? 85 percent? Of your company's standard cost of manufacture, what are the relative standard percentages for material, labor, and burden? What has been the trend of these numbers for the past three years—up or down? Why?
- What was your company's dollar and percentage *variance* last year, and this year, from the standard cost of manufacture? What relative percentages and dollars of that total manufacturing variance were caused by labor rate variance, labor efficiency, and by scrap, rework, and warranty expense? And, again, what are the trends? And what, if anything, do these numbers mean to you as the personnel manager?
- What is your company's inventory-to-sales ratio? What should it be in your industry? And why does the answer to this question have significance to you as the personnel manager?
- What are your company's research, development, and engineering costs as a percent of sales? How much of that expense is covered by general development funds versus local funding?
- What is your company's general and administrative (G&A) expense as a percent of sales? What are the cost elements which comprise your G&A, and what is their trend—up or down—and in which elements?
- What is your company's book-to-bill rate for the past six months? (That is, is your company's order input running higher or lower than sales?) What significance does that ratio have to you as the personnel manager?
- What is your company's forecasted book-to-bill rate versus budget for the next six

months? What effect will that forecast have on your company's production back-log? What importance does that information have for you as the personnel manager?

- And a dozen other similar-type questions concerning your company's operational statistics.

A GOLD MINE
OF REVEALING INFORMATION

Buried—but not too deeply—in the *answers* to those questions is a gold mine of revealing statistics, a plethora of information that will quickly alert a business-oriented personnel manager to existing or developing problems and/or promising opportunities. From this information, the personnel manager (independent of his chief executive) can assess and selectively investigate personnel matters that are vital to his company's well-being.

Assessing Vital Signs of Corporate Health

Buried in your company's voluminous operating statistics are startling clues that will enable the business-oriented personnel manager to assess the following vital signs of corporate health or corporate malaise: the *quality* of your work force; its *productivity;* its *actual cost* compared to established job *standard* rates; whether foremen are using higher-rated job classifications to perform lower-rated work, or vice versa; the amount of *overtime* being worked (being *worked,* that is; not necessarily being *required*); the possible adverse effect of *labor turnover, absenteeism,* or *unfilled job requisitions* on factory efficiency and productivity; established *pay rates* in relation to your market's *fluctuating sales prices* (and what this might mean in your next labor negotiations); the *strength and performance* of one product line, or one manufacturing department, versus another; the viability or weakness of certain clauses in your *collective bargaining agreement;* the optimum level of *employment for tomorrow's business;* possible *impending layoffs* or *requirements for new hires.* And so much more.

The answers to the questions I have posed to you dispassionately portray the current economic health of your company, and, when objectively interpreted, will project a fairly accurate prognosis for your company's near-term growth, stagnation, or decline.

WOULDN'T IT BE NICE?

Remember that your boss, the chief executive, is poring over these same financial and operating statistics like a hawk—to him, they mean corporate success or failure and perhaps the future of his own career. Wouldn't it be nice for you—*and for him*—if you could go into his office and recommend, in view of certain operating trends which you have noted in the company's financial statements, that he should consider taking certain personnel actions? Wouldn't it be nice if *you* initiated those recommendations *before* your boss came down to you with a directive to take action which you could, and *should*, have anticipated yourself? You bet it would!

When Was the Last Time?

But let's ask ourselves one last question. When was the last time that you, the personnel manager, *seriously read and studied* your company's profit and loss statement and balance sheet with all of their supporting detail?

Heaven knows, ITT grinds out literally tons of such material every month. The pity is that, generally, only three or four people in each ITT unit—probably the president, the comptroller, and the manufacturing or operations director—really study that statistical material, make judgments, and take management action.

It is possible that you, the personnel manager, a key member of top management, *may not even receive these essential operating statements.* Or if you do, perhaps you limit your perusal to a quick glance at the bottom line to note actual net income versus budget. And from this particular bit of extremely limited knowledge, you generalize that your company is doing well or that it may be experiencing a few problems.

Why Shouldn't You?

Why shouldn't you, the personnel manager, be one of those few informed, forward-looking people in your company who analyze the past and present, and who take action for the future? Instead of having your boss *come to you* with directives to lay off or to hire people, or to take a variety of other personnel actions, *you* could have gone to *him* first. Would your president have liked that? If your recommendations were based on economic operating facts, might he have responded favorably to your ideas? Might you have moved up a notch in your president's estimation? Rhetorical questions, of course! The fact is, unfortunately, that the *average* personnel manager *reacts* to events rather than *shapes* events.

Why Don't You Try It?

"Terrific," you say! "Great idea!" The paradox is that very, very few personnel people actually do what I have just suggested. They either haven't trained themselves to do it, or they won't take the time to do it. But when you get back home, why don't you try it—just to see what happens? If you do your homework thoroughly and knowledgeably, I guarantee that your president will respond positively to your ideas, and I guarantee renewed respect for the personnel department of your company.

A personnel manager who *does not know* or who *does not understand* the answers to those questions I posed to you—or worse, one who *does not even suspect* that such questions should be asked—is, and will remain, a personnel journeyman of pedestrian caliber. Instead of being a vigorous and productive key contributor to the management success of his company, the uninformed, nonbusiness-oriented personnel executive is virtually a management eunuch.

THE CRUX OF MY MESSAGE

There are many personnel managers who know a great deal about labor relations, compensation, recruiting, industrial safety and security, EEO requirements, personnel legislation, and all other aspects of personnel administration.

However, one subject which has regrettably eluded many otherwise professional personnel people is the understanding of how, and why, their company makes a profit or suffers a loss.

And this brings me to the crux of my message to you today. My thesis is that too many personnel managers simply don't understand, or even bother to find out, how their company's business is run.

WHY PERSONNEL MANAGEMENT AS A CAREER?

"Because I Like People"

In interviewing personnel people over the years, it has been interesting to note their response to the somewhat sophomoric, but yet revealing question: *"Why did you choose personnel management as a career?"* The response to this question comes in many forms, but it can often be translated: *"Because I like people."* This answer is not "wrong," of course, but neither is it complete. Interest in and sensitivity to people are essential in performing effective personnel work. However, the personnel manager must recognize that the personnel job is an integral part of a total business organization *whose primary objective is to make a profit.*

A More Acceptable Answer

A more acceptable answer, among many, to the question *"Why did you choose personnel management as a career?"* is: "Because I enjoy and am competent at developing and motivating people at all levels so that they consistently produce the best work of which they are capable, thereby contributing to the company's growth and profit."

Business Exists Primarily to Make a Profit

Obviously, the personnel manager must assure that people are treated fairly and equitably, that they are motivated and rewarded, that their complaints and aspirations are heard and appropriately acted upon, and that their jobs present the opportunity for satisfaction and a feeling of personal accomplishment. *However, the personnel manager must always bear in mind that business exists primarily to make a profit; business does not exist solely to make people happy.*

A WELL-BALANCED VIEW
FOR PEOPLE AND PROFIT

Both for People and for Profit

Tunnel vision by the personnel manager which disproportionately focuses on people-pacification will adversely affect the achievement of profit. Conversely, of course, blind concentration on profit to the exclusion of the *realistic* recognition of people is equally objectionable. The truly effective personnel manager is one who can achieve a well-balanced, pragmatic view of his concerns *both* for people and for profit.

Distinction between People and Profit

To be productive, people must feel wanted and needed. You want that. I want that. And so do all the other people in our companies. As psychologist William James has written: The most profound principle of human nature is the congenital desire of each of us to be appreciated.

On the other hand, people must be made clearly—sometimes, painfully—aware of their responsibility to contribute, through their best performance, to the company's success and profit. Each employee must produce *at least* equally to the burden he places on the payroll. It is the pragmatic recognition of this distinction between people-satisfaction and profit-accomplishment which characterizes the truly effective personnel manager. Some personnel managers, unfortunately, are unable to achieve this difficult, but essential, balance. I don't know the formula for success in business, but I can give you the formula for failure: Try to please everybody.

THE PERSONNEL MANAGER
MUST UNDERSTAND HOW BUSINESS WORKS

A Working Knowledge
of Diverse Responsibilities

A personnel manager is not expected to be a master of marketing, nor a CPA, nor a creative engineer, nor a manufacturing expert, but he should be expected to understand and to have a working knowledge of how those diverse responsibilities are carried out successfully. He must understand the daily and unique operating problems which confront each functional department head in his company. Unless the personnel manager's opinions reflect this understanding and working knowledge, they are almost useless to the chief executive.

The Factory Is Responsible for Profit
(Isn't It?)

The personnel manager's views and recommendations concerning various courses of action which the company is planning must consider the profit-and-loss impact of such recommendations. Some personnel managers do not seem to understand this. They myopically view their personnel responsibilities as being only vaguely, if at all, related to profit and loss. The personnel job, they often mistakenly believe, is to take care of people. Their job, they think, does not include helping to make a profit. After all, personnel is part of the G&A or overhead expense. It is the factory that is supposed to make the profit.

Failure to Concentrate
on Contribution to Profit

Personnel people with this distorted point of view spend a disproportionate amount of their time on compensation surveys that invariably demonstrate that the company's rates and fringe benefits are lower than the area; on gainless personnel reports and analyses that very few people read; on company picnics, bond drives, and Christmas parties; and on esoteric psychological exercises which most line managers don't understand. Meanwhile, these personnel managers fail to concentrate on those essential aspects of their responsibilities which will structure the company with the most qualified and productive people and on other vital personnel activities which will contribute to profit.

Conversely, a personnel manager who really understands how his company's business functions, and how each manager shares in the operational success (or failure) of that business, will be a valuable asset to his company.

SPECIFIC ACTIVITIES
OF A PROFESSIONAL
PERSONNEL MANAGER

And now I'd like to discuss with you some more specific ideas about what, in my opinion, a personnel manager should be, the characteristics and activities which truly mark him as a professional working partner with his chief executive. These activities are:

- Being the eyes and ears of the chief executive
- Evaluating executive candidates
- Planning *individual* employee development
- Counseling top managers
- Removing unproductive employees
- Assuring promotions from within
- Acting as the ultimate guardian of the company's right to manage the business

THE EYES AND EARS
OF THE CHIEF EXECUTIVE

What's Going on and What to Do about It?

The personnel manager must be the "eyes and ears" (and frequently the voice) of the chief executive. He must know what is going on in the company, what people are really thinking and why, and how company actions and decisions are affecting employee attitudes toward the company and its management. Second, he must evaluate this intelligence: Is it real, or is it idle conversation? Is a complaint serious, or is it harmless griping? Third, it is insufficient merely to report this evaluated intelligence to the chief executive. The personnel manager must also recommend well-conceived, pragmatic actions which will effectively counteract unfavorable trends in employee attitude. Further, these recommendations, before being presented to the chief executive, should have been coordinated with and agreed to by the involved operating executives.

Not an Obsequious Tattletale

As the "eyes and ears" of the chief executive, the personnel manager should not be an obsequious tattletale. However, he must be a continually reliable source of information concerning employee attitudes and thinking *at all levels* of the company. A personnel manager who does not keep the president informed on what is being said and discussed at all levels of the company is failing an important responsibility.

EVALUATING EXECUTIVE CANDIDATES

An Intelligent Evaluation

The personnel manager must have the ability to *intelligently* evaluate and recommend candidates for executive positions. He should not simply screen resumes and accept the candidates served up to him by a highly paid outside search agency. It is totally unacceptable merely to conduct perfunctory interviews, select two or three candidates, telephonically check a few references (which are always highly favorable), and then have the chief executive decide which candidate to hire. The personnel manager should already have reached a selection decision, and he must advise the chief executive beforehand of this choice and the reasons supporting it.

Concentrate on Six or Seven Key People

The personnel manager must recognize that if six or seven highly qualified and compatible executives can be placed at the top of his company, they in turn will staff their functions with people of similar caliber. Therefore, the personnel manager should first concentrate on the selection of those six or seven key people, and thereafter he must assure that those executives are continually motivated and realistically satisfied. In this respect, the personnel manager has an exciting, creative opportunity to help mold the management team into a strong support system for the chief executive in the achievement of the company's objectives.

It Is Necessary to Object Beforehand

When an unqualified or undeserving manager, supervisor, or executive is thrust unilaterally into a position, the personnel manager who stands by in a semidetached manner, as if disclaiming responsibility for the selection, is failing in his job. It is always necessary for the personnel manager to object *beforehand* to the appointment of an unsuitable candidate, *no matter who recommended the candidate,* and to present firm, objective, business-oriented reasons supporting his judgment.

"The Operating People Insisted on Their Own Choice"

Personnel people occasionally admit in public (and frequently lament in private): "We objected to hiring Mr. So-And-So, but the operating people insisted on making their own choice." This distressing copout is an absolutely unacceptable abdication of personnel responsibility. If the personnel manager were one who had gained the confidence of the operating executives through his past performance, I can assure you that the operating people would be very reluctant to hire anyone to whom the personnel manager seriously objected.

Be Advocate as Well as Judge

On occasions when the operating people *do* persist in the face of the personnel manager's objections, then he must openly, diplomatically, and constructively present his objections to the chief executive *before* a final selection is made. Moreover, the personnel manager must be advocate as well as judge. He must immediately, or within a limited time span, propose a candidate who is more viable than the one he has rejected.

A Measurable Responsibility

But instead of pressing on with their recommendations, personnel people all too frequently retreat into the convenient, totally unproductive "What can *I* do about it" syndrome. An affirmative recommendation on key personnel selection carries with it the responsibility for the ultimate success or failure of that recommendation. Many personnel people seem to avoid that measurable responsibility.

The Cost of a Selection Mistake

Consider the cost to our company of the selection of a key executive with a salary of $75,000 who turns out to be the wrong choice. First, we paid an executive search firm a fee of about $23,000 (30 percent) in addition to their out-of-pocket expenses of, let's say, $10,000. Our company paid the new executive's relocation costs, which these days can run anywhere from $50,000 to $100,000.

It took six months to discover that the newly hired executive was the wrong choice, and then it took six months to remove him diplomatically. Those 12 months translate into a salary cost of $75,000 and fringe benefit costs of $30,000 (40 percent). The grand total of the financial penalty paid for this selection mistake comes to a staggering $215,000!

And to add insult to injury—or to throw good money after bad—*the whole costly selection process must now be repeated*, this time resulting, hopefully, in the proper choice of candidate. In addition, the time lost, the delay of company plans, and the upset among other managers must be considered as intangible but serious costs.

Who needs a measurable responsibility with an approximate half-million-dollar price tag for failure? Is there any wonder why some personnel managers avoid making a clear, unequivocal recommendation on executive personnel selection?

PLANNING INDIVIDUAL EMPLOYEE DEVELOPMENT

Usually Limited to Outside Seminars

One of the least understood and perhaps the most poorly practiced aspects of personnel work is employee development. The *average* personnel manager's action plan for employee development is limited to the suggestion that a certain number of people—often selected for no objective reason except that they can be spared from their jobs for a week—should attend outside seminars each year. Such seminars can be beneficial, of course, but they are the least personalized and, therefore, the least productive segment of employee development.

Individual Management Development Is Required

When you ask the *average* personnel manager what he is doing to develop management employees, he will usually list a variety of seminars and courses which various people are scheduled to attend. An interesting non-event occurs, however, when you ask the personnel manager to show you the *individual* management development file on, let's say, John Smith, the assistant director of engineering. The personnel manager—99 times out of 100—will reply that he has no such file. If so, then I maintain that neither does that personnel manager have any effective management development program for John Smith or anyone else.

In such an *individualized* file—if he had it—there would be a memorandum of understanding and objectives among the personnel manager, John Smith, and John Smith's supervisor. In this written plan, they would have explored Smith's personal interests, made a realistic evaluation of Smith's chances of achieving his management ambitions, and then would have structured a mutually agreed-upon management development program with him. This program might include specific work assignments, temporary exposures to other facets of the company's business, perhaps an after-hours advanced degree program, scheduled private conversations with other company executives during which they could explain their functions and problems, periodic milestone counseling sessions with the personnel manager, and yes, of course, *some* outside seminars. Without such *individualized* planning and followup, I maintain that there is no effective management development program at that personnel manager's company.

Individual Development Is Difficult and Time-Consuming

It is mandatory that the personnel manager identify those people who are, *or could become,* significant contributors to the company's business. Then, he must devise *individual* development plans for and with those people. For example, it may be beneficial for a research and development engineer to spend some full or part-time in the marketing function. It may be productive to place a manufacturing manager in engineering for a period of time. It may be advantageous to create several "assistant to" positions for management "comers" where they can obtain a broader overall view and understanding of the company.

This type of *individual* employee development is difficult and time-consuming to plan and implement effectively and harmoniously. In addition to structuring an *individual* program with periodic *individual* employee counseling on a continuing basis, it requires coordination among department heads who may not immediately see the benefit of disrupting their own functions. Personalized employee development also requires the personnel manager to exercise imagination and creativity.

A Euphemistic "Program"

Because of these bothersome reasons, most personnel people avoid making the effort, or they establish some meaningless, euphemistic "program" of outside seminars merely for the record, despite the fact that employee development is one of the most important and mutually rewarding responsibilities of the personnel function.

COUNSELING TOP MANAGERS

Another vital personnel responsibility, in my opinion, is counseling the company's 10, 15, or perhaps even 30 top managers concerning their working relations with their fellow executives. This counseling must be conducted in such a manner that all managers feel free to speak frankly with the personnel manager, confident that their comments and concerns will not be bruited about to other managers.

And yet, the personnel manager must use the knowledge obtained from one executive in order to counsel other executives as to their working relationships with that person. Obviously, this counseling must be discreetly and judiciously handled, and it represents a real opportunity for the personnel manager who *is* sincerely interested in people. It requires, however, a business-oriented personnel manager who can understand the working problems of various management disciplines and who can rise above petty bickering, gossip, and personal jealousies to get to the heart of any human relations problem which may be impeding the maximum effectiveness of the company's management team.

Manager of the CEO

And here, I might add a thought that is not as generally prevalent in personnel circles as it should be. There is another important counseling role that the personnel manager can play: that of the *manager of the chief executive.* In most ITT units and divisions the chief executive officer is located some geographical distance from his boss. Therefore, there is no one to tell the chief executive how his management style is going over with his organization, whether there are a few chinks in his armor that need repairing or strengthening. There is no one to keep a professional eye on sensitive personnel issues that may escape the awareness of a busy division president. The counseling of the chief executive concerning his personal impact on the company—good or bad—is an advisory role that a strong personnel manager can handle very well. To be effective at it, of course, the personnel manager must already have gained the chief executive's confidence.

Before assuming the role of manager of the CEO, it would be prudent to ascertain whether your boss is smart enough and "big" enough to want his personnel manager to fulfill what can be a very valuable function. There may be a few chief executives who would agree with the sentiments expressed by Jimmy Hoffa in his bribery trial testimony some years ago: "I may have faults, but being wrong ain't one of them." If your CEO has that imperious attitude, forget about trying to counsel. He won't be around for long anyway.

REMOVING UNPRODUCTIVE EMPLOYEES

The Average Personnel Manager Won't

Unless prodded or directed, the *average* personnel manager will rarely initiate a recommendation to remove marginal or downright unproductive employees. Why? Because it creates problems for him. The *average* personnel manager mistakenly believes that such negative recommendations, if acted upon, will disturb employee morale, provoke personnel insecurity, possibly lead to unionization, or might even result in that ultimate personnel anathema: a discrimination charge.

Selective Removal Actually Improves Morale

The positive fact is that the removal of a marginal, unproductive, or unnecessary surplus employee, provided it is legally and ethically handled, almost always *improves* the morale of the average and above-average employees, who are, after all, the people the company most wants to retain. It is demotivating to a good, productive employee to observe a fellow worker who is consistently dogging it—and getting away with it.

It is the personnel manager's responsibility to see that the level of employee performance and productivity is always as high as possible, even when achievement of that objective requires the unilateral removal of unsatisfactory employees.

ASSURING PROMOTIONS FROM WITHIN

A Desirable Objective
Sometimes Creates Conflicts

The personnel manager must absolutely assure, whenever it is at all possible, that promotions occur from within the company. At times, this desirable objective may cause unexpected and confusing conflicts which the personnel manager must quickly resolve.

For example, some department managers who are deeply engrossed in dealing with the problems of their own functions don't want to lose a good worker, even when they know that their refusal may represent the loss of a desired promotion to a deserving employee. The personnel manager must handle this situation tactfully, but firmly, to assure that outstanding contributors are promoted from within the company. Such high-performing employees must be promoted, or they will very soon find another employer who will recognize and reward their talent and ambition.

When a New Manager Must Be Brought in from Outside

When it *does* become necessary to bring in a new manager from outside because there is no qualified employee in-house, then the personnel manager must assure that the outsider's arrival is handled in a straightforward manner, yet with professional diplomacy and with full explanation and counseling to the insiders who had aspired to the position.

Avoid Political Expediency

The personnel manager cannot be swayed by what is politically expedient in such matters. If he loses the confidence of other executives by bowing to unilateral and biased selection influences inside or outside the company, his fellow executives will not seek the personnel manager's advice and counsel in the future. They will not soon forget that the personnel manager did what was politically expedient rather than what was right.

ULTIMATE GUARDIAN OF THE RIGHT TO MANAGE

The Personnel Manager's Own Thinking

It is the personnel manager's responsibility to assure that all employee work rules, personnel actions, and labor contracts preserve management's absolute right to manage the business. Moreover, the personnel manager must promulgate this essential management requirement as his own thinking, not solely as the directive of the chief executive.

"The Front Office" Made Me Do It

Ineffective personnel managers mistakenly attempt to maintain their own personal relations with employees or labor unions by attributing the imposition of any unpopular work rules, personnel actions, or rigid contract enforcement to "the front office." In doing so, these personnel managers are actually avoiding their own responsibilities.

When Overruled, Carry out the Order

On the other hand, an effective personnel manager will always disagree with the chief executive whenever a proposed work rule, contract change, management directive, or personnel action is more harmful than helpful to the company's well-being. But after having stated his case (more than once, if necessary) and being overruled, the personnel manager must then carry out the order as if it were his *own* decision. Expressing self-serving disagreement to other employees, especially to management peers, or benignly disavowing any personal responsibility for the decisions of the chief executive, only weakens the personnel manager's image and effectiveness in the company. Sooner or later, I can assure you, that type of personnel manager will also lose the confidence of the "front office."

PERSONNEL:
A MAGNET FOR DISPARATE DISCIPLINES

How the Company's Functions Fit Together

The R&D engineer must know the product; the marketing director must know the company's market and its customers; the accountant must know how to keep the books and offer financial advice; the head of manufacturing must understand production. The personnel manager, however, must know how, and why, all these functions fit together in his company. He should be the *management magnet* which helps the chief executive draw these disparate disciplines, objectives, and personalities into a unified, productive team. Unless the personnel manager understands thoroughly how his company's business is run, he cannot possibly generate this magnetism.

Doomed to a Plebeian Role

Many personnel managers lack this magnetic ability; some seem unaware that they should have it. Without this "magnetism," which cannot be achieved without understanding how his company's business is run, the personnel manager will be relegated to the plebeian role of keeper of the personnel files, the arranger of employee activities, the processor of wage increases, and the handler of insurance claims. These personnel managers then bemoan the fact that they seem to have so little influence on their company's management decisions. They wonder why they are never admitted to the inner circle of their company's management.

A BUSINESS-ORIENTED PERSONNEL MANAGER
IS A TREASURE

A well-informed, well-balanced, common-sense, pragmatic personnel manager who understands how his company's business operates is a treasure, a tremendous asset to his company, probably a greater asset than even he realizes.

A chief executive who is fortunate enough to have such a business-oriented personnel manager as a working partner will rely heavily and regularly on that personnel manager for advice, opinions, and recommendations. That business-oriented personnel manager will become, and will remain, an important, respected and influential contributor to his company's success, an executive who will be consulted on every major management issue.

A sensible chief executive wants to extend that status to his personnel manager, but only in direct ratio to the personnel manager's willingness and demonstrated ability to earn it.

AN INTERVIEW
WITH BOB BERRA

What kind of training is necessary for personnel work?

I haven't checked the curricula in schools in quite a while, but I have some fairly strong ideas about what they ought to do. I think the things that make for a successful personnel executive are pretty much the same things that make for success in anything else. In personnel, you've got to have analytical skills and you've got to be good at communications. You'd also better be willing to take on numbers. We have too many people who figure you never have to worry about the bottom line.

If I had the opportunity to set a curriculum for a personnel course, I'd probably run a balance of economics, some behavioral science exposure, certainly some finance and a bit of liberal arts to give the perspective and background that I think is necessary, particularly as we look to the future. That, combined with a fairly good understanding of political science, would permit the individual not only to do a professional job but to cope with the increasing social and economic problems of today and tomorrow.

A study of personnel curriculum in this issue reveals that practitioners now rank the need for ethics courses lower than they did 10 years ago. Does this seem right to you?

I'm sorry to hear that, but there may not be any particular correlation between a personnel practitioner's view of ethics as a course and his or her daily coming to grips with the definition of ethics. It's one of the key impact areas that personnel has to bring into focus for the company. In our organization we're really focused on this matter of ethics. There should be a real concern for business, and particularly the people of business, to take the responsibility to define ethics.

How does that tie into the controversy about the social responsibility of business versus bottom line thinking?

Most of our problems stem from lack of understanding about what

"An Interview with Bob Berra," reprinted from the February 1976 issue of The Personnel Administrator, copyright 1976, The American Society for Personnel Administration, 606 North Washington Street, Alexandria, VA 22314.

really goes on in business. Of course we're concerned about the bottom line because we have to be, but no reasonable person would think that a business could survive in the long run without a balanced concern for its social obligations on the one hand and its financial health on the other. The employees, the stockholders, the government itself, the local community—all of these have to be put in balance. That's the challenge of management today. Social responsibility in the major companies is something that is clearly important.

Where does the personnel function fit as you look at business in the future?

I'm very optimistic about the role that we play and will play. In just the past five to seven years, I've seen a significant difference in the role of the personnel professional, in the way top management views personnel capabilities and the increasing capability of the personnel executive to make a significant contribution. Our problem now is to make sure that our ability to deliver keeps pace with management's requests for help. I don't think there's any question that the role we are now playing is going to become increasingly important.

Ideally, isn't the personnel executive a change agent who sparks much of this?

The function I see the top personnel executive filling today is a combination of roles that I find hard to contain within the present definition of personnel. First, the personnel executive has to be a competent professional, able to do the things he or she is being paid to do and able to organize people to get that job done. Once that's done, a key role is being a member of top management's inner council—a general advisor or sounding board for the CEO and for other members of the executive group who indeed must have someone knowledgeable as an anticipator of trends in these areas.

What are the possibilities for advancement?

There's nothing to preclude a personnel executive from moving into operations or into other kinds of staff work or broadening the scope of present responsibilities. A natural evolutionary route would be for the personnel professional to become the vice president of administration with a variety of functions reporting to him. There's no reason why a personnel person can't move up and there is much less tendency on the part of top management to assume that if you're in personnel, you can't do top administrative jobs. I don't see any limit to upward mobility in the next 15 years.

But personnel is a career in itself, isn't it?

Oh yes, and I think many people have decided that. It's a major responsibility and not everybody can or wants to be president. If a person can be a top personnel executive in a company, that's an honorable place to cap a career.

What about the relationship with the CEO and top management?

The real concern is the attitude of the chief executive officer. I get my job done just as easily reporting directly or through an intermediate as long as the CEO takes a strong interest in the function. More and more top management posts will go to personnel people in time. But the profession has to do some things more aggressively than we've done in the past if indeed that's what we want to happen. This includes a better understanding of the business or entity we serve, a clear understanding of the company's overall objectives, a realization of the need to balance the needs of the human resources with the other company resources. We are going to have to do our homework better—to be as knowledgeable as possible.

There's an old saying—"fortune favors the prepared mind." And I agree. If we are going to break out of the personnel function and do broader things, we're going to have to be more creative in the development of sensible people-oriented programs in such areas as motivation and environment. And if personnel executives are going to move into other kinds of top management posts, they're going to have to have the courage to speak out, to make sure that the CEO and other members of top management get a balanced point of view. It's our job to make sure that the people needs of the organization are understood. And we must keep those needs in balance with the company's ability to pay.

What do you see as the biggest single area of concern facing personnel today?

If you want to speak generally, I would emphasize two things. First is the problem of learning how to cope with rapid change. I know that this has become something of a cliche but things *are* changing rapidly. We have to be flexible and not get married to a particular course of action once we've committed ourselves to it. We have to constantly be getting feedback and fine tuning to modify what's going on or change what we thought was a grand idea.

Secondly, we have to deal more effectively with people. The expectations of people are rising faster than our ability to accommodate them. In 1966 I predicted that the coming decade would be the decade of education.

That turned out to be true. But I also said that although I knew we were going to make great strides forward, I wasn't sure whether the caliber was going to be such that we could be completely positive about the progress. That turned out to be true. In 1965 I was afraid that within 10 years we would be a group of people "academically all dressed up with no place to go." I also expressed concern that we would "know enough to be afraid and not enough to do anything about it." You could build a whole concept on that because that's what is happening.

You called it an insidious sense of insecurity for the mass of people. Do you still see it that way?

If you go back in history, man was probably most secure when he understood his environment. I don't even understand the simple concept of radio. I don't understand much of what goes on around me in terms of mechanical things. I'm a slave, if you will, to somebody else. If my automobile doesn't start when I turn the key, I'm lost. That can erode your security.

One person who made a significant impact on American society was Eli Whitney, primarily because he introduced the concept of interchangeable parts. So long as an individual could make a whole gun, for example, he felt good about it, he could see the result when he was finished. But once we decided that one person could make all the barrels, one all the stocks and one all the triggers, no one person had security or the feeling of satisfaction that he could do something entirely. Division of labor is something that goes with increased productivity. But again there's a need for balance. As Americans we have to consider the trade offs that are inevitable between maximizing personal satisfaction and the creation of more material things at affordable prices.

Can you give us your thoughts on measuring personnel leadership?

We can measure the value and effectiveness of individual personnel programs better than we used to, but we need to get better at it. But the higher the personnel executive goes in an organization, the more intangible is his role and thus the more difficult it is to measure his contribution precisely. In some ways, this is an ambivalent role because personnel executives have to have a degree of charisma in dealing with people who report to them. After all, they are the managers of an organization. They have to get things done through people, to program, to plan, to motivate, and, from that standpoint of leadership, they have as important roles as any other managers. On the other hand, they must take a more passive role in relating to their colleagues in the executive suite because to really do the job, they must serve as counsellors, sounding boards, supportive influences, if you will, which top managers need in defining their own roles in the organization. Top personnel executives can't play that role very well if their colleagues sense they are competing with them for the next job.

How do you measure the personnel intangibles?

How do you measure a person's scope of understanding, their interest, if you will, their sensitivity, their guts? How do you measure all those things when that's really how it all comes together to achieve an effective generalist at the top level? We all have more or less of those things and none of us have all of them to the same degree. I don't know how to measure these intangibles accurately.

There is a difference between an individual's ability to do a job and the results he gets. Let me use an analogy. Job evaluation defines what the job is but doesn't say how well the person is going to do it. We use salary ranges to determine what we'll pay them within that area of responsibility once we have decided through the evaluation how important it is—how well they're doing.

Motivation is internally generated. There has to be a gap between what a person wants to be and what they see themselves as being. As long as there is a gap between their present image of themselves and what they would want to be, they're motivated as individuals. No matter how motivated an individual may be, he or she must still have a certain amount of talent to achieve. You can have a hell of an image gap and not achieve because you just don't have the capability to do a job. Individual motivation is only important when you're able to put it into practice. If you're a member of a large group and the work environment doesn't recognize individual effort, then you've got another kind of problem. How can we develop an atmosphere which will spur people on to greater achievement? Here are some of the things I feel are important:

1. Establish clear-cut objectives and standards. The individual must know what is expected of him or her.
2. Evaluate the individual's progress against these standards and in terms of whether he is on target toward his objectives.
3. Discuss their progress or lack of it with them as often as is possible—help them to make necessary adjustments.
4. Take prompt corrective action—including discipline—when necessary. Good discipline is essential to any healthy environment.
5. Use rewards promptly and amply when results are good. Rewards must be tied to the specific result and commensurate with the contribution. There has to be differentiation between those who contribute and those who do not. Otherwise, the tendency is to skip into mediocrity because there is no advantage to being better than the next person.

6. Encourage and appreciate excellence among your people. Frequently when you expect great things of people, they will deliver even beyond their own expectations.

7. Consider your expectations for the person in terms of his capability. Be pleased if he appears to exceed your concept of his ability. You may have gauged him wrongly. Savor the person with high talent who produces much, but be appreciative of the lesser talented person who lives up to the last ounce of their capacity.

8. Try to assign discrete beginnings and endings, i.e., intermediate goals where possible—to give the feeling of achievement. A series of small successes can build confidence and expand horizons. If as the current image improves, expectations continue to rise, a high motivation level can be sustained.

9. Give the person the opportunity to fail on occasion, particularly in less critical areas and after he has had a few successes to build his ego enamel.

10. Give employees an understanding of the total goals of the organization and the part which they are contributing and can contribute to the success of the total plan. This provides them with a sense of involvement so essential to their needs to grow and develop.

Do you see the role of personnel expanding to generate open, honest communications at all levels within a company?

Personnel is certainly one of the major forces that enables an organization to get its communication arteries unclogged. But personnel itself should not be looked upon as the *agent of communication*. Rather, it should be looked upon as that part of the organization which focuses the need and provides the mechanism and vehicles by which proper communications are achieved. The best kind of communication within an organization is always the belly-to-belly kind of thing that comes from boss to subordinate and back, all up and down the line in all areas.

The second and perhaps more critical aspect is the chief executive's willingness and his or her ability to articulate what the company's purpose is and what role the individual can play in achieving that purpose. Too often the employees just don't understand what's in it for them. I have a hope that some day we will get to the point where in any plant or location in Monsanto an individual can look at that entity which he serves, be it a plant or sales office, and say this: this is truly the "goose that lays the golden egg." To the extent that I contribute to the success of this particular entity and to our country's well being, I can assure myself a comfortable standard of living, a comfortable old age and education for my children and an opportunity to personally grow and develop. You have communication at its best when you have that kind of feeling.

A third aspect is to define the other communities that need to be communicated with—the outside world, the community, the customers, the financial community, the suppliers, the stockholders, the retirees, the government. We have to take all of these into account. Personnel plays a very important role, to be sure, but I don't think it's the only role.

It's often said that the personnel specialist doesn't know anything about business. Do you agree?

First of all, we have to talk about the level of the personnel person we're addressing. If one is new in the function, just on board, he or she may have a somewhat limited knowledge of business. By the time one reaches the job of chief personnel officer of a company, there is no choice but to understand the business—what makes it run as it does. If you don't, then you're not accepted as a part of the top management group. More and more companies are putting chief personnel officers on their internal boards, many of them on the full board as well. That does two things: it gives the personnel chief an opportunity to interface with the other people who are running the operation and it puts a great burden on him if he doesn't do his homework, if he doesn't learn and grow himself. Those who fail to grasp the nature of their business will not carry their weight and, in time, will probably not succeed.

Do you see a change in the role of professional societies like ASPA in the next decade?

Yes, I do, depending on the vitality of the organization. I've always stressed the emphasis on size in ASPA. This does not mean that I am not aware of the importance of quality. But I would have to say that until ASPA got to be 12 to 15,000 members, we didn't really have much clout. No one really listened to us. Size also controls our ability to attract resources. We couldn't have as capable a staff of people when we had limited funds. If a society such as ours is vital, if it has enough resources to make things happen, then I see it as being a very powerful force in the future. I don't think we have overstated at all the expanding role that we're beginning to play in Washington.

Size is one measuring stick, but doesn't the society become a change agent in this growth structure?

Yes and there's another thing that the society does that I think we lose sight of. I'm beginning to feel a little bit of an anachronism at the ASPA meetings. I'm probably the most senior man there in terms of service. I've often thought of getting off the board but I don't want to lose my sense of responsibility to the profession by not helping the younger people move forward. We see this happening in some chapters in the cities. People come in and are very active in the chapter. Then they reach an area of top responsibility and get too involved. We no longer see them. We *must* keep people involved at all levels. It's almost impossible for me to get away for an ASPA meeting because of the demands of my job. But I do it for two reasons: first, because I enjoy it; and secondly, because it's my responsibility.

WHAT LINE MANAGEMENT EXPECTS
OF HUMAN RESOURCE MANAGERS

Herbert Hubben

When it comes to management expectations, you've all heard the story of the college basketball coach who was asked by a fledgling sports writer, "What do you expect of your players?" The big-time coach looked at the lad with some pity and said, "I expect them to win." Management, too, expects its team to win. And the companies that win depend upon people, not numbers, records, computers, forms and schedules. There's got to be a goal, a plan, a lot of physical equipment—but there has to be a balance and the chief executive officer and his immediate team are the people who provide that balance, and who set the tone and style for the whole company. That style depends on philosophy and motivation much more than on job descriptions or dotted-line relationships. It depends on the value system of the organization and the person who heads it.

TEN RULES FOR HUMAN RESOURCE
MANAGEMENT SUCCESS

Be Professional in the Depth and Currency of Your Knowledge of Your Field

The art of management is based on a vast and ever-changing variety of functional skills and knowledge, ranging from personal communications to econometric forecasting. Management will assume that each functional specialist is as up-to-date and thoroughly grounded as possible in the discipline of his or her job responsibility. You must relearn the details of your profession constantly. It has been said that every professional learns five new jobs in his or her career. This is hard work and requires a lot of dedication. The absence of such professional dedication produces the people who spend their lives in college recruiting, or job evaluation, or labor statistics. It's like my good friend, Charley, who spent 25 years in the Person-

Herbert Hubben, "What Line Management Expects of Human Resources Managers," reprinted by permission of the publisher from Human Resource Planning, *Vol. 6, No. 3, 1983. Copyright 1983 by the Human Resources Planning Society.*

nel Department. Of him, it was said, "He doesn't have 25 years of experience; he's had one year of experience 25 times." Promotions and transfers come to those who have demonstrated an eagerness and an ability to take on new challenges and, in relatively short order, master the concepts and skills of new assignments.

Be Professional in Your Attitudes, Viewpoints and Behavior

This revolves around maturity and selflessness. Your advice and counsel to management must be devoid of personal interest, prejudice and organizational politics. You will be asked for recommendations about people, about organizational changes and about compensation adjustments, sometimes involving your friends or even you. Your recommendations have to be clean. There can be no suspicion that you're carrying out some secret or personal objective. There is also a recognizable difference between politics and diplomacy . . . between currying favors and demonstrating a skill in communications. There are times to call a spade a spade, other times to call it a shovel, and other times to refer to it as a sharp-bladed instrument for disconfiguration . . . or maybe just avoid the subject altogether.

Your personal credibility can be as strong as steel or as fragile as china. It's an asset that is not worth risking in a bone-headed effort to transfer someone you personally dislike. Like Humpty-Dumpty, a cracked credibility can't be put together again.

Let me conclude this comment about Rule 2 by simply identifying the relevance of another subject that has had adequate media and entertainment coverage recently. That's sex in the office. You may be very progressive and liberal about that subject and perhaps I am, but the executive making people decisions—perhaps involving you—is likely not to be. Don't be foolish.

Learn as Much about the Business as You Can

It always surprises me to find professionals in the people business who know or care little about the product end of the business. In a manufacturing organization, for instance, each product requires research, development, manufacturing, marketing, financing and distribution. The human resource professionals in that organization will do an infinitely better job of supporting the staffing, compensation and motivation programs in that organization if they can understand, explain and participate in decisions concerning the products, or at least engage in intelligent discussions. Obviously, there is also a greater likelihood of your own promotion into senior management positions if your knowledge about the business and your ability to make people decisions reflects a general management judgment rather than narrow, specialized experience or a point of view. The human resource professional is sitting on a unique corporate perch that allows a full and wide-ranging scope of the company's activities. The real professionals use that perch as a launching pad, not a roost.

Lead the Way with New Ideas and Programs, but Make Sure We're Doing the Basics Well First

We all want to be innovative, to be out in front. It would be nice to get our organization's performance in the human resources area to such a smooth level of performance that we're always ready to try the latest ideas discussed in the professional literature. You would get a lot of satisfaction out of that, and it's fun to talk about at the Country Club. However, before the talented quarterback can unleash a fancy flea-flicker he's got to be sure that his team can block and tackle. You can't score in sports without doing the basics spectacularly well. You can't win in business without knowing your playbook inside-out. It takes a real professional to know the difference between a new direction and a gimmick.

At the same time, it's your responsibility to assure that your senior executives are informed about the leading edge of thought and practice in the human resources area. You can do this without outside speakers, seminars, circulating relevant papers and non-stop personal communications. You are not doing your job if your boss comes in and asks you about transactional analysis or behavior reinforcement and you reply, with an indifferent shrug of the shoulders, that you've never heard of them.

Once in a while, one of these advanced programs makes sense for your company because it meets a particular need, one that would make a full-scale selling campaign by you to try it appropriate. Be aware, however, that you really can't do that too often and, further, you'd better be confident about the program and the results you expect.

Think and Act Like a Member of the Management Team

It is not only important that you become integrated into the total management structure, but also that you understand and accept the value and importance of the American enterprise system and your role in it. We do not need spokesmen for the down-trodden and underprivileged of the world on the Management Committee. Not only are your contributions to the decision-making process likely to be ignored, you also run the risk of losing whatever influence you may have had or could have in the future.

There are already multitudes of skilled and strident spokesmen for every conceivable minority viewpoint known. Your fellow executives are constantly battered from the outside by pressures and opinions that they find difficult to understand, much less accept. I'm never surprised to get an appeal for funds from a group dealing with an illness I never heard of. I hear regularly from the Procrastinators' Society to invite me to the 1976 Annual Meeting.

Simply put, there is no place in the professional business organization for discordant and challenging voices over social concerns. Before you become critical of that viewpoint, or dismiss me as a throwback, stop and ponder the impact on a family when one member acts continually like an outsider and challenges and denigrates the long-established values that the family holds dear. It's hard to take, and it's a very human characteristic to be resentful of such a presence.

Show the Way in Managing and Controlling Your Own Department

Like Caesar's wife, human resources is in the unfortunate position of having to be above reproach. Wouldn't it be great if, in the organization, there is at least this one department which: manages to evaluate its jobs correctly; appraises people's performance on schedule and well; stays within the published guidelines; sets objectives, reviews objectives, and sends its staff to needed training programs. If this same department did all of this within budget and without a constant clamor for more people it would certainly be well regarded by management and envied by colleagues at all levels. If, at the same time, this department happened to be the human resources function, there would be hope for us all.

The human resources professional must keep his or her own house in good order. Just as young children are far more likely to follow their parents' example rather than their advice, so, too, will every function of the organization look to the human resources department to take the lead in human resources management.

Be Loyal to the Organization

While it would be nice to command the personal loyalty of every person who works for you, this is neither necessary nor particularly reasonable. Personal loyalty can and must be earned by demonstrated competence and superior qualities. But we can and should demand organizational loyalty. By this I mean that you do not publicly denigrate the company, its practices, its products and its people no matter how frustrated, underpaid, tired, or angry you may be. As a matter of fact, you should use social and outside business opportunities to express the pride you have in the company and to promote its products and policies. This is particularly true of human resources people, whose extensive contacts with the outside world could have a significant impact on recruiting and on the company's reputation in the community.

You are presumed, and rightly so, to possess privileged information and if you cannot speak well of the company, you must know what you're talking about. If for some reason, you cannot bring yourself to defend the company at a cocktail party or rap session, perhaps it's time to update your resume.

No Surprises, Please

Give me the good news first, if you want, but also give me the bad news. It is the duty of every professional to keep appropriate people informed of the news, events, and numbers that they need to do their job. We are all constantly faced with the unexpected . . . questions from bosses, peers and subordinates . . . questions from investment analysts . . . questions from the media . . . that demand accurate and timely information. I am always reminded of the consternation of a chief executive officer who learned that there had been a major fire at one of his plants from the newspaper reporter who asked for his comments. It seemed that someone in the company had felt that the news could wait until after a dinner party.

Let me know what's going on. Trust me to have a balanced reaction to bad news, and I will come to trust you. I have no objection, for example, to seeing one of my subordinates in deep conversation with my boss as long as I have full confidence that if anything was discussed that I ought to know about, I'll hear it from my subordinate. If you have the self-confidence to let me know the bad news, I promise to practice self control in not killing the bearer of bad news.

Believe in Something and Fight for It

You are entitled to beliefs that may not agree with mine. You are also entitled to push for the implementation of those beliefs and undertake to persuade me or other members of the management team that your view should be the organizational stand. There is also, of course, a time for debate and a time for decision. During the debate, we need your input, your ideas, your dissension. Top management does not have a corner on brains and wisdom and most senior executives understand and appreciate the value of hearing opposing points of view. During the debate, don't be afraid to kick and scratch and get a little red in the face.

Once the decision has been made, you are expected to be a part of the whole and help make it work successfully. The debate is over and there are no appeals. If you find that you are unable to accept the decision, you owe it to the organization, and to yourself, to remove yourself from the situation. That does not necessarily mean that you resign, but it could. The point is that you must be able to maintain the obligation of loyalty we spoke about earlier.

Maintain Yourself as a Whole Person

It is important to you and to your employer that you keep yourself in good health, physically and emotionally. It is not in anyone's benefit for you to work so hard or so intently that you undermine your health, your family situation or your emotional stability. This is why we insist on people taking vacations, annual medical examinations . . . Why we strive for pleasant working conditions and reasonable work loads. It is also why we tend to frown on unusual extracurricular activities. Coaching a Little League baseball team is fun and rewarding; coaching three hockey teams, the girls' diving team and the High School chess squad while chairing the annual Church Fund Drive and the Girl Scout cookie sale just might affect your job performance. It almost goes without saying that it is much more satisfying to make those personal decisions for yourself rather than force the organization to intervene.

CONCLUSION

Whether you find these rules easy or difficult to apply in your own situation depends on so many individual factors that it's difficult to be more specific. I hope that they are clear and you have no great difficulty in grasping the basic meaning.

It may be useful to point out that while I've referred to human resources activities in industry, these basic rules apply to any organization. Whether you work for a university, a labor union, the government or any other profit or non-profit institution, the rules are universal.

Let me note that I've said nothing about the usual human resources programs. It is not your job to plan people needs, to recruit, to train, to utilize, to motivate, to compensate fairly and to discipline wisely. That's my job and it's the job of every manager who employs people for the purpose of accomplishing a task. It is also your job, but more importantly, it's your job to help me and others get that done. You're the program designers and the quality controllers.

Almost every organization has physical, financial and human assets. The physical and financial assets are cold, solid, uncommunicative and available to all at the same price.

The human assets are what make the difference between winners and losers. Think of yourselves as human assets managers . . . and you won't go wrong.

SELECTION AND PERFORMANCE CRITERIA FOR A CHIEF HUMAN RESOURCES EXECUTIVE . . . A PRESIDENTIAL PERSPECTIVE

Editor's Note: A special feature of AMA's 48th Annual Human Resources Conference, held in New York City on March 9 to 11, 1977, was a Presidents' Round Table at which four chief executive officers discussed what they expect from and look for in a chief human resources executive. Participants in this one-hour discussion were Evelyn Berezin, president, Redactron Corporation, a subsidiary of Burroughs Corporation; David W. Hughes, president and chief executive officer, National Oats Company; George G. Raymond, president, The Raymond Corporation; Peter G. Scotese, president and chief executive officer, Springs Mills, Inc; and, as moderator, Robert F. Pearse, professor of behavioral sciences, Boston University, School of Management. *Personnel* taped the presentations and discussion. The article that follows is based on these short presentations and on edited excerpts from the discussion. It was submitted to the participants for their review prior to its publication.

Pearse: Before we begin our discussion, I would like to set the stage by mentioning two things. First, as I am sure most of you are aware, a major national magazine last year called personnel and human resources executives the "new corporate heroes." This appellation was chosen to reflect the fact that the human resources function is more and more being considered a significant contributor to corporate profitability, growth, and survival. Few here will dispute that.

Second, if we as human resources executives review where we are today, we find that we have much better tools and techniques with which to work than we did 15 or 10 years ago in manpower planning, training and development, selection and staffing, and even compensation systems. The availability of these tools should make it a little easier for us to be "heroes." At the very least, we have little excuse for failure.

Now let's turn to the first of our panelists, Dave Hughes.

"Selection and Performance Criteria for a Chief Human Resources Executive . . . A Presidential Perspective," reprinted, by permission of the publisher, from Personnel, *May–June 1977,* © *1977 by AMACOM, a division of American Management Associations, New York. All rights reserved. Panelists are Evelyn Berezin, David W. Hughes, George G. Raymond, and Peter G. Scotese.*

ESSENTIAL CHARACTERISTICS
OF A HUMAN RESOURCES OFFICER

Hughes: I would like first to outline those characteristics and qualities I feel are essential for the person serving as an organization's top human resources officer. Then I will review some of the training and selection criteria I believe to be important.

In the discussion that follows I have assumed that the qualities of integrity and mental ability, which are basic and necessary for those holding a key position in any organization, are present. That true, I consider these additional characteristics as essential in a human resources officer:

- Curiosity, not only about the human resources profession, but also about the business served. This characteristic is critical.
- The highest personal and professional expectations for the contribution the human resources function can make to the company.
- Creativity that, when coupled with the officer's risk-taking ability, enables the function to contribute in many unique ways to the growth of the company.
- Business instincts. I think a good human resources professional is a business person first and a specialist second. Paradoxically, perhaps, I think a strong and totally professional commitment to the human resources function and to the incredible contribution it can make to the management process of any company is also essential.
- A human resources professional must be approachable and compassionate—but dare not be a bleeding heart. He or she must be able to relate effectively to all personnel of the organization, whether blue collar workers or senior executives.

All of these characteristics are vitally important, but three additional characteristics, pragmatism, articulateness, and guts, are in my opinion *most* critical. Too many personnel professionals are rigid or too structured and are thus often not pragmatic in their problem-solving techniques. This quickly leads to a lack of the credibility that is absolutely essential to this function. Further, the human resources professional must be able to communicate effectively with all levels of management or he or she will never be able to persuade management to follow some changed course of action. And last, the human resources officer must have made the commitment to stand by those personnel actions that he or she knows inherently and professionally are correct; such courage is a *sine qua non.*

I have said that techniques and approaches for the effective use of human resources represent the last and most critically important management science—and I use that term very loosely—that must and will be conquered by the management profession. Effective human resources management is *the* critical skill of the successful manager. Management teams that do not learn how to optimize their use of human resources will *not* succeed in their management tasks.

In considering candidates for the position of top human resources officer, I believe several factors are worthy of your consideration. The top human resources officer must:

- Be an effective manager.
- Be willing to demand, and have a professional record of demanding, the highest levels of personal performance both of himself and of the human resources staff.
- Be reasonably well informed about all functions of the business. There is no function in a business that offers greater opportunity for in-depth knowledge of each other function, and of the total business operation, than human resources. Those in the human resources function who are curious, pragmatic, and professional will take advantage of this opportunity—and succeed. Those who are not will be marginal contributors.
- Have had experience at all levels of the organization so that he or she will be able to understand, relate to, and play a significant role in the management process of the company and to know the opportunities the company offers to its employees. I am suspicious of the value of the suggestions made by individuals who have not worked in human resources management at the plant level. Corporate staff people, in almost all circumstances in my experience, simply cannot understand or appreciate the day-to-day problems experienced by the plant human resources professional.
- Have in his or her background responsibility for both making and implementing decisions. Such an action orientation is of greater importance to me than is having experience in only developing solutions for problems. To be sure, a professional human resources manager must be a strong problem solver and planner. That, however, is only 50 percent of the battle. He or she must be equally competent in executing the plan to solve the problem.

When I have identified a candidate who has what I consider the necessary characteristics and experience required for success in the top human resources position, the selection process boils down to ensuring that the personal chemistry of the candidate fits the climate in which he or she will serve. The importance of this match is widely accepted but is nonetheless probably the most frequently violated concept in all employee selection. When it is overlooked in selecting the top human resources professional of a company, it is disastrous. All reasonable efforts must be made to ensure that the chemistry of the company fits that of any potential top human resources officer and that the personal chemistry of the candidate fits that of the company.

STRATEGIC PLANNING
AND THE HUMAN RESOURCES OFFICER

Berezin: In our company we believe that the head of the human resources function must contribute to the long-term plan of the company. We spend a great deal of time examining long-term alternatives and planning business strategies. We use the capabilities of the human resources officer to help us consider the critical staffing aspects of any plans or strategies we might develop. We have one-year, five-year, and ten-year plans. We must determine what talent we will have to bring into the company from the outside and who we will have to develop internally to help us implement our plans.

We review our short-term plans quarterly. The human resources officer is very actively involved in these reviews, particularly when shortfalls may be attributable to human resources problems.

Attributes we look for in our human resources officer are, first, objectivity in gathering and interpreting the information that helps to explain how well or how badly we're doing and where the problems are. At the same time, we are asking this executive for his or her subjective responses to the problems we face and the information we get. This is particularly necessary to me because I have found that as I have climbed higher in the organization, it has gotten much more difficult for me to know what is going on, how people feel, what they're thinking. I count on the human resources officer to keep in touch with the pulse of the organization.

I also expect the top human resources person to know the capabilities of our people throughout the company so we can move them ahead as rapidly as their talents will allow. After all, the growth of our company has been very rapid, from a start in 1972 to annual sales of $20 million three years later. One problem we had during this period of rapid growth has been in the very fast development of our people. That growth was necessary if they were to be able to take on major responsibilities with comparatively little experience. So we have really needed in our human resources officer someone who could understand the difficulties of moving people ahead in a rapidly growing organization.

There is one other point I would like to make. My company *does* attempt to bring people into the company primarily at the lowest levels—directly from school—and to develop people within the company rather than hire from the outside for higher-level jobs. We therefore need in our human resources officer someone who can develop good human resources plans and who can then get young people with the talents and interests we need into the company and train them. . . .

Raymond: We look for a variety of skills and knowledge in our human resources officer:

- Basic knowledge of personnel and training.
- Exposure to experimental learning and consulting skills.
- Management training followed by practical first-line experience.
- Creativity in experimental learning and long-range planning.
- Knowledge of behavioral theories and practices.
- Consulting experience—primarily consulting in the areas of people management.
- Public speaking.
- Consumer contact—what's going on in the world of the user of our equipment and services.

- First-level staff experience in the employment, wage and salary, and training areas.

The organization of our human resources function is unusual. To the usual activities of industrial relations, including personnel, manpower planning and development, career planning, and behavioral activities, we have added corporate strategy and planning and administrative services. This is an officer-level responsibility carrying full officer-level influence on our management team. But do not misunderstand. We have not delegated strategy and planning to a staff organization. Staff provides the framework and coordination, but the line officers are responsible for the actual planning. The human resources organization, however, ensures that all our people are involved in a coordinated way in our planning activities. . . .

NECESSARY ATTRIBUTES
FOR A HUMAN RESOURCES OFFICER:
ANOTHER VIEW

Scotese: . . . What attributes, in general, should any company consider in seeking a human resources officer? Here are a few guidelines that I would recommend:

- The chief human resources executive of an enterprise should, first of all, be a sound business generalist. This means that he or she should have a broad understanding of the objectives of the enterprise. It also means that the person should have the ability to contribute importantly to the development of strategies that will enable the enterprise to achieve its objectives.
- The successful human resources executive must be able to think well conceptually and be effective in dealing with fresh, innovative ideas or concepts.
- The human resources executive must believe in communication, must understand the importance and the possibilities of communication, and must be an effective communicator.
- The person must have a broad understanding of the changing environment and a flexibility of mind that permits creative responses to changing conditions and values affecting people, their goals, and their expectations.
- The human resources executive must be a discriminating, tough-minded thinker, able to perceive and to differentiate between what is of real value and what is simply faddish or superficial. This requires a basic independence of mind and a well-developed personal system of values.
- Such an executive must have a "bottom line" point of view, an understanding of costs versus payback, and a sound grasp of the real value of an idea measured against basic corporate objectives.
- Last, the chief human resources executive must be able to sell ideas to management.

Underlying all of these points, and implicit in everything I have said, is the basic fact that the chief human resources executive of any enterprise must have an in-depth understanding of people and a genuine interest in people, as contrasted with statistics, procedures, and rules. This will not manifest itself in back-slapping, big warm smiles, and earnest talk about caring for people. Instead, it will be demonstrated in effective action that produces meaningful, positive results for the employees of the organization.

There was a time when the management of human resources was mainly administrative and bureaucratic. The function was oriented to statistics and records and paper work. Now it is changing, under the pressure of two divergent forces.

On the one hand, the complexity of the business environment places a premium on action-oriented movers and doers who are creative problem solvers. Such people are flexible managers able to deal with sophisticated problems and unusual challenges.

On the other hand, the highly technical requirements of government regulations demand an unusual knowledge of the details of ERISA, OSHA, Affirmative Action, and many other constraints and guidelines.

This two-way pull places human resources management in a tug-of-war between creative generalism and technical specialization. The stakes are high. The investment riding on human resources today is enormous. In this atmosphere, the tough-minded but creative generalist must win. If you have what it takes, there's room at the top. . . .

Biographies

Kenneth R. Andrews

Koby Antupit Photographers

Kenneth R. Andrews is Donald K. David Professor of Business Administration at Harvard University and, until August 1985, was the editor of the *Harvard Business Review*. He was educated at Wesleyan University (BA, 1936; MA, 1937) and was awarded the PhD degree from the University of Illinois in 1948. He served five years in the Air Force during World War II. He has been on the faculty of the Harvard Business School since 1946 with intermittent additional appointments at universities abroad. At various times he has chaired the Business Policy area, the General Management faculty, and the Advanced Management Program. He recently completed a 10-year term as Master of Leverett House of Harvard College. His principal field is business policy, and his special interests are corporate strategy formulation and implementation and management development. His current research is concerned with the effectiveness of corporate boards of directors.

Andrews' board experience includes current membership on five corporate boards, among which is the Xerox Corporation. He was earlier a director of two other companies and a trustee of Wesleyan University for 18 years. He is currently chairman of the board of the Harvard University Press and a member of the boards of the

American Productivity Center and the National Center of Economic Education for Children. His consulting activities have focused on strategic planning, corporate organization, executive development, and management training. He was senior consultant, professional development and education, for the General Electric Company for eight years. He is a member of the advisory committee of the Whittemore School of Business and Economics, University of New Hampshire. His articles and books are mostly about corporate strategy, boards of directors, and executive education, and include case and textbooks in business policy. *Nook Farm: Mark Twain's Hartford Circle* (1950) and *The Concept of Corporate Strategy* (revised edition, 1980) are his two most diverse and best known books.

Robert N. Beck

As executive vice-president of Bank of America's Human Resource Division in San Francisco, Robert N. Beck has worldwide responsibility for all human resource matters for the corporation and its subsidiaries. Beck assumed this position in August 1982, after serving as director of Benefits and Personnel Services for International Business Machines (IBM) for the previous four years.

Joining IBM in 1967 as a personnel trainee, Beck was named manager of Employee Relations Research for Corporate Staff in 1971. A year later, he was named manager of Personnel and Communications for the Advanced Systems Development Division. He became director of personnel for the division in 1973. For the next five years, Beck held positions as director of Compensation for the Corporation and director of personnel for the General Business Group/International. In 1978, he was named IBM director of Benefits and Personnel Services.

Beck earned his bachelor's degree in business administration and master's degree in behavioral science and industrial relations at San Diego State University. He served in the U.S. Navy from 1961 to 1963 and later managed supermarkets for Winn-Dixie and Safeway.

Beck is a member of various key committees within the bank including: Social Policy Committee; Human Resources Management Committee; BankAmerica Foundation board of trustees; chairman of the Employee Benefits Administration Committee; Employee Benefits Finance Committee; and secretary to the Executive Personnel and Compensation Committee of BankAmerica's board of directors.

He also serves as a board member and advisor on a large number of professional, educational, and business organizations and foundations. He frequently lectures at leading universities across the United States, and he has been actively involved for several years in the fields of health care and aging. He has published numerous articles and co-authored two books.

In 1985, in recognition of his creative approaches and outstanding performance, Beck received the American Society for Personnel Administration's award of professional excellence for human resource management.

R. L. Berra

Robert L. Berra is currently senior vice-president of administration for Monsanto Company in St. Louis, Missouri. In his present assignment he is responsible for public affairs, corporate marketing, and corporate personnel among other functions.

He has spent most of his career with Monsanto in various personnel assignments including division and plant positions and corporate vice-president of personnel. He was also vice-president of Personnel and Public Relations for Foremost-McKesson Inc. in San Francisco, California from 1970 to 1974.

He holds a BS degree in business from St. Louis University and an MBA from the Harvard Business School.

He has served as president of the American Society for Personnel Administration (ASPA) and president of the ASPA Foundation. He served as chairman of the Committee to Visit Personnel at Harvard University. He is presently an advisory member of the Monsanto board of directors, and is a member of the boards of Fisher Controls International and Monsanto Oil Company.

He was a 1977 recipient of the St. Louis University Alumni Merit Award and was honored as Personnel Professional of the Year by ASPA in 1983.

He lectures regularly at major universities throughout the country and is a member of the Adjunct Faculty of Washington University in St. Louis.

Irving Bluestone

Irving Bluestone served as vice-president of the International Union, United Automobile, Aerospace & Agricultural Implement Workers of America (UAW) from 1972 until his retirement in 1980. From 1970 until his retirement, he served as director of the UAW General Motors Department where he supervised activities related to negotiation and administration of the UAW-GM contract, covering 400,000 workers. He was involved in all national contract negotiations with G.M. from 1948 until his retirement. He also participated in national contract negotiations at Ford, Chrysler, American Motors, auto supplier companies, and aerospace firms.

From 1961 to 1970, Bluestone served as administrative assistant to UAW President Walter P. Reuther; he was involved in all major negotiations and in general administration work of the total union. From 1955 to 1961, he was administrative assistant to UAW Vice-President Leonard Woodcock and was involved in negotiations with General Motors Corporation and supervised the Aerospace Department of the union. Before 1955, he was an international representative for UAW, serving in the National G.M. Department from 1947 to 1955, and as a staff representative in Region 9A from 1945 to 1947, providing service to UAW local unions from Philadelphia to Boston.

Bluestone received a BA degree from City College of New York, where he graduated Phi Beta Kappa, and he pursued graduate studies at the University of Bern in Switzerland.

Among his current community activities are: co-chairman of the Economic Alliance for Michigan; member, Commission on Engineering and Technical Systems, National Research Council, National Academy of Sciences; member, board of directors, Work in America Institute; member, Advisory Committee, Harman Fellowship Program, Harvard University; member, executive board, Michigan Quality of Worklife Council; member, Advisory Committee to the Archives of Labor History and Urban Affairs, Wayne State University; lifetime member of the NAACP; member, National Trade Union Council for Human Rights; member, Industrial Relations Research Association, Detroit chapter, IRRA.

He is also a member of the board of directors of the employee-owned Weirton Steel Corporation and of Waterbury Rolling Mills, Inc.

James F. Bolt

James F. Bolt is president and founder of Human Resource Associates (HRA), a consulting firm offering broad services in the field of human resources, with particular emphasis on the customized design of executive education and development programs.

Prior to founding HRA, Bolt was with the Xerox Corporation for 16 years. As corporate director of Human Resource Planning and Development, he had companywide responsibility for education and training, human resource planning, employment, management succession planning, and quality of work-life activities. Earlier in his Xerox career, Bolt held several key line and staff marketing positions.

Bolt is a member of the faculty of the Duke University Strategic Human Resources Management Program. Bolt also serves as the executive director of the Executive Development Network. The network membership includes senior executives responsible for executive development in 20 Fortune 100 companies. He is also a member of the Human Resource Planning Society, the American Management Association, the American Society for Training and Development, and the American Society for Personnel Administration.

Bolt is the author of "Job Security: An Idea Whose Time Has Come" (*Harvard Business Review,* November/December 1983), recognized as one of the best articles of 1983 by the McKinsey Foundation for Management Research, and "Tailor Executive Development to Strategy" (*Harvard Business Review,* November/December 1985). He is coauthor of "How to Close the Gap in Human Performance" (*Management Review,* January 1982), and he is author of "Management Resource Planning: Keys to Success" (*Human Resource Planning Journal,* Fall 1982).

Fosten A. Boyle

Fosten A. Boyle is corporate vice-president of Human Resources for Honeywell Inc. In this position, Boyle is responsible for establishing policy and programs on major human resource issues and providing leadership for the human resource function throughout the company. Boyle has been with Honeywell for 20 years in a variety of human resource assignments.

Boyle holds a bachelor's degree in industrial relations from the University of Minnesota and completed the program for management development at the Harvard Business School. He is currently on the board of trustees at Dunwoody Institute, serves as co-chairman of the Labor/Management Council for the City of Minneapolis, serves as chairman of the Employer Corporate Council of the Minnesota Coalition on Health Care Costs, and is the program chairman for the Twin Cities Industrial Relations Executive Council. He is also a member of the Twin Cities Personnel Association and the American Society of Personnel Administration.

Walton E. Burdick

Walton E. Burdick is IBM vice-president of personnel. After graduating from Cornell University, he joined IBM in Endicott in 1955.

He subsequently held a number of management personnel positions and was promoted to IBM director of personnel plans and programs in November 1970. He was elected a vice-president in June 1972. He was appointed assistant group executive, finance and planning, General Business Group in August 1977. He was named IBM vice-president of personnel in August 1980.

Bachrach

Frederic W. Cook

Frederic Cook is a member of Frederic W. Cook & Co., a firm that provides management compensation consulting services to corporations. The firm has been in business since 1973, has about 25 employees, and has offices in New York and Chicago. Prior to forming the firm, Cook was a principal with Towers, Perrin, Forster & Crosby, a firm which he joined in 1966 following service in the U.S. Marine Corps and graduation from Dartmouth College.

Bachrach

Graef S. Crystal

Graef S. Crystal is a vice-president and coordinating practice leader for Towers, Perrin, Forster & Crosby. He not only serves as an executive compensation consultant to the senior managements and/or board compensation committees of 35 multibillion-dollar companies, but he also has functional responsibility for TPF&C's worldwide consulting practices in executive compensation, salary administration, compensation surveys, and sales compensation.

Crystal joined TPF&C in 1969 from Booz, Allen & Hamilton. Prior to that, he held compensation director positions with Pfizer International and General Dynamics.

He has written extensively on executive compensation topics, contributing frequently to *The New York Times, The Wall Street Journal*, and other major business periodicals.

Crystal has written four books, the most recent of which is *Questions and Answers on Executive Compensation: How to Get What You're Worth*. In addition, he has contributed chapters to seven other books, including three encyclopedia works.

Crystal is listed in *Who's Who in Finance and Industry* and also *Who's Who in the East*. He is a former regional president of the American Compensation Association and has been honored by that organization with a life membership. A 1956 industrial psychology graduate of the University of California at Berkeley, Crystal received a master of arts degree in the same field from Occidental College in Los Angeles.

Stanley M. Davis

Stanley Davis's interests span three areas: organizational behavior, international management, and management policy. He completed his bachelor's degree at Brandeis University and holds his MA and PhD degrees in sociology from Washington University. He served for a number of years on the faculty of the Harvard Graduate School of Business Administration, was a professor of management at Columbia University, and is now a research professor at the School of Management at Boston University. The author of several books, including *Matrix* (with Paul Lawrence), *Managing and Organizing Multinational Corporations,* and *Managing Corporate Culture,* he also contributes regularly to scholarly journals. Davis has extensive consulting experience and has conducted corporate executive education programs as well.

Edward A. DeCroce

Eileen M. DeCoursey

Before Eileen DeCoursey founded Executive Research Associates in Denver, Colorado, she was, from 1975 to 1985, vice-president of Employee Relations for Manville Corporation.

In this position, DeCoursey was responsible for the design and development of corporate-wide personnel policies, procedures and programs, including recruiting, compensation, benefits, affirmative action, management development, and training. She was also actively been involved in seeking legislative solutions to occupational health problems.

Prior to joining Manville, DeCoursey served as vice-president and executive assistant to the chairman of Squibb Corporation, a position which included extensive work in personnel planning, employee benefits, compensation, and personnel policies.

A native of Livingston, New Jersey, DeCoursey received her BS degree from New Jersey State.

She is a member of the board of directors of the First Colorado Bank and Trust, Denver; Loretto Heights College; and the Institute for Health; a member of the Personnel Roundtable; the Human Resources Roundtable Group; Advisory Council on Management and Personnel Research of the Conference Board; the Human Resources Strategies and Issues Council of ASPA; American Pension Conference; and American Compensation Association.

Clifford J. Ehrlich

Clifford Ehrlich, senior vice-president of Human Resources for the Marriott Corporation, is a graduate of Brown University and Boston College Law School. He was employed by Monsanto Company for 13 years in various personnel positions before joining Marriott in 1973. In April 1978, he was promoted into his current position. Listed in *Who's Who in America*, Ehrlich is a member of the Organization Planning Council of the Conference Board, a member of the Labor Law Committee of the U.S. Chamber of Commerce, and a member and past president of The Personnel Council for the Food Service and Lodging Industry. His activities in the Washington, D.C. area have included work with the American Red Cross and Junior Achievement.

Boston University Photo Services

Fred K. Foulkes

Fred Foulkes received the BA degree from Princeton University and the MBA and DBA degrees from Harvard University. He was a member of the Harvard Business School faculty before joining the faculty of Boston University. Prior to entering teaching, he was employed by Chrysler Corporation and the New York Telephone Company. He is a member of the board of directors of three companies and a trustee of the Profit Sharing Research Foundation.

He has taught courses in organizational behavior, university administration, and labor and personnel relations. He currently teaches Strategic Management of Personnel and Labor Relations, an elective in the MBA program, and management policy.

His publications include *Creating More Meaningful Work*, The American Management Association, 1969; "Some Observations on Career Plans" (*Harvard Business School Bulletin*, March/April 1972); "Search for Solution," in *Where Have All The Robots Gone?*, Harold L. Sheppard and Neal Herrick (The Free Press, 1972); "Learning to Live with OSHA" (*Harvard Business Review*, November/ December 1973); "Transferring Professional Training Models: The Case Method for Theological Education?" (*Theological Education*, Spring 1974); "The Expanding Role of the Personnel Function" (*Harvard Business Review*, March/April 1975); "Organizing and Staffing the Personnel Function," with Henry M. Morgan (*Harvard Business Review*, May/June 1977); "How Top Nonunion Companies Manage Employees" (*Harvard Business Review*, September/October 1981); "People Make Robots Work," with Jeffrey L. Hirsch (*Harvard Business Review*, January/ February 1984); and "Marketing Strategies to Maintain

Full Employment," with Anne Whitman *(Harvard Business Review,* July/August 1985).

In 1979, Foulkes completed an exploratory field study of the personnel policies and practices of 26 large U.S. corporations that are either predominantly or entirely nonunion. The book, entitled *Personnel Policies in Large Nonunion Companies,* was published by Prentice-Hall in 1980.

In 1981, with E. Robert Livernash, Foulkes completed a textbook entitled *Human Resources Management: Text and Cases* (Prentice-Hall, 1982). Aimed at the future general manager rather than the personnel specialist, the book consists of eight introductory chapters and over 20 case studies.

Foulkes was editor-in-chief and contributing author to *Employee Benefits Handbook* (Warren, Gorham and Lamont, 1982).

Douglas A. Fraser

Douglas A. Fraser has been called "the man who never lost touch" and "the labor leader everyone respects." He rose through the ranks to become the UAW's sixth International president, a positon he held until his retirement in May of 1983. Fraser is the last of the "pioneer generation" of UAW presidents.

He was born in a working class district in Glasgow, Scotland and came to the United States with his parents when he was six years old; the family settled in Detroit. After attending Chadsey High School, he went to work as a metal finisher in the DeSoto plant of Chrysler Corp. at the age of 18.

Doug, as he is known to all those around him, became active in UAW Local 227. He was elected to various local offices, including steward, chief steward, recording secretary and, finally, local president in 1943. He served three terms in that position.

In 1947, Fraser was appointed to the staff of the UAW and assigned to the union's Chrysler Department. He caught the eye of then UAW President Walter P. Reuther who selected him as an administrative assistant in 1951—a position he held for eight years. While serving in that capacity, he was involved in many major negotiations.

Fraser was elected co-director of Region 1A in January 1959, and in 1962, convention delegates elected him to the union's International Executive Board as a member-at-large. He was re-elected to that position in 1964, 1966, and 1968.

He was elected an international vice-president in 1970, and president of the union at the May 1977 convention.

In 1964, Fraser, along with Reuther, led the union's bargaining committee at Chrysler where UAW won its historic early retirement program. In 1967, he again led negotiations at Chrysler and won the first U.S.–Canada wage parity agreement.

In 1973, Fraser and then UAW President Leonard Woodcock led the bargaining team at Chrysler setting the pattern for the auto industry that year after a successful nine-day strike. Contract gains included restrictions on compulsory overtime, a comprehensive health and safety program, an improved "30-and-Out" early retirement plan, dental care, and accelerated arbitration, to mention just a few. The Woodcock–Fraser team also led the union's Chrysler negotiators in 1976.

During the 1979 round of auto negotiations—which Fraser headed for the first time in the role of president of the union—the UAW achieved another breakthrough: frequent incremental increases in pension benefits for current and future retirees. Other gains included substantially reduced worktime and improvements in the cost-of-living allowance formula.

Another historic breakthrough that year was achieved when the UAW won union representation on the Chrysler board of directors. Fraser was elected to the board in May of 1980 after indicating clearly in the proxy statement to stockholders that he would serve on the board as a representative of the Chrysler workers. He served in that position until May of 1984, agreeing to remain on the board for a one-year transition period after his retirement as UAW president. The union's participation is based on the principle, in Fraser's words, that "workers must have a say in the corporate decision-making process that so affects their lives."

In 1981, Fraser moved to strengthen the labor movement by leading the UAW back into the AFL-CIO after a 13-year absence from the federation. He served on the Executive Council of the AFL-CIO for three years.

Fraser is an officer or member of many labor, civic, and governmental bodies including chairman of the Health Security Action Council; the board of directors of the National Bank of Washington; the Hyatt Clark Corp., a worker-owned company; the Full Employment Action Council; the Villers Foundation; the Detroit Economic Growth Corp.; the Economic Club of Detroit; and the National Urban Coalition. In addition, he serves on the board of trustees of the Aspen Institute for Humanistic Studies. He is also on the executive committee of the Leadership Conference on Civil Rights and the board of governors of the United Way of America. He is currently serving as co-chair, with Chrysler Chairman Lee Iacocca, of the Michigan Governor's Commission on Jobs and Economic Development.

Although retired as UAW president, Fraser maintains an active career. In addition to his public service, Fraser is a professor of labor studies at Wayne State University and is currently the Jerry Wurf fellow and lecturer at the John F. Kennedy School at Harvard University. He previously served as a visiting professor at the University of Michigan.

Paul C. Gordon

Paul Gordon is a vice-president of ITT Corporation and chairman and president of Federal Electric Corporation, headquartered at Paramus, N.J. After joining ITT in 1957, Gordon served in various personnel positions until 1965 when he was appointed general manager of a divisional manufacturing plant. Since 1967, Gordon has served as president of various ITT companies in California, Pennsylvania, and New Jersey. In his present position, Gordon is responsible for some 7000 employees working in the United States and overseas. The companies in his group provide technical and support services as well as international construction work. Gordon received a BS degree in business administration, cum laude, from the University of Notre Dame and earned his MBA from the New York University Graduate School of Business Administration. His other activities include vice-chairman of the board of the Commerce & Industry Association of New Jersey, chairman of the board of the Foundation for Free Enterprise, the Associate Board of United Jersey Banks, and the board of governors of Ramapo College of New Jersey.

Andrew S. Grove

After receiving his Bachelor of Chemical Engineering degree from City College of New York in 1960, Andrew Grove went on to obtain his PhD from the University of California at Berkeley in 1963. He then worked until 1968 as a scientist at the Research and Development Laboratory of Fairchild Semiconductor, where he participated in work that led to major developments in semiconductors. He currently holds several patents pertaining to surface-controlled semiconductor devices and has written over 40 technical papers.

In July 1968, Grove participated in the founding of Intel Corporation where, after serving as vice-president and director of operations, he became executive vice-president in January 1975 and chief operating officer in April 1976. In April 1979, Grove was named president of Intel and remains chief operating officer.

Grove, a fellow of the Institute of Electrical and

Electronic Engineers, is a recipient of the Certificate of Merit from the Franklin Institute and a member of the National Academy of Engineering. He is the author of a widely used text, *Physics and Technology of Semiconductor Devices.*

Excerpts from his latest book, *High Output Management,* have appeared in *The New York Times, The Wall Street Journal, Fortune, Computer World, Across the Board,* and *Research Management.*

Bruce D. Henderson

Bruce Henderson is a professor of management in the Owen Graduate School of Business Administration of Vanderbilt University. He is also chairman of the board of the Boston Consulting Group, which he founded. He received his BE at Vanderbilt University. He also attended the University of Virginia and Harvard Business School. He received an honorary doctorate of laws from Babson College. He has been a member of the Visiting Committee of the Vanderbilt University School of Engineering for the past 15 years.

Before founding the Boston Consulting Group, he spent four years as the senior vice-president of Arthur D. Little Inc. in charge of their Management Services Division.

A major part of his previous career was spent with Westinghouse Electric Company, where he was elected a vice-president in 1953. At that time, he was the youngest vice-president that Westinghouse had elected in more than 50 years. He served as vice-president of Purchases and Traffic, and as vice-president and general manager of the Airconditioning Division and the Transformer Division. He also served on the Westinghouse Corporate Management Committee.

Henderson's first consulting assignment was as a member of a five-man task force appointed by President Eisenhower to evaluate the effects of the Marshall Plan on West Germany.

He is the author of several books on strategy and more than two hundred essays known as "perspectives." These have been distributed worldwide and translated into several languages. (The article published here is one of these perspectives.) He was the author of a book in 1967 on the effect of experience on cost, now known as the experience curve, which has had a major effect on business strategy.

He now serves on the editorial board of the *Strategic Management Journal,* the advisory board of the *Journal of Business Strategy,* and the board of directors of the Strategic Management Society.

James Alan Henderson

James Henderson attended Culver Military Academy in Culver, Indiana, and graduated in 1952 *cum laude* with honors in five subjects. In 1956, he graduated from Princeton University.

In the U.S. Navy from 1956 to 1961, he served three years on a destroyer leader, taught two years at the Naval Academy, and achieved the rank of lieutenant. In 1963, he graduated "with high distinction" from the Harvard Business School. He holds an honorary degree in Humane Letters from Wilberforce University.

In 1963–64, he was a staff member of the American Research and Development Corporation in Boston and a member of the faculty of Harvard Business School. At Harvard, he co-authored a textbook *Creative Collective Bargaining*. He joined Cummins in 1964, became executive vice-president and chief operating officer in 1971, and became president in 1977. He is also a director.

Henderson is a director of American Information Technologies (Ameritech), Inland Steel Co., and Hayes-Albion Corp. He is president of the Culver Educational Foundation Board of Trustees—the governing body for the distinguished Culver Military Academy, Culver Girls Academy, and Culver Summer Schools in Northern Indiana. A charter trustee of Princeton University, he is chairman of the university's $330 million fund drive. He is also a founding director of the local community foundation, the Heritage Fund of Bartholomew County.

Herbert Hubben

Herbert Hubben is vice-president–International of Eaton Corporation, a manufacturer of advanced technology products serving worldwide industrial and transportation markets, with its world headquarters in Cleveland, Ohio. He was previously vice-president of Management Resources from September 1974 to December 1980.

Born in Germany, Hubben came to the United States in 1933. He attained his BS in economics at Antioch College in 1948 and his MS from Cornell University in industrial and labor relations in 1950.

Hubben has worked for the U.S. Atomic Energy Commission, has been a college professor at George Washington University, and spent seven years with McKinsey and Company, the management consulting firm, including two years in Geneva, Switzerland, as manager of that office.

He came to Eaton from Corning Glass Works, Corning, New York where he served as vice-president–Personnel, Corning Glass international and corporate director–Personnel Resources from 1966 to 1974.

He is chairman of the Northern Ohio District Export Council, and president of the Cleveland World Trade Association. He is on the Board of the National Foreign Trade Council (New York City), the Greater Cleveland Growth Association, and the Cleveland Council on World Affairs. He is on the editorial board of the *International Marketing Review*.

Homer S. Klock II

Homer Klock attained his BA in economics from Hobart College.

From 1954 to 1966 Klock was responsible for a variety of business staff and employee relations functions in research and development and corporate staff activities at Burroughs Corporation. He then became vice-president of employee relations, chemical group, at Celanese Corporation, where he directed a decentralized human resource function in a group of four companies with 9000 employees in 44 facilities worldwide. He represented the chemical group in corporate policy committees and provided strategic planning for group-wide human resource needs.

In 1979 Klock become the principal and director of human resources for Morgan Stanley & Co. Incorporated. As such, he directed the human resources function and acted as counselor to senior management in shareholder strategy, executive compensation, benefit planning, and executive selection and promotion.

At present Klock is executive vice-president and a member of the board of directors of the Sports Training Institute, where he is responsible for new business development, employee relations, and manpower planning.

Klock is affiliated with the American College of Sports Medicine, New York Industrial Relations Association, and Wall Street Personnel Management Association, of which he is the former chairman.

Alan F. Lafley

Alan F. Lafley is a managing director of Korn/Ferry International and visiting professor of business administration and executive-in-residence at the University of Michigan Graduate School of Business Administration. Prior to joining Korn/Ferry, Lafley was executive vice-president of the Chase Manhattan Bank where he was in charge of the bank's corporate-wide human resources function.

Lafley began his career in 1951 at General Electric

where he served as manager of Employee Relations for the Small Motors Division and then as manager of Union Relations for GE's largest plant in Schenectady, New York. In 1962, he was assigned responsibility for Employee Relations for the Hotpoint Division, and was named Manager of Employee Relations for the Aircraft Engine Group in 1966. Lafley joined Ebasco Corporation in 1968 as vice-president of personnel, returned to GE as manager of Executive Manpower and Compensation in 1968, and then served as vice-president of personnel with the Clark Equipment Company, Inc. before joining the Chase in 1975.

He holds a BBA degree from Clarkson University and an MBA from the University of Michigan.

Edward E. Lawler III

After graduation from the University of California at Berkeley in 1964, Edward Lawler joined the faculty of Yale University as assistant professor of industrial administration and psychology. Three years later he was promoted to associate professor.

Lawler moved to the University of Michigan in 1972 as professor of psychology and also became a program director in the Survey Research Center at the Institute for Social Research. He has been a visiting scientist at the Human Affairs Research Centers at the Batelle Memorial Institute in Seattle, Washington, since 1971 and has also held a Fullbright Fellowship at the London Graduate School of Business. In 1978, he became a professor in the Business School at the University of Southern California. During 1979, he founded and became the director of the University's Center for Effective Organizations. In 1982, he was named professor of research at the University of Southern California.

Lawler is a member of many professional organizations in his field and is on the editorial board of five major journals. He is the author and co-author of over 100 articles and eleven books. His most recent books include *Motivation in Work Organizations* (Brooks/Cole, 1973), *Behavior in Organizations* (McGraw-Hill, 1975), *Information and Control in Organizations* (Goodyear, 1976), *Managing Organizational Behavior* (Little, Brown, 1979), *Organizational Assessment* (John Wiley & Sons, 1980), *Pay and Organization Development* (Addison Wesley, 1981), *Assessing Organizational Change* (Wiley-Interscience, 1983), and *Managing Creation* (Wiley-Interscience, 1983).

Ian C. MacMillan

Ian C. MacMillan is director of the Center for Entrepreneurial Studies and professor of management at the Graduate School of Business at New York University. Previously he was at Columbia and Northwestern Business Schools. He received his BS at the University of Witwatersrand, and his MBA and DBA at the University of South Africa. Prior to joining the academic world, he was a chemical engineer and gained experience in gold and uranium mines, chemical and explosive factories, oil refineries, soap and food manufacturers, and the South African Atomic Energy Board. He has been a director of several companies in the travel and import/export business in South Africa, Canada, Hong Kong, and Japan. He has also consulted with a number of companies, including Du Pont, General Electric, I.B.M., Metropolitan Life, Citibank, Combustion Engineering, and Materials Research Corporation. He has published numerous articles and books on organizational politics, new ventures, and strategy formulation. His articles have appeared in the *Journal of Business Strategy, Harvard Business Review, Sloan Management Review, Strategic Management Journal, Academy of Management Journal, Management Science,* and *California Management Review.*

©1985 Thomas Victor

David J. McLaughlin

David J. McLaughlin is a noted author, speaker, and consultant. He presently serves as the head of McLaughlin and Company, Inc., a business research and management consulting firm that specializes in human resource management. McLaughlin is also the executive director of the Senior Personnel Executives Forum, a nonprofit association of the top human resource executives in some 30 multibillion-dollar companies.

Prior to establishing McLaughlin and Company, McLaughlin served in a senior capacity with two of the country's largest consulting organizations. He was a partner in McKinsey & Company, Inc. from 1969 to 1978, with worldwide accountability for the firm's executive resource management practice. From 1981 to 1984 he was with Hay Associates, where he was the general partner responsible for the strategic direction of the practices and accountable for the Compensation Information Center. He was a member of the U.S. Executive Committee, the Worldwide Director Group, and Hay Group Policy and Planning Committee. Earlier in his career, McLaughlin held a variety of positions in industry, including executive positions with Eastern Airlines, where he was initially staff vice-president of Personnel Relations, and later vice-president of Planning.

McLaughlin is a prolific writer and public speaker. He is the author of *The Executive Money Map* (McGraw-Hill), and he organized and published two professional compendiums: *Executive Compensation in the 1980's* and *Compensation and Company Performance* (Pentacle Press). He has also written over two dozen articles, the most recent of which were "Take the Personnel Challenge," *Personnel Journal* (1984) and "Executive Compensation: Myths and Legends," *New Management* (1983). McLaughlin has addressed a wide variety of both domestic and international conferences over the years including major events organized by the American Compensation Association, The Conference Board, *Business Week, Industry Week,* the American Management Association, the American Program Bureau, and over a dozen industry associations.

Donald W. Meals

Donald Meals is a behavioral scientist who has contributed to the planning, development, and evaluation of a wide variety of systems where people, their needs, and their contributions are important. He has been a contributor to long-range planning projects for military and industrial organizations in the United States and in developing countries. Among the projects he has carried out is a strategic plan for a national broadcast organization and the master plan for a new technological university. Currently, he is developing and applying techniques for identifying adjustments in management systems needed to support the implementation of strategic plans. Special emphasis is being given to aligning human resources and their management with strategic objectives.

He received both an MA and a PhD in psychology at the University of Pennsylvania following undergraduate work in engineering. Graduate education concentrated on experimental work and included a summer as a research associate in the psychological laboratory of the University of Cambridge, Cambridge, England. He has studied and taught in the Wharton School of the University of Pennsylvania and was a research fellow at Harvard University. Meals teaches human resource management in the Arthur D. Little Management Education Institute, Inc. graduate-level programs for managers in developing countries. During his professional career, Meals has been a university instructor, applied research analyst, and manager of interdisciplinary research groups involved in systems analysis and long-range planning.

Professional activities include membership in the

Operations Research Society of America, the American
Psychological Association, and the Society of Sigma Xi.
Meals has contributed to symposia on planning, evaluation, and systems analysis. He has published in the
professional literature of the fields of operations research, psychology, and education.

Henry M. Morgan

Henry Morgan, Dean of the School of Management at
Boston University, was previously on the faculties of the
Massachusetts Institute of Technology and the Harvard
Graduate School of Business Administration. His extensive management experience includes service as president and director of H. M. Morgan Co., Inc.; president
and general manager of KLH Research and Development
Corporation; and manager of human relations for Polaroid Corporation. He presently sits on the boards of
directors or serves as consultant to numerous organizations. Morgan's current research interests involve the re-
sponsiveness of business organizations to the social
environment and effective management of the personnel
function. He holds his S.B., S.M., and Sc.D. degrees
from M.I.T.

Robert H. Murphy

Robert Murphy is currently vice-president of Management and Organization at Rockwell International's corporate headquarters in Pittsburgh. Murphy has moved
through successive positions ranging from staffing and
manpower planning manager—Space Division; manager
of finance administration—Corporate Finance; director—Salaried Personnel Automotive Group; corporate
director of personnel—Europe and Middle East; and
vice-president of personnel—Automotive Operations.
He has been exposed to the full spectrum of Rockwell
businesses and the challenge of managing in diverse
business environments.

In his current position he works with Rockwell's
chairman and CEO and president and COO in shaping
company policy and direction for the company's organization and management effectiveness.

Murphy's expertise in the human resources field
has contributed to Rockwell's recognition by others such
as *Business Week* in his May 1982 conference speech entitled "A Line Manager's View of the Human Resources
Role of the 80's." Murphy's contributions are also rec-

ognized in a recent publication entitled *Succession Planning in Leading Companies* by Walt Mahler with a detailed description of Rockwell's Management Succession and Development Planning Program.

Murphy received a BS degree in industrial psychology from California State University in 1962 and an MBA degree in finance and general management from Michigan State University in 1976.

Preston S. Parish

Preston S. Parish, former vice-chairman of the board and chairman of the Executive Committee, The Upjohn Company, Kalamazoo, Michigan, has recently retired after serving with the company since 1949. Parish's career with The Upjohn Company encompassed production, personnel relations, international, and administrative responsibilities. He was elected a director in 1955, vice-president in 1958, executive vice-president in 1960, vice-chairman of the board, and chairman of the Executive Committee in November 1969.

After graduating from Williams College, Williamstown, Massachusetts, in 1941, Parish enlisted in the U.S. Marine Corps and was commissioned a lieutenant in November 1941. He was released to inactive duty as a major in 1946.

Parish continues to serve on The Upjohn Company Board, and as a director of the American National Holding Company, Kalamazoo; director and chairman of Kal-Aero, Inc., Kalamazoo; director of Van Dusen Air, Inc., Minneapolis; and director of National Energy Associates, San Francisco.

He is also a trustee and chairman of the W. E. Upjohn Unemployment Trustee Corporation, Kalamazoo; a director of the National Business Aviation Association, Washington, D.C.; and a trustee of Williams College, Williamstown, Massachusetts.

Parish has had a continuing interest in education and is actively involved as chairman of the board of Jobs for Michigan's Graduates, Inc., and director of Jobs for America's Graduates, Inc. He is a former member of the advisory board of the Foundation for Student Communication, and former vice-chairman of the National Board of Junior Achievement.

In addition to his business and other interests, Parish's hobbies include aircraft renovation (he is a director of the EAA Air Museum Foundation and a trustee and chairman of the Kalamazoo Aviation History Museum), flying, and outdoor sports.

Douglas M. Reid

Douglas M. Reid is vice-president of personnel for Xerox Corporation, Stamford, Conn.

Reid joined Xerox in 1963 as a compensation specialist and has held several positions in the personnel department. In 1973, Reid was named vice-president of personnel for the former Information Systems Group. He became director of international personnel in January 1977. Reid assumed his present position in September 1978.

Before joining Xerox, Reid held various personnel and industrial relations posts with Ford Motor Company of Canada, Limited.

Reid is a member of the advisory committee to the School of Industrial and Labor Relations at Cornell University. He is also a member of the board of directors of Xerox of Canada, Inc.

A native of Windsor, Ontario, Canada, Reid received a BA degree in business administration from the University of Western Ontario, London, Canada in 1958, and a master of industrial and labor relations degree from Cornell University, Ithaca, New York in 1960. Reid attended the Advanced Management Program at the Harvard Business School in the spring of 1981. He served in the Canadian Army from 1954 to 1957.

Bouley Studio

John W. Rogers Jr.

John Rogers is presently vice-president of International Human Resources for Stanhome Inc., a multinational direct marketing firm based in Westfield, Massachusetts. In addition to responsibility for international compensation and benefits, labor relations, and executive recruitment, he is charged with manpower and succession planning.

Prior to joining Stanhome, Rogers was from 1975 until 1979 on the personnel staff of Arthur D. Little, Inc. in Cambridge, Massachusetts. His primary responsibilities were international staffing and compensation.

Rogers' other experience includes work as a personnel manager for a textile manufacturing firm in both the United States and Canada (1972–1975), and a brief period in the U.S. Foreign Service (1971–1972).

He received his PhD from Johns Hopkins University and a BA from Harvard University. He also did graduate work at the University of Paris.

He has taught at the Arthur D. Little Management Education Institute, The Johns Hopkins University, and Westfield State College.

Richard A. Chase, Inc.

Leonard A. Schlesinger

Leonard Schlesinger is Executive Vice President and Managing Officer of Au Bon Pain, a Boston-based national chain of French bakery cafes. Prior to joining the company, he was associate professor of business administration at the Harvard Business School where his teaching and research was in organizational behavior and human resource management. He received his bachelor's degree from Brown University, an MBA in corporate and labor relations from Columbia University, and a doctorate in organizational behavior from the Harvard Business School. Prior to joining the Harvard faculty in 1978, he served in a number of manufacturing, industrial relations, and organization development positions with Procter and Gamble and held the position of Associate Coordinator of Youth Services in the State of Rhode Island.

The bulk of Schlesinger's research has focused on (1) organizational innovations designed to foster employee productivity and quality of work life, (2) the strategic readaptation of organization in response to changes in technology, markets, regulation, and/or workforce demographics, and (3) the management of human resources in diversified companies. He is author of several books and articles in scholarly and management-oriented journals.

Schlesinger is a member of the Academy of Management, the Organizational Behavior Teaching Society (member of the board), and the Human Resource Planning Society (member of the board). He also serves as a member of the editorial boards of the *Organizational Behavior Teaching Review*, the *Academy of Management Review*, and *Human Resource Management*.

As a management consultant, Schlesinger has worked with a wide variety of organizations in the United States, Canada, and Mexico.

Randall S. Schuler

Randall S. Schuler is an associate professor of human resource management at the Graduate School of Business, New York University. His interests are stress and time management, in addition to personnel and human resource management, and the relationship between human resource management and strategy. He is coauthor of a personnel and human resource management textbook (West Publishing, 1984) and coauthor of *Managing Job Stress* (Little, Brown & Company, 1981). In addition, he has contributed many chapters for various books including *Current and Future Perspectives on Stress in Personnel Management*, edited by Roland and Ferris (Allyn & Bacon, 1982), and is coauthor of *Human Resource Management Practices in the 1980s* along with coeditor, Stephen Carroll (Bureau of National Affairs, 1983).

Howard M. Schwartz

Howard Schwartz, a senior vice president at Management Analysis Center, Inc., with over 15 years of consulting experience, directs the firm's work in the area of managing strategic change. He pioneered work that allows top management to systematically assess the impact of their corporate culture in the direction, pace, and cost of major strategic change. His recent project work has focused on helping top executives to build strategically and value driven organizations, and to design effective organizational structures, management process, and measurements systems to implement major redirections.

Much of his work in the past 10 years has focused on the financial services, telecommunications, and energy businesses. In financial services he has worked extensively with seven of the 15 largest banks, developing and implementing business strategies for the retail consumer business, the commercial and middle market, trust services, large corporate cash management services, international corporate services and functional strategies for operations, funding and human resources support groups.

In the telecommunications industry his work has focused on designing organizational structures and management processes to implement strategies for communications equipment, network services, and regulated local service businesses. His work in the energy field has emphasized marketing and distribution strategy and improving the design and effectiveness of large, decentralized marketing organizations. His other industrial experience includes major strategic studies in the entertainment industry and organizational effectiveness work for photographic, computer, home building, and industrial equipment manufacturers.

Before joining MAC, Mr. Schwartz was a Ford Foundation-MIT Sloan Fellow in Colombia, S.A.

Donald N. Scobel

Donald Scobel was educated at Antioch College (BS in chemistry) and Cornell (MS in industrial and labor relations). He spent 25 years with the Eaton Corporation, first at a Michigan plant and then at its headquarter's city of Cleveland, Ohio. There, he spent most of his early years in labor relations, steeped in the adversarial battles . . . then his latter years in organizational development as described in the "Factory Blues" article. Since 1979, he has been director of his own consulting firm called the Creative Worklife Center. He has worked with over 50 companies to help improve the quality of opportunity at work and the performance of the organization. He has written a book called *Creative Worklife* (Gulf Publishing, 1981). The Harvard Business Review published his second article ("Business and Labor: From Adversaries To Allies") in 1982. He is currently writing a book on *Employee Views For Vitalizing Worklife*.

Lord Sieff of Brimpton, OBE, MA

Lord Marcus J. Sieff is the recently retired chairman of Marks and Spencer plc.

Born in 1913, a son of the late Lord Sieff (Israel M. Sieff) and grandson of Michael Marks, the founder of Marks and Spencer, Marcus J. Sieff was educated at Manchester Grammar School, St. Paul's, and Corpus Christi, Cambridge. He joined Marks and Spencer in 1935.

He played a major role in streamlining administration, in the "good housekeeping" campaign of the 50s, and in building up the food business. He was appointed assistant managing director in 1963, vice-chairman in 1965, and joint managing director in 1967. He became chairman and chief executive officer in 1972.

At his own request, Lord Sieff relinquished his duties as chief executive officer and joint managing director in April 1983, and as chairman in July 1984 when, at the request of the board, he became president. He remains a director.

His term as chairman was marked by extensive merchandise development and the company's expansion overseas. One of Lord Sieff's contributions was to strengthen and further develop Marks and Spencer's policy of good human relations with staff, suppliers, and the community.

He is a nonexecutive director of N.M. Rothschild & Sons and chairman of FIBI Financial Trust, the British subsidiary of The First International Bank of Israel.

During the war, he served with the Royal Artillery and, as a colonel, held operational and staff appointments; he was awarded the OBE in 1944.

He was created a Knight Batchelor in 1971 "for services to export" and a Life Peer in 1980.

In 1974, Lord Sieff received Management Centre Europe's first award for "an outstanding contribution to the social responsibility of business in Europe"; in 1976 he was presented with the Hambro Award for the Businessman of the Year and in 1978 the Aim's National Free Enterprise Award. In 1982, he received the "International Retailer of the Year" award of the National Retail Merchants Association of USA. In 1984, he was awarded the British Institute of Management's 1983 Gold Medal.

In 1982, Lord Sieff was the recipient of the B'nai B'rith International Humanitarian Award. He has been connected with the development of first Palestine and then Israel for over 50 years. He is an honorary fellow of the Weizmann Institute of Science in Israel and chairman of its international board of governors.

He was elected an honorary fellow of Corpus Christi College, Cambridge, in 1975. He was awarded an honorary LL.D. by St. Andrews University in 1983 and an honorary doctorate by Babson College, Massachusetts, in 1984. He became a patron of the Royal College of Surgeons in 1977 and an honorary fellow in 1984. He is vice-president of the Policy Studies Institute.

Edson W. Spencer

Edson Spencer attended the University of Michigan, was an officer in the U.S. Naval Reserve, and graduated from Williams College in 1948. He spent two years as a Rhodes scholar at Oxford University in England.

In 1954, after working in Venezuela for three years, Spencer joined Honeywell. He served in the Aeronautical Division, and for five years, from 1959 to 1964, was Honeywell's Far East regional manager in Tokyo. After returning to Minneapolis in 1965, Spencer became corporate vice-president of international operations. He was named an executive vice-president and elected a director of the company in 1969. In October 1974 he was elected president and chief executive officer, and in May 1978 he became chairman of the board of directors.

Spencer holds a directorship in Norwest Corporation and is a member of the board of trustees of the Ford Foundation and the Mayo Foundation. He is chairman of the Advisory Council on Japan–U.S. Economic Relations.

Ray Stata

Ray Stata, one of the founders of Analog Devices in 1965, has been president of the company since 1971 and chairman of the board since 1973. Prior to the formation of Analog Devices, he was a founder of Solid State Instruments and became vice president of Marketing for Kollmorgen Corporation's Inland Controls Division when that company acquired Solid State Instruments.

Stata is active in the high-technology industry and in public service. He was a founder and first president of the Massachusetts High Technology Council, where he helped devise and implement the Massachusetts Social Contract between state government and high-technology industry. He is currently a member of MHTC's Executive Committee and chairman of its Technical Education Committee.

Stata also served as a member of the Massachusetts Board of Regents of Higher Education and on the Commission on Higher Education and the Economy of New England, a study group created by the New England Board of Higher Education. He holds a BSEE and MSEE from M.I.T. and serves on that institution's Visiting Committee of the Department of Electrical Engineering and Computer Science; he is on the Advisory Board of the Center for Advanced Engineering Study at M.I.T. In June of 1984 he was elected a member of the M.I.T. Corporation.

Stata has received three honorary doctorates and is a co-author of *Global Stakes* (Ballinger Press, 1982) and *The Innovators* (Harper & Row, 1984).

Eric W. Vetter

Eric Vetter is responsible for a variety of human resource activities at The Crocker Bank in San Francisco including human resource planning, professional training, management development, performance appraisal, organizational effectiveness, executive and college recruiting, and quality of work life. He joined the bank in 1983 as senior vice-president for Human Resources Development.

Prior to joining Crocker, he was senior vice-president for Human Resources at Gould Inc. and a vice-president of Russell Reynolds Associates, an executive recruiting firm. He also served as a faculty member and as an associate dean of the Graduate School of Business of Northwestern University and Tulane University.

Vetter was educated at the University of Michigan where he received his BA, MBA, and PhD degrees. He is the author of *Manpower Planning for High Talent Personnel*, a pioneer work in the field. He also has written related articles in this field and on the subject of management development. During his 15 years in the academic community, he engaged in numerous consulting studies on organization behavior, employee attitudes, and management development.

While in Chicago, he was a director of the United Way/Crusade of Mercy of Metropolitan Chicago and of Suburban Chicago and a member of the executive committee of both organizations. He is a founding director of the Human Resource Planning Society.

James W. Walker

Bachrach

James Walker is a vice-president and director of Human Resource Consulting Services in Cresap, McCormick, and Paget, the general management consulting division of Towers, Perrin, Forster & Crosby. He is responsible for guiding the development of the firm's services in human resource management.

His responsibilities include direction of client assignments in such areas as:

- Studies of corporate human resource strategy and re-direction of human resource practices and programs to meet changing needs
- Studies of organization and staffing, including forecasting of future staffing requirements and availability
- Projects to help clients improve organizational effectiveness, particularly through better coordinated organization and job design, performance management, communications, and employee development
- Audits of the roles, organization, and effectiveness of the human resource function
- Design and implementation of processes for management succession and development, particularly in decentralized corporations.

He has worked with many of the larger industrial and banking corporations in the United States and Canada.

Walker is widely known for his writing, consulting, and other professional activities in human resource planning. He is the author of *Human Resource Planning*, a book published in 1980 by McGraw-Hill and the winner of the 1980 Book Award of the American Society of Personnel Administration. He is also author of *The End of Mandatory Retirement: Management Implications* (1978), which was published in Japanese, and *The Challenge of Human Resource Planning* (1979).

A 1963 graduate of Millikin University (Illinois), Walker earned an MA and PhD in business administration from the University of Iowa in 1964 and 1967, respectively. Prior to joining TPF&C in 1971, he served on the business faculties of Indiana University and San Diego State University. In 1978–79, he was a visiting professor at Arizona State University. He has been active in professional activities and speaks frequently to management and professional groups. He was a founder and charter president of the Human Resource Planning Society.

Richard A. Chase, Inc.

Richard E. Walton

Richard Walton writes extensively in the areas of work innovations and conflict resolution. Recently, his research efforts have been devoted to the development of high-commitment organizations, innovative approaches to labor-management relations, and the development of organizationally sensitive information technology.

Walton taught at Purdue University before joining the Harvard faculty in 1968. From 1969 to 1976 he served as the director of the Division of Research at the Harvard Business School. He consults with industrial firms and is a member of the board of directors of the Berol Corporation.

Walton received a BS in political science from Purdue University in 1953 and did post-graduate study in economics and political science at Victoria University in New Zealand in 1953. He received an MS in economics from Purdue University in 1954 and a Doctor of Business Administration from Harvard University in 1959. He held a post-doctorate in social psychology at the University of Michigan during 1962–1963.

Arnold R. Weber

Arnold Weber received his BA in economics and his MA in industrial relations from the University of Illinois in 1950 and 1952, respectively. In 1958, he received his PhD in economics from M.I.T.

His academic appointments have included professorships in industrial relations at M.I.T., Stanford University, and the Graduate School of Business at the University of Chicago; the director of the doctoral program at the Graduate School of Business at the University of Chicago in 1961–1963; the dean of the Graduate School of Industrial Administration of Carnegie-Mellon University in 1973–1977; the provost of Carnegie-Mellon in 1977–1980; the president of the University of Colorado in

1980; and the president of Northwestern University in 1984.

Among his many professional appointments are the following: member of the U.S. Council for the World Communications Year (1983), member of the President's National Productivity Advisory Committee (1982–1983), member of the Economic Advisory Committee to the U.S. Secretary of Commerce (1980–1982), economic consultant to the Secretary of the Treasury (1976–1979), member of the Advisory Council on Social Security (1974–1975), academic advisor on the Board of Governors of the Federal Reserve System (1973–1984), and executive director of the Cost of Living Council and special assistant to the President (1971).

Weber has served on the board of directors for PepsiCo., Inc., Super Valu Stores, Inc., and Rio Grande Industries, and he has held membership in the National Academy of Public Administration, Industrial Relations Research Association, and the American Economics Association.

Among his many books are the following: *Union Decision-making and Collective Bargaining* (University of Illinois, 1953), *The Structure of Collective Bargaining: Problems and Perspectives* (ed.) (The Free Press, 1961), *Strategies for the Displaced Worker*, with George P. Shultz (Harper & Row, 1966), and *The Price of Public Service: Executive, Legislative and Judicial Compensation* (The Brookings Institution, 1979). He has also published numerous articles.

Name Index

Subject Index